Surprise Billing Handbook

A GUIDE FOR LAWYERS AND PROVIDERS

Joseph R. Rivet and
Jessica L. Gustafson

AMERICAN BAR ASSOCIATION
Health Law Section

Cover design by Mary Anne Kulchawik/ABA Design

Printed in the United States of America.

29 28 27 26 25   5 4 3 2 1

ISBN 978-1-63905-582-1

Contents

I. INTRODUCTION

Medical debts are a significant problem for many Americans. According to a Kaiser Family Foundation (KFF) Health Care Debt Survey, 41 percent of adults have a health care debt due to medical or dental bills.[1] These medical debts often arise from a surprise medical bill. A surprise medical bill is "an unexpected bill from a health care provider or facility that occurs when a covered person received medical services from a provider or facility that, usually unknown to the participant, beneficiary, or enrollee, is a nonparticipating provider or facility with respect to the individual's coverage."[2]

II. FEDERAL NO SURPRISES ACT

To address the issue of surprise medical bills, the Consolidated Appropriations Act of 2021 (CAA), which contains the federal No Surprises Act (NSA), was enacted on December 27, 2020.[3] The NSA "provides federal protections against surprise billing and limits out-of-network cost sharing under many of the circumstances in which surprise bills arise most frequently."[4] Implementing regulations to the NSA were issued in phases and can be found at 45 C.F.R. Part 149:

- First, on July 13, 2021, the Office of Personnel Management (OPM) and the Department of the Treasury, Department of Labor, and Department of Health and Human Services (HHS) (together, the Departments) issued an interim final rule (Part 1 IFR) implementing the provisions of the NSA "that protect participants, beneficiaries and enrollees in group health plans and group and individual health insurance coverage[5] from surprise medical bills when they receive emergency services, non-emergency services from non-participating providers at participating facilities and air ambulance services from nonparticipating providers of air ambulance services, under certain circumstances."[6] These scenarios are those where surprise medical bills historically have occurred most frequently. The provisions of the Part 1 IFR applicable to health care providers, facilities, and providers of air-ambulance services were applicable on January 1, 2022, and the provisions of the Part 1 IFR applicable to health benefit plans were applicable to contract years beginning on or after January 1, 2022.[7]

1 *See* Lunna Lopes et al., *Health Care Debt in the U.S.: The Broad Consequences of Medical and Dental Bills,* KFF (June 16, 2022), https://www.kff.org/report-section/kff-health-care-debt-survey-appendix/.

2 86 Fed. Reg. 36872, 36874 (July 13, 2021), https://www.govinfo.gov/content/pkg/FR-2021-07-13/pdf/2021-14379.pdf.

3 *See* CAA, Pub. L. No. 116–260 (2020), Division BB, Title I, https://www.congress.gov/116/plaws/publ260/PLAW-116publ260.pdf.

4 86 Fed. Reg. at 36875.

5 Of significance, the NSA applies to ERISA plans, which state laws do not govern.

6 86 Fed. Reg. at 36872.

7 *Id.*

- Next, on October 7, 2021, the OPM and the Departments issued a second interim final rule (Part 2 IFR) implementing provisions of the NSA that "provide for a Federal independent dispute resolution (IDR) (Federal IDR) process to permit group health plans and health issuers offering group or individual health insurance coverage and nonparticipating providers, facilities, and providers of air ambulance services to determine the out-of-network rate for items and services that are emergency services, nonemergency services furnished by non-participating providers at participating facilities, and air ambulance services furnished by nonparticipating providers of air ambulance services, under certain circumstances . . . [and] address good faith estimates of health care items and services for uninsured or self-pay individuals and the associated patient-provider dispute resolution process."[8]
- Implementation of the NSA proved controversial, and multiple lawsuits followed. On February 23, 2022, in *Texas Medical Association et al. v. United States Department of Health and Human Services*,[9] and on July 26, 2022, in *LifeNet, Inc. v. United States Department of Health and Human Services*,[10] the U.S. District Court for the Eastern District of Texas vacated portions of the Part 2 IFR related to payment determinations made under the Federal IDR process. Accordingly, on August 19, 2022, the Departments issued a final rule titled "Requirements Related to Surprise Billing Final Rules,"[11] which finalizes the Part 1 IFR and Part 2 IFR provisions and accounts for the court's decisions.
- On December 21, 2023, the Departments issued a final rule setting forth the "Federal Independent Dispute Resolution (IDR) Process Administrative Fee and Certified IDR Entity Fee Ranges."[12]
- Concerning NSA requirements governing health plans, on November 23, 2021, the OPM, the Internal Revenue Service (IRS), the Departments, the Centers for Medicare and Medicaid Services (CMS), and the Employee Benefits Security Administration published an IFR governing "Prescription Drug and Health Care Spending," which implements requirements for group health plans and issuers to submit certain information about prescription drug and health care spending.[13]

---

8 86 Fed. Reg. 55980 (Oct. 7, 2021), https://www.govinfo.gov/content/pkg/FR-2021-10-07/pdf/2021-21441.pdf.

9 Texas Med. Ass'n et al. v. United States Dep't of Health & Hum. Servs., 587 F. Supp. 3d 528 (E.D. Tex. 2022).

10 LifeNet, Inc. v. United States Dep't of Health & Hum. Servs., 617 F. Supp. 3d 547 (E.D. Tex. 2022).

11 87 Fed. Reg. 52618 (Aug. 26, 2022), https://www.govinfo.gov/content/pkg/FR-2022-08-26/pdf/2022-18202.pdf.

12 88 Fed. Reg. 88494 (Dec. 21, 2023) https://www.govinfo.gov/content/pkg/FR-2023-12-21/pdf/2023-27931.pdf.

13 86 Fed. Reg. 66662 (Nov. 23, 2021), https://www.govinfo.gov/content/pkg/FR-2021-11-23/pdf/2021-25183.pdf.

The regulations lay the foundation for federal patient protections against surprise medical bills. However, note that a Request for Information (RFI) and additional proposed rules have been issued over time, which have not yet been finalized.[14] In addition, legal challenges to the NSA remain ongoing.[15] Attorneys representing individuals, providers, facilities, and health plans are well advised to closely monitor communications from the OPM and the Departments for any changes to the statute or its implementation as the proposed rules may be finalized and litigation unfolds.

A. Protections against Balance Billing for Consumers Covered by Group or Individual Health Insurance

1. Emergency Services and Air Ambulance Services

Federal regulations set forth at 45 C.F.R. §§ 149.110 and 149.130 govern the prevention of surprise medical bills for emergency services and air ambulance services, respectively, to patients covered by group or individual health insurance. Under the NSA, if a group health plan or health insurance issuer provides or covers any benefits with respect to services provided in (1) an emergency department of a hospital, or (2) an independent freestanding emergency department,[16] or (3) air ambulance services, then the plan or issuer must cover emergency services without any prior authorization determination, regardless of whether the provider or facility is a participating provider or facility, and regardless of any other term or condition of coverage. If emergency services are provided to a patient by a nonparticipating provider or facility, the NSA further requires that the services be provided without any more restrictive limitations or requirements on coverage than apply to the same services provided by a participating provider or participating facility. The cost-sharing and balance-billing restrictions discussed later in Section II.A.3 apply.[17]

14 *See* https://www.cms.gov/nosurprises/policies-and-resources/overview-of-rules-fact-sheets, providing a list of and links to rules and fact sheets issued by the OPM and the Departments related to the NSA.

15 *See, e.g.*, No Surprises Act, O'Neill Institute, https://litigationtracker.law.georgetown.edu/issues/no-surprises-act/ (last visited Oct. 20, 2024).

16 If, under state licensure laws, urgent care centers are permitted to provide emergency services and the urgent care center is geographically separate and distinct from a hospital, the NSA applies to such urgent care centers offering emergency services. In such cases, even if an urgent care center does not operate as an emergency center, it would fall within the definition of an independent freestanding emergency department for purposes of the Part 1 IFR. 86 Fed. Reg. at 36878.

17 45 C.F.R. §§ 149.110,149.130.

Under the NSA, the terms "emergency services," "emergency medical condition,"[18] and "to stabilize"[19] generally have the same meanings as provided under the Emergency Medical Treatment and Labor Act (EMTALA).[20] "Emergency services" include the following:

(A) An appropriate medical screening examination . . . that is within the capability of the emergency department of a hospital or of an independent freestanding emergency department, as applicable, including ancillary services routinely available to the emergency department, to evaluate such emergency medical condition; and

(B) Within the capabilities of the staff and facilities at the hospital or the independent freestanding emergency department, as applicable, such further medical examination and treatment . . . to stabilize the patient (regardless of the department of the hospital in which such further examination or treatment is furnished).[21]

After a patient's condition has stabilized after receiving emergency services, the cost-sharing and balance-billing restrictions discussed in Section II.A.3 extend to any items or services provided as part of that patient's subsequent outpatient, outpatient observation, or inpatient hospital stay, unless the following four conditions are met:[22]

(1) The attending emergency physician or treating provider determines that the participant, beneficiary, or enrollee is able to travel using nonmedical transportation or nonemergency medical transportation to an available participating provider or facility located within a reasonable travel distance, taking into account the individual's medical condition . . .[23]

---

18 Whether a patient is suffering from an "emergency medical condition" is determined from a layperson's point of view. An "emergency medical condition" includes "a medical condition, including a mental health condition or substance use disorder, manifesting itself by acute symptoms of sufficient severity (including severe pain) such that a prudent layperson, who possesses an average knowledge of health and medicine, could reasonably expect the absence of immediate medical attention to result in a condition [described in EMTALA, and] (i) refers to placing the health of the individual (or, with respect to a pregnant woman, the health of the woman or her unborn child) in serious jeopardy, clause (ii) refers to serious impairment to bodily functions, and clause (iii) refers to serious dysfunction of any bodily organ or part." 45 C.F.R. § 149.110(c)(1).

19 With respect to an emergency medical condition, 45 C.F.R. §149.110(c)(3) defines the term "stabilize" to have "the meaning given such term in section 1867(e)(3) of the Social Security Act (42 U.S.C. 1395dd(e)(3))." Section 1867(e)(3) of the Social Security Act provides the following definition:

(A) The term "to stabilize" means . . . to provide such medical treatment of the condition as may be necessary to assure, within a reasonable medical probability, that no material deterioration of the condition is likely to result from or occur during the transfer of the individual from a facility, or [with respect to a pregnant woman having contractions] to deliver (including the placenta) . . .

20 86 Fed. Reg. at 36768.

21 45 C.F.R. § 149.110(C)(2).

22 *Id.* § 149.410(b).

23 The attending emergency physician's or treating provider's determination is binding on the facility for purposes of this requirement.

(2) The provider or facility furnishing such additional items and services satisfies the notice and consent criteria (discussed in Section II.A.2.a).

(3) The participant, beneficiary, or enrollee (or an authorized representative of such individual) is in a condition to receive the information described (in the notice and consent) as determined by the attending emergency physician or treating provider using appropriate medical judgment, and to provide informed consent . . .

(4) The provider or facility satisfies any additional requirements or prohibitions as may be imposed under state law.[24]

2. *Nonemergency Services Performed by a Nonparticipating Provider at a Participating Facility*[25]

The NSA also prevents surprise medical bills to patients covered by group or individual health insurance for nonemergency services provided by a nonparticipating provider at a participating facility.[26] A participating health care facility includes a contractual relationship, directly or indirectly, with a group health plan or issuer offering group or individual coverage. Protections extend to situations where a single case agreement is entered between a health care facility and a plan or issuer.[27] Health care facilities governed by this section of the NSA include hospitals, hospital outpatient departments, critical access hospitals, and ambulatory surgical centers.[28] When nonemergency services are provided to a patient by a nonparticipating provider at a participating facility, a group health plan or health insurance issuer cannot impose a cost-sharing requirement that is greater than required of a patient receiving services from a participating provider, unless the notice and consent requirements discussed in the following subsection are satisfied.[29] Otherwise, the cost-sharing and balance-billing restrictions limitations discussed in Section II.A.3 apply.

a. Notice and Consent

When a nonparticipating provider, in adherence to the notice and consent process, provides a nonemergency item or service and issues a proper notice and obtains consent, it may balance bill the beneficiary. The notice and consent exception, a critical part of these regulations, does not apply to emergency services (other than

---

24 This provision is intended to address those scenarios where a state has imposed stricter standards than imposed by the NSA. 86 Fed. Reg. at 36881. 45 C.F.R. § 149.410 (b).

25 *See generally* 45 C.F.R. § 149.420 governing balance billing in cases of nonemergency services performed by nonparticipating providers at certain participating health facilities.

26 45 C.F.R. § 149.420.

27 *Id.* § 149.30.

28 *Id.* Urgent care centers are not included in the definition of nonemergency facilities due to the variation in state law definitions. 86 Fed. Reg. at 36882–36883.

29 45 C.F.R. § 149.30.

post-stabilization services) or air ambulance services under most circumstances.[30] Additionally, a nonparticipating provider, in their commitment to these regulations, cannot issue a notice and consent for items or services related to emergency medicine, anesthesiology, pathology, radiology, neonatology, and laboratory services, regardless of whether such items or services are provided by a physician or a nonphysician practitioner, assistant surgeon, hospitalist, or intensivist.[31] Furthermore, notice and consent, a process that ensures transparency and patient understanding, cannot be issued if there is a lack of a participating provider who can provide the item or service at a facility.[32]

b. Timing of Notice

When an item or service is scheduled at least 72 hours before the date of service, a notice must be issued to the patient no later than 72 hours prior to the date of service. If an item or service is scheduled within 72 hours of the date of service, the notice must be issued on the date the appointment is made.[33] In cases where a patient is provided notice on the same date on which items or services are to be furnished, the notice must be provided at least three hours before the nonparticipating provider furnishes the item or service.[34] The Departments believe this timeframe is sufficient to obtain the patient's voluntary informed consent.[35]

c. Form of Notice

The notice must be made using the form specified by HHS and available in the 15 most common languages in the geographic region of the applicable facility.[36] The notice must be written and provided in paper form or electronically (as chosen by the patient).[37] The notice and consent must include the following elements:

- A statement that the health care provider is a nonparticipating provider with respect to the patient's health plan or coverage.
- The good faith estimated amount that such nonparticipating provider may charge the patient for the items and services reasonably expected to be provided to the patient.

---

30 86 Fed. Reg. at 36905.
31 *Id.* at 36911.
32 *Id. See also* 45 C.F.R. § 149.420(b).
33 86 Fed. Reg. at 36907.
34 *Id. See also* 45 C.F.R. § 149.420(c).
35 86 Fed. Reg. at 36907.
36 45 C.F.R. § 149.420(c), (f). HHS standard notice and consent documents are available at https://www.cms.gov/files/document/standard-notice-consent-forms-nonparticipating-providers-emergency-facilities-regarding-consumer.pdf.
37 86 Fed. Reg. at 36907.

- A statement that prior authorization or other care management limitations may be required.
- A statement that the patient's consent to receive an item or service from a nonparticipating provider is optional and that the patient may instead seek care from a participating provider.

d. Consent

As with the notice, nonparticipating providers must use the consent document specified by HHS to document the patient's consent to balance billing. The patient must sign the consent before the item or service is furnished within the timeframes just discussed. The consent serves as an acknowledgment that the patient has been provided with written notice and is informed of the anticipated charges. The consent form must include an acknowledgment that the patient was provided the opportunity to receive the notice and consent either electronically or in paper form. The notice and consent must include two dates: (1) the date when the notice was received and (2) the date on which the notice and consent were signed.[38]

e. Retention of Notice and Consent Forms

The facility must retain the notice and consent documents for seven years from the date the item or service is provided.[39] The date the patient signed a notice may not be the threshold date on which to base the appropriate destruction date of the document because a signed notice and consent may often be obtained on a date prior to the date the item or service is provided.

3. Cost-Sharing and Balance-Billing Limitations

a. The Patient's Payment Obligation: The Cost-Sharing Amount

(1) Emergency Services

If a group health plan or health insurance issuer provides or covers any benefits with respect to services in (1) an emergency department of a hospital, or (2) an independent freestanding emergency department,[40] or (3) air ambulance services, the

---

38 45 C.F.R. § 149.420(e) and 86 Fed. Reg. at 36908–36909. Standard notice and consent documents are available at https://www.cms.gov/files/document/standard-notice-consent-forms-nonparticipating-providers-emergency-facilities-regarding-consumer.pdf.

39 *See* NSA, Section 104.

40 If, under state licensure laws, urgent care centers are permitted to provide emergency services and the urgent care center is geographically separate and distinct from a hospital, the NSA applies to such urgent care centers offering emergency services. In such cases, even if an urgent care center does not operate as an emergency center, it would fall within the definition of an independent freestanding emergency department for purposes of the Part 1 IFR. 86 Fed. Reg. at 36878.

cost-sharing requirement for any such services performed by a nonparticipating provider or nonparticipating emergency facility must not be greater than the cost-sharing requirement that would apply if such services were provided by a participating provider or participating emergency facility.[41]

(2) Nonemergency Services

If a group health plan or health insurance issuer provides or covers any benefits for nonemergency items and services furnished at a participating facility, unless a nonparticipating provider satisfies the notice and consent criteria discussed in Section II.A.2.a herein, the plan or issuer may not impose a cost-sharing requirement for such items and services that is greater than the cost-sharing requirement that would apply if a participating provider had furnished the items or services.[42] Any such cost-sharing payments must be counted toward any in-network deductible or out-of-pocket maximums in the same manner as if such cost-sharing payments were made with respect to services furnished by a participating provider or facility.[43]

(3) Recognized Amount

A patient's cost-sharing amount for emergency services received from a nonparticipating provider or facility and for nonemergency services received from a nonparticipating provider at a participating facility is calculated as if the total amount that would have been charged for the services by a participating facility or participating provider were the recognized amount (Recognized Amount) for such services.[44] The Recognized Amount is (1) the amount determined by an applicable All-Payer Model Agreement[45] or (2) if there is no applicable All-Payer Model Agreement, then the amount determined by a "specified state law" (Specified State Law), or (3) if there is no applicable All-Payer Model Agreement or Specified State Law, than the lesser of the amount billed by the provider or facility or the "qualifying payment amount" (QPA) for such item or service.[46]

- An All-Payer Model Agreement is an agreement between CMS and a state "to test and operate new ways to structure the payment for the medical care of residents of the state. In an All-Payer Model Agreement, the rates for an item or service covered by the Agreement will generally be the same for all patients,

41 45 C.F.R. § 149.110.
42 *Id.* § 149.120.
43 *Id.*
44 *See id.* §§ 149.110, 149.120.
45 *See* 42 U.S.C. §§ 1315(a) *et seq.*
46 *See* 45 Fed. Reg. § 149.30.

regardless of the type of insurance they have."[47] Very few states have an All-Payer Model Agreement with CMS.[48]

- However, many states have adopted Specified State Laws that provide surprise billing protections to certain patients in those states.[49] A Specified State Law is defined as follows:

  Specified State law means a State law that provides for a method for determining the total amount payable under a group health plan or group or individual health insurance coverage offered by a health insurance issuer to the extent such State law applies for an item or service furnished by a nonparticipating provider or nonparticipating emergency facility (including where it applies because the State has allowed a plan that is not otherwise subject to applicable State law an opportunity to opt in, subject to section 514 of the Employee Retirement Income Security Act of 1974). A group health plan that opts in to such a specified State law must do so for all items and services to which the specified State law applies and in a manner determined by the applicable State authority, and must prominently display in its plan materials describing the coverage of out-of-network services a statement that the plan has opted in to the specified State law, identify the relevant State (or States), and include a general description of the items and services provided by nonparticipating facilities and providers that are covered by the specified State law.[50]

  Specified State Laws are included at the conclusion of this book.

- Generally, the QPA is based on the median contracted rates by the plan or issuer for the same or similar item or service in the same or similar specialty provided in the same geographic region.[51]

---

47 U.S. Dep't of Health & Hum. Servs., No Surprises Act Consumer Advocate Toolkit Glossary, https://www.cms.gov/files/document/nsa-toolkit-glossary.pdf (last revised Sept. 2023).

48 *See, e.g., States Advancing All-Payer Health Equity Approaches and Development (AHEAD) Model*, CMS.gov, https://www.cms.gov/priorities/innovation/innovation-models/ahead (last visited Oct. 20, 2024).

49 *See, e.g.*, Nadia Stovicek, *Map: No Surprises Act Enforcement*, The Commonwealth Fund, https://www.commonwealthfund.org/publications/maps-and-interactives/2022/feb/map-no-surprises-act (last visited Oct. 20, 2024).

50 45 C.F.R. § 149.30.

51 The calculation of the QPA is complex. *See id.* § 149.140. Generally, the QPA is based on the median contracted rates by the plan or issuer on January 31, 2019, for the same or similar item or service in the same or similar specialty provided in a geographic region which the item or service was furnished. The median contracted rate is to be determined with respect to all group health plans of the plan sponsor or all group or individual health insurance that is offered in the same insurance market. The Departments require a minimum of three contracted rates to calculate a median rate. In cases where there is insufficient information the act allows for an alternative method by use of a third-party database. The use of the alternative method is limited to use when the plan or issuer cannot rely on contracted rates as a reflection of the market dynamics in a geographic region.

The Recognized Amount is not used to determine a patient's cost-sharing obligation for patients receiving services from a nonparticipating air ambulance provider. Instead, the cost-sharing requirement is that which would apply if the services were rendered by a participating air ambulance provider, and any coinsurance or deductible must be based on rates that would apply for such services if they were provided by a participating air ambulance provider.[52]

b. The Plan's Payment Obligation: The Out-of-Network Rate

The NSA also establishes requirements related to the total amount a plan or issuer must pay for items and services (Out-of-Network Rate (OON Rate)). The OON Rate for an item or service provided by a nonparticipating provider or facility is determined in a manner similar to the Recognized Amount. The OON Rate is (1) the amount that a state has approved under an All-Payer Model Agreement,[53] or (2) if an All-Payer Model Agreement does not exist, the amount determined under a Specified State Law for such item or service, but (3) in the absence of an All-Payer Model Agreement or Specified State Law, then the amount that is the OON Rate for such item or service is (a) the amount agreed on between the provider or facility and the plan or coverage or (b) the amount determined by the Federal IDR entity.[54] CMS has published a chart summarizing the entity responsible for determining the OON Rate in each state.[55]

c. Open Negotiation and Federal IDR Procedure to Determine the Plan or Issuer's Payment Obligation[56]

(1) Open Negotiation

The NSA requires plans and issuers to send an initial payment or notice of denial of payment no more than 30 days after a nonparticipating provider or facility submits its claim for items and services falling within the statute's purview.[57] Together with its payment or denial of payment, the plan or issuer must notify the provider or facility of the opportunity to enter into open negotiation to determine the OON Rate.[58]

---

52 45 C.F.R. § 149.130 and 86 Fed. Reg. at 86883.

53 *See* 42 U.S.C. §§ 1315(a) *et seq.*

54 45 C.F.R. §§ 149.30, 149.510(b).

55 *See* Chart for Determining the Applicability for the Federal Independent Dispute Resolution (IDR) Process, https://www.cms.gov/files/document/caa-federal-idr-applicability-chart.pdf (last visited Oct. 20, 2024).

56 *See generally* Federal Independent Dispute Resolution (IDR) Process Guidance for Disputing Parties (Dec. 2023 update to Oct. 2022 guidance), https://www.cms.gov/files/document/federal-independent-dispute-resolution-guidance-disputing-parties.pdf.

57 *Id.* at Section 3.1.2.

58 45 C.F.R. § 149.510(b).

Either party may initiate the open negotiation process by providing written notice to the other party within 30 business days of receipt of the initial payment or notice of denial of payment.[59] The Departments have issued a standard Open Negotiation Notice that a party must use to notify the other of the party's desire to enter into open negotiation.[60] During this 30-business-day open negotiation period, the Departments encourage (but do not require) the parties to come to an agreement regarding the OON Rate.[61]

(2) IDR Initiation

If the parties do not reach an agreement, the Federal IDR process may be used to determine the OON Rate for the items or services. Either the nonparticipating provider or facility, or the plan or issuer, may initiate the Federal IDR process during the four-business-day period starting on the day after the open negotiation period ends (i.e., on the 31st business day following the start of the open negotiation period).[62] However, note that the parties are permitted to continue negotiations following the completion of the open negotiation period.[63]

To initiate the Federal IDR process, the initiating party must submit a notice to the other party and to the Departments through the Federal IDR portal.[64] The Departments have issued a standard Notice of IDR Initiation form that the parties are required to use.[65]

(3) Selection of IDR Entity

The parties must jointly select an IDR entity no later than three business days following IDR initiation.[66] The initiating party must notify the Departments of the IDR entity selection (or failure to select an IDR entity) by submitting notice to

---

59 *Id.* Notice may be sent electronically (by email) provided that (1) the initiating party has a good faith belief that the electronic method is readily accessible to by the other party; and (2) the notice is provided free of charge in paper form upon request. *Id.*

60 https://www.dol.gov/sites/dolgov/files/ebsa/laws-and-regulations/laws/no-surprises-act/surprise-billing-part-ii-information-collection-documents-attachment-2.pdf.

61 86 Fed. Reg. at 55991.

62 45 C.F.R. § 149.510(b).

63 86 Fed. Reg. at 55993. If the parties are successful in agreeing upon the OON Rate, the initiating party must notify the Departments. The Notice of Agreement must include the data elements published by the Departments, which are available at https://www.dol.gov/sites/dolgov/files/ebsa/laws-and-regulations/laws/no-surprises-act/surprise-billing-part-ii-information-collection-documents-attachment-5.pdf.

64 *See*ENDING SURPRISE MEDICAL BILLS, CMS.GOV, https://www.cms.gov/nosurprises, and 45 C.F.R. § 149.510(b)(2).

65 https://www.dol.gov/sites/dolgov/files/ebsa/laws-and-regulations/laws/no-surprises-act/surprise-billing-part-ii-information-collection-documents-attachment-3.pdf.

66 45 C.F.R. § 149.510(c)(1)(i). A list of certified IDR entities is available at https://www.cms.gov/nosurprises/Help-resolve-payment-disputes/certified-IDRE-list.

the Departments through the Federal IDR portal.[67] If the parties cannot jointly select a certified IDR entity, then the Departments will select the IDR entity.[68] The IDR entity cannot have a conflict of interest with either party: The IDR entity may not be an employee or agent of either party and cannot have any material familial, financial, or professional relationship with either party.[69] Within three business days of selection as the IDR entity, the IDR entity must review the Notice of IDR Initiation and (1) attest that it meets the regulatory criteria to serve as the IDR entity (and has no conflict of interest) and (2) determine whether the federal IDR process applies.[70] If the IDR entity cannot provide the attestation, the parties must select another IDR entity.[71]

(4) Offers

Within ten days after the IDR entity is selected, both parties must provide an offer for a payment amount for the item or service expressed as both a dollar amount and a percentage of the QPA.[72] Along with the offer, the parties are required to supply additional information including (1) the size of the facility or provider practice, (2) the specialty of the facility or provider practice, (3) the coverage area of the plan or issuer, and (4) any additional information requested by the IDR entity.[73]

The NSA allows the batching of claims for IDR.[74] The benefit of batching claims is to take like-type claims and bring them forward as part of a single determination. The batching option is to encourage efficiency where possible. To be eligible to batch claims, the claims subject to the IDR must meet the following requirements: the services and items must be furnished by the same provider or facility; payment for the item or services is required by the same group health plan or issuer; the items and services must be related to the treatment of similar conditions; and all of the services must have been furnished during the 30-day period following the date of the first claim determination. The bundled payment will be handled as part of a single determination.[75]

---

67 45 C.F.R. § 149.510(c)(1)(iii). Selection of Certified IDR Entity Data Elements are available at https://www.dol.gov/sites/dolgov/files/ebsa/laws-and-regulations/laws/no-surprises-act/surprise-billing-part-ii-information-collection-documents-attachment-4.pdf.

68 45 C.F.R. § 149.510(c)(1)(i).

69 NSA, Section 103. *See also* 45 C.F.R. § 149.510(c)(1)(iv).

70 45 C.F.R. § 149.510(c)(1)(v).

71 *Id.* § 149.510(c)(4).

72 *Id.*

73 *Id.* The Departments have published guidance regarding the data elements to be supplied along with the offer, which are available at https://www.dol.gov/sites/dolgov/files/ebsa/laws-and-regulations/laws/no-surprises-act/surprise-billing-part-ii-information-collection-documents-attachment-6.pdf.

74 45 C.F.R. § 149.510(c)(3).

75 *Id.*

(5) IDR Determination

Within 30 business days of the selection of the IDR entity, the IDR entity must select one of the offers as the final payment determination (without modification) and provide notice to the parties of the determination.[76] The IDR entity's determination will be binding on the parties absent evidence of fraud or material misrepresentation of material facts to the IDR entity.[77]

In making its determination, the IDR entity may consider the following:

- The QPAs for the applicable year for the same or similar item or service;
- The level of training, experience, and quality outcomes measurement of the provider or facility providing the item or service under review;
- The market share held by the nonparticipating provider or facility or of the plan or issuer in the geographic region in which the item or service under review was provided;
- The acuity of the individual receiving the item or service or the complexity of providing the item or service;
- The teaching status, case mix, and scope of service furnished by the nonparticipating facility; and
- The demonstration of good faith efforts (or lack thereof) made by the nonparticipating provider or facility or the plan or issuer to enter into network agreements.[78]

The IDR is prohibited from considering the usual and customary charges; the amount that the provider or facility would have billed in respect to the item or service; or the payment or reimbursement rate payable by a public payer, including Medicare, Medicaid, Children's Health Insurance Program, and Tricare.[79]

(6) Cost of IDR

The cost of IDR comprises the IDR entity fee as well as an administrative fee:

- *IDR Entity Fee.* Each party must pay the entire IDR entity fee when the offers are submitted to a certified IDR entity.[80] The IDR entity will hold the funds in

---

76 *Id.* § 149.510(c)(4). The Departments have published guidance outlining the data elements that will be included in an IDR entity's written decision, which is available at https://www.dol.gov/sites/dolgov/files/ebsa/laws-and-regulations/laws/no-surprises-act/surprise-billing-part-ii-information-collection-documents-attachment-11.pdf.

77 *Id.* § 149.510(c)(4).

78 *Id.* For air ambulance, in addition to the considerations outlined in 45 C.F.R. § 149.510(c)(4)(iii), in evaluating which offer to select, the IDR entity also may consider the ambulance vehicle type (aircraft) and the clinical capability level of the vehicle (aircraft). Additionally, the population density of the pickup location can also be a consideration in determining the acceptance of payment, such as urban, rural, suburban, or frontier. These are the only additions regarding the IDR process for air ambulance under the NSA. 86 Fed. Reg. at 56998–56999 and 45 C.F.R. § 149.520(b)(2).

79 45 C.F.R. § 149.510(c)(4)(v).

80 *Id.* § 149.510(d)(1).

trust until the IDR entity makes a written determination, at which time the IDR entity will refund the IDR entity fee to the prevailing party.[81] Should the parties reach an agreement on the OON Rate prior to the certified IDR entity issuing its decision, the certified IDR entity will return half of each party's certified IDR entity fee, unless directed otherwise by the parties.[82]

- *Administrative Fee.* Each party to an IDR determination must pay a nonrefundable administrative fee to the Departments when the IDR entity is selected.[83]

(7) Timing of Payment

Once a certified IDR entity has issued a written determination of the OON Rate, payment must be made to the nonparticipating provider or facility within 30 calendar days of the final determination.[84]

Plans and issuers of claims are to process the claim utilizing the proper No Surprises Act Remittance Advice Remark Codes (RARCs). The RARCs provide specific information that explains how the claim was adjusted. There are unique RARCs for claims impacted by adjustments made regarding the NSA. (See Appendix for the current list of NSA RARCs.)

(8) 90-Calendar-Day Suspension Period

Once there is a determination by the IDR entity, the initiating party is prohibited from submitting another Notice of IDR Initiation involving the same other party and the same or similar items or services for 90 calendar days.[85] This suspension period is intended as a "cooling off" timeframe between disputes.[86]

4. Notice Posted on Provider/Facility Website[87]

All health care providers and facilities must publicly make available, and post on their websites, a one-page notice in clear and understandable language outlining the requirements and prohibitions under the NSA regarding balance billing in cases of emergency services and balance billing in cases of nonemergency services performed by nonparticipating providers at participating facilities.[88]

Additionally, the notice must include information (1) about any state law requirements on the provider or facility regarding the amounts the provider or facility may

81 *Id.*
82 *Id.* § 149.510(c)(2).
83 *Id.* § 149.510(d)(2).
84 *Id.* § 149.510(c)(ix).
85 *Id.* § 149.510(c)(vii).
86 86 Fed. Reg. at 5600.
87 *See generally* 45 C.F.R. § 149.430.
88 *Id.*

charge a participant, beneficiary, or enrollee of a group health plan or health coverage with respect to which the provider or facility does not have a contractual relationship; and (2) on contacting state and federal agencies if an individual believes that the provider or facility has violated any of the requirements stated in the notice.[89]

5. *Enforcement*

If an individual believes that a health care provider, provider of air ambulance services, or health care facility has failed to abide by the protections of the NSA, he or she may file a written or oral complaint indicating that a potential violation has occurred.[90] The Centers for Medicare and Medicaid Services (CMS) have published a website containing instructions for submitting a complaint online or by phone.[91] A response to a filed complaint is required to be issued within 60 days. Based on the nature of the complaint, CMS may:

- Refer the complainant to another appropriate state or federal resolution process or regulatory authority with enforcement jurisdiction over the matter;
- Refer the health care provider, air ambulance provider, or health care facility for an investigation for enforcement action under 45 C.F.R. Part 150; or
- Explain to the complainant any resolution and/or corrective action taken.[92]

Note that the NSA supplements, but does not replace, state surprise billing laws. As described by CMS:

> Enforcement of state laws is handled by the respective state agencies, such as a state's department of insurance. States have primary enforcement authority over health insurance issuers, facilities, and providers (including air ambulance services providers) with respect to the No Surprises Act. The Centers for Medicare & Medicaid Services (CMS) directly enforces any provision that a state fails to substantially enforce. If the applicable state authority lacks the authority but wants to participate in the enforcement of a provision, the applicable state authority may enter into an agreement with CMS regarding enforcement.
>
> If a participant or beneficiary is covered by a self-insured group health plan (such as a health plan provided by an employer to its employees, a state will not be able to enforce its surprise billing protections unless the plan has opted into the state's surprise billing law.[93]

89 *Id.*

90 *See* 45 C.F.R. § 149.450.

91 https://www.cms.gov/medical-bill-rights/help/submit-a-complaint.

92 *See* 45 C.F.R. § 149.450.

93 U.S. Dep't of Health & Hum. Servs., Questions and Answers on the No Surprises Act and State Laws, https://www.cms.gov/files/document/nsa-state-laws-q-and-a.pdf (last revised Aug. 2023).

Although state surprise billing laws generally do not apply to ERISA plans, ERISA does not prohibit state laws from allowing self-insured, ERISA-covered plans to choose to voluntarily comply with them.[94]

The NSA provides civil monetary penalties up to $10,000 to providers, air ambulance, and facilities.[95] The penalty applies to each violation of the NSA and can be substantial in the event of numerous violations. However, there are exceptions under the NSA for which penalties may be waived. For example, a provider, facility, or air ambulance can show that it did not knowingly violate and could not have reasonably known it violated the NSA.[96]

If a violation is found, within 30 days, the provider, facility, or air ambulance must withdraw the bill violating the NSA and reimburse the health plan or enrollee as applicable. The reimbursement amount must be equal to the difference between the amount billed and the amount allowed under the provisions, including interest.[97]

B. Protections for the Uninsured

1. *Good Faith Estimates (GFE) for Uninsured (or Self-Pay) Individuals*

The NSA also creates protections against surprise medical bills for uninsured and self-pay individuals.[98] Upon scheduling an item or service, or upon an individual's request, health care providers and facilities must inquire about the individual's health coverage status and provide a GFE of the expected charges for furnishing the items or services with the expected billing and diagnostic codes.[99] The Part 2 IFR sets forth requirements for providing GFEs to individuals who are not enrolled in a plan or coverage and are not seeking to file a claim with the plan or coverage (i.e., uninsured or self-pay individuals).[100] The requirements are codified at 45 C.F.R. § 149.610.

---

94 No Surprises Act Consumer Advocate Toolkit Glossary, *supra* note 47.

95 *See* NSA, Section 104.

96 *Id.*

97 *Id.*

98 *Id.*, Section 111.

99 86 Fed. Reg. at 56013.

100 *Id.* The NSA also requires that providers and facilities furnish GFE to insured individuals' plans or issuers. *See* NSA, Section 111. However, acknowledging that the Departments had received feedback from stakeholders that establishing the technical infrastructure necessary to transmit such information to plans or issuers had proven challenging, the Departments concluded that HHS would defer enforcement of the requirement until such time rulemaking for such requirement had been fully implemented. 86 Fed. Reg. at 55984.

A "convening health care provider" or "convening health care facility" (defined as the provider or facility that receives the request for a GFE and who would be responsible to schedule the primary item or service[101]) is required to:

- Inquire whether the individual is enrolled in a plan or coverage and is seeking to have a claim submitted to such plan or coverage for the item or service;
- Inform all uninsured or self-pay individuals of the availability of a GFE of expected charges upon scheduling an item or service or upon request (the convening health care provider or convening health care facility must treat any inquiry regarding potential costs as a request for GFE); and
- Timely provide a GFE to the individual.[102]

a. Notice of the Availability of a GFE

The convening provider or health care facility must inform uninsured or self-pay individuals of the availability of a GFE for expected charges.[103] This notice must be provided both orally (when questions surrounding the cost of items or services are raised) and in writing.[104] The written notice must be displayed in a clear and understandable manner in multiple locations:

- On the convening provider's or convening facility's website, in an easily searchable location from a public search engine;
- In a convening provider's office; and
- At a location where scheduling or questions surrounding the cost of items or services occur.[105]

HHS has developed a model notice; however, use of the model notice is not required.[106]

b. Content of the GFE

The GFE must include the following information:

- Patient name and date of birth;
- A description of the primary item or service and the date such item or service is scheduled to be provided as well as an itemized list of items or services

101 42 C.F.R. § 149.610(a)(2).

102 *Id.* § 149.610(b).

103 *Id. See also* U.S. Dep't of Health & Hum. Servs., Sample Notice of Uninsured (or Self-Pay) Individual's Right to Receive a Good Faith Estimate, https://www.cms.gov/files/document/nsa-gfe-required-notice.pdf (last revised Aug. 2023).

104 *Id.*

105 *Id.*

106 *Id. See also* U.S. Dep't of Health & Hum. Servs., Sample Good Faith Estimate for Uninsured (or Self-Pay) Individuals, https://www.cms.gov/files/document/nsa-sample-good-faith-estimate.pdf (last revised Aug. 2023).

grouped by provider or facility that are reasonably expected to be provided during a defined period of care (including those items and services to be provided by a co-provider or co-facility, i.e., a provider or facility that is not the convening health care provider or convening health care facility[107]). Note that these services may include the following: encounters, procedures, tests, prescription drugs, durable medical equipment and supplies, or fees;[108]

- Applicable diagnosis codes, expected service codes, and expected charges;
- The name, NPI, and TIN of each provider or facility represented in the GFE, and the state(s) where the items or services are expected to be provided;
- A list of items or services that are expected to require separate scheduling; and
- Disclaimers related to the limitations of the GFE.[109]

c. Timely Notice of the GFE

The GFE must be provided to an uninsured or self-pay individual within the following timeframes:

- In scenarios where an item or service is planned to be furnished at least three business days after scheduling, the GFE must be provided within one business day after the date of scheduling;[110]
- In scenarios where an item or service is planned to be furnished at least ten business days after scheduling (or if a GFE is requested by an individual for an item or service that is not yet scheduled), the GFE must be provided within three business days from the date of scheduling or request.[111]

If the convening health care provider or convening health care facility anticipates that an uninsured or self-pay individual also will require care from a co-provider or co-facility, the convening health care provider or convening health care facility has the responsibility to request a GFE from the co-provider or co-facility no later than one business day following scheduling an item or service or the individual's request.[112] The convening health care provider or convening health care facility will notify the co-provider or co-facility of the date the GFE information must be received.[113]

---

107 45 C.F.R. § 149.610(a)(2).

108 *See*CMS Ctr. for Consumer Info. & Ins. Oversight, The No Surprises Act's Good Faith Estimates and Patient-Provider Dispute Resolution Requirements, https://www.cms.gov/files/document/gfe-and-ppdr-requirements-slides.pdf (last visited Oct. 20, 2024).

109 45 C.F.R. § 149.610(c). *See also* Sample Good Faith Estimate for Uninsured (or Self-Pay) Individuals, *supra* note 106.

110 45 C.F.R. § 149.610(b).

111 *Id.*

112 *Id.*

113 *Id.*

If the scope of information included in a GFE changes, the convening health care provider or convening health care facility is required to furnish the individual with a new GFE no later than one business day before the item or service is scheduled.[114] Furthermore, if the expected providers or facilities represented in a GFE change within one business day before an item or service is scheduled, and a replacement provider or replacement facility is to render the item or service, the replacement provider or replacement facility must accept the GFE as the expected charges.[115]

2. *Patient-Provider Dispute Resolution (PPDR)*

The NSA requires HHS to establish a PPDR process for an uninsured (or self-pay) individual to use if he or she receives a GFE and is billed in an amount "substantially in excess" of the expected charges contained in the GFE.[116] "Substantially in excess" means at least $400 more than the total amount of expected charges listed on the GFE.[117] The PPDR process is outlined at 45 C.F.R. § 149.620.

a. Initiating PPDR

An individual can initiate the PPDR process by submitting a notice to HHS within 120 calendar days of receiving an initial bill from the provider or facility (hereafter, the PPDR initiation notice).[118] The PPDR initiation notice may be submitted online,[119] by fax, or by mail (and the submission must be postmarked within 120 calendar days from receipt of the initial bill).[120] The PPDR initiation notice must satisfy certain content requirements, including the following:

(A) Information sufficient to identify the item or service under dispute, including the date the item or service was provided, and a description of the item or service;
(B) A copy of the provider or facility bill for the item and service under dispute (the copy can be a photocopy or an electronic image so long as the document is readable);
(C) A copy of the good faith estimate for the item or service under dispute (the copy can be a photocopy or an electronic image so long as the document is readable);

114 *Id.*
115 *Id.*
116 *See* NSA, Section 112.
117 45 C.F.R. § 149.620(a)(2)(ii).
118 *Id.* § 149.620(c).
119 *Id.* § 149.620(c)(1). *See also* The No Surprises Act Protects People from Unexpected Medical Bills, CMS.gov, https://www.cms.gov/nosurprises/consumers/medical-bill-disagreements-if-you-are-uninsured (last visited Oct. 20, 2024).
120 45 C.F.R. § 149.620(c)(1).

(D) If not included on the good faith estimate, contact information of the provider or facility involved, including, if available, name, email address, phone number, and mailing address;
(E) The State where the items or services in dispute were furnished; and
(F) The uninsured (or self-pay) individual's communication preference, through the Federal IDR portal, or electronic or paper mail.[121]

HHS has developed a standard form that must be used as the PPDR initiation notice.[122] An administrative fee for the selected dispute resolution (SDR) entity must be submitted with the PPDR initiation notice.[123]

b. Selecting the SDR Entity

Once HHS receives the PPDR initiation notice, it will select an SDR entity.[124] If the selected SDR entity has a conflict of interest, it must notify HHS no later than three business days following selection, and HHS will select a different SDR entity from the remaining pool of SDR entities. Selection will occur in a round-robin format.[125]

If no conflict exists, the SDR entity will notify the individual and the provider or facility that a PPDR initiation notice was received and is under review.[126] While the PPDR process is ongoing, the provider or facility is prohibited from moving bills for the items or services into collection or threatening to do so.[127] The provider or facility must defer accrual of any late fees on the unpaid bill amounts until the conclusion of PPDR.[128]

The SDR entity shall review the PPDR initiation notice to ensure the disputed items and services meet eligibility criteria and the PPDR initiation notice contains the required information.[129]

- If the SDR entity determines that an item or service is *ineligible* for PPDR or the initiation notice is incomplete, the SDR entity will issue an insufficiency notice,

121 *Id.* § 149.620(c)(2).
122 *See* PPDR Form Notice, https://nsa-idr.cms.gov/billdisputes/s/.
123 45 C.F.R. § 149.620(c)(1).
124 *Id.* § 149.620(e).
125 *Id.*
126 *Id.* § 149.620(c)(3). *See also* Standard Notice: Selected Dispute Resolution (SDR) Entity Notification to Health Care Providers and Facilities and Uninsured (or Self-Pay) Individuals, https://www.reginfo.gov/public/do/DownloadDocument?objectID=129464501. Following selection of the SDR entity, and even if the SDR entity has not identified a conflict of interest, either party may attest that a conflict of interest exists, in which case the SDR entity must notify HHS no later than three business days following receipt of the attestation. HHS will select a different SDR entity. 86 Fed. Reg. at 56035.
127 45 C.F.R. § 149.620(c)(5).
128 *Id.*
129 *Id.* § 149.620(c)(4).

and the individual will be provided 21 calendar days to submit missing information or other information to demonstrate the item or service is eligible for PPDR.[130]

- If the SDR entity determines that an item or service is *eligible* for PPDR, the SDR entity must notify both parties and request that the provider or facility provide certain information within ten business days, including:
  - A copy of the GFE;
  - A copy of the billed charges provided to the individual; and
  - Documentation demonstrating that the difference between the billed charges and the expected charges in the GFE reflects the cost of a medically necessary item or service and is based on unforeseen circumstances that could not have reasonably been anticipated by the provider or facility when the GFE was provided.[131]

c. Payment Determination

(1) Determination of the Payment Amount through Settlement

In the event the parties agree to settle the dispute before the date the SDR entity issues a payment determination, the provider or facility must notify the SDR entity through the Federal IDR portal or by mail as soon as possible, but no later than three business days after the date of the agreement.[132] Any settlement must reflect that the provider or facility applied a reduction to the amount owed equal to at least half of the administrative fee.[133]

(2) Determination of the Payment Amount through PPDR

The SDR entity will use the expected charges as listed in the GFE as the presumed appropriate amount, unless the provider or facility provides credible information justifying the difference between the billed charges and the expected charges in the GFE by demonstrating that the difference: (1) reflects the cost of a medically necessary item or service; and (2) is based on unforeseen circumstances that could not have been reasonably anticipated by the provider or facility when the GFE was provided.[134]

---

130 *Id.* HHS has developed *Standard Notice: Ineligible for Patient-Provider Dispute Resolution or Additional Information Needed,* which is available at https://www.reginfo.gov/public/do/DownloadDocument?objectID=120309201.

131 86 Fed. Reg. at 56033. A list and description of the data elements to be supplied is available at https://www.reginfo.gov/public/do/DownloadDocument?objectID=120309201.

132 45 C.F.R. § 149.620(f)(1). HHS has developed a Standard Notice of Settlement and Standard Notice of Receipt of Dispute Settlement, both of which are available at https://www.cms.gov/files/document/payment-settlement-form-patient-disputes.pdf.

133 86 Fed. Reg. at 56036.

134 45 C.F.R. § 149.620(f)(2).

For an item or service where the billed charge is more than the expected charge listed in the GFE, the SDR entity will determine the payment amount as follows:

- If the SDE entity determines the provider or facility *has **not** provided* credible information:
  - *For an item or service listed in the GFE,* the amount the individual will be required to pay will be equal to the expected charge for the item or service as listed in the GFE.
  - *For an item or service **not** listed in the GFE,* the amount the individual will be required to pay will be $0.[135]
- If the SDE entity determines the provider or facility *has provided* credible information:
  - *For an item or service listed in the GFE,* the amount the individual will be required to pay will be equal to the lesser of (1) the billed charge or (2) the median payment amount for the same or similar service in the geographic area that is reflected in an independent database (or if the amount in the independent database is less than the expected charge in the GFE, then the amount listed in the GFE).
  - *For an item or service **not** listed in the GFE,* the amount the individual will be required to pay will be equal to the lesser of (1) the billed charge or (2) the median payment amount for the same or similar service in the geographic area that is reflected in an independent database.[136]

d. Notice of Determination

Once a final payment determination amount has been calculated, the SDR entity must inform the parties through the Federal IDR portal or by mail of the final payment determination and the justification for the determination.[137] The determination made by an SDR entity will be binding on the parties absent a fraudulent claim or evidence of misrepresentation of facts presented to the SDR entity.[138]

C. Health Plan Requirements

Health plans will not escape the requirements of the NSA. Implementation and enforcement of certain provisions of the statute have been delayed.[139] Where implementation has not been delayed, health plans must make efforts to comply with

135 *Id.* § 149.620(f)(3).

136 *Id.*

137 *Id.*

138 *Id.* § 149.620(f)(4).

139 The CMS No Surprises Act website provides guidance to plans and issuers related to NSA requirements. It is available at https://www.cms.gov/nosurprises/plans-and-issuers-requirements-and-resources.

applicable sections of the NSA in good faith. Additional guidance will be provided through future rulemaking.[140]

Reporting requirements related to prescription drug and health care spending were adopted by way of IFR published in November 2021 and are codified at 45 C.F.R. §§ 149.710 *et seq.* and require a group health plan or health insurance issuer offering group or individual health insurance coverage to submit an annual report to the Secretary, Secretary of Treasury, and Secretary of Labor on prescription drug and health care spending, premiums, and enrollment.[141]

III. CONCLUSION

Stakeholders mostly agree that the NSA has proven successful in protecting individuals from surprise medical bills.[142] However, the status of the NSA's implementation remains in flux. Attorneys representing individuals, providers, facilities, and health plans must remain diligent to monitor communications for the OPM and the Departments for any changes to the NSA and its regulations as additional rulemaking is finalized and in response to pending litigation. In addition, changes to the NSA may occur in response to changes in state laws.

140 *See, e.g.*, guidance regarding NSA Title I Sections 113, 114, 115, and 116, Title II and Title III: FAQs about Affordable Care Act and Consolidated Appropriations Act, 2021 Implementation Part 49 (Aug. 20, 2021), https://www.dol.gov/sites/dolgov/files/EBSA/about-ebsa/our-activities/resource-center/faqs/aca-part-49.pdf. All CAA enforcement letters are posted on the CCIIO CAA page under the title "Enforcement." https://www.cms.gov/marketplace/about/oversight/other-insurance-protections/consolidated-appropriations-act-2021-caa.

141 CMS has made available templates, FAQs, and additional sub-regulatory guidance, which are available at https://www.cms.gov/marketplace/about/oversight/other-insurance-protections/prescription-drug-data-collection-rxdc.

142 *See, e.g.*, Jack Hoadley et al., *No Surprises Act: Perspectives on the Status of Consumer Protections against Balance Billing*, Urban Inst., Ctr. on Health Ins. Reforms (Apr. 2023), https://www.urban.org/sites/default/files/2023-04/No%20Surprises%20Act%20Perspectives%20on%20the%20Status%20of%20the%20Consumer%20Protections%20Against%20Balance%20Billing.pdf.

AT-A-GLANCE: STATE BALANCE-BILLING LAWS AND ADMINISTRATIVE RULES

State	*Balance-Billing Law*	*Out-of-Network Reimbursement*	*Arbitration*	*State Agency*	*State Statute / Administrative Code*
Alabama	No	—	—	Department of Insurance	—
Alaska	No, but IDR available for state-regulated plans	80th percentile for out-of-network reimbursement for state-regulated plans	Provider complaint process through Alaska Division of insurance for state-regulated plans	Division of Insurance	**Statute:** None for balance billing **Admin. Code:** 3 AAC 26.110
Arizona	Yes	Amount determined by negotiation/IDR	"Surprise out of network billing dispute resolution program"	Department of Insurance	**Statute:** ARS 20-3111 through 3119 **Admin. Code:** AAC R9-29-302, 303, AAC R20-6-2401
Arkansas	No	—	—	Insurance Department	—
California	Yes	Local average contracted rate or 125% of Medicare	IDR through Department of Insurance	Department of Insurance	**Statute:** Cal. Health & Safety Code 1371.30, 1371.31; Cal. Ins. Code 10112.8, 10112.81, 10112.82 **Admin. Code:** 28 CCR 1300.71.31
Colorado	Yes	105% of median in-network rate for emergency, 110% of median or 60th percentile for nonemergency	Yes	Division of Insurance	**Statute:** CRS 12-30-112, 113, CRS 10-16-704, CRS 25.3-122 **Admin. Code:** 3 CCR 702-4 Series 4-2
Connecticut	Yes	80th percentile of all charges for same/similar in geographic area	According to contract terms	Department of Insurance	**Statute:** Conn. Gen. Stat. 38a-477aa **Admin. Code:** Regs., Conn. State Agencies 38a-472f-2

(Continued)

State	*Balance-Billing Law*	*Out-of-Network Reimbursement*	*Arbitration*	*State Agency*	*State Statute / Administrative Code*
Delaware	Yes	Previously agreed rate or negotiated rate	Optional	Department of Insurance	**Statute:** 18 Del. C. 3348, 3349, 3564, 3370A, 3571S **Admin. Code:** CDR 18-1400-1403
Florida	No, but disclosure of possible balance billing required	—	—	Office of Insurance Regulation	**Statute:** Fla. Stat. 641.3154, 627.6471 **Admin. Code:** None
Georgia	Yes	Median contracted amount as calculated by vendor chosen by Commissioner	Arbitration by Commissioner	Office of Insurance and Safety Fire Commissioner	**Statute:** OCGA 33-20E-7 **Admin. Code:** Ga. Comp. R. & Regs. R. 120-2-106-.10, .05, .06
Hawaii	Yes, HMOs and Mutual Benefit Societies Only	No	ADR through Commissioner	Insurance Division	**Statute:** HRS 431:26-104 **Admin. Code:** None
Idaho	No	—	—	Department of Insurance	—
Illinois	Yes	Negotiated/arbitrated between parties	Yes, from DOI approved list of arbitrators	Department of Insurance	**Statute:** 215 ILCS 5/356z.3a **Admin. Code:** None
Indiana	Yes	No	No	Department of Insurance	**Statute:** Burns Ind. Code. Ann. 27-1-45-8 **Admin. Code:** None
Iowa	Yes, Emergency or HMO/PPO enrollees only	No	No	Insurance Division	**Statute:** Iowa Code 514C.16 **Admin. Code:** None
Kansas	No	—	—	Insurance Department	—

(Continued)

(Continued)

State	*Balance-Billing Law*	*Out-of-Network Reimbursement*	*Arbitration*	*State Agency*	*State Statute / Administrative Code*
Kentucky	No	—	—	Department of Insurance	—
Louisiana	No	—	—	Department of Insurance	**Statute:** La RS 22:1874 – specifically allows charges for noncontracted services **Admin. Code:** None
Maine	Yes	Negotiated price – in case of arbitration, arbitrator chooses between three different reimbursement calculations	Yes	Bureau of Insurance	**Statute:** 22 MRS 1718-D, 24-A MRS 4303-C, 4303-E **Admin. Code:** CMR 02-031-365
Maryland	HMOs, PPO/EPO, or ground ambulances governed by Maryland law only	HMOs only – 125% of HMO rate, 140% of Medicare rate, various for PPOs	Complaint with Insurance Admin. or civil suit	Insurance Administration	**Statute:** MD. Health-General Code Ann 19-710.1, MD Insurance Code Ann 14-205.2 **Admin. Code:** COMAR 10.02.01.01–10.02.01.11
Massachusetts	Yes	Same as No Surprises Act	Federal IDR through No Surprises Act	Division of Insurance	**Statute:** ALM GL ch. 176O sec. 6 **Admin. Code:** None
Michigan	Yes	Median payer contracted rate OR 150% of Medicare, whichever is greater	Yes, only for complicated emergency services	Department of Financial Services	**Statute:** MCL §§ 333.24501–333.24504; 333.24507; 333.24509–24511; 333.24513 **Admin. Code:** R 500.241–R 500.245

(Continued)

State	*Balance-Billing Law*	*Out-of-Network Reimbursement*	*Arbitration*	*State Agency*	*State Statute / Administrative Code*
Minnesota	Yes	Negotiated between provider/carrier	Federal IDR through No Surprises Act	Insurance Division, Department of Commerce	**Statute:** Minn. Stat. 62Q.556, 62K.11, 62J.811 **Admin. Code:** None
Mississippi	Yes	No	No	Insurance Department	**Statute:** Miss. Code Ann. 83-9-5(1)(i) **Admin. Code:** None
Missouri	Yes	Reasonable Amount	Yes	Department of Insurance	**Statute:** R.S. MO. 376.690, 376.1367 **Admin. Code:** 20 CSR 400-14.100, 22 CSR 10-2.010
Montana	No	—	—	Office of the Montana State Auditor, Commissioner of Securities and Insurance	—
Nebraska	Yes, for Emergency Services Only	Contracted rate OR 175% of Medicare reimbursement	Mediation	Department of Insurance	**Statute:** NRS §§ 44-6834–44-6850; 25-2930–25-2942 **Admin. Code:** None
Nevada	Yes	Previously contracted rate OR 108–115% of reimbursement	Yes, if negotiation fails	Division of Insurance	**Statute:** NRS 439B.745, 439B.748–439B.751, 439B.754 **Admin. Code:** None
New Hampshire	Yes, emergency, anesthesiology, radiology, or pathology services only	Commercially reasonable rate	No, insurance commissioner has exclusive jurisdiction under RSA 420-J:8-e	Insurance Department	**Statute:** NH Rev. Stat. § 329:31-b **Admin. Code:** None

(*Continued*)

(Continued)

State	*Balance-Billing Law*	*Out-of-Network Reimbursement*	*Arbitration*	*State Agency*	*State Statute / Administrative Code*
New Jersey	Yes, MCOs only	Contracted rate	Yes, but no provision to consider in-network rate	Department of Banking and Insurance	**Statute:** NJ ST 30:4D-7ff(d), 26:2S-6.1 **Admin. Code:** NJ ADC 11:3-29.6
New Mexico	Yes, for emergency care and nonemergency when medically necessary and not available in-network, or if there is inability to choose	Reimbursement calculation repealed	Grievances adjudicated through Superintendent after internal remedies exhausted	Office of Superintendent of Insurance	**Statute:** NM ST §59A-57A-3, 59A-57A-4, 59A-57A-10 **Admin. Code:** NMAC 13.10.33.9, 13.10.33.10, 13.10.33.12, 13.10.16.10
New York	Yes	Contracted rate	Yes	Department of Financial Services	**Statute:** NY CLS Fin. Serv. §§ 601–607 **Admin. Code:** 23 NYCRR 400.0–400.10
North Carolina	No, not in emergency services context	—	—	Department of Insurance	—
North Dakota	No	—	—	Insurance Department	—
Ohio	Yes	Greatest of the following amounts: (1) amount negotiated with in-network providers in that geographic area, (2) amount for the service calculated using same method as health benefit plan, and (3) amount that would've been paid under Medicare	Yes, if service was within one year and billed amount exceeds $750	Department of Insurance	**Statute:** OH ST § 3902.51–3902.54, §4769.02 **Admin. Code:** None

(Continued)

State	*Balance-Billing Law*	*Out-of-Network Reimbursement*	*Arbitration*	*State Agency*	*State Statute / Administrative Code*
Oklahoma	No	—	—	Insurance Department	—
Oregon	Yes, in Insurance Code by legislative action but not added to ORS chapter 743B	Calculated using OAR 836-053-1610 for non-anesthesia, calculated using OAR 836-053-1615 for anesthesia claims	Federal IDR	Division of Financial Regulation	**Statute:** ORS § 743B.287 **Admin. Code:** OAR 836-053-1605, 836-053-1610, 836-053-1615
Pennsylvania	No	—	—	Insurance Department	—
Rhode Island	No	—	—	Insurance Division, Department of Business Regulation	—
South Carolina	No	—	—	Department of Insurance	—
South Dakota	No	—	—	Department of Labor and Regulation	—
Tennessee	No	—	—	Department of Commerce and Insurance	—
Texas	Yes, MCO/PPO only	Usual and customary rate	Arbitration for providers, mediation for facilities	Department of Insurance	**Statute:** TX INS § 752.0001–752.0003, 1275.051–1275.054, 1467.001-.006, 1467.050-.060, 1467.081–.089 **Admin. Code:** 26 TAC § 509.67; § 564.28, 28 TAC 21.5010-.5013, 21.5020-.5023, 25 TAC 133.46

(Continued)

(Continued)

State	*Balance-Billing Law*	*Out-of-Network Reimbursement*	*Arbitration*	*State Agency*	*State Statute / Administrative Code*
Utah	Yes, MCOs and emergency care only	Like amount as the reimbursement for contracted provider	—	Insurance Department	**Statute:** UT ST §§ 31A-26-301.5, 31A-45-501, 31A-2-216, 31A-22-627 **Admin. Code:** None
Vermont	No	—	—	Department of Financial Regulation	—
Virginia	Yes	Commercially reasonable amount	Yes, carrier/provider shall provide written notice to the Commission and party no later than 10 days after good faith negotiation	State Corporation Commission	**Statute:** VA ST § 38.2-3445.01-02; 38.3-3445.2 § 38.2-5801; § 38.2-3445.04 **Admin. Code:** 14 VA ADC 5-405-30, 5-405-40
Washington	Yes	Commercially reasonable amount as determined by arbitrator	Services other than air ambulance services are subject to IDR under public health services act	Office of the Insurance Commissioner	**Statute:** WA ST 48.49.005–48.49.040 **Admin. Code:** WA ADC 284-43B-010 – 284-43B-090
West Virginia	No	—	—	Offices of the Insurance Commissioner	—
Wisconsin	No	—	—	Office of the Commissioner of Insurance	—
Wyoming	No	—	—	Wyoming Department of Insurance	—

APPENDIX A: REMITTANCE ADVICE REMARK CODES RELATED TO THE NO SURPRISES ACT

Remittance Advice Remark Codes (RARCs) may be used by plans and issuers to communicate information about claims to providers and facilities, subject to state law.

The following RARCs related to the No Surprises Act have been approved by the RARC Committee and are effective as of March 1, 2022.

For a complete and regularly updated list of RARCs, please see https://x12.org/codes/remittance-advice-remark-codes.

The No Surprises Act Provisions that Apply to the Claim	
RARC #	RARC Text
N864	Alert: This claim is subject to the No Surprises Act provisions that apply to emergency services.
N865	Alert: This claim is subject to the No Surprises Act provisions that apply to nonemergency services furnished by nonparticipating providers during a patient visit to a participating facility.
N866	Alert: This claim is subject to the No Surprises Act provisions that apply to services furnished by nonparticipating providers of air ambulance services.
How Cost Sharing Was Calculated under the No Surprises Act	
RARC #	RARC Text
N862	Alert: Member cost share is in compliance with the No Surprises Act, and is calculated using the lesser of the QPA or billed charge.
N867	Alert: Cost sharing was calculated based on a specified state law, in accordance with the No Surprises Act.
N868	Alert: Cost sharing was calculated based on an All-Payer Model Agreement, in accordance with the No Surprises Act.
N869	Alert: Cost sharing was calculated based on the qualifying payment amount, in accordance with the No Surprises Act.
N870	Alert: In accordance with the No Surprises Act, cost sharing was based on the billed amount because the billed amount was lower than the qualifying payment amount.
Initial Payment Amount	
RARC #	RARC Text
N871	Alert: This initial payment was calculated based on a specified state law, in accordance with the No Surprises Act.
N877	Alert: This initial payment is provided in accordance with the No Surprises Act. The provider or facility may initiate open negotiation if they desire to negotiate a higher out-of-network rate.
Final Payment Amount	
RARC #	RARC Text
N863	Alert: This claim is subject to the No Surprises Act (NSA). The amount paid is the final out-of-network rate and was calculated based on an All-Payer Model Agreement, in accordance with the NSA.

(*Continued*)

(Continued)

N872	Alert: This final payment was calculated based on a specified state law, in accordance with the No Surprises Act.
N873	Alert: This final payment was calculated based on an All-Payer Model Agreement, in accordance with the No Surprises Act.
N874	Alert: This final payment was determined through open negotiation, in accordance with the No Surprises Act.
N875	Alert: This final payment equals the amount selected as the out-of- network rate by a Federal Independent Dispute Resolution Entity, in accordance with the No Surprises Act.
Denial of Payment	
RARC #	RARC Text
N876	Alert: This item or service is covered under the plan. This is a notice of denial of payment provided in accordance with the No Surprises Act. The provider or facility may initiate open negotiation if they desire to negotiate a higher out-of-network rate than the amount paid by the patient in cost sharing.
Notice and Consent	
RARC #	RARC Text
N878	Alert: The provider or facility specified that notice was provided and consent to balance bill obtained, but notice and consent was not provided and obtained in a manner consistent with applicable federal law. Thus, cost sharing and the total amount paid have been calculated based on the requirements under the No Surprises Act, and balance billing is prohibited.
N879	Alert: The notice and consent to balance bill, and to be charged out-of-network cost sharing, that was obtained from the patient with regard to the billed services, is not permitted for these services. Thus, cost sharing and the total amount paid have been calculated based on the requirements under the No Surprises Act, and balance billing is prohibited.
Miscellaneous	
RARC #	RARC Text
N830	Alert: The charge[s] for this service was processed in accordance with federal/state, balance-billing/no-surprise billing regulations. As such, any amount identified with OA, CO, or PI cannot be collected from the member and may be considered provider liability or be billable to a subsequent payer. Any amount the provider collected over the identified PR amount must be refunded to the patient within applicable federal/state timeframes. Payment amounts are eligible for dispute pursuant to any federal/state documented appeal/grievance process(es).
N859	Alert: The federal No Surprises Act was applied to the processing of this claim. Payment amounts are eligible for dispute pursuant to any federal documented appeal/grievance/dispute resolution process(es).

For more on health care payment and remittance advice, please see https://www.cms.gov/Regulations-and-Guidance/Administrative-Simplification/Transactions/HealthCarePaymentandRemittanceAdviceandElectronicFundsTransfer or https://www.cms.gov/Medicare/Billing/ElectronicBillingEDITrans/Remittance.

APPENDIX B: BALANCE BILLING LAWS BY STATE

TITLE 3 ALASKA ADMINISTRATIVE CODE

§ 26.110 Additional standards for prompt, fair, and equitable settlements of health claims

(a) A person who provides coverage in this state for health care services or supplies on an expense incurred basis for which benefits are based on an amount that is less than the actual amount billed for the health care services or supplies shall

(1) for a vaccine covered by an insurance policy that is an included vaccine and purchased by a provider instead of obtained from the state under the statewide immunization program established under AS 18.09.200, determine the final payment for the covered vaccine at an amount equal to or greater than the cost of the state-purchased vaccine under the statewide immunization program; in this paragraph, "included vaccine" has the meaning given in AS 18.09.990;

(2) provide an explanation of the basis of payments in clear and simple terms with any claim payment and document the provided explanation in the claim file; and

(3) provide an explanation of the basis of payments in the health insurance policy, including any payments for which a covered individual may be responsible, and include on any schedule or summary of benefits page accompanying the policy a statement regarding whether the covered individual is responsible for any amount billed for a health care service or supply item that exceeds the final payment.

(b) This section does not apply to workers' compensation claims.

(c) If a person who is required to include a coordination of benefits provision under AS 21.42.205 provides coverage on a secondary basis,

(1) absent evidence of fraud, the secondary insurer must accept the primary insurer's precertification, utilization review, or other managed care requirement determination and may not deny, delay, or reduce benefits under its policy for a covered person who has met the primary insurer's precertification, utilization review, or other managed care requirement; and

(2) the secondary insurer must calculate its covered benefits at no greater cost to the covered person than if the health care services were obtained from the secondary insurer's participating provider if

(A) the secondary policy provides benefits through a provider network but the primary insurer's policy does not provide coverage through a provider network;

(B) both the primary policy and the secondary policy provide benefits through provider networks but the covered person obtains health care services from a provider that is in the provider network of the primary insurer but not the provider network of the secondary insurer; or

(C) both the primary policy and the secondary policy provide benefits through provider networks but the covered person obtains health care services from a provider that is not part of the provider network of the primary insurer or the secondary insurer because no provider in the primary insurer's provider network is able to meet the particular health need of the covered person.

(d) A health care insurer shall give written notice to a health care provider, health care facility, or consumer at least 30 calendar days before the insurer seeks recovery of an overpayment. The notice must include adequate information for the health care provider, health care facility, or consumer to identify the specific claim and the specific reason for the recovery. A health care insurer may not initiate recovery of an overpayment more than 365 days after the date the original payment was made to a health care provider, health care facility, or consumer, or its agents, unless the health care insurer has clear and documented reason to believe that the health care provider, the health care facility, or consumer, or its agents has committed fraud or other intentional misconduct.

(e) A health care insurer shall provide a health care provider, health care facility, or consumer with an opportunity to challenge the recovery of an overpayment, including sharing of claims information, and shall establish written policies and procedures for a health care provider, health care facility, or consumer to follow in order to challenge the recovery of an overpayment.

(f) If a health insurance policy provides in-network and out-of-network benefits, the policy must provide at a minimum the in-network benefit level for the following:

(1) emergency services;

(2) services or supplies provided by an out-of-network health care provider or health care facility, if an in-network health care provider or health care facility is not reasonably accessible as defined in the policy;

(3) services provided by an out-of-network health care provider as part of a covered stay at an in-network health care facility when a covered individual does not have or is not given a choice of health care provider.

(g) An insurer may require a covered individual to purchase specialty drugs from a specific in-network health care provider in order to receive benefits under a health insurance policy, unless the specialty drug is not available from the health care provider when needed and a delay in receiving the drug would threaten the efficacy of treatment or the life of the covered individual.

(h) An insurer may require a covered individual to receive transplant services from an in-network health care provider in order to receive benefits under a health insurance policy, unless transplant services are not available from a network health care provider when needed and a delay in receiving the transplant services would threaten the efficacy of treatment or the life of the covered individual.

(i) An insurer may not process claims based on a procedure code that differs from the procedure code specified in the claim unless agreed upon by the health care provider that provided the service or supply.

(j) If an insurer provides benefits to a domestic partner, then the insurer may not unfairly discriminate on the basis of gender and must provide benefits to both same and opposite gender domestic partners.

(k) If an insurer, for purposes of negotiating discounts with a health care provider, delays payment of an otherwise clean claim beyond the timeframes under AS 21.36.495, the insurer is subject to the 15 percent interest penalty under AS 21.36.495(c) or (d).

(l) An insurer may not reduce the payment on a current claim for an overpayment on a previous claim unless the reduction
   (1) is determined to be in compliance with (d) and (e) of this section; and
   (2) does not result in a reduction on the amount allowed on any other claims of the covered individual.

ARIZONA REVISED STATUTES

§ 20-3111 Definitions

In this article, unless the context otherwise requires:

1. "Arbitration" means a dispute resolution process in which an impartial arbitrator determines the dollar amount a health care provider is entitled to receive for payment of a surprise out-of-network bill.
2. "Arbitrator" means an impartial person who is appointed to conduct an arbitration.
3. "Billing company" means any affiliated or unaffiliated company that is hired by a health care provider or health care facility to coordinate the payment of bills with health insurers and to generate or bill and collect payment from enrollees on the health care provider's or health care facility's behalf.
4. "Contracted provider" means a health care provider that has entered into a contract with a health insurer to provide health care services to the health insurer's enrollees at agreed on rates.
5. "Cost sharing requirements" means an enrollee's applicable out-of-network coinsurance, copayment and deductible requirements under a health plan based on the adjudicated claim.
6. "Emergency services" has the same meaning prescribed in section 20-2801.
7. "Enrollee" means an individual who is eligible to receive benefits through a health plan.
8. "Health care facility" has the same meaning prescribed in section 36-437.
9. "Health care provider" means a person who is licensed, registered or certified as a health care professional under title 32 or a laboratory or durable medical equipment provider that furnishes services to a patient in a network facility and that separately bills the patient for the services.
10. "Health care services" means treatment, services, medications, tests, equipment, devices, durable medical equipment, laboratory services or supplies rendered or provided to an enrollee for the purpose of diagnosing, preventing, alleviating, curing or healing human disease, illness or injury.
11. "Health insurer" means a disability insurer, group disability insurer, blanket disability insurer, hospital service corporation or medical service corporation that provides health insurance in this state.
12. "Health plan" means a group or individual health plan that finances or furnishes health care services and that is issued by a health insurer.
13. "Network facility" means a health care facility that has entered into a contract with a health insurer to provide health care services to the health insurer's enrollees at agreed on rates.
14. "Surprise out-of-network bill" means a bill for a health care service that was provided in a network facility by a health care provider that is not a contracted provider and that meets one of the requirements listed in section 20-3113.

§ 20-3112 Applicability

This article does not apply to:

1. Health care services that are not covered by the enrollee's health plan.
2. Limited benefit coverage as defined in section 20-1137.
3. Charges for health care services that are subject to a direct payment agreement under section 32-3216 or 36-437.
4. Health plans that do not include coverage for out-of-network health care services, unless otherwise required by law.
5. State health and accident coverage for full-time officers and employees of this state and their dependents that is provided pursuant to title 38, chapter 4, article 4.
6. A self-funded or self-insured employee benefit plan if the regulation of that plan is preempted by the employee retirement income security act of 1974 (P.L. 93-406; 88 Stat. 829; 29 United States Code section 1144(b)).

§ 20-3113 Surprise out-of-network bill: requirements; notice

A. A bill for a health care service that was provided in a network facility by a health care provider that is not a contracted provider must meet one of the following requirements to qualify as a surprise out-of-network bill:
   1. The bill was for emergency services, including under circumstances described by section 20-2803, subsection A and health care services directly related to the emergency services that are provided during an inpatient admission to any network facility.
   2. The bill was for a health care service that was not provided in the case of an emergency and the health care provider or the provider's representative did not provide to the enrollee, or did not provide to the enrollee within a reasonable amount of time before the enrollee received the services, a written dated disclosure that contained the following information:
      (a) Notice that contains the name of the billing health care provider and that states the health care provider is not a contracted provider.
      (b) The estimated total cost to be billed by the health care provider or the provider's representative.
      (c) Notice that the enrollee or the enrollee's authorized representative is not required to sign the disclosure to obtain medical care but if the enrollee or the enrollee's representative signs the disclosure, the enrollee may have waived any rights to dispute resolution under this article.
   3. The bill was for a health care service that was not provided in the case of an emergency and the enrollee received the disclosure prescribed in paragraph 2 of this subsection, but the enrollee or the enrollee's authorized representative chose not to sign the disclosure.

B. Notwithstanding any provision of this article, a health insurer and any health plan offered by a health insurer shall comply with chapter 17, article 1 of this title.

§ 20-3114 Dispute resolution; settlement teleconference; arbitration; surprise out-of-network bills

A. An enrollee who has received a surprise out-of-network bill and who disputes the amount of the bill may seek dispute resolution of the bill by filing a request for arbitration with the department not later than one year after the date of service noted in the surprise out-of-network bill, except as otherwise provided in this section, if all of the following apply:

1. The enrollee has resolved any health care appeal pursuant to chapter 15, article 2 of this title that the enrollee may have had against the health insurer following the health insurer's initial adjudication of the claim. The one-year time period for requesting arbitration is tolled from the date that the enrollee files a health care appeal until the date of final resolution of the appeal.
2. The enrollee has not instituted a civil lawsuit or other legal action against the insurer or health care provider related to the same surprise out-of-network bill or the health care services provided.
3. The amount of the surprise out-of-network bill for which the enrollee is responsible for all related health care services provided by the health care provider whether contained in one or multiple bills, after deduction of the enrollee's cost sharing requirements and the insurer's allowable reimbursement, is at least one thousand dollars.

B. If an enrollee requests dispute resolution of a surprise out-of-network bill, the enrollee or the enrollee's authorized representative shall participate in an informal settlement teleconference and may participate in the arbitration of the bill. If the enrollee or enrollee's authorized representative fails to attend the informal settlement teleconference, the conference shall be terminated and the enrollee, within fourteen days after the first scheduled informal settlement teleconference, may request that the department reschedule the informal settlement teleconference. If the enrollee does not request that the department reschedule the informal settlement teleconference, the enrollee forfeits the right to arbitrate the surprise out-of-network bill. The health care provider or the provider's representative and the health insurer shall participate in the informal settlement teleconference and the arbitration.

C. An enrollee may not seek dispute resolution of a bill if the enrollee or the enrollee's authorized representative signed the disclosure prescribed in section 20-3113, subsection A, paragraph 2 and the amount actually billed to the enrollee is less than or equal to the estimated total cost provided in the disclosure.

§ 20-3115 Conduct of arbitration proceedings

A. The department shall develop a simple, fair, efficient and cost-effective arbitration procedure for surprise out-of-network bill disputes and specify time frames, standards and other details of the arbitration proceeding, including procedures for scheduling and notifying the parties of the settlement teleconference required by subsection E of this section. The department shall contract with one or more entities to provide arbitrators who are qualified under section 20-3116 for this process. Department staff may not serve as arbitrators.

B. An enrollee may request arbitration of a surprise out-of-network bill by submitting a request for arbitration to the department on a form prescribed by the department, which shall include contact, billing and payment information regarding the surprise out-of-network bill and any other information the department believes is necessary to confirm that the bill qualifies for arbitration. The form shall be made available on the department's website.

C. Within fifteen days after receipt of a request for arbitration, the department shall do one of the following:

1. Determine that the surprise out-of-network bill qualifies for arbitration under this article and notify the enrollee, health insurer and health care provider that the request qualifies.
2. Determine that the surprise out-of-network bill does not qualify for arbitration under this article and notify the enrollee that the surprise out-of-network bill does not qualify and state the reason for the determination.
3. If the department cannot determine whether the surprise out-of-network bill qualifies for arbitration, request in writing any additional information from the enrollee, health insurer or health care provider or its billing company that is needed to determine whether the surprise out-of-network bill qualifies for arbitration and all of the following apply:
   (a) The enrollee, health insurer or health care provider or its billing company shall respond to the department's request for additional information within fifteen days after the date of the department's request.
   (b) Within seven days after receipt of the additional requested information, the department shall determine whether the surprise out-of-network bill qualifies for arbitration and send the notices required under this subsection.
   (c) If the health insurer or health care provider or its billing company fails to respond within the time frame specified in subdivision (a) of this paragraph to a department request for information, the department shall deem the request for arbitration as eligible for arbitration. If the enrollee fails to respond within the time frame specified in subdivision (a) of this paragraph, the request for arbitration is denied.

D. The determination by the department of whether a surprise out-of-network bill qualifies for arbitration is a final and binding decision with no right of appeal to the department. The department's determination is solely an administrative remedy and does not bar any private right or cause of action for or on behalf of any enrollee, provider or other person. The court shall decide the matter, including any interpretation of statute or rule, without deference to any previous determination that may have been made on the question by the department.

E. In an effort to settle the surprise out-of-network bill before arbitration, the department shall arrange an informal settlement teleconference within thirty days after the department sends the notices required by this section. The department is not a party to and may not participate in the informal settlement teleconference. As part of the settlement teleconference the health insurer shall provide to the parties the enrollee's cost sharing requirements under the enrollee's health plan based on the adjudicated claim. The insurer shall notify the department whether the informal settlement teleconference resulted in settlement of the disputed surprise out-of-network bill and, if settlement was reached, notify the department of the terms of the settlement within seven days.

F. If after proper notice from the department or contracted entity either the health insurer or health care provider or the provider's representative fails to participate in the teleconference, the other party may notify the department to immediately initiate arbitration and the nonparticipating party shall be required to pay the total cost of the arbitration.

G. On receipt of notice that the dispute has not settled or that a party has failed to participate in the teleconference, the department shall appoint an arbitrator and shall notify the parties of the arbitration and the appointed arbitrator. The department's notice shall specify whether one party is responsible for the total cost of the arbitration pursuant to subsection F of this section. The health insurer and health care provider must agree on the arbitrator and may mutually agree to use an arbitrator who is not on the department's list. If either the health insurer or health care provider objects to the arbitrator, and the parties are unable to agree on a mutually acceptable alternative arbitrator, the department or contracted entity shall randomly assign three arbitrators. The health insurer and the health care provider shall each strike one arbitrator, and the last arbitrator shall conduct the arbitration unless there are two arbitrators remaining, in which case the department or contracted entity shall randomly assign the arbitrator.

H. Before the arbitration:
   1. The enrollee shall pay or make arrangements in writing to pay the health care provider the total amount of the enrollee's cost sharing requirements that is due for the health care services that are the subject of the surprise out-of-network bill as stated by the health insurer in the settlement teleconference.
   2. The enrollee shall pay any amount that has been received by the enrollee from the enrollee's health insurer as payment for the out-of-network health care services that were provided by the health care provider.
   3. If a health insurer pays for out-of-network health care services directly to a health care provider, the health insurer that has not remitted its payment for the out-of-network health care services shall remit the amount due to the health care provider.

I. Arbitration of any surprise out-of-network bill shall be conducted telephonically unless otherwise agreed by all of the required participants.

J. Arbitration of the surprise out-of-network bill shall take place with or without the enrollee's participation.

K. The arbitrator shall determine the amount the health care provider is entitled to receive as payment for the health care services. The arbitrator shall allow each party to provide information the arbitrator reasonably determines to be relevant in evaluating the surprise out-of-network bill, including the following information:

1. The average contracted amount that the health insurer pays for the health care services at issue in the county where the health care services were performed.
2. The average amount that the health care provider has contracted to accept for the health care services at issue in the county where the services were performed.
3. The amount that Medicare and Medicaid pay for the health care services at issue.
4. The health care provider's direct pay rate for the health care services at issue, if any, under section 32-3216.
5. Any information that would be evaluated in determining whether a fee is reasonable under title 32 and not excessive for the health care services at issue, including the usual and customary charges for the health care services at issue performed by a health care provider in the same or similar specialty and provided in the same geographic area.
6. Any other reliable databases or sources of information on the amount paid for the health care services at issue in the county where the services were performed.

L. Except on the agreement of the parties participating in the arbitration, the arbitration shall be conducted within one hundred twenty days after the department's notice of arbitration.

M. Except on the agreement of the parties participating in the arbitration, the arbitration may not last more than four hours.

N. The arbitrator shall issue a final written decision within ten business days following the arbitration hearing. The arbitrator shall provide a copy of the decision to the enrollee, the health insurer and the health care provider or its billing company or authorized representative.

O. All pricing information provided by health insurers and health care providers in connection with the arbitration of a surprise out-of-network bill is confidential and may not be disclosed by the arbitrator or any other party participating in the arbitration or used by anyone, other than the providing party, for any purpose other than to resolve the surprise out-of-network bill.

P. All information received by the department or contracted entity in connection with an arbitration is confidential and may not be disclosed by the department or contracted entity to any person other than the arbitrator.

Q. A claim that is the subject of an arbitration request is not subject to article 1 of this chapter during the pendency of the arbitration. A health insurer shall remit its portion of the payment resulting from the informal settlement teleconference or the amount awarded by the arbitrator within thirty days after resolution of the claim.

R. A claim that is reprocessed by an insurer as a result of a settlement, arbitration decision or other action under this article is not in violation of section 20-3102, subsection N.

S. Notwithstanding any informal settlement or the arbitrator's decision under this article, the enrollee is responsible for only the amount of the enrollee's cost sharing requirements and any amount received by the enrollee from the enrollee's health insurer as payment for the out-of-network health care services that were provided by the health care provider, and the health care provider may not issue, either directly or through its billing company, any additional balance bill to the enrollee related to the health care service that was the subject of the informal settlement teleconference or arbitration.

T. Unless all the parties otherwise agree or unless required by subsection F of this section, the health insurer and the health care provider shall share the costs of the arbitration equally, and the enrollee is not responsible for any portion of the cost of the arbitration. The health insurer and health care provider shall make payment arrangements with the arbitrator for their respective share of the costs of the arbitration.

§ 20-3116 Arbitrator qualifications

To qualify as an arbitrator, a person shall have at least three years' experience in health care services claims and shall comply with any other qualifications established by the department.

§ 20-3117 Dispute resolution; notice of rights

A. The department in conjunction with the appropriate health care boards shall prescribe the notice outlining an enrollee's rights to dispute surprise out-of-network bills under this article.

B. Health insurers shall include the notice prescribed pursuant to subsection A of this section in each explanation of benefits or other similar claim adjudication notice that is issued to enrollees and that involves covered services provided by a noncontracted health care provider.

C. If an enrollee contacts a health care provider, a provider's representative or a billing company regarding a dispute involving a surprise out-of-network bill, the health care provider, the provider's representative or the billing company shall provide written notice as prescribed in subsection A of this section to the enrollee of the dispute resolution process.

D. The department shall post on its website information for health care consumers regarding what constitutes a surprise out-of-network bill, how to try to avoid a surprise out-of-network bill and how the dispute resolution process may be used to resolve a surprise out-of-network bill.

§ 20-3118 Surprise out-of-network bills; annual report

A. On or before December 31, 2019, and each December 31 thereafter, the department shall report on the resolution of disputed surprise out-of-network bills. The report shall include:

   1. The total number of inquiries regarding dispute resolution of surprise out-of-network bills.

2. The total number of requests that did not qualify for dispute resolution and the reasons why the disputed bills did not qualify.
3. The number of requests that qualified for dispute resolution.
4. The most common requests for dispute resolution by health care provider specialty area.
5. The most common requests for dispute resolution by health care service.
6. The number of requests for dispute resolution by geographic area in this state.
7. The most common requests for dispute resolution based on the type of health care facility in which the health care services were provided.
8. The number of requests for dispute resolution that were settled during a settlement teleconference.
9. The number of requests for dispute resolution that were settled during arbitration.
10. The number of times a health insurer, a health care provider or the provider's representative or an enrollee failed to attend the settlement teleconference.
11. The average percentage by which disputed surprise out-of-network bills were reduced from the initially billed amount.
12. Any additional information that the department determines is relevant in evaluating the effectiveness of the dispute resolution process.

B. The department shall submit the report to the governor, the president of the senate and the speaker of the house of representatives and shall provide a copy of the report to the secretary of state.

§ 20-3119 Right of civil action

An enrollee who is aggrieved by an arbitration decision regarding a disputed surprise out-of-network bill may file a civil action in superior court not later than one year after the date of the disputed decision to obtain appropriate relief with respect to the same surprise out-of-network bill.

ARIZONA ADMINISTRATIVE CODE

§ R20-6-2401 Definitions

The definitions in A.R.S. § 20-3111 and this Section apply to this Article.

1. "Allowed Amount" is the amount reimbursable for a covered service under the terms of the enrollee's benefit plan. The allowed amount includes both the amount payable by the insurer and the amount of the enrollee's cost sharing requirements.

2. "Alternative Arbitrator" is an individual who is mutually agreeable to the health insurer and health care provider to act as the arbitrator of a surprise out-of-network billing dispute. If the person is contracted with the State of Arizona to conduct arbitration proceedings, the provisions of that contract shall apply. Department staff may not serve as an Alternative Arbitrator.
3. "Amount of the enrollee's cost sharing requirements" means the amount determined by the insurer prior to the dispute resolution process to be owed by the enrollee for out-of-network copayment, coinsurance and deductible pursuant to the enrollee's health care policy.
4. "Arbitrator" has the same meaning as A.R.S. § 20-3111(2) and may include a mediator, arbitrator or other alternative dispute resolution professional who is contracted with the Department to arbitrate a surprise out-of-network billing dispute. Department staff may not serve as an Arbitrator.
5. "A.R.S. § 20-3113 Disclosure" means a written, dated document that contains the following information:
   a. The name of the billing health care provider;
   b. A statement that the health care provider is not a contracted provider;
   c. The estimated total cost to be billed by the health care provider or the provider's representative for the health care services being provided;
   d. A notice that the enrollee or the enrollee's authorized representative is not required to sign the A.R.S. § 20-3113 Disclosure to obtain health care services;
   e. A notice that if the enrollee or the enrollee's authorized representative signs the A.R.S. § 20-3113 Disclosure, they may have waived any rights to request arbitration of a qualifying surprise out-of-network bill.
6. "Balance bill" means all charges that exceed the enrollee's cost sharing requirements and the amount paid by the insurer.
7. "Date of service" means the latest date on which the health care provider rendered a related health care service that is the subject of a qualifying surprise out-of-network bill.
8. "Days" as used in this Article means calendar days unless specified as business days and does not include the day of the filing of a document.
9. "Department" means the Arizona Department of Insurance and Financial Institutions or an entity with which it contracts to administer the out-of-network claim dispute resolution process.
10. "Enrollee's authorized representative" means a person to whom an enrollee has given express written consent to represent the enrollee, the enrollee's parent or legal guardian, a person appointed by the court to act on behalf of the enrollee or the enrollee's legal representative. An enrollee's authorized representative shall not be someone who represents the provider's interests.
11. "Final resolution of a health care appeal" means that a member has a final decision under the review process provided by A.R.S. Title 20, Chapter 15, Article 2.

12. "Informal Settlement Teleconference" means a teleconference arranged by the Department that is held to settle the enrollee's qualifying surprise out-of-network bill prior to an Arbitration being scheduled. The parties to the Informal Settlement Teleconference are:
    (a) the enrollee or the enrollee's authorized representative;
    (b) the health insurer; and
    (c) the provider or the provider's representative.
13. "Qualifying surprise out-of-network bill" is a surprise out-of-network bill for health care services provided on or after January 1, 2019, that is disputed by the enrollee and:
    a. Is for health care services covered by the enrollee's health plan;
    b. Is for health care services provided in a network health care facility;
    c. Is for health care services performed by a provider who is not contracted to participate in the network that serves the enrollee's health plan;
    d. The enrollee has resolved any health care appeal pursuant to A.R.S. Title 20, Chapter 15, Article 2, that the enrollee may have had against the insurer following the health insurer's initial adjudication of the claim;
    e. The enrollee has not instituted a civil lawsuit or other legal action against the insurer or health care provider related to the surprise out-of-network bill or the health care services provided;
    f. The amount of the surprise out-of-network bill for which the enrollee is responsible for all related health care services provided by the health care provider whether contained in one or multiple bills, after deduction of the enrollee's cost sharing requirements and the insurer's allowable reimbursement, is at least $1,000.00; and
    g. One of the following applies:
        i. The bill is for emergency services, including under circumstances described by A.R.S. § 20-2803(A);
        ii. The bill is for health care services directly related to the emergency services that are provided during an inpatient admission to any network facility;
        iii. The bill is for a health care service that was not provided in the case of an emergency and the health care provider or provider's representative did not provide the enrollee a written dated A.R.S. § 20-3113 Disclosure;
        iv. The bill is for a health care service that was not provided in the case of an emergency and the health care provider or provider's representative did not provide the enrollee a written dated A.R.S. § 20-3113 Disclosure within a reasonable amount of time before the enrollee received the service;
        v. The bill is for a health care service that was not provided in the case of an emergency and the health care provider or provider's representative provided the enrollee a written dated A.R.S. § 20-3113 Disclosure ("Disclosure") and the enrollee or the

enrollee's authorized representative chose not to sign the Disclosure;

vi. The bill is for a health care service that was not provided in the case of an emergency and the health care provider or provider's representative provided the enrollee a written dated A.R.S. § 20-3113 Disclosure ("Disclosure") and the enrollee or the enrollee's authorized representative signed the Disclosure but the amount actually billed to the enrollee is greater than the estimated cost provided in the signed Disclosure.

§ R20-6-2402 Request for arbitration

A. Request for Arbitration. An enrollee may request dispute resolution of a surprise out-of-network bill by filing a timely Request for Arbitration with the Department on a Request for Arbitration form available on the Department's website.

B. Deadline for filing a Request for Arbitration with the Department. A Request for Arbitration must be received by the Department within one year after the date of service listed on the surprise out-of-network bill. If the enrollee filed a health care appeal pursuant to A.R.S. Title 20, Chapter 15, Article 2, the one year deadline is tolled from the date the enrollee filed the health care appeal to the date of the final resolution of the appeal.

C. Evaluation of the Request for Arbitration by the Department. Within 15 days after receipt of a Request for Arbitration, the Department shall do one of the following:

1. Determine that the surprise out-of-network bill is a qualifying surprise out-of-network bill and notify the enrollee, health insurer and health care provider that the Request for Arbitration qualifies for Arbitration;
2. Determine that the surprise out-of-network bill is not a qualifying surprise out-of-network bill and notify the enrollee of the reason for the Department's determination;
3. Determine that the Request for Arbitration is incomplete, or
4. Return the Request for Arbitration to the enrollee without making a determination if the enrollee's request should instead be filed as a health care appeal within the meaning of A.R.S. Title 20, Chapter 15, Article 2.

D. Request for additional information for an incomplete Request for Arbitration. If the Department determines that the Request for Arbitration is incomplete, the Department may send a written request for additional information to the enrollee, health insurer, health care provider or health care provider's billing company.

E. Time to respond to the Department's Request for Additional Information. The enrollee, health insurer, health care provider or the health care provider's billing company shall have 15 days from the date of the request to respond to the Department's Request for Additional Information.

F. Failure to respond to the Department's Request for Additional Information.
   1. If the enrollee fails to respond to the Department's Request for Additional Information, the Department shall deny the enrollee's Request for Arbitration.
   2. If either the health insurer or the health care provider or health care provider's billing company fail to respond to the Department's Request for Additional Information, the Department shall deem that the enrollee's Request for Arbitration qualifies for arbitration.

G. Receipt of Additional Information. Upon receipt of the additional information requested by the Department under subsection (D) of this Section, the Department shall determine, within seven days, whether the enrollee's Request for Arbitration qualifies for Arbitration and send the notice required under subsection (C)(1) or subsection (C)(2) of this Section, whichever applies.

H. Final Determination. The Department's determination whether an enrollee's Request for Arbitration qualifies for Arbitration is a final decision and not an appealable agency action within the meaning of A.R.S. § 41-1092(3). A claim that is the subject of a qualifying surprise out-of-network bill is not subject to the timely payment of claims law during the pendency of the Arbitration.

I. Enrollee's payment responsibility.
   1. Notwithstanding any informal settlement or Arbitrator's Final Written Decision, the enrollee is responsible for only the following:
      a. The amount of the enrollee's cost sharing requirements; and
      b. Any amount received by the enrollee from the enrollee's health insurer as payment for the health care services at issue in a qualifying surprise out-of-network bill.
   2. A health care provider may not issue, either directly or indirectly through its billing company, any additional balance bill to the enrollee for the same health care services.

§ R20-6-2403 Informal settlement teleconference

A. Deadline to arrange the Informal Settlement Teleconference. Upon a determination that an enrollee has made a Request for Arbitration that qualifies for Arbitration, the Department shall arrange an Informal Settlement Teleconference between the parties within 30 days of notifying the enrollee that the enrollee's Request for Arbitration qualifies for Arbitration required by Section R20-6-2402(C)(1).

B. Notice of Informal Settlement Teleconference. At least 14 days prior to the scheduled date, the Department shall send a Notice of Informal Settlement Teleconference to the enrollee, the enrollee's authorized representative, the health insurer, the health care provider and the health care provider's representative informing them of the date, time and instructions on how to participate in the Informal Settlement Teleconference.

C. Health Insurer documentation. On or before the Informal Settlement Teleconference, the health insurer shall provide to the parties the enrollee's cost sharing requirements under the enrollee's health plan based on the qualifying surprise out-of-network bill.

D. Consequences of non-participation in the Informal Settlement Teleconference. If a party fails to participate in the Informal Settlement Teleconference, it shall be subject to the following consequences:

1. If the health insurer, provider or provider's representative fails to participate in an Informal Settlement Teleconference scheduled by the Department, the participating party may notify the Department which shall promptly schedule the Arbitration. The non-participating party shall pay the entire cost of the Arbitration.
2. If the enrollee or the enrollee's authorized representative fails to participate in the original Informal Settlement Teleconference, the original Informal Settlement Teleconference is terminated.
3. If the enrollee or the enrollee's authorized representative fails to participate in a rescheduled Informal Settlement Teleconference, the enrollee's Request for Arbitration is terminated.

E. One-time opportunity for the enrollee to reschedule the Informal Settlement Teleconference. If the enrollee or the enrollee's representative fails to participate in the Informal Settlement Teleconference originally scheduled by the Department, the enrollee may request that the Department reschedule the Informal Settlement Conference. The enrollee's request to reschedule must be received by the Department within 14 days after the originally scheduled Informal Settlement Teleconference. Failure to submit a request to the Department to reschedule the Informal Settlement Teleconference within the 14 day period terminates the enrollee's Request for Arbitration.

F. Notification to the Department after the Informal Settlement Teleconference: Within seven days after the date of the Informal Settlement Teleconference, the health insurer shall:

1. Notify the Department whether a settlement was reached between the parties; and
2. If a settlement was reached, notify the Department of the terms of the settlement on a form prescribed by the Department.

G. Failure to settle. If the parties fail to settle the qualifying surprise out-of-network bill at the Informal Settlement Teleconference, the Department shall arrange for the Arbitration.

H. Settlement. If the parties settle the qualifying surprise out-of-network bill at the Informal Settlement Teleconference, the health insurer shall remit its portion of the payment to the health care provider within 30 days after the Informal Settlement Teleconference. A claim that is reprocessed by a health insurer as a result of informal settlement is not in violation of A.R.S. § 20-3102(L).

§ R20-6-2404 Arbitrators

A. Contracted entities. The Department shall contract with one or more persons to provide Arbitrators. The Department must have a list of at least four Arbitrators to assign to Arbitrations. The Department shall publish the list of contracted entities and a list of each entity's qualified Arbitrators on its website.

B. Arbitrator Qualifications. Any person contracting with the Department must be able to provide Arbitrators who possess at least three years of experience in health care services claims.

C. Alternative Arbitrators. A health insurer and provider may mutually agree to use an Alternative Arbitrator if either the health insurer or the health care provider objects to an Arbitrator appointed by the Department.

D. Appointment of an Arbitrator.
   1. The Department shall appoint an Arbitrator for each Arbitration.
   2. If the health insurer and health care provider do not agree to the Arbitrator appointed by the Department, they shall either:
      a. Mutually agree to use an Alternative Arbitrator; or
      b. Participate in the following procedure:
         i. The Department shall assign three Arbitrators.
         ii. The health insurer shall strike one Arbitrator.
         iii. The health care provider shall strike one Arbitrator.
         iv. If one Arbitrator remains, the Department shall appoint the remaining Arbitrator to the Arbitration.
         v. If the health insurer and health care provider strike the same Arbitrator, the Department shall randomly assign the Arbitrator from the remaining two Arbitrators.

§ R20-6-2405 Before the arbitration

A. Enrollee's duties. Before the Arbitration, the enrollee shall:
   1. Pay or make arrangements in writing to pay to the health care provider the amount stated by the health insurer in the Informal Settlement Teleconference which shall be the total amount of the enrollee's cost sharing requirements due for the health care services that are the subject of the qualifying surprise out-of-network bill.
   2. Pay to the health care provider any amount that the enrollee has received from the health insurer as payment for the health care services that are the subject of the qualifying surprise out-of-network bill.

B. Health insurer's duties. Before the Arbitration, the health insurer shall remit any amount due to the health care provider if the health care insurer pays for out-of-network services directly to health care providers and the health insurer has not remitted any amounts due.

§ R20-6-2406 The arbitration

A. Conduct of Arbitration. An Arbitration of a qualifying out-of-network surprise bill shall be conducted:

1. Telephonically unless the parties agree otherwise;
2. With or without the enrollee's participation;
3. Within 120 days after the Department's Notice of Arbitration unless agreed otherwise by the parties; and
4. For a maximum duration of four hours unless agreed otherwise by the parties.

B. Arbitrator's Determination. The Arbitrator or Alternative Arbitrator shall determine the amount the health care provider is entitled to receive as payment for the health care services that are the subject of the qualifying surprise out-of-network bill.

C. Allowable Evidence. The Arbitrator or Alternative Arbitrator shall allow each party to provide relevant information for evaluating the qualifying surprise out-of-network bill including:

1. The average contracted amount that the health insurer pays for the health care services at issue in the county where the health care provider performed the health care services;
2. The average amount that the health care provider has contracted to accept for the health care services at issue in the county where the health care provider performed the services;
3. The amount Medicare and Medicaid pay for the health care services at issue;
4. The health care provider's direct pay rate for the health care services at issue, if any, under A.R.S. § 32-3216;
5. Any information that would be evaluated in determining whether a fee is reasonable under title 32 and not excessive for the health care services at issue, including the usual and customary charges for the health care services at issue performed by a health care provider in the same or similar specialty and provided in the same geographic area; and
6. Any other reliable sources of information, including databases, that provide the amount paid for the health care services at issue in the county where the health care provider performed the services.

D. Final Written Decision. Within 10 business days following the Arbitration, the Arbitrator or Alternative Arbitrator shall issue a Final Written Decision and provide a copy to the enrollee, the health insurer, the health care provider, the health care provider's billing company (if applicable) and the health care provider's authorized representative (if applicable).

E. Payment of the claim. The health insurer shall remit its portion of the payment awarded by the Arbitrator or Alternative Arbitrator to the health care provider within 30 days of the date of the Final Written Decision. A claim that is reprocessed by a health insurer as a result of the Arbitration is not in violation of A.R.S. § 20-3102(L).

F. Payment of the Costs of Arbitration. The health insurer and health care provider shall make payment arrangements with the Arbitrator or Alternative Arbitrator to pay their respective shares of the costs of the Arbitration within 30 days after the date of the Final Written Decision. The respective shares of the costs of Arbitration are determined as follows:
   1. The enrollee is not responsible for any portion of the cost of the Arbitration.
   2. The health insurer and the health care provider shall share the costs of the Arbitration equally unless one of the following exceptions applies:
      a. The health insurer and health care provider agree to share the costs of the Arbitration in non-equal portions.
      b. The health insurer pays the entire cost of the Arbitration for failing to participate in the Informal Settlement Teleconference after receiving proper notice from the Department.
      c. The health care provider or the health care provider's representative pays the entire cost of the Arbitration for failing to participate in the Informal Settlement Teleconference after receiving proper notice from the Department.

G. Confidentiality. In connection with the Arbitration of a qualifying surprise out-of-network bill, all of the following apply:
   1. All pricing information provided by a health insurer or health care provider is confidential.
   2. Pricing information provided by a health insurer or health care provider may not be disclosed by the Arbitrator, Alternative Arbitrator or any other party participating in the Arbitration.
   3. Pricing information provided by a health insurer or health care provider may not be used by anyone, except the party providing the information, for any purpose other than to resolve the qualifying surprise out-of-network bill.
   4. All information received by the Department in connection with the Arbitration is confidential and may not be disclosed to any person except the Arbitrator or Alternative Arbitrator.

H. Arbitrator's Report. At the conclusion of each Arbitration, the Arbitrator shall produce a report to the Department that contains the following information:
   1. Date of Arbitration;
   2. Date the Arbitrator issued the Final Written Decision;
   3. Whether the parties settled the qualifying surprise out-of-network bill during the Arbitration;
   4. The initial amount billed by the health care provider;
   5. The payment amount awarded to the health care provider; and
   6. Any other information the Department may request an Arbitrator to report prior to an Arbitration.

CALIFORNIA HEALTH AND SAFETY CODE

§ 1371.30 Independent dispute resolution process for noncontracting individual health professional

(a)

(1) By September 1, 2017, the department shall establish an independent dispute resolution process for the purpose of processing and resolving a claim dispute between a health care service plan and a noncontracting individual health professional for services subject to subdivision (a) of Section 1371.9.

(2) Prior to initiating the independent dispute resolution process, the parties shall complete the plan's internal process.

(3) If either the noncontracting individual health professional or the plan appeals a claim to the department's independent dispute resolution process, the other party shall participate in the appeal process as described in this section.

(b)

(1) The department shall establish uniform written procedures for the submission, receipt, processing, and resolution of claim payment disputes pursuant to this section and any other guidelines for implementing this section. These procedures shall include a process for each party to submit into evidence information that will be kept confidential from the other party, in order to preserve the confidentiality of the source contract.

(2) The department shall establish reasonable and necessary fees for the purpose of administering this section, to be paid by both parties.

(3) In establishing the independent dispute resolution process, the department shall permit the bundling of claims submitted to the same plan or the same delegated entity for the same or similar services by the same noncontracting individual health professional.

(4) The department shall permit a physician group, independent practice association, or other entity authorized to act on behalf of a noncontracting individual health professional to initiate and participate in the independent dispute resolution process.

(5)

(A) In deciding the dispute, the independent organization shall conduct a de novo review and base its decision regarding the appropriate reimbursement solely on the information and documents timely submitted into evidence by the parties to the dispute.

(B) The independent organization shall assign reviewers to each case based on their relevant education, background, and medical claims payment and clinical experience.

(c)

(1) The department may contract with one or more independent organizations to conduct the proceedings. The independent organization handling a dispute shall be independent of either party to the dispute.

(2) The department shall establish conflict-of-interest standards, consistent with the purposes of this section, that an organization shall meet in order to qualify to administer the independent dispute resolution program. The conflict-of-interest standards shall be consistent with the standards pursuant to subdivisions (c) and (d) of Section 1374.32.

(3) The department may contract with the same independent organization or organizations as the Department of Insurance.

(4) The department shall provide, upon the request of an interested person, a copy of all nonproprietary information, as determined by the director, filed with the department by an independent organization seeking to contract with the department to administer the independent dispute resolution process pursuant to this section. The department may charge a nominal fee to cover the costs of providing a copy of the information pursuant to this paragraph.

(5) The independent organization retained to conduct proceedings shall be deemed to be consultants for purposes of Section 43.98 of the Civil Code.

(6) Contracts entered into pursuant to the authority in this subdivision shall be exempt from Part 2 (commencing with Section 10100) of Division 2 of the Public Contract Code, Section 19130 of the Government Code, and Chapter 6 (commencing with Section 14825) of Part 5.5 of Division 3 of the Government Code and shall be exempt from the review or approval of any division of the Department of General Services.

(d) The decision obtained through the department's independent dispute resolution process shall be binding on both parties. The plan shall implement the decision obtained through the independent dispute resolution process. If dissatisfied, either party may pursue any right, remedy, or penalty established under any other applicable law.

(e) This section shall not apply to a Medi-Cal managed health care service plan or any entity that enters into a contract with the State Department of Health Care Services pursuant to Chapter 7 (commencing with Section 14000), Chapter 8 (commencing with Section 14200), and Chapter 8.75 (commencing with Section 14591) of Part 3 of Division 9 of the Welfare and Institutions Code.

(f) If a health care service plan delegates payment functions to a contracted entity, including, but not limited to, a medical group or independent practice association, then the delegated entity shall comply with this section.

(g) This section shall not apply to emergency services and care, as defined in Section 1317.1.

(h) The definitions in subdivision (f) of Section 1371.9 shall apply for purposes of this section.

(i) This section shall not be construed to alter a health care service plan's obligations pursuant to Sections 1371 and 1371.4.

(j) Notwithstanding Chapter 3.5 (commencing with Section 11340) of Part 1 of Division 3 of Title 2 of the Government Code, the department may implement, interpret, or make specific this section by means of all-plan letters or similar instructions, without taking regulatory action, until the time regulations are adopted.

(k) By January 1, 2019, the department shall provide a report to the Governor, the President pro Tempore of the Senate, the Speaker of the Assembly, and the Senate and Assembly Committees on Health of the data and information provided in the independent dispute resolution process in a manner and format specified by the Legislature.

§ 1371.31 Reimbursement rate for noncontracting individual health professional; reporting requirements; exemptions

(a)

(1) For services rendered subject to Section 1371.9, effective July 1, 2017, unless otherwise agreed to by the noncontracting individual health professional and the plan, the plan shall reimburse the greater of the average contracted rate or 125 percent of the amount Medicare reimburses on a fee-for-service basis for the same or similar services in the general geographic region in which the services were rendered. For the purposes of this section, "average contracted rate" means the average of the contracted commercial rates paid by the health plan or delegated entity for the same or similar services in the geographic region. This subdivision does not apply to subdivision (c) of Section 1371.9 or subdivision (b) of this section.

(2)

(A) By July 1, 2017, each health care service plan and its delegated entities shall provide to the department all of the following:

(i) Data listing its average contracted rates for the plan for services most frequently subject to Section 1371.9 in each geographic region in which the services are rendered for the calendar year 2015.

(ii) Its methodology for determining the average contracted rate for the plan for services subject to Section 1371.9. The methodology to determine an average contracted rate shall ensure that the plan includes the highest and lowest contracted rates for the calendar year 2015.

(iii) The policies and procedures used to determine the average contracted rates under this subdivision.

(B) For each calendar year after the plan's initial submission of the average contracted rate as specified in subparagraph (A) and until the standardized methodology under paragraph (3) is specified, a health care service plan and the plan's delegated entities shall adjust the rate initially established pursuant to this subdivision by the Consumer Price Index for Medical Care Services, as published by the United States Bureau of Labor Statistics.

(3)

(A) By January 1, 2019, the department shall specify a methodology that plans and delegated entities shall use to determine the average contracted rates for services most frequently subject to Section 1371.9. This methodology shall take into account, at a minimum, information from the independent dispute resolution process, the specialty of the individual health professional, and the geographic region in which the services are rendered. The methodology to determine an average contracted rate shall ensure that the plan includes the highest and lowest contracted rates.

(B) Health care service plans and delegated entities shall provide to the department the policies and procedures used to determine the average contracted rates in compliance with subparagraph (A).

(C) If, based on the health care service plan's model, a health care service plan does not pay a statistically significant number or dollar amount of claims for services covered under Section 1371.9, the health care service plan shall demonstrate to the department that it has access to a statistically credible database reflecting rates paid to noncontracting individual health professionals for services provided in a geographic region and shall use that database to determine an average contracted rate required pursuant to paragraph (1).

(D) The department shall review the information filed pursuant to this subdivision as part of its examination of fiscal and administrative affairs pursuant to Section 1382.

(E) The average contracted rate data submitted pursuant to this section shall be confidential and not subject to disclosure under the California Public Records Act (Division 10 (commencing with Section 7920.000) of Title 1 of the Government Code).

(F) In developing the standardized methodology under this subdivision, the department shall consult with interested parties throughout the process of developing the standards, including the Department of Insurance, representatives of health plans, insurers, health care providers, hospitals, consumer advocates, and other stakeholders it deems appropriate. The department shall hold the first stakeholder meeting no later than July 1, 2017.

(4) A health care service plan shall include in its reports submitted to the department pursuant to Section 1367.035 and regulations adopted pursuant to that section, in a manner specified by the department, the number of payments made to noncontracting individual health professionals for services at a contracting health facility and subject to Section 1371.9, as well as other data sufficient to determine the proportion of noncontracting individual health professionals to contracting individual health professionals at contracting health facilities, as defined in subdivision (f) of Section 1371.9. The department shall include a summary of this information in its January 1, 2019, report required pursuant to subdivision (k) of Section 1371.30 and its findings regarding the impact of the act that added this section on health care service plan contracting and network adequacy.

(5) A health care service plan that provides services subject to Section 1371.9 shall meet the network adequacy requirements set forth in this chapter, including, but not limited to, subdivisions (d) and (e) of Section 1367 of this code and in Exhibits (H) and (I) of subdivision (d) of Section 1300.51 of, and Sections 1300.67.2 and 1300.67.2.1 of, Title 28 of the California Code of Regulations, including, but not limited to, inpatient hospital services and specialist physician services, and if necessary, the department may adopt additional regulations related to those services. This section shall not be construed to limit the director's authority under this chapter.

(6) For purposes of this section for Medicare fee-for-service reimbursement, geographic regions shall be the geographic regions specified for physician reimbursement for Medicare fee-for-service by the United States Department of Health and Human Services.

(7) A health care service plan shall authorize and permit assignment of the enrollee's right, if any, to any reimbursement for health care services covered under the plan contract to a noncontracting individual health professional who furnishes the health care services rendered subject to Section 1371.9. Lack of assignment pursuant to this paragraph shall not be construed to limit the applicability of this section, Section 1371.30, or Section 1371.9.

(8) A noncontracting individual health professional, health care service plan, or health care service plan's delegated entity who disputes the claim reimbursement under this section shall utilize the independent dispute resolution process described in Section 1371.30.

(b) If nonemergency services are provided by a noncontracting individual health professional consistent with subdivision (c) of Section 1371.9 to an enrollee who has voluntarily chosen to use the enrollee's out-of-network benefit for services covered by a plan that includes coverage for out-of-network benefits, unless otherwise agreed to by the plan and the noncontracting individual health professional, the amount paid by the health care service plan shall be the amount set forth in the enrollee's evidence of coverage. This payment is not subject to the independent dispute resolution process described in Section 1371.30.

(c) If a health care service plan delegates the responsibility for payment of claims to a contracted entity, including, but not limited to, a medical group or independent practice association, then the entity to which that responsibility is delegated shall comply with the requirements of this section.

(d)

(1) A payment made by the health care service plan to the noncontracting health care professional for nonemergency services as required by Section 1371.9 and this section, in addition to the applicable cost sharing owed by the enrollee, shall constitute payment in full for nonemergency services rendered unless either party uses the independent dispute resolution process or other lawful means pursuant to Section 1371.30.

(2) Notwithstanding any other law, the amounts paid by a plan for services under this section shall not constitute the prevailing or customary charges, the usual fees to the general public, or other charges for other payers for an individual health professional.

(3) This subdivision shall not preclude the use of the independent dispute resolution process pursuant to Section 1371.30.

(e) This section shall not apply to a Medi-Cal managed health care service plan or any other entity that enters into a contract with the State Department of Health Care Services pursuant to Chapter 7 (commencing with Section 14000), Chapter 8 (commencing with Section 14200), and Chapter 8.75 (commencing with Section 14591) of Part 3 of Division 9 of the Welfare and Institutions Code.

(f) This section shall not apply to emergency services and care, as defined in Section 1317.1.

(g) The definitions in subdivision (f) of Section 1371.9 shall apply for purposes of this section.

(h) This section shall not be construed to alter a health care service plan's obligations pursuant to Sections 1371 and 1371.4.

§ 1371.9 "In-network cost-sharing amount" for services provided by noncontracting individual health professional; exemptions

(a)

(1) Except as provided in subdivision (c), a health care service plan contract issued, amended, or renewed on or after July 1, 2017, shall provide that if an enrollee receives covered services from a contracting health facility at which, or as a result of which, the enrollee receives services provided by a noncontracting individual health professional, the enrollee shall pay no more than the same cost sharing that the enrollee would pay

for the same covered services received from a contracting individual health professional. This amount shall be referred to as the "in-network cost-sharing amount."

(2) An enrollee shall not owe the noncontracting individual health professional more than the in-network cost-sharing amount for services subject to this section. At the time of payment by the plan to the noncontracting individual health professional, the plan shall inform the enrollee and the noncontracting individual health professional of the in-network cost-sharing amount owed by the enrollee.

(3) A noncontracting individual health professional shall not bill or collect any amount from the enrollee for services subject to this section except for the in-network cost-sharing amount. Any communication from the noncontracting individual health professional to the enrollee prior to the receipt of information about the in-network cost-sharing amount pursuant to paragraph (2) shall include a notice in 12-point bold type stating that the communication is not a bill and informing the enrollee that the enrollee shall not pay until he or she is informed by his or her health care service plan of any applicable cost sharing.

(4)

(A) If the noncontracting individual health professional has received more than the in-network cost-sharing amount from the enrollee for services subject to this section, the noncontracting individual health professional shall refund any overpayment to the enrollee within 30 calendar days after receiving payment from the enrollee.

(B) If the noncontracting individual health professional does not refund any overpayment to the enrollee within 30 calendar days after being informed of the enrollee's in-network cost-sharing amount, interest shall accrue at the rate of 15 percent per annum beginning with the date payment was received from the enrollee.

(C) A noncontracting individual health professional shall automatically include in his or her refund to the enrollee all interest that has accrued pursuant to this section without requiring the enrollee to submit a request for the interest amount.

(b) Except for services subject to subdivision (c), the following shall apply:

(1) Any cost sharing paid by the enrollee for the services subject to this section shall count toward the limit on annual out-of-pocket expenses established under Section 1367.006.

(2) Cost sharing arising from services subject to this section shall be counted toward any deductible in the same manner as cost sharing would be attributed to a contracting individual health professional.

(3) The cost sharing paid by the enrollee pursuant to this section shall satisfy the enrollee's obligation to pay cost sharing for the health service and shall constitute "applicable cost sharing owed by the enrollee."

(c) For services subject to this section, if an enrollee has a health care service plan that includes coverage for out-of-network benefits, a noncontracting individual health professional may bill or collect from the enrollee the out-of-network cost sharing, if applicable, only when the enrollee consents in writing and that written consent demonstrates satisfaction of all the following criteria:

(1) At least 24 hours in advance of care, the enrollee shall consent in writing to receive services from the identified noncontracting individual health professional.

(2) The consent shall be obtained by the noncontracting individual health professional in a document that is separate from the document used to obtain the consent for any other part of the care or procedure. The consent shall not be obtained by the facility or any representative of the facility. The consent shall not be obtained at the time of admission or at any time when the enrollee is being prepared for surgery or any other procedure.

(3) At the time consent is provided, the noncontracting individual health professional shall give the enrollee a written estimate of the enrollee's total out-of-pocket cost of care. The written estimate shall be based on the professional's billed charges for the service to be provided. The noncontracting individual health professional shall not attempt to collect more than the estimated amount without receiving separate written consent from the enrollee or the enrollee's authorized representative, unless circumstances arise during delivery of services that were unforeseeable at the time the estimate was given that would require the provider to change the estimate.

(4) The consent shall advise the enrollee that he or she may elect to seek care from a contracted provider or may contact the enrollee's health care service plan in order to arrange to receive the health service from a contracted provider for lower out-of-pocket costs.

(5) The consent and estimate shall be provided to the enrollee in the language spoken by the enrollee, if the language is a Medi-Cal threshold language, as defined in subdivision (d) of Section 128552.

(6) The consent shall also advise the enrollee that any costs incurred as a result of the enrollee's use of the out-of-network benefit shall be in addition to in-network cost-sharing amounts and may not count toward the annual out-of-pocket maximum on in-network benefits or a deductible, if any, for in-network benefits.

(d) A noncontracting individual health professional who fails to comply with the requirements of subdivision (c) has not obtained written consent for purposes of this section. Under those circumstances, subdivisions (a) and (b) shall apply and subdivision (c) shall not apply.

(e)

(1) A noncontracting individual health professional may advance to collections only the in-network cost-sharing amount, as determined by the

plan pursuant to subdivision (a) or the out-of-network cost-sharing amount owed pursuant to subdivision (c), that the enrollee has failed to pay.

(2) The noncontracting individual health professional, or any entity acting on his or her behalf, including any assignee of the debt, shall not report adverse information to a consumer credit reporting agency or commence civil action against the enrollee for a minimum of 150 days after the initial billing regarding amounts owed by the enrollee under subdivision (a) or (c).

(3) With respect to an enrollee, the noncontracting individual health professional, or any entity acting on his or her behalf, including any assignee of the debt, shall not use wage garnishments or liens on primary residences as a means of collecting unpaid bills under this section.

(f) For purposes of this section and Sections 1371.30 and 1371.31, the following definitions shall apply:

(1) "Contracting health facility" means a health facility that is contracted with the enrollee's health care service plan to provide services under the enrollee's plan contract. A contracting health care facility includes, but is not limited to, the following providers:

(A) A licensed hospital.

(B) An ambulatory surgery or other outpatient setting, as described in subdivision (a), (d), (e), (g), or (h) of Section 1248.1.

(C) A laboratory.

(D) A radiology or imaging center.

(2) "Cost sharing" includes any copayment, coinsurance, or deductible, or any other form of cost sharing paid by the enrollee other than premium or share of premium.

(3) "Individual health professional" means a physician and surgeon or other professional who is licensed by this state to deliver or furnish health care services. For this purpose, an "individual health professional" shall not include a dentist, licensed pursuant to the Dental Practice Act (Chapter 4 (commencing with Section 1600) of Division 2 of the Business and Professions Code).

(4) "In-network cost-sharing amount" means an amount no more than the same cost sharing the enrollee would pay for the same covered service received from a contracting health professional. The in-network cost-sharing amount with respect to an enrollee with coinsurance shall be based on the amount paid by the plan pursuant to paragraph (1) of subdivision (a) of Section 1371.31.

(5) "Noncontracting individual health professional" means a physician and surgeon or other professional who is licensed by the state to deliver or furnish health care services and who is not contracted with the enrollee's health care service product. For this purpose, a "noncontracting individual health professional" shall not include a dentist, licensed pursuant

to the Dental Practice Act (Chapter 4 (commencing with Section 1600) of Division 2 of the Business and Professions Code). Application of this definition is not precluded by a noncontracting individual health professional's affiliation with a group.

(g) This section shall not be construed to require a health care service plan to cover services not required by law or by the terms and conditions of the health care service plan contract.

(h) This section shall not be construed to exempt a plan or provider from the requirements under Section 1371.4 or 1373.96, nor abrogate the holding in Prospect Medical Group, Inc. v. Northridge Emergency Medical Group (2009) 45 Cal.4th 497.

(i) If a health care service plan delegates payment functions to a contracted entity, including, but not limited to, a medical group or independent practice association, the delegated entity shall comply with this section.

(j) This section shall not apply to a Medi-Cal managed health care service plan or any other entity that enters into a contract with the State Department of Health Care Services pursuant to Chapter 7 (commencing with Section 14000), Chapter 8 (commencing with Section 14200), and Chapter 8.75 (commencing with Section 14591) of Part 3 of Division 9 of the Welfare and Institutions Code.

(k) This section shall not apply to emergency services and care, as defined in Section 1317.1.

2016 CALIFORNIA ASSEMBLY BILL 72

The people of the State of California do enact as follows:

Section 1

Section 1371.30 is added to the Health and Safety Code, immediately following Section 1371.3, to read:

§ 1371.30

(a)

(1) By September 1, 2017, the department shall establish an independent dispute resolution process for the purpose of processing and resolving a claim dispute between a health care service plan and a noncontracting individual health professional for services subject to subdivision (a) of Section 1371.9.

(2) Prior to initiating the independent dispute resolution process, the parties shall complete the plan's internal process.

(3) If either the noncontracting individual health professional or the plan appeals a claim to the department's independent dispute resolution

process, the other party shall participate in the appeal process as described in this section.

(b)

(1) The department shall establish uniform written procedures for the submission, receipt, processing, and resolution of claim payment disputes pursuant to this section and any other guidelines for implementing this section.

(2) The department shall establish reasonable and necessary fees for the purpose of administering this section, to be paid by both parties.

(3) In establishing the independent dispute resolution process, the department shall permit the bundling of claims submitted to the same plan or the same delegated entity for the same or similar services by the same noncontracting individual health professional.

(4) The department shall permit a physician group, independent practice association, or other entity authorized to act on behalf of a noncontracting individual health professional to initiate and participate in the independent dispute resolution process.

(5) In deciding the dispute, the independent organization shall base its decision regarding the appropriate reimbursement on all relevant information.

(c)

(1) The department may contract with one or more independent organizations to conduct the proceedings. The independent organization handling a dispute shall be independent of either party to the dispute.

(2) The department shall establish conflict-of-interest standards, consistent with the purposes of this section, that an organization shall meet in order to qualify to administer the independent dispute resolution program. The conflict-of-interest standards shall be consistent with the standards pursuant to subdivisions (c) and (d) of Section 1374.32.

(3) The department may contract with the same independent organization or organizations as the Department of Insurance.

(4) The department shall provide, upon the request of an interested person, a copy of all nonproprietary information, as determined by the director, filed with the department by an independent organization seeking to contract with the department to administer the independent dispute resolution process pursuant to this section. The department may charge a nominal fee to cover the costs of providing a copy of the information pursuant to this paragraph.

(5) The independent organization retained to conduct proceedings shall be deemed to be consultants for purposes of Section 43.98 of the Civil Code.

(6) Contracts entered into pursuant to the authority in this subdivision shall be exempt from Part 2 (commencing with Section 10100) of Division 2 of the Public Contract Code, Section 19130 of the

Government Code, and Chapter 6 (commencing with Section 14825) of Part 5.5 of Division 3 of the Government Code and shall be exempt from the review or approval of any division of the Department of General Services.

(d) The decision obtained through the department's independent dispute resolution process shall be binding on both parties. The plan shall implement the decision obtained through the independent dispute resolution process. If dissatisfied, either party may pursue any right, remedy, or penalty established under any other applicable law.

(e) This section shall not apply to a Medi-Cal managed health care service plan or any entity that enters into a contract with the State Department of Health Care Services pursuant to Chapter 7 (commencing with Section 14000), Chapter 8 (commencing with Section 14200), and Chapter 8.75 (commencing with Section 14591) of Part 3 of Division 9 of the Welfare and Institutions Code.

(f) If a health care service plan delegates payment functions to a contracted entity, including, but not limited to, a medical group or independent practice association, then the delegated entity shall comply with this section.

(g) This section shall not apply to emergency services and care, as defined in Section 1317.1.

(h) The definitions in subdivision (f) of Section 1371.9 shall apply for purposes of this section.

(i) This section shall not be construed to alter a health care service plan's obligations pursuant to Sections 1371 and 1371.4.

(j) Notwithstanding Chapter 3.5 (commencing with Section 11340) of Part 1 of Division 3 of Title 2 of the Government Code, the department may implement, interpret, or make specific this section by means of all-plan letters or similar instructions, without taking regulatory action, until the time regulations are adopted.

(k) By January 1, 2019, the department shall provide a report to the Governor, the President pro Tempore of the Senate, the Speaker of the Assembly, and the Senate and Assembly Committees on Health of the data and information provided in the independent dispute resolution process in a manner and format specified by the Legislature.

Section 2

Section 1371.31 is added to the Health and Safety Code, to read:

§ 1371.31

(a)

(1) For services rendered subject to Section 1371.9, effective July 1, 2017, unless otherwise agreed to by the noncontracting individual health

professional and the plan, the plan shall reimburse the greater of the average contracted rate or 125 percent of the amount Medicare reimburses on a fee-for-service basis for the same or similar services in the general geographic region in which the services were rendered. For the purposes of this section, "average contracted rate" means the average of the contracted commercial rates paid by the health plan or delegated entity for the same or similar services in the geographic region. This subdivision does not apply to subdivision (c) of Section 1371.9 or subdivision (b) of this section.

(2)

(A) By July 1, 2017, each health care service plan and its delegated entities shall provide to the department all of the following:

(i) Data listing its average contracted rates for the plan for services most frequently subject to Section 1371.9 in each geographic region in which the services are rendered for the calendar year 2015.

(ii) Its methodology for determining the average contracted rate for the plan for services subject to Section 1371.9. The methodology to determine an average contracted rate shall ensure that the plan includes the highest and lowest contracted rates for the calendar year 2015.

(iii) The policies and procedures used to determine the average contracted rates under this subdivision.

(B) For each calendar year after the plan's initial submission of the average contracted rate as specified in subparagraph (A) and until the standardized methodology under paragraph (3) is specified, a health care service plan and the plan's delegated entities shall adjust the rate initially established pursuant to this subdivision by the Consumer Price Index for Medical Care Services, as published by the United States Bureau of Labor Statistics.

(3)

(A) By January 1, 2019, the department shall specify a methodology that plans and delegated entities shall use to determine the average contracted rates for services most frequently subject to Section 1371.9. This methodology shall take into account, at a minimum, information from the independent dispute resolution process, the specialty of the individual health professional, and the geographic region in which the services are rendered. The methodology to determine an average contracted rate shall ensure that the plan includes the highest and lowest contracted rates.

(B) Health care service plans and delegated entities shall provide to the department the policies and procedures used to determine the average contracted rates in compliance with subparagraph (A).

(C) If, based on the health care service plan's model, a health care service plan does not pay a statistically significant number or dollar amount of claims for services covered under Section 1371.9, the health care service plan shall demonstrate to the department that it has access to a statistically credible database reflecting rates paid to noncontracting individual health professionals for services provided in a geographic region and shall use that database to determine an average contracted rate required pursuant to paragraph (1).

(D) The department shall review the information filed pursuant to this subdivision as part of its examination of fiscal and administrative affairs pursuant to Section 1382.

(E) The average contracted rate data submitted pursuant to this section shall be confidential and not subject to disclosure under the California Public Records Act (Chapter 3.5 (commencing with Section 6250) of Division 7 of Title 1 of the Government Code).

(F) In developing the standardized methodology under this subdivision, the department shall consult with interested parties throughout the process of developing the standards, including the Department of Insurance, representatives of health plans, insurers, health care providers, hospitals, consumer advocates, and other stakeholders it deems appropriate. The department shall hold the first stakeholder meeting no later than July 1, 2017.

(4) A health care service plan shall include in its reports submitted to the department pursuant to Section 1367.035 and regulations adopted pursuant to that section, in a manner specified by the department, the number of payments made to noncontracting individual health professionals for services at a contracting health facility and subject to Section 1371.9, as well as other data sufficient to determine the proportion of noncontracting individual health professionals to contracting individual health professionals at contracting health facilities, as defined in subdivision (f) of Section 1371.9. The department shall include a summary of this information in its January 1, 2019, report required pursuant to subdivision (k) of Section 1371.30 and its findings regarding the impact of the act that added this section on health care service plan contracting and network adequacy.

(5) A health care service plan that provides services subject to Section 1371.9 shall meet the network adequacy requirements set forth in this chapter, including, but not limited to, subdivisions (d) and (e) of Section 1367 of this code and in Exhibits (H) and (I) of subdivision (d) of Section 1300.51 of, and Sections 1300.67.2 and 1300.67.2.1 of, Title 28 of the California Code of Regulations, including, but not limited to, inpatient hospital services and specialist physician services, and if necessary, the department may adopt additional regulations related to those

services. This section shall not be construed to limit the director's authority under this chapter.

(6) For purposes of this section for Medicare fee-for-service reimbursement, geographic regions shall be the geographic regions specified for physician reimbursement for Medicare fee-for-service by the United States Department of Health and Human Services.

(7) A health care service plan shall authorize and permit assignment of the enrollee's right, if any, to any reimbursement for health care services covered under the plan contract to a noncontracting individual health professional who furnishes the health care services rendered subject to Section 1371.9. Lack of assignment pursuant to this paragraph shall not be construed to limit the applicability of this section, Section 1371.30, or Section 1371.9.

(8) A noncontracting individual health professional, health care service plan, or health care service plan's delegated entity who disputes the claim reimbursement under this section shall utilize the independent dispute resolution process described in Section 1371.30.

(b) If nonemergency services are provided by a noncontracting individual health professional consistent with subdivision (c) of Section 1371.9 to an enrollee who has voluntarily chosen to use his or her out-of-network benefit for services covered by a plan that includes coverage for out-of-network benefits, unless otherwise agreed to by the plan and the noncontracting individual health professional, the amount paid by the health care service plan shall be the amount set forth in the enrollee's evidence of coverage. This payment is not subject to the independent dispute resolution process described in Section 1371.30.

(c) If a health care service plan delegates the responsibility for payment of claims to a contracted entity, including, but not limited to, a medical group or independent practice association, then the entity to which that responsibility is delegated shall comply with the requirements of this section.

(d)

(1) A payment made by the health care service plan to the noncontracting health care professional for nonemergency services as required by Section 1371.9 and this section, in addition to the applicable cost sharing owed by the enrollee, shall constitute payment in full for nonemergency services rendered unless either party uses the independent dispute resolution process or other lawful means pursuant to Section 1371.30.

(2) Notwithstanding any other law, the amounts paid by a plan for services under this section shall not constitute the prevailing or customary charges, the usual fees to the general public, or other charges for other payers for an individual health professional.

(3) This subdivision shall not preclude the use of the independent dispute resolution process pursuant to Section 1371.30.

(e) This section shall not apply to a Medi-Cal managed health care service plan or any other entity that enters into a contract with the State Department of Health Care Services pursuant to Chapter 7 (commencing with Section 14000), Chapter 8 (commencing with Section 14200), and Chapter 8.75 (commencing with Section 14591) of Part 3 of Division 9 of the Welfare and Institutions Code.
(f) This section shall not apply to emergency services and care, as defined in Section 1317.1.
(g) The definitions in subdivision (f) of Section 1371.9 shall apply for purposes of this section.
(h) This section shall not be construed to alter a health care service plan's obligations pursuant to Sections 1371 and 1371.4.

Section 3

Section 1371.9 is added to the Health and Safety Code, to read:

§ 1371.9

(a)

(1) Except as provided in subdivision (c), a health care service plan contract issued, amended, or renewed on or after July 1, 2017, shall provide that if an enrollee receives covered services from a contracting health facility at which, or as a result of which, the enrollee receives services provided by a noncontracting individual health professional, the enrollee shall pay no more than the same cost sharing that the enrollee would pay for the same covered services received from a contracting individual health professional. This amount shall be referred to as the "in-network cost-sharing amount."

(2) An enrollee shall not owe the noncontracting individual health professional more than the in-network cost-sharing amount for services subject to this section. At the time of payment by the plan to the noncontracting individual health professional, the plan shall inform the enrollee and the noncontracting individual health professional of the in-network cost-sharing amount owed by the enrollee.

(3) A noncontracting individual health professional shall not bill or collect any amount from the enrollee for services subject to this section except for the in-network cost-sharing amount. Any communication from the noncontracting individual health professional to the enrollee prior to the receipt of information about the in-network cost-sharing amount pursuant to paragraph (2) shall include a notice in 12-point bold type stating that the communication is not a bill and informing the enrollee that the enrollee shall not pay until he or she is informed by his or her health care service plan of any applicable cost sharing.

(4)

(A) If the noncontracting individual health professional has received more than the in-network cost-sharing amount from the enrollee for services subject to this section, the noncontracting individual health professional shall refund any overpayment to the enrollee within 30 calendar days after receiving payment from the enrollee.

(B) If the noncontracting individual health professional does not refund any overpayment to the enrollee within 30 calendar days after being informed of the enrollee's in-network cost-sharing amount, interest shall accrue at the rate of 15 percent per annum beginning with the date payment was received from the enrollee.

(C) A noncontracting individual health professional shall automatically include in his or her refund to the enrollee all interest that has accrued pursuant to this section without requiring the enrollee to submit a request for the interest amount.

(b) Except for services subject to subdivision (c), the following shall apply:

(1) Any cost sharing paid by the enrollee for the services subject to this section shall count toward the limit on annual out-of-pocket expenses established under Section 1367.006.

(2) Cost sharing arising from services subject to this section shall be counted toward any deductible in the same manner as cost sharing would be attributed to a contracting individual health professional.

(3) The cost sharing paid by the enrollee pursuant to this section shall satisfy the enrollee's obligation to pay cost sharing for the health service and shall constitute "applicable cost sharing owed by the enrollee."

(c) For services subject to this section, if an enrollee has a health care service plan that includes coverage for out-of-network benefits, a noncontracting individual health professional may bill or collect from the enrollee the out-of-network cost sharing, if applicable, only when the enrollee consents in writing and that written consent demonstrates satisfaction of all the following criteria:

(1) At least 24 hours in advance of care, the enrollee shall consent in writing to receive services from the identified noncontracting individual health professional.

(2) The consent shall be obtained by the noncontracting individual health professional in a document that is separate from the document used to obtain the consent for any other part of the care or procedure. The consent shall not be obtained by the facility or any representative of the facility. The consent shall not be obtained at the time of admission or at any time when the enrollee is being prepared for surgery or any other procedure.

(3) At the time consent is provided, the noncontracting individual health professional shall give the enrollee a written estimate of the enrollee's

total out-of-pocket cost of care. The written estimate shall be based on the professional's billed charges for the service to be provided. The noncontracting individual health professional shall not attempt to collect more than the estimated amount without receiving separate written consent from the enrollee or the enrollee's authorized representative, unless circumstances arise during delivery of services that were unforeseeable at the time the estimate was given that would require the provider to change the estimate.

(4) The consent shall advise the enrollee that he or she may elect to seek care from a contracted provider or may contact the enrollee's health care service plan in order to arrange to receive the health service from a contracted provider for lower out-of-pocket costs.

(5) The consent and estimate shall be provided to the enrollee in the language spoken by the enrollee, if the language is a Medi-Cal threshold language, as defined in subdivision (d) of Section 128552.

(6) The consent shall also advise the enrollee that any costs incurred as a result of the enrollee's use of the out-of-network benefit shall be in addition to in-network cost-sharing amounts and may not count toward the annual out-of-pocket maximum on in-network benefits or a deductible, if any, for in-network benefits.

(d) A noncontracting individual health professional who fails to comply with the requirements of subdivision (c) has not obtained written consent for purposes of this section. Under those circumstances, subdivisions (a) and (b) shall apply and subdivision (c) shall not apply.

(e)

(1) A noncontracting individual health professional may advance to collections only the in-network cost-sharing amount, as determined by the plan pursuant to subdivision (a) or the out-of-network cost-sharing amount owed pursuant to subdivision (c), that the enrollee has failed to pay.

(2) The noncontracting individual health professional, or any entity acting on his or her behalf, including any assignee of the debt, shall not report adverse information to a consumer credit reporting agency or commence civil action against the enrollee for a minimum of 150 days after the initial billing regarding amounts owed by the enrollee under subdivision (a) or (c).

(3) With respect to an enrollee, the noncontracting individual health professional, or any entity acting on his or her behalf, including any assignee of the debt, shall not use wage garnishments or liens on primary residences as a means of collecting unpaid bills under this section.

(f) For purposes of this section and Sections 1371.30 and 1371.31, the following definitions shall apply:

(1) "Contracting health facility" means a health facility that is contracted with the enrollee's health care service plan to provide services under the enrollee's plan contract. A contracting health care facility includes, but is not limited to, the following providers:
(A) A licensed hospital.
(B) An ambulatory surgery or other outpatient setting, as described in subdivision (a), (d), (e), (g), or (h) of Section 1248.1.
(C) A laboratory.
(D) A radiology or imaging center.

(2) "Cost sharing" includes any copayment, coinsurance, or deductible, or any other form of cost sharing paid by the enrollee other than premium or share of premium.

(3) "Individual health professional" means a physician and surgeon or other professional who is licensed by this state to deliver or furnish health care services. For this purpose, an "individual health professional" shall not include a dentist, licensed pursuant to the Dental Practice Act (Chapter 4 (commencing with Section 1600) of Division 2 of the Business and Professions Code).

(4) "In-network cost-sharing amount" means an amount no more than the same cost sharing the enrollee would pay for the same covered service received from a contracting health professional. The in-network cost-sharing amount with respect to an enrollee with coinsurance shall be based on the amount paid by the plan pursuant to paragraph (1) of subdivision (a) of Section 1371.31.

(5) "Noncontracting individual health professional" means a physician and surgeon or other professional who is licensed by the state to deliver or furnish health care services and who is not contracted with the enrollee's health care service product. For this purpose, a "noncontracting individual health professional" shall not include a dentist, licensed pursuant to the Dental Practice Act (Chapter 4 (commencing with Section 1600) of Division 2 of the Business and Professions Code). Application of this definition is not precluded by a noncontracting individual health professional's affiliation with a group.

(g) This section shall not be construed to require a health care service plan to cover services not required by law or by the terms and conditions of the health care service plan contract.

(h) This section shall not be construed to exempt a plan or provider from the requirements under Section 1371.4 or 1373.96, nor abrogate the holding in Prospect Medical Group, Inc. v. Northridge Emergency Medical Group (2009) 45 Cal. 4th 497.

(i) If a health care service plan delegates payment functions to a contracted entity, including, but not limited to, a medical group or independent practice association, the delegated entity shall comply with this section.

(j) This section shall not apply to a Medi-Cal managed health care service plan or any other entity that enters into a contract with the State Department of

Health Care Services pursuant to Chapter 7 (commencing with Section 14000), Chapter 8 (commencing with Section 14200), and Chapter 8.75 (commencing with Section 14591) of Part 3 of Division 9 of the Welfare and Institutions Code.

(k) This section shall not apply to emergency services and care, as defined in Section 1317.1.

Section 4

Section 10112.8 is added to the Insurance Code, to read:

§ 10112.8

(a)

(1) Except as provided in subdivision (c), a health insurance policy issued, amended, or renewed on or after July 1, 2017, that provides benefits through contracts with providers at alternative rates of payment pursuant to Section 10133, shall provide that if an insured receives covered services from a contracting health facility at which, or as a result of which, the insured receives services provided by a noncontracting individual health professional, the insured shall pay no more than the same cost sharing that the insured would pay for the same covered services received from a contracting individual health professional. This amount shall be referred to as the "in-network cost-sharing amount."

(2) Except as provided in subdivision (c), an insured shall not owe the noncontracting individual health professional more than the in-network cost-sharing amount for services subject to this section. At the time of payment by the insurer to the noncontracting individual health professional, the insurer shall inform the insured and the noncontracting individual health professional of the in-network cost-sharing amount owed by the insured.

(3) A noncontracting individual health professional shall not bill or collect any amount from the insured for services subject to this section except the in-network cost-sharing amount. Any communication from the noncontracting individual health professional to the insured prior to the receipt of information about the in-network cost-sharing amount pursuant to paragraph (2) shall include a notice in 12-point bold type stating that the communication is not a bill and informing the insured that the insured shall not pay until he or she is informed by his or her insurer of any applicable cost sharing.

(4)

(A) If the noncontracting individual health professional has received more than the in-network cost-sharing amount from the insured for services subject to this section, the noncontracting individual health professional shall refund any overpayment to the insured within 30 calendar days after receiving payment from the insured.

(B) If the noncontracting individual health professional does not refund any overpayment to the insured within 30 calendar days after being informed of the insured's in-network cost-sharing amount, interest shall accrue at the rate of 15 percent per annum beginning with the date payment was received from the insured.

(C) A noncontracting individual health professional shall automatically include in his or her refund to the insured all interest that has accrued pursuant to this section without requiring the insured to submit a request for the interest amount.

(b) Except for services subject to subdivision (c), the following shall apply:

(1) Any cost sharing paid by the insured for the services subject to this section shall count toward the limit on annual out-of-pocket expenses established under Section 10112.28.

(2) Cost sharing arising from services subject to this section shall be counted toward any deductible in the same manner as cost sharing would be attributed to a contracting individual health professional.

(3) The cost sharing paid by the insured pursuant to this section shall satisfy the insured's obligation to pay cost sharing for the health service and shall constitute "applicable cost sharing owed by the insured."

(c) For services subject to this section, if an insured has an insurance contract that includes coverage for out-of-network benefits, a noncontracting individual health professional may bill or collect from the insured the out-of-network cost sharing, if applicable, only when the insured consents in writing and that written consent demonstrates satisfaction of all the following criteria:

(1) At least 24 hours in advance of care, the insured shall consent in writing to receive services from the identified noncontracting individual health professional.

(2) The consent shall be obtained by the noncontracting individual health professional in a document that is separate from the document used to obtain the consent for any other part of the care or procedure. The consent shall not be obtained by the facility or any representative of the facility. The consent shall not be obtained at the time of admission or at any time when the enrollee is being prepared for surgery or any other procedure.

(3) At the time consent is provided the noncontracting individual health professional shall give the insured a written estimate of the insured's total out-of-pocket cost of care. The written estimate shall be based on the professional's billed charges for the service to be provided. The noncontracting individual health professional shall not attempt to collect more than the estimated amount without receiving separate written consent from the insured or the insured's authorized representative, unless circumstances arise during delivery of services that were

unforeseeable at the time the estimate was given that would require the provider to change the estimate.

(4) The consent shall advise the insured that he or she may elect to seek care from a contracted provider or may contact the insured's insurer in order to arrange to receive the health service from a contracted provider for lower out-of-pocket costs.

(5) The consent and estimate shall be provided to the insured in the language spoken by the insured, if the language is a Medi-Cal threshold language, as defined in subdivision (d) of Section 128552 of the Health and Safety Code.

(6) The consent shall also advise the insured that any costs incurred as a result of the insured's use of the out-of-network benefit shall be in addition to in-network cost-sharing amounts and may not count toward the annual out-of-pocket maximum on in-network benefits or a deductible, if any, for in-network benefits.

(d) A noncontracting individual health professional who fails to comply with provisions of this subdivision has not obtained written consent for purposes of this section. Under those circumstances, subdivisions (a) and (b) shall apply and subdivision (c) shall not apply.

(e)

(1) A noncontracting individual health professional may advance to collections only the in-network cost-sharing amount, as determined by the insurer pursuant to subdivision (a) or the out-of-network cost-sharing amount owed pursuant to subdivision (c), that the insured has failed to pay.

(2) The noncontracting individual health professional, or any entity acting on his or her behalf, including any assignee of the debt, shall not report adverse information to a consumer credit reporting agency or commence civil action against the insured for a minimum of 150 days after the initial billing regarding amounts owed by the insured under subdivision (a) or (c).

(3) With respect to an insured, a noncontracting individual health professional, or any entity acting on his or her behalf, including any assignee of the debt, shall not use wage garnishments or liens on primary residences as a means of collecting unpaid bills under this section.

(f) For purposes of this section and Sections 10112.81 and 10112.82, the following definitions shall apply:

(1) "Contracting health facility" means a health facility that is contracted with the insured's health insurer to provide services under the insured's policy. A contracting health care facility includes, but is not limited to, the following providers:

(A) A licensed hospital.

(B) An ambulatory surgery or other outpatient setting, as described in subdivision (a), (d), (e), (g), or (h) of Section 1248.1 of the Health and Safety Code.

(C) A laboratory.

(D) A radiology or imaging center.

(2) "Cost sharing" includes any copayment, coinsurance, or deductible, or any other form of cost sharing paid by the insured other than premium or share of premium.

(3) "Individual health professional" means a physician and surgeon or other professional who is licensed by the state to deliver or furnish health care services. For this purpose, an "individual health professional" shall not include a dentist, licensed pursuant to the Dental Practice Act (Chapter 4 (commencing with Section 1600) of Division 2 of the Business and Professions Code).

(4) "In-network cost-sharing amount" means an amount no more than the same cost sharing the insured would pay for the same covered service received from a contracting health professional. The in-network cost-sharing amount with respect to an insured with coinsurance shall be based on the amount paid by the insurer pursuant to paragraph (1) of subdivision (a) of Section 10112.82.

(5) "Noncontracting individual health professional" means a physician and surgeon or other professional who is licensed by the state to deliver or furnish health care services and who is not contracted with the insured's health insurance product. For this purpose, a "noncontracting individual health professional" shall not include a dentist, licensed pursuant to the Dental Practice Act (Chapter 4 (commencing with Section 1600) of Division 2 of the Business and Professions Code). Application of this definition is not precluded by a noncontracting individual health professional's affiliation with a group.

(g) This section shall not be construed to require an insurer to cover services not required by law or by the terms and conditions of the health insurance policy.

(h) If a health insurer delegates payment functions to a contracted entity, including, but not limited to, a medical group or independent practice association, the delegated entity shall comply with this section.

(i) This section shall not apply to emergency services and care, as defined in Section 1317.1 of the Health and Safety Code.

Section 5

Section 10112.81 is added to the Insurance Code, to read:

§ 10112.81

(a)

(1) By September 1, 2017, the commissioner shall establish an independent dispute resolution process for the purpose of processing and resolving

a claim dispute between a health insurer and a noncontracting individual health professional for services subject to subdivision (a) of Section 10112.8.

(2) Prior to initiating the independent dispute resolution process, the parties shall complete the insurer's internal process.

(3) If either the noncontracting individual health professional or the insurer appeals a claim to the department's independent dispute resolution process, the other party shall participate in the appeal process as described in this section.

(b)

(1) The commissioner shall establish uniform written procedures for the submission, receipt, processing, and resolution of claim payment disputes pursuant to this section and any other guidelines for implementing this section.

(2) The commissioner shall establish reasonable and necessary fees for the purpose of administering this section, to be paid by both parties.

(3) In establishing the independent dispute resolution process, the commissioner shall permit the bundling of claims submitted to the same insurer or the same delegated entity for the same or similar services by the same noncontracting individual health professional.

(4) The commissioner shall permit a physician group, independent practice association, or other entity authorized to act on behalf of a noncontracting individual health professional to initiate and participate in the independent dispute resolution process.

(5) In deciding the dispute, the independent organization shall base its decision regarding the appropriate reimbursement on all relevant information.

(c)

(1) The commissioner may contract with one or more independent organizations to conduct the proceedings. The independent organization handling a dispute shall be independent of either party to the dispute.

(2) The commissioner shall establish conflict-of-interest standards, consistent with the purposes of this section, that an organization shall meet in order to qualify to administer the independent dispute resolution program. The conflict-of-interest standards shall be consistent with the standards pursuant to subdivisions (c) and (d) of Section 10169.2.

(3) The commissioner may contract with the same independent organization or organizations as the State Department of Managed Health Care.

(4) The commissioner shall provide, upon the request of an interested person, a copy of all nonproprietary information, as determined by the commissioner, filed with the department by an independent organization seeking to contract with the department to administer the independent dispute resolution process pursuant to this section. The

department may charge a nominal fee to cover the costs of providing a copy of the information pursuant to this paragraph.

(5) Contracts entered into pursuant to the authority in this subdivision shall be exempt from Part 2 (commencing with Section 10100) of Division 2 of the Public Contract Code, Section 19130 of the Government Code, and Chapter 6 (commencing with Section 14825) of Part 5.5 of Division 3 of the Government Code and shall be exempt from the review or approval of any division of the Department of General Services.

(d) The decision obtained through the commissioner's independent dispute resolution process shall be binding on both parties. The insurer shall implement the decision obtained through the independent dispute resolution process. If dissatisfied, either party may pursue any right, remedy, or penalty established under any other applicable law.

(e) If a health insurer delegates payment functions to a contracted entity, including, but not limited to, a medical group or independent practice association, then the delegated entity shall comply with this section.

(f) This section shall not apply to emergency services and care, as defined in Section 1317.1 of the Health and Safety Code.

(g) The definitions in subdivision (f) of Section 10112.8 shall apply for purposes of this section.

(h) This section shall not be construed to alter a health insurer's obligations pursuant to Section 10123.13.

(i) Notwithstanding Chapter 3.5 (commencing with Section 11340) of Part 1 of Division 3 of Title 2 of the Government Code, the commissioner may implement, interpret, or make specific this section by issuing guidance, without taking regulatory action, until the time regulations are adopted.

(j) By January 1, 2019, the commissioner shall provide a report to the Governor, the President pro Tempore of the Senate, the Speaker of the Assembly, and the Senate and Assembly Committees on Health of the data and information provided in the independent dispute resolution process in a manner and format specified by the Legislature.

Section 6

Section 10112.82 is added to the Insurance Code, to read:

§ 10112.82

(a)

(1) For services rendered subject to Section 10112.8, effective July 1, 2017, unless otherwise agreed to by the noncontracting individual health professional and the insurer, the insurer shall reimburse the greater of the average contracted rate or 125 percent of the amount Medicare

reimburses on a fee-for-service basis for the same or similar services in the general geographic region in which the services were rendered. For the purposes of this section, "average contracted rate" means the average of the contracted commercial rates paid by the health insurer for the same or similar services in the geographic region. This subdivision does not apply to subdivision (c) of Section 10112.8 or subdivision (b) of this section.

(2)

(A) By July 1, 2017, each health insurer shall provide to the commissioner all of the following:
   (i) Data listing its average contracted rates for the insurer for services most frequently subject to Section 10112.8 in each geographic region in which the services are rendered for the calendar year 2015.
   (ii) Its methodology for determining the average contracted rate for the insurer for services subject to Section 10112.8. The methodology to determine an average contracted rate shall ensure that the insurer includes the highest and lowest contracted rates for the calendar year 2015.
   (iii) The policies and procedures used to determine the average contracted rates under this subdivision.

(B) For each calendar year after the health insurer's initial submission of the average contracted rate as specified in subparagraph (A) and until the standardized methodology under paragraph (3) is specified, a health insurer shall adjust the rate initially established pursuant to this subdivision by the Consumer Price Index for Medical Care Services, as published by the United States Bureau of Labor Statistics.

(3)

(A) By January 1, 2019, the commissioner shall specify a methodology that insurers shall use to determine the average contracted rates for services most frequently subject to Section 10112.8. This methodology shall take into account, at a minimum, information from the independent dispute resolution process, the specialty of the individual health professional, and the geographic region in which the services are rendered. The methodology to determine an average contracted rate shall ensure that the insurer includes the highest and lowest contracted rates.

(B) Insurers shall provide to the commissioner the policies and procedures used to determine the average contracted rates in compliance with subparagraph (A).

(C) The average contracted rate data submitted pursuant to this section shall be confidential and not subject to disclosure under the

California Public Records Act (Chapter 3.5 (commencing with Section 6250) of Division 7 of Title 1 of the Government Code).

(D) In developing the standardized methodology under this subdivision, the commissioner shall consult with interested parties throughout the process of developing the standards, including the Department of Managed Health Care, representatives of health plans, insurers, health care providers, hospitals, consumer advocates, and other stakeholders it deems appropriate. The commissioner shall hold the first stakeholder meeting no later than July 1, 2017.

(4) A health insurer shall include in its reports submitted to the commissioner pursuant to Section 10133.5 and regulations adopted pursuant to that section, in a manner specified by the department, the number of payments made to noncontracting individual health professionals for services at a contracting health facility and subject to Section 10112.8, as well as other data sufficient to determine the proportion of noncontracting individual health professionals to contracting individual health professionals at contracting health facilities, as defined in subdivision (f) of Section 10112.8. The commissioner shall include a summary of this information in its January 1, 2019, report required pursuant to subdivision (j) of Section 10112.81 and its findings regarding the impact of the act that added this section on health insurer contracting and network adequacy.

(5) A health insurer that provides services subject to Section 10112.8 shall meet the network adequacy requirements set forth in this chapter, including, but not limited to, Section 10133.5 of this code and Sections 2240.1 and 2240.7 of Title 10 of the California Code of Regulations, including, but not limited to, inpatient hospital services and specialist physician services, and if necessary, the commissioner may adopt additional regulations related to those services. This section shall not be construed to limit the commissioner's authority under this chapter.

(6) For the purposes of this section, for average contracted rates for individual and small group coverage, geographic region shall be the geographic regions listed in subparagraph (A) of paragraph (2) of subdivision (a) of Section 10753.14. For purposes of this section for Medicare fee-for-service reimbursement, geographic regions shall be the geographic regions specified for physician reimbursement for Medicare fee-for-service by the United States Department of Health and Human Services.

(7) A health insurer shall authorize and permit assignment of the insured's right, if any, to any reimbursement for health care services covered under the health insurance policy to a noncontracting individual health professional who furnishes the health care services rendered subject to Section 10112.8. Lack of assignment pursuant to this paragraph shall

not be construed to limit the applicability of this section, Section 10112.8, or Section 10112.81.

(8) A noncontracting individual health professional or health insurer who disputes the claim reimbursement under this section shall utilize the independent dispute resolution process described in Section 10112.81.

(b) If nonemergency services are provided by a noncontracting individual health professional consistent with subdivision (c) of Section 10112.8 to an insured who has voluntarily chosen to use his or her out-of-network benefit for services covered by an insurer that includes coverage for out-of-network benefits, unless otherwise agreed to by the insurer and the noncontracting individual health professional, the amount paid by the insurer shall be the amount set forth in the insured's policy. This payment is not subject to the independent dispute resolution process described in Section 10112.81.

(c) If a health insurer delegates the responsibility for payment of claims to a contracted entity, including, but not limited to, a medical group or independent practice association, then the entity to which that responsibility is delegated shall comply with the requirements of this section.

(d)

(1) A payment made by the health insurer to the noncontracting health care professional for nonemergency services as required by Section 10112.8 and this section, in addition to the applicable cost sharing owed by the insured, shall constitute payment in full for nonemergency services rendered unless either party uses the dispute resolution process or other lawful means pursuant to Section 10112.81.

(2) Notwithstanding any other law, the amounts paid by an insurer for services under this section shall not constitute the prevailing or customary charges, the usual fees to the general public, or other charges for other payers for an individual health professional.

(3) This subdivision shall not preclude the use of the independent dispute resolution process pursuant to Section 10112.81.

(e) This section shall not apply to emergency services and care, as defined in Section 1317.1 of the Health and Safety Code.

(f) The definitions in subdivision (f) of Section 10112.8 shall apply for purposes of this section.

(g) This section shall not be construed to alter a health insurer's obligations pursuant to Section 10123.13.

Section 7

The Legislature finds and declares that Sections 2 and 6 of this act, which add Section 1371.31 to the Health and Safety Code and Section 10112.82 to the Insurance Code, respectively, impose a limitation on the public's right of access to the meetings of public bodies or the writings of public officials and agencies within the meaning of Section 3 of Article I of the California Constitution. Pursuant to that constitutional provision, the Legislature makes the following findings to demonstrate the interest protected by this limitation and the need for protecting that interest:

In order to protect confidential rate information used by health care service plans and health insurers and to protect the integrity of the competitive market, it is necessary that this act limit the public's right of access to that information.

Section 8

No reimbursement is required by this act pursuant to Section 6 of Article XIII B of the California Constitution because the only costs that may be incurred by a local agency or school district will be incurred because this act creates a new crime or infraction, eliminates a crime or infraction, or changes the penalty for a crime or infraction, within the meaning of Section 17556 of the Government Code, or changes the definition of a crime within the meaning of Section 6 of Article XIII B of the California Constitution.

COLORADO REVISED STATUTES

§ 10-16-704 Network adequacy—required disclosures—balance billing—rules—legislative declaration—definitions

(1) A carrier providing a managed care plan shall maintain a network that is sufficient in numbers and types of providers to assure that all covered benefits to covered persons will be accessible without unreasonable delay. In the case of emergency services, covered persons shall have access to health-care services twenty-four hours per day, seven days per week. Sufficiency shall be determined in accordance with the requirements of this section and may be established by reference to any reasonable criteria used by the carrier, including but not limited to:

(a) Provider-covered person ratios by specialty, which may include the use of providers through telehealth for services that may appropriately be provided through telehealth;

(b) Primary care provider-covered person ratios;

(c) Geographic accessibility, which in some circumstances may require the crossing of county or state lines;

(d) Waiting times for appointments with participating providers;

(e) Hours of operation;

(f) The volume of technological and specialty services available to serve the needs of covered persons requiring covered technologically advanced or specialty care; and

(g) An adequate number of accessible acute care hospital services within a reasonable distance, travel time, or both.

(1.5)

(a)

(I) The commissioner shall promulgate rules, consistent with federal law, to:

(A) Require a carrier providing managed care plans to include essential community providers in the carrier's network; or

(B) Allow a carrier providing managed care plans that provides a majority of covered professional services through physicians employed by the carrier or through a single contracted medical group to comply with the alternate standard for essential community providers permitted under federal law.

(II) For purposes of the rules, "essential community providers" includes providers that serve predominately low-income, medically underserved individuals, such as health-care providers defined in the federal law and under part 4 of article 5 of title 25.5; except that nothing in this subsection (1.5) requires any carrier to provide coverage for any specific medical procedure.

(b) The commissioner may promulgate rules to require carriers to be accredited by an accrediting entity recognized by the United States department of health and human services.

(2)

(a) In any case where the carrier has no participating providers to provide a covered benefit, the carrier shall arrange for a referral to a provider with the necessary expertise and ensure that the covered person obtains the covered benefit at no greater cost to the covered person than if the benefit were obtained from participating providers.

(b)

(I) A carrier offering a managed care plan with out-of-network benefits, that is not a health maintenance organization or a health maintenance organization with a point of service plan, may require that a covered person travel a reasonable distance beyond the requirements of subsection (6) of this section for care within an adequate provider network in order to receive services from a participating provider. This paragraph (b) shall only apply if:

(A) The covered person resides outside of a metropolitan statistical area or primary metropolitan statistical area and the carrier has no participating providers to provide covered benefits in such geographic area; and

(B) The carrier demonstrates upon request by the commissioner, that the carrier has made unsuccessful good faith efforts to contract with local providers on reasonable terms.

(II) Subsection (2)(b)(I) of this section shall not apply to:

(A) Emergency services or primary care providers; and

(B) Cases in which the covered person is so severely ill or impaired that such person is unable to move from place to place without the aide of a mechanical device; has a physical or mental condition, verified by a physician licensed to practice medicine in this state or practicing medicine pursuant to section 12-240-107 (3)(i), that substantially limits the person's ability to move from place to place; or suffers from a physical hardship such that travel would threaten the safety or welfare of the covered person as verified by the covered person's in-network treating physician. Decisions in which a carrier contests the covered person's ability to travel may be appealed pursuant to section 10-16-113 or 10-16-113.5.

(c)

(I) In cases where, as a result of the provisions of subparagraph (I) of paragraph (b) of this subsection (2), a covered person is required to travel a reasonable distance beyond the requirements of subsection (6) of this section for an adequate network in order to receive services from a participating provider, and the covered person knowingly seeks services from a nonparticipating provider, the carrier shall be responsible to pay to the provider the lesser of:

(A) The nonparticipating provider's bill charges;

(B) A negotiated rate; or

(C) In the absence of a negotiated rate, the greater of the carrier's average in-network rate for the relevant geographic area or the usual, customary, and reasonable rate for such geographic area. Nothing in this paragraph (c) shall require either a carrier or a nonparticipating provider to attempt to negotiate a reimbursement rate.

(II) Upon request the carrier shall disclose to the covered person or the nonparticipating provider whether the amount reimbursed to the nonparticipating provider was the nonparticipating provider's billed charges, a negotiated rate, or the greater of the carrier's average in-network rate for the relevant geographic area or the usual, customary, and reasonable rate for such geographic area.

(III) A nonparticipating provider may balance bill the covered person in the event that the reimbursement rate described in subparagraph (I) of this paragraph (c) is not equal to the billed charges.

(IV) The commissioner shall promulgate rules defining the relevant geographic area for the purposes of sub-subparagraph (C) of subparagraph (I) of this paragraph (c). In the promulgation of such rules, the commissioner shall group together counties with similar demographic and economic characteristics. Such characteristics shall include, but not be limited to, average per capita income, the cost of housing, general cost of living, poverty and unemployment levels, or the primary economic base of the county.

(d) The carrier shall provide, in conspicuous, bold-faced type, an understandable disclosure in policy contract materials, certificates of coverage for a policyholder, and marketing materials about the following:

(I) Specific counties of the state where there are no participating providers;

(II) The circumstances under which the covered person may be balanced billed by nonparticipating providers; and

(III) The mechanisms to obtain the carrier's reimbursement rates to nonparticipating providers for specific covered health-care services.

(e)

(I) A carrier shall make available upon request from the covered person or the nonparticipating provider, from whom the covered person is seeking treatment, the carrier's usual, customary, and reasonable rate for reimbursement for specific health-care services.

(II) The commissioner may, upon receipt of one or more complaints from a covered person or a covered person's nonparticipating treating provider, review the carrier's usual, customary, and reasonable rate to determine if the rate is established pursuant to an appropriate methodology that is based on generally accepted industry standards and practices.

(III) The carrier's methodology for determining usual, customary, and reasonable reimbursement rates shall be applied in a uniform manner statewide; except that geographic adjustments may be made apart from the standard methodology.

(f) Repealed.

(g) A health maintenance organization offering health benefits in this state may:

(I) Offer health benefit coverage in accordance with paragraph (i) of this subsection (2) to a small employer that is not located, or whose employees do not work or reside, within the health maintenance organization's geographic service area;

(II) Offer health benefit coverage in accordance with paragraph (i) of this subsection (2) in a geographic area within the carrier's service area in which a health maintenance organization is unable to maintain an adequate network and is able to demonstrate to the commissioner upon request that the carrier has made unsuccessful good faith efforts to contract with local providers on reasonable terms; or

(III) Offer coverage pursuant to this paragraph (g) within a geographic area consistent with the requirements of section 10-16-105 (1) and (4).

(h) The health maintenance organization shall provide a disclosure to a small employer and its employees who purchase health insurance coverage under the circumstance described in this paragraph (h). Such disclosure shall also be given in writing to all interested policyholders and certificate holders as part of the sales and marketing materials before the insurer or entity approves an application for insurance from an insured. The disclosure shall contain the following statement: "Interested policyholders, certificate holders, and enrollees are hereby given notice that this small group policy requires that an insured travel outside of the geographic area to receive covered health benefits." The carrier shall, in a conspicuous location on the policy contract materials, certificates of coverage for a policyholder, and marketing materials, provide the disclosure required by this paragraph (h) in bold-faced, twelve-point type and all capital letters.

(i)

(I) A health maintenance organization that offers coverage pursuant to this section may require that a covered person travel a reasonable distance beyond the area specified under subsection (6) of this section in order to receive services from a participating provider. Except for emergency services and benefits available for out-of-network services, in such cases where the covered person is required to travel a reasonable distance to receive services from a participating provider and knowingly seeks services from a nonparticipating provider, the health maintenance organization shall be responsible to pay for the lesser of:

(A) The provider's billed charges;

(B) A negotiated rate; or

(C) In the absence of a negotiated rate, the greater of the health maintenance organization's average in-network rate for the relevant geographic area or the usual, customary, and reasonable rate for such geographic area.

(II) Upon request, the health maintenance organization shall disclose to the covered person or the nonparticipating provider whether the amount reimbursed to the nonparticipating provider was the nonparticipating provider's billed charges, a negotiated rate, or the greater of the carrier's average in-network rate for the relevant geographic area or the usual, customary, and reasonable rate for such geographic area.

(j) Nothing in paragraph (i) of this subsection (2) shall require either a carrier or a nonparticipating provider to attempt to negotiate a reimbursement rate.

(k) A nonparticipating provider may balance bill the covered person in the event that the reimbursement rate described in paragraph (i) of this subsection (2) is not equal to the provider's billed charges.

(l) The provisions of subsection (2)(i) of this section shall not apply to cases in which the covered person is so severely ill or impaired that such person is unable to move from place to place without the aid of a mechanical device; has a physical or mental condition, verified by a physician licensed to practice medicine in this state or practicing medicine pursuant to section 12-240-107 (3)(i), that substantially limits the person's ability to move from place to place; or suffers from a physical hardship such that travel would threaten the safety or welfare of the covered person as verified by the covered person's in-network treating physician. Decisions in which a carrier contests the covered person's ability to travel may be appealed pursuant to section 10-16-113 or 10-16-113.5.

(m) Notwithstanding any other provision of law, on and after September 1, 2006, for the duration of the term of a policy in effect when the insured pays the amount charged for a covered health-care service and seeks reimbursement from a carrier for such covered health-care service, the insured shall be liable for no more than the in-network copayment, coinsurance, and deductible for such service if:

(I) The insured seeks reimbursement from the carrier within twelve months after the provision of the service;

(II) Preauthorization is not required for the particular type of service provided; and

(III) A contract between the provider and the carrier was in place when the service was provided.

(2.5)

(a) In the event of a material change to the carrier's network that could result in the application of subparagraph (I) of paragraph (b) of subsection (2) of this section, the carrier shall provide at least forty-five days prior to the change, in conspicuous bold-faced type, an understandable disclosure to all affected covered persons about the following:

(I) Specific network changes in the geographic area;

(II) The circumstances under which the covered person may be balance billed by nonparticipating providers; and

(III) The mechanisms to obtain the carrier's reimbursement rates to a nonparticipating provider for specific covered health-care services.

(b) In the event of a material change to the carrier's network that could result in the application of subparagraph (I) of paragraph (b) of subsection (2) of this section, the carrier shall provide notice of the change to the commissioner at least fifteen days prior to the change. Such notice may be provided by electronic means.

(c) In the event that a network of a managed care plan with out-of-network benefits that is not a health maintenance organization or a health maintenance organization with a point of service plan changes, and notice to covered persons is provided pursuant to section 10-16-705 (7), such notice shall include an understandable disclosure of:

(I) The circumstances under which the covered person may be balance billed by nonparticipating providers; and

(II) The mechanisms to obtain the carrier's reimbursement rate to nonparticipating providers for specific covered health-care services.

(d) In the event that a contract with a participating provider terminates or is terminated, notification to covered persons shall be provided pursuant to section 10-16-705 (7).

(2.7)

(a) Nothing in subsection (2) or (2.5) of this section shall delay access to health-care services.

(b) Nothing in subparagraph (I) of paragraph (b) of subsection (2) of this section shall exempt a carrier from having a participating provider for all covered benefits. In any case where the carrier has no participating providers to provide a covered benefit, the provisions of paragraph (a) of subsection (2) of this section shall apply.

(3)

(a)

(I) In 1997, the general assembly enacted this part 7 with the express intent to incorporate consumer protections into the creation and maintenance of provider networks and to establish standards to assure the adequacy, accessibility, and quality of health-care services offered under a managed care plan.

(II) The general assembly hereby finds, determines, and declares that there are situations in which insured consumers receive health-care services, including procedures approved by their insurance carrier, in a network facility, with a primary provider that is a network provider, but in which other health-care professionals assisting with such procedures may not be in-network providers. In such situations, the consumer is not aware that the assisting providers are out-of-network providers. Further, the consumer may have little or no direct contact with the assisting health-care professionals. The division of insurance has interpreted the network adequacy provisions in this section, along with the provisions related to relationships between an insurer and a health-care provider in section 10-16-705, to hold the consumer harmless for additional charges from out-of-network providers for care rendered in a network facility. The division of insurance's interpretation of these statutes was challenged by an insurer and invalidated by a division of the Colorado court of appeals in *Pacific Life & Annuity Co. v. Colorado Div. of Ins.*, no. 04CA2169 (slip op.) (Feb. 23, 2006).

(III) The general assembly finds, determines, and declares that the division has correctly interpreted this section to protect a covered person from the additional expense charged by a provider who is an out-of-network provider, and has properly required carriers to hold the covered person harmless. The division does not have regulatory authority over all health plans. Some consumers are enrolled in self-funded health insurance programs that are governed under the federal "Employee Retirement Income Security Act of 1974", 29 U.S.C. sec. 1001 et seq. Therefore, health-care facilities, carriers, and providers must provide consumers with disclosures about the potential impact of receiving services from an out-of-network provider or health-care facility and their rights under this section. Covered persons must have access to accurate information about their health-care bills and their payment obligations in order to enable them to make informed decisions about their health care and financial obligations.

(IV) Repealed.

(V) Therefore, the general assembly finds, determines, and declares that the purpose of Senate Bill 06-213 is to codify the interpretation of the division of insurance that holds consumers harmless for charges over and above the in-network rates for services rendered in a network facility.

(b) When a covered person receives services or treatment in accordance with plan provisions at an in-network facility, the benefit level for all covered services and treatment received through the facility shall be the in-network benefit. Covered services or treatment rendered at an in-network facility, including covered ancillary services or treatment rendered by an out-of-network provider performing the services or treatment at an in-network facility, shall be covered at no greater cost to the covered person than if the services or treatment were obtained from an in-network provider. A payment made by a covered person pursuant to this subsection (3)(b) must be applied to the covered person's in-network deductibles and out-of-pocket maximum amounts and in the same manner as if the cost-sharing payments were made to an in-network provider at an in-network facility.

(c) Repealed.

(d)

(I) If a covered person receives covered services at an in-network facility from an out-of-network provider, the carrier shall pay the out-of-network provider directly and in accordance with this subsection (3)(d). At the time of the disposition of the claim, the carrier shall advise the out-of-network provider and the covered person of any required coinsurance, deductible, or copayment.

(II) When the requirements of subsection (3)(b) of this section apply, the carrier shall reimburse the out-of-network provider directly in accordance with section 10-16-106.5 the greater of:

(A) One hundred ten percent of the carrier's median in-network rate of reimbursement for that service in the same geographic area; or

(B) The sixtieth percentile of the in-network rate of reimbursement for the same service in the same geographic area for the prior year based on commercial claims data from the all-payer health claims database created in section 25.5-1-204.

(III) Payment made by a carrier in compliance with this subsection (3)(d) is presumed to be payment in full for the services provided, except for any coinsurance, deductible, or copayment amount required to be paid by the covered person.

(IV) This subsection (3)(d) does not preclude the carrier and the out-of-network provider from voluntarily negotiating an independent reimbursement rate. If the negotiations fail, the reimbursement rate required by subsection (3)(d)(II) of this section applies.

(V) This subsection (3)(d) does not apply when a covered person has received notice and given consent as required by section 12-30-112 or 25-3-121, as applicable, to use an out-of-network provider in compliance with the federal "No Surprises Act".

(VI) Repealed.

(4) When a treatment or procedure has been preauthorized by the plan, benefits cannot be retrospectively denied except for fraud and abuse. If a health carrier provides preauthorization for treatment or procedures that are not covered benefits under the plan, the carrier shall provide the benefits as authorized with no penalty to the covered person.

(4.5)

(a) All claims paid by a carrier shall be considered final unless adjustments are made pursuant to this subsection (4.5).

(b) Except as otherwise provided in this subsection (4.5), adjustments to claims by the provider or the carrier shall be made within the time period set out in a contract between the provider and the carrier. Such time period shall be the same for the provider and the carrier and shall not exceed twelve months after the date of the original explanation of benefits.

(c) Except as otherwise provided in this subsection (4.5), if there is no contract between a provider and a carrier, adjustments to claims paid to providers shall be made within twelve months after the date of the original explanation of benefits. The time period for adjustments shall be the same for the provider and the carrier.

(d)

(I) Adjustments to claims paid under a risk assumption or risk sharing agreement shall be made within six months after the last date of service for a period for which a settlement is being reconciled. The period for which a settlement is reconciled shall not exceed twelve months.

(II) For purposes of this paragraph (d), "risk assumption" and "risk sharing" refer to a transaction whereby the chance of loss, including the expenses for the delivery of service, with respect to the health care of a person is transferred to or shared with another entity in return for full consideration. Such transactions include, but are not limited to, full or partial capitation agreements, withholds, risk corridors, and indemnification agreements. Such transactions do not include fee-for-service arrangements, per diem payments, and diagnostic-related group payment agreements.

(e) Adjustments to claims related to coordination of benefits with federally funded health benefit plans, including Medicare and Medicaid, shall be made within thirty-six months after the date of service.

(f) A carrier shall not retroactively adjust a claim based on eligibility if the provider received verification of eligibility within two business days prior to the delivery of services, unless the policyholder notified the carrier of an individual's ineligibility pursuant to section 10-16-103.5 (1).

(g)

(I)

(A) In circumstances where a carrier determines that a premium has not been received during a grace period required by section 10-16-202 (4) for an individual policy, the carrier may report to the provider that eligibility is contingent on payment of the premium due and that eligibility cannot be confirmed for the period that the premium is outstanding. In such cases, a carrier shall comply with the requirements of section 10-16-705 (12)(b) and (12)(c).

(B) If a carrier fails to report to the provider that eligibility is contingent on payment of premium due pursuant to sub-subparagraph (A) of this subparagraph (I), the carrier shall comply with paragraph (f) of this section.

(II) In circumstances where the provider receives information from the carrier that coverage is contingent upon receipt of a premium, the requirements of section 10-16-705 (3) shall not apply and the provider may collect payment for services from the enrollee.

(III) If the provider has collected payment from the enrollee and subsequently receives payment from the carrier, the provider shall reimburse the enrollee less any applicable copayments, deductibles, or coinsurance amounts.

(h) In circumstances where a carrier determines that a premium has not been received during a grace period required by section 10-16-214 (3) for a group policy, the carrier may report to the provider that the carrier is not required to pay for health-care services rendered to an enrollee during a time in which the carrier can demonstrate that the policyholder has secured coverage with another carrier.

(i) Nothing in this subsection (4.5) shall prohibit the carrier from requiring the enrollee to reimburse the carrier for claims paid by the carrier to the provider if:

(I) A change in eligibility status has occurred making the enrollee ineligible for coverage on the date services were provided; or

(II) An enrollee has committed fraud or material misrepresentation in applying for coverage or in receiving or filing for benefits.

(j) A carrier shall not retroactively adjust a claim based on eligibility if the provision of benefits is a required policy provision pursuant to section 10-16-202 (4) or 10-16-214 (3), unless the policyholder notified the carrier of an individual's ineligibility pursuant to section 10-16-103.5 (1).

(k) Nothing in this subsection (4.5) shall be construed to require a grace period for the payment of premiums to a health maintenance organization.

(l)

(I) Any adjustment made by the carrier that recovers carrier overpayments to a provider shall include a written notice to the provider and shall contain a complete and specific explanation of such adjustments and information regarding the carrier's provider dispute resolution procedures pursuant to section 10-16-705 (13). Such notice shall be made to both the provider and the enrollee to the extent that the adjustment will result in enrollee liability. Notice to the enrollee required by this paragraph (l) shall include information regarding the carrier's enrollee appeals procedure rather than the carrier's provider dispute resolution procedures.

(II)

(A) For claims adjusted by the carrier due to coordination of benefits, in addition to the requirements of this paragraph (l), upon request of the provider, the carrier shall provide all available information regarding the party responsible for payment of the claim to the provider.

(B) The carrier shall provide notice to the provider with the explanation of benefits regarding the availability of the information related to the party responsible for payment of the claim.

(m) Adjustments to claims made in cases where a carrier, pursuant to section 10-1-128 (5)(a)(IV), has reported fraud or abuse committed by the provider, shall not be subject to the requirements of this subsection (4.5).

(5) A managed care plan shall not deny benefits for emergency services previously rendered, based upon the covered person's failure to provide subsequent notification in accordance with plan provisions, where the covered person's medical condition prevented timely notification.

(5.5)

(a) Notwithstanding any provision of law, a carrier that provides any benefits with respect to emergency services shall cover the emergency services:

(I) Without the need for any prior authorization determination;

(II) Regardless of whether the health-care provider furnishing emergency services is a participating provider with respect to emergency services;

(III) For services provided out of network;

(IV) Without imposing any administrative requirement or limitation on coverage that is more restrictive than the requirements or limitations that apply to emergency services received from in-network providers; and

(V) At the in-network benefit level, with the same coinsurance, deductible, or copayment requirements as would apply if the emergency services were provided by an in-network provider or at an in-network facility, and at no greater cost to the covered person than if the emergency services were obtained from an in-network provider at an in-network facility. Any payment made by a covered person pursuant to this subsection (5.5)(a)(V) must be applied to the covered person's in-network deductibles and in-network out-of-pocket maximum amounts and in the same manner as if the cost-sharing payments were made to an in-network provider or an in-network facility.

(a.5)

(I) A carrier shall:

(A) Cover post-stabilization services provided by an out-of-network provider or at an out-of-network facility at no greater cost to the covered person than the cost that would apply, and with the same coinsurance, deductible, or copayment requirements as the requirements that would apply, if the post-stabilization services were obtained from an in-network provider or at an in-network facility; and

(B) Reimburse the out-of-network provider for post-stabilization services in accordance with subsection (3)(d)(II) of this section and the out-of-network facility in accordance with subsection (5.5)(b) of this section.

(II) Any payment made by a covered person pursuant to subsection (5.5)(a.5)(I) of this section must be applied to the covered person's in-network deductibles and in-network out-of-pocket maximum amounts.

(b)

(I) If a covered person receives emergency services at an out-of-network facility, other than any out-of-network facility operated by the Denver health and hospital authority pursuant to article 29 of title 25, the carrier shall reimburse the out-of-network provider in accordance with subsection (3)(d)(II) of this section and reimburse the out-of-network facility directly in accordance with section 10-16-106.5 the greater of:

(A) One hundred five percent of the carrier's median in-network rate of reimbursement for that service provided in a similar facility or setting in the same geographic area; or

(B) The median in-network rate of reimbursement for the same service provided in a similar facility or setting in the same geographic area for the prior year based on claims data from the Colorado all-payer health claims database created in section 25.5-1-204.

(II) If a covered person receives emergency services at any out-of-network facility operated by the Denver health and hospital authority created in section 25-29-103, the carrier shall reimburse the out-of-network facility directly in accordance with section 10-16-106.5 the greater of:

(A) The carrier's median in-network rate of reimbursement for the same service provided in a similar facility or setting in the same geographic area;

(B) Two hundred fifty percent of the Medicare reimbursement rate for the same service provided in a similar facility or setting in the same geographic area; or

(C) The median in-network rate of reimbursement for the same service provided in a similar facility or setting in the same geographic area for the prior year based on claims data from the Colorado all-payer health claims database described in section 25.5-1-204.

(III) Payment made by a carrier in compliance with this subsection (5.5)(b) is presumed to be payment in full for the services provided, except for any coinsurance, deductible, or copayment amount required to be paid by the covered person.

(c) This subsection (5.5) does not preclude the carrier and the out-of-network facility and the carrier and the provider from voluntarily negotiating an independent reimbursement rate. If the negotiations fail, the reimbursement rate required by subsection (5.5)(b) of this section applies.

(d)

(I) Subsections (5.5)(a), (5.5)(b), and (5.5)(c) of this section do not apply to service agencies, as defined in section 25-3.5-103 (11.5), providing ambulance services, as defined in section 25-3.5-103 (3).

(II)

(A) The commissioner shall promulgate rules to identify and implement a payment methodology that applies to service agencies described in subsection (5.5)(d)(I) of this section, except for service agencies that are publicly funded fire agencies.

(B) The commissioner shall make the payment methodology available to the public on the division's website. The rules must be equitable to service agencies and carriers; hold consumers harmless except for any applicable coinsurance, deductible, or copayment amounts; and be based on a cost-based model that includes direct payment to service agencies as described in subsection (5.5)(d)(I) of this section.

(C) The division may contract with a neutral third-party that has no financial interest in providers, emergency service providers, or carriers to conduct the analysis to identify and implement the payment methodology.

(e) Repealed.

(6) The carrier shall establish and maintain adequate arrangements to ensure reasonable proximity of participating providers to covered persons and shall only market a network plan in a geographic area where network providers are accessible without unreasonable delay. In determining whether a health carrier has complied with this subsection (6), consideration shall be given to the relative availability of health-care providers in the service area under consideration.

(7) A carrier shall monitor, on an ongoing basis, the capacity and legal authority of the participating providers and facilities with which it contracts to furnish all covered benefits to covered persons.

(8) No managed care plan shall deny or restrict in-network covered benefits to a covered person solely because the covered person obtained treatment outside the network. This protection shall be disclosed in writing to the covered person. Nothing in this subsection (8) shall be construed to require a managed care plan to pay for any benefit obtained outside the plan's network unless the contract or certificate provides for that out-of-network benefit.

(9) Beginning January 1, 1998, a carrier shall maintain and make available upon request of the commissioner, the executive director of the department of public health and environment, or the executive director of the department of health care policy and financing, in a manner and form that reflects the requirements specified in paragraphs (a) to (k) of this subsection (9), an access plan for each managed care network that the carrier offers in this state. The carrier shall make the access plans, absent confidential information as specified in section 24-72-204 (3), C.R.S., available on its business premises and shall provide them to any interested party upon request. In addition, all health benefit plans and marketing materials shall clearly disclose the existence and availability of the access plan. All rights and responsibilities of the covered person under the health benefit plan, however, shall be included in the contract provisions, regardless of whether or not such provisions are also specified in the access plan. The carrier shall prepare an access plan prior to offering a new

managed care network and shall update an existing access plan whenever the carrier makes any material change to an existing managed care network, but not less than annually. The access plan of a carrier offering a managed care plan shall demonstrate the following:

(a) An adequate number of accessible acute care hospital services, within a reasonable distance or travel time, or both;

(a.3) An adequate number of accessible primary care providers within a reasonable distance or travel time, or both;

(a.5) An adequate number of accessible specialists and sub-specialists within a reasonable distance or travel time, or both, or who may be available through the use of telehealth;

(a.7) Geographic accessibility, which in some circumstances may require the crossing of county or state lines;

(a.9) If the covered person has a pharmacy benefit, an adequate number of pharmacy providers within a reasonable distance, travel time, delivery time, or all three. Nothing in this paragraph (a.9) shall preclude the use of a retail or mail-order pharmacy provider.

(b) A carrier offering a managed care plan shall maintain procedures for making referrals within and outside its network that, at a minimum, must include the following:

- (I) A comprehensive listing, made available to covered persons and primary care providers, of the plan's network participating providers and facilities;
- (II)
  - (A) A provision that referral options cannot be restricted to less than all providers in the network that are qualified to provide covered specialty services; except that a health maintenance organization may offer variable deductibles and copayments to encourage the selection of certain providers.
  - (B) A health maintenance organization that offers variable deductibles and copayments shall provide adequate and clear disclosure, as required by law, of variable deductibles and copayments to enrollees, and the amount of any deductible or copayment shall be reflected on the benefit card provided to the enrollees.
- (III) Timely referrals for access to specialty care;
- (IV) A process for expediting the referral process when indicated by medical condition; and
- (V)
  - (A) A provision that referrals approved by the plan cannot be retrospectively denied except for fraud or abuse;
  - (B) A provision that referrals approved by the plan cannot be changed after the preauthorization is provided unless there is evidence of fraud or abuse.

(c) The carrier's process for monitoring and assuring on an ongoing basis the sufficiency of the network to meet the health-care needs of populations that enroll in managed care plans;

(d) The carrier's quality assurance standards, adequate to identify, evaluate, and remedy problems relating to access, continuity, and quality of care;

(e) The carrier's efforts to address the needs of covered persons with limited English proficiency and illiteracy, with diverse cultural and ethnic backgrounds, and with physical and mental disabilities;

(f) The carrier's methods for determining the health-care needs of covered persons, tracking and assessing clinical outcomes from network services, and evaluating consumer satisfaction with services provided;

(g) The carrier's method for informing covered persons of the plan's services and features, including but not limited to the following:

(I) The plan's grievance procedures, which shall be in conformance with division rules concerning prompt investigation of health claims involving utilization review and grievance procedures;

(II) The extent to which specialty medical services, including physical therapy, occupational therapy, and rehabilitation services are available;

(III) The plan's process for choosing and changing network providers; and

(IV) The plan's procedures for providing and approving emergency and medical care;

(h) The carrier's system for ensuring the coordination and continuity of care for covered persons referred to specialty providers;

(i) The carrier's process for enabling covered persons to change primary care professionals;

(j) The carrier's proposed plan for providing continuity of care in the event of contract termination between the carrier and any of its participating providers or in the event of the carrier's insolvency or other inability to continue operations. The description shall explain how covered persons will be notified of the contract termination or the carrier's insolvency or other cessation of operations and transferred to other providers in a timely manner.

(k) Any other information required by the commissioner to determine compliance with the provisions of this part 7.

(10)

(a) In determining the reasonableness of travel time and distances for the purposes of this section, consideration shall be given to differences in travel times for rural areas as opposed to urban areas, the relative availability of health-care providers, the location where the majority of people in the area access nonemergency services, and the managed care plan's good faith efforts to contract with local providers at reasonable rates.

(b) The commissioner, upon the commissioner's authority or upon review of one or more complaints, may require the carrier to demonstrate the adequacy of the network's plan as specified in subsection (9) of this section.

(c) The commissioner may utilize the remedies outlined in section 10-3-1108 for failing to provide proper disclosures to covered persons pursuant to subsection (2) or (2.5) of this section.

(11) The division of insurance, in cooperation with the chief medical officer for the state, shall evaluate a carrier's network adequacy plan concerning the use of telehealth for providers who are specialists and sub-specialists for rural areas. The division and chief medical officer shall conduct the review in a timely fashion so as not to delay access to health-care services.

(12)

(a) On and after January 1, 2020, carriers shall develop and provide disclosures to covered persons about the potential effects of receiving emergency or nonemergency services from an out-of-network provider or at an out-of-network facility. The disclosures must, at a minimum, comply with the federal "No Surprises Act" and the rules adopted under subsection (12)(b) of this section.

(b) The commissioner, in consultation with the state board of health created in section 25-1-103 and the applicable regulators of health-care occupations and professions, shall adopt rules to specify the list of the ancillary services for which an out-of-network provider or out-of-network facility must not balance bill a covered person and the disclosure requirements under this subsection (12).

(c) Receipt of the disclosures required by this subsection (12) does not waive a covered person's protections under subsection (3) or (5.5) of this section or the right to benefits under the health benefit plan at the in-network benefit level for all covered services and treatment received.

(13)

(a) When a carrier makes a payment to a provider or a health-care facility pursuant to subsection (3)(d) or (5.5)(b) of this section, the provider or the facility may request, and the commissioner shall collect, data from the carrier to evaluate the carrier's compliance in paying the highest rate required. The information requested may include the methodology for determining the carrier's median in-network rate or reimbursement for each service in the same geographic area.

(b) Repealed.

(14) [Repealed by 2024 amendment.]

(15)

(a)

(I) If a provider or a health-care facility believes that a payment made pursuant to subsection (3) or (5.5) of this section or section 12-30-113 or a health-care facility believes that a payment made pursuant to subsection (5.5) of this section or section 25-3-122 (3) was not sufficient given the complexity and circumstances of the services provided, the provider or the health-care facility may initiate arbitration by filing a request for arbitration with the commissioner and the carrier. A provider or health-care facility must submit a request for the arbitration of a claim within ninety days after the receipt of payment for that claim.

(II) Prior to arbitration under subsection (15)(a)(I) of this section, if requested by the carrier and the provider or health-care facility, the commissioner may arrange an informal settlement teleconference to be held within thirty days after the request for arbitration. The parties shall notify the commissioner of the results of the settlement conference.

(III) Upon receipt of notice that the settlement teleconference was unsuccessful, the commissioner shall appoint an arbitrator and notify the parties of the arbitration.

(b) The commissioner shall promulgate rules to implement an arbitration process that establishes a standard arbitration form and includes the selection of an arbitrator from a list of qualified arbitrators developed pursuant to the rules. Qualified arbitrators must be independent; not be affiliated with a carrier, health-care facility, or provider, or any professional association of carriers, health-care facilities, or providers; not have a personal, professional, or financial conflict with any parties to the arbitration; and have experience in health-care billing and reimbursement rates.

(c) Within thirty days after the commissioner appoints an arbitrator and notifies the parties of the arbitration, both parties shall submit to the arbitrator, in writing, each party's final offer and each party's argument. The arbitrator shall pick one of the two amounts submitted by the parties as the arbitrator's final and binding decision. The decision must be in writing and made within forty-five days after the arbitrator's appointment. In making the decision, the arbitrator shall consider the circumstances and complexity of the particular case, including the following areas:

(I) The provider's level of training, education, experience, and specialization or subspecialization; and

(II) The previously contracted rate, if the provider had a contract with the carrier that was terminated or expired within one year prior to the dispute.

(d) If the arbitrator's decision made pursuant to subsection (15)(c) of this section requires additional payment by the carrier above the amount paid, the carrier shall pay the provider in accordance with section 10-16-106.5. A carrier shall not recalculate a covered person's cost-sharing amount based on an additional payment required or made as a result of an arbitration decision.

(e) The party whose final offer amount was not selected by the arbitrator shall pay the arbitrator's expenses and fees. If the parties reach a settlement after an arbitrator is appointed but before the arbitrator makes a final decision, the parties shall split the costs of the arbitration equally unless otherwise agreed by the parties.

(16) [Repealed by 2024 amendment.]

(17) The commissioner shall post on the division's website information on the state and federal agencies that a covered person may contact if a provider, facility, or carrier violates this section.

(18) The commissioner may adopt rules to implement this section, including rules necessary to implement the requirements of the federal "No Surprises Act".

(19) As used in this section:

(a) "Ancillary services" means:

(I) Diagnostic services, including radiology and laboratory services, unless excluded by rule of the secretary of the United States department of health and human services pursuant to 42 U.S.C. sec. 300gg-132 (b)(3);

(II) Items and services related to emergency medicine, anesthesiology, pathology, radiology, and neonatology, whether or not provided by a physician or nonphysician provider, unless excluded by rule of the secretary of the United States department of health and human services pursuant to section 2799B-2 (b)(3) of the federal "No Surprises Act";

(III) Items and services provided by assistant surgeons, hospitalists, and intensivists, unless excluded by rule of the secretary of the United States department of health and human services pursuant to section 2799B-2 (b)(3) of the federal "No Surprises Act";

(IV) Items and services provided by an out-of-network provider if there is no in-network provider who can furnish the needed services at the facility; and

(V) Any other items and services provided by specialty providers as established by rule of the commissioner.

(b) "Applicable regulators of health-care occupations and professions" means the:

(I) Colorado state board of chiropractic examiners created in section 12-215-104;

(II) Colorado dental board created in section 12-220-105;

(III) Colorado medical board created in section 12-240-105;

(IV) State board of psychologist examiners created in section 12-245-302;

(V) State board of social work examiners created in section 12-245-402;

(VI) State board of marriage and family therapist examiners created in section 12-245-502;

(VII) State board of licensed professional counselor examiners created in section 12-245-602;
(VIII) State board of unlicensed psychotherapists created in section 12-245-702;
(IX) State board of addiction counselor examiners created in section 12-245-802;
(X) State board of nursing created in section 12-255-105;
(XI) Board of examiners of nursing home administrators created in section 12-265-106;
(XII) State board of optometry created in section 12-275-107;
(XIII) State board of pharmacy created in section 12-280-104;
(XIV) State physical therapy board created in section 12-285-105;
(XV) Colorado podiatry board created in section 12-290-105; and
(XVI) The director of the division of professions and occupations in the department of regulatory agencies.

(c) "Balance bill" means:
(I) The amount that an out-of-network provider may charge a covered person for the provision of health-care services, which amount equals the difference between the amount paid by the carrier for the health-care services and the amount of the out-of-network provider's billed charge for the health-care services; and
(II) The act of a nonparticipating provider charging a covered person the difference between the billed amount and the amount the carrier paid the provider.

(d) "Emergency medical condition" means a medical condition that manifests itself by acute symptoms of sufficient severity, including severe pain, that a prudent layperson with an average knowledge of health and medicine could reasonably expect, in the absence of immediate medical attention, to result in:
(I) Serious jeopardy to the health of the individual or, with respect to a pregnant woman, the health of the woman or unborn child;
(II) Serious impairment to bodily functions; or
(III) Serious dysfunction of any bodily organ or part.

(e)
(I) "Emergency services", with respect to an emergency medical condition, means:
(A) A medical screening examination that is within the capability of the emergency department of a hospital or a free-standing emergency department, as applicable, including ancillary services routinely available to the emergency department to evaluate the emergency medical condition; and
(B) Within the capabilities of the staff and facilities available at the hospital, regardless of the department in which

further examination or treatment is furnished, or the free-standing emergency department, as applicable, further medical examination and treatment as are required to stabilize the patient to ensure, within reasonable medical probability, that no material deterioration of the condition is likely to result from or occur during the transfer of the patient from a facility.

(II) For a covered person who is provided services described in subsections (19)(e)(I)(A) and (19)(e)(I)(B) of this section with respect to an emergency medical condition, unless each of the conditions in subsection (19)(e)(III) of this section are met, the term "emergency services" includes services that are:

(A) Covered under the health benefit plan; and

(B) Provided by a nonparticipating provider or nonparticipating emergency facility, regardless of the department or the facility in which the items or services are provided, after the covered person is stabilized and as part of the outpatient observation or inpatient or outpatient stay, with respect to the emergency visit in which the services described in subsection (19)(e)(I) of this section are provided.

(III) For the purposes of subsection (19)(e)(II) of this section, the conditions described in this subsection (19)(e)(III), with respect to a covered individual who is stabilized and furnished additional items and services described in subsection (19)(e)(II) of this section after the stabilization by a provider or facility are the following:

(A) The out-of-network provider or out-of-network facility determines the covered person is able to travel using non-medical transportation or nonemergency medical transportation;

(B) The out-of-network provider or out-of-network facility has provided the covered person with notice and obtained consent as required by section 12-30-112 or 25-3-121, as applicable;

(C) The covered person is in a condition to receive the notice and consent described in section 12-30-112 or 25-3-121 and to provide informed consent; and

(D) The out-of-network provider or out-of-network facility is in compliance with, at a minimum, other requirements established in 42 U.S.C. sec. 300gg-111 and any federal regulations adopted pursuant to 42 U.S.C. sec. 300gg-111.

(f) "Federal 'No Surprises Act'" means the federal "No Surprises Act", Pub. L. 116-260, as amended.

(g) "Freestanding emergency department" has the same meaning as set forth in section 25-1.5-114 (5).

(h) "Geographic area" means a specific area in this state as established by the commissioner by rule.

(i) "In-network facility" means a participating provider that is a health-care facility.

(j) "In-network provider" means a participating provider who is an individual.

(k) "Medicare reimbursement rate" means the reimbursement rate for a particular health-care service provided under the "Health Insurance for the Aged Act", Title XVIII of the federal "Social Security Act", 42 U.S.C. sec. 1395 et seq., as amended.

(l) "Negotiated rate" means the rate mutually agreed upon between the carrier and the provider in a specific instance.

(m) "Stabilized" means the condition of a patient in which, within reasonable medical probability, no material deterioration of the condition is likely to result from or occur during the transfer of the patient from one facility or department to another.

(n) "Usual, customary, and reasonable rate" means a rate established pursuant to an appropriate methodology that is based on generally accepted industry standards and practices.

§ 12-30-112 Health-care providers—required disclosures—balance billing—deceptive trade practice—rules—definitions

(1) As used in this section and section 12-30-113:

(a) "Ancillary services" means:

(I) Diagnostic services, including radiology and laboratory services, unless excluded by rule of the secretary of the United States department of health and human services pursuant to 42 U.S.C. sec. 300gg-132 (b)(3);

(II) Items and services related to emergency medicine, anesthesiology, pathology, radiology, and neonatology, whether or not provided by a physician or nonphysician provider, unless excluded by rule of the secretary of the United States department of health and human services pursuant to section 2799B-2 (b)(3) of the federal "No Surprises Act";

(III) Items and services provided by assistant surgeons, hospitalists, and intensivists, unless excluded by rule of the secretary of the United States department of health and human services pursuant to section 2799B-2 (b)(3) of the federal "No Surprises Act";

(IV) Items and services provided by an out-of-network provider if there is no in-network provider who can furnish the needed services at the facility; and

(V) Any other items and services provided by specialty providers as established by rule of the commissioner of insurance.

(a.3) "Balance bill" has the same meaning as set forth in section 10-16-704 (19)(c).

(a.5) "Carrier" has the same meaning as set forth in section 10-16-102 (8).

(b) "Covered person" has the same meaning as defined in section 10-16-102 (15).

(c) "Emergency services" has the same meaning as set forth in section 10-16-704 (19)(e).

(c.5) "Federal 'No Surprises Act'" means the federal "No Surprises Act", Pub. L. 116-260, as amended.

(d) "Geographic area" has the same meaning as set forth in section 10-16-704 (19)(h).

(e) "Health benefit plan" has the same meaning as defined in section 10-16-102 (32).

(f) "Medicare reimbursement rate" has the same meaning as set forth in section 10-16-704 (19)(k).

(g) "Out-of-network provider" means a health-care provider that is not a participating provider.

(h) "Participating provider" has the same meaning as set forth in section 10-16-102 (46).

(2) On and after January 1, 2020, health-care providers shall develop and provide disclosures to consumers about the potential effects of receiving emergency or nonemergency services from an out-of-network provider. The disclosures must comply with the rules adopted pursuant to subsection (3) of this section.

(3) The regulator, in consultation with the commissioner of insurance and the state board of health created in section 25-1-103, shall adopt rules that specify the requirements for health-care providers to develop and provide consumer disclosures in accordance with this section. The regulator shall ensure that the rules, at a minimum, comply with the notice and consent requirements in subsection (3.5) of this section and the federal "No Surprises Act".

(3.5)

(a) An out-of-network provider may balance bill a covered person for post-stabilization services in accordance with section 10-16-704 and covered nonemergency services in an in-network facility that are not ancillary services if:

(I) The out-of-network provider provides written notice that the provider will balance bill a covered person at least seventy-two hours in advance of the date of service, if the appointment was scheduled at least seventy-two hours in advance, or at least three hours before the scheduled appointment, if the appointment was made less than seventy-two hours in advance, in either paper or electronic format as selected by the covered person. The notice must be available in the fifteen most common languages in the geographic region in which the out-of-network provider is located. The notice must state:

(A) If applicable, that the health-care provider is out of network with respect to the covered person's health benefit plan;

(B) Effective upon the implementation date of the applicable federal rules, a good-faith estimate of the amount of the charges for which the covered person may be responsible;

(C) That the estimate or consent to treatment does not constitute a contract for services;

(D) If the facility is a participating provider and the health-care provider is an out-of-network provider, a list of participating providers at the facility who are able to provide the same services;

(E) Information about whether prior authorization or other care management limitations may be required in advance of receiving the requested services; and

(F) That consent to receive the services from an out-of-network provider is optional and that the covered person may seek services from a participating provider, in which case the cost-sharing responsibility of the covered person would not exceed the responsibility for in-network benefits under the covered person's health benefit plan;

(II) The out-of-network provider obtains signed consent from the covered person that acknowledges that the covered person has been:

(A) Provided with written notice of the covered person's financial responsibility, in the format and language selected by the covered person and within the applicable periods specified in subsection (3.5)(a)(I) of this section; and

(B) Provided written notice that the payment by the covered person for health-care services provided by the out-of-network provider may not accrue toward meeting any limitation that the health benefit plan places on cost sharing, including an explanation that the payment may not apply to an in-network deductible.

(b) If the notice in subsection (3.5)(a)(I) of this section is received within ten days before a scheduled service, the covered person may elect to use the out-of-network provider at the in-network benefit level, and the provider must be reimbursed for the services in accordance with section 10-16-704 (3)(d)(II).

(c) The notice and consent required by this subsection (3.5) must include the date and the time at which the covered person received the written notice and the date on which the consent form was signed. The out-of-network provider shall provide a signed copy of the consent form to the covered person through regular or electronic mail.

(d) An out-of-network provider that obtains a signed consent with respect to furnishing an item or service shall retain the signed consent for at least a seven-year period after the date on which such item or service is furnished.

(3.7) An out-of-network provider shall not balance bill a covered person for services if the provisions of section 10-16-705 (4.5)(c)(II) apply.

(4) Receipt of the disclosures required by this section does not waive a consumer's protections under section 10-16-704 (3) or (5.5) or the consumer's right to benefits under the consumer's health benefit plan at the in-network benefit level for all covered services and treatment received.

(5) This section does not apply to service agencies, as defined in section 25-3.5-103 (11.5), that are publicly funded fire agencies.

(6) A violation of this section is a deceptive trade practice pursuant to section 6-1-105 (1)(xxx).

§ 12-30-113 Out-of-network health-care providers—out-of-network services—billing—payment—deceptive trade practice

(1) If an out-of-network health-care provider provides emergency services or covered nonemergency services to a covered person at an in-network facility, the out-of-network provider shall:

(a) Submit a claim for the entire cost of the services to the covered person's carrier; and

(b) Not bill or collect payment from a covered person for any outstanding balance for covered services not paid by the carrier, except for the applicable in-network coinsurance, deductible, or copayment amount required to be paid by the covered person.

(2)

(a) If an out-of-network health-care provider provides covered nonemergency services at an in-network facility or emergency services at an out-of-network or in-network facility and the health-care provider receives payment from the covered person for services for which the covered person is not responsible pursuant to section 10-16-704 (3)(b) or (5.5), the health-care provider shall reimburse the covered person within sixty calendar days after the date that the overpayment was reported to the provider.

(b) An out-of-network health-care provider that fails to reimburse a covered person as required by subsection (2)(a) of this section for an overpayment shall pay interest on the overpayment at the rate of ten percent per annum beginning on the date the provider received the notice of the overpayment. The covered person is not required to request the accrued interest from the out-of-network health-care provider in order to receive interest with the reimbursement amount.

(3) An out-of-network health-care provider shall provide a covered person a written estimate of the amount for which the covered person may be responsible for covered nonemergency services within three business days after a request from the covered person.

(4)

(a) An out-of-network health-care provider must send a claim for a covered service to the carrier within one hundred eighty days after the receipt of insurance information in order to receive reimbursement as specified in this subsection (4)(a). The reimbursement rate is the greater of:

(I) One hundred ten percent of the carrier's median in-network rate of reimbursement for that service provided in the same geographic area; or

(II) The sixtieth percentile of the in-network rate of reimbursement for the same service in the same geographic area for the prior year based on claims data from the all-payer health claims database described in section 25.5-1-204.

(b) If the out-of-network health-care provider submits a claim for covered services after the one-hundred-eighty-day period specified in subsection (4)(a) of this section, the carrier shall reimburse the health-care provider one hundred twenty-five percent of the Medicare reimbursement rate for the same services in the same geographic area.

(c) The health-care provider shall not bill a covered person any outstanding balance for a covered service not paid for by the carrier, except for any coinsurance, deductible, or copayment amount required to be paid by the covered person.

(5) A health-care provider may initiate arbitration pursuant to section 10-16-704 (15) if the health-care provider believes the payment made pursuant to subsection (4) of this section is not sufficient.

(6) A violation of this section is a deceptive trade practice pursuant to section 6-1-105 (1)(xxx).

RULE 3 COLORADO CODE OF REGULATIONS

§ 713-1.31 Concerning health care provider disclosures to consumers about the potential effects of receiving emergency or nonemergency services from an out-of-network provider

A. Basis: The basis for the Board's promulgation of these rules and regulations is sections 12-20-204, 12-30-112, and 12-240-106(1)(a), C.R.S., in consultation with the Commissioner of Insurance and the State Board of Health.

B. Purpose: The purpose of these rules and regulations is to establish requirements for health care providers to provide disclosures to consumers about the potential effects of receiving emergency or non-emergency services from an out-of-network provider.

C. Definitions, for purposes of this Rule, are as follows:

   1. "Publicly available" means, for the purposes of this regulation, searchable on the health care provider's public website, displayed in a manner that is easily accessible, without barriers, and that ensures that the information is accessible to the general public, including that it is findable through public search engines. The health care provider's public website must be accessible free of charge, without having to establish a user account, password, or other credentials, accept any terms or conditions, and without having to submit any personal identifying information.

D. Disclosure requirements.

   1. An out of network provider may balance bill a covered person for post-stabilization services in accordance with section 10-16-704, C.R.S., and covered nonemergency services in an in-network facility that are not ancillary services if the provider meets the requirements set forth in section 12-30-112(3.5), C.R.S. If a consumer has incurred a claim for emergency or nonemergency health care services from an out-of-network provider, the health care provider shall provide the disclosures contained in Appendix C in compliance with section 12-30-112(3.5), C.R.S.
   2. The health care provider shall provide the disclosure contained in Appendix C as set forth in section 12-30-112(3.5), C.R.S.:

E. Noncompliance with this Rule may result in the imposition of any of discipline made available by section 12-240-125, C.R.S.

§ 713-1-C Appendix C: your rights and protections against surprise medical bills

When you get emergency care or get treated by an out-of-network provider at an in-network hospital or ambulatory surgical center, you are protected from surprise billing or balance billing.

What is "balance billing" (sometimes called "surprise billing")?

When you see a doctor or other health care provider, you may owe certain out-of-pocket costs, like a copayment, coinsurance, or deductible. You may have additional costs or have to pay the entire bill if you see a provider or visit a health care facility that isn't in your health plan's network.

"Out-of-network" means providers and facilities that haven't signed a contract with your health plan to provide services. Out-of-network providers may be allowed to bill you for the difference between what your plan pays and the full amount charged for a service. This is called "balance billing." This amount is likely more than in-network costs for the same service and might not count toward your plan's deductible or annual out-of-pocket limit.

"Surprise billing" is an unexpected balance bill. This can happen when you can't control who is involved in your care—like when you have an emergency or when you schedule a visit at an in-network facility but are unexpectedly treated by an out-of-network provider. Surprise medical bills could cost thousands of dollars depending on the procedure or service.

You're protected from balance billing for:

Emergency services

If you have an emergency medical condition and get emergency services from an out-of-network provider or facility, the most they can bill you is your plan's in-network cost-sharing amount (such as copayments, coinsurance, and deductibles). You can't be balance billed for these emergency services. This includes services you may get after you're in stable condition, unless you give written consent and give up your protections not to be balanced billed for these post-stabilization services.

If you believe you've been wrongly billed by a healthcare provider, please contact the Colorado Medical Board at dora_medicalboard@state.co.us or at 303-894-7800.

Visit the CMS No Surprises Act website (https://www.cms.gov/nosurprises/consumers) for more information about your rights under federal law.

Visit section 12-30-112, C.R.S., for more information about your rights under state law.

Certain services at an in-network hospital or ambulatory surgical center

When you get services from an in-network hospital or ambulatory surgical center, certain providers there may be out-of-network. In these cases, the most those providers can bill you is your plan's in-network cost-sharing amount. This applies to emergency medicine, anesthesia, pathology, radiology, laboratory, neonatology, assistant surgeon, hospitalist, or intensivist services. These providers can't balance bill you and may not ask you to give up your protections not to be balance billed.

If you get other types of services at these in-network facilities, out-of-network providers can't balance bill you, unless you give written consent and give up your protections.

You're *never* required to give up your protections from balance billing. You also aren't required to get out-of-network care. You can choose a provider or facility in your plan's network.

When balance billing isn't allowed, you also have these protections:

- You're only responsible for paying your share of the cost (like the copayments, coinsurance, and deductible that you would pay if the provider or facility was in-network). Your health plan will pay any additional costs to out-of-network providers and facilities directly.
- Generally, your health plan must:
  - Cover emergency services without requiring you to get approval for services in advance (also known as "prior authorization").
  - Cover emergency services by out-of-network providers.
  - Base what you owe the provider or facility (cost-sharing) on what it would pay an in-network provider or facility and show that amount in your explanation of benefits.
  - Count any amount you pay for emergency services or out-of-network services toward your in-network deductible and out-of-pocket limit.

If you believe you've been wrongly billed by a healthcare provider, please contact the Colorado Medical Board at dora_medicalboard@state.co.us or at 303-894-7800.

Visit the CMS No Surprises Act website (https://www.cms.gov/nosurprises/consumers) for more information about your rights under federal law. Visit section 12-30-112, C.R.S., for more information about your rights under state law. The federal phone number for information and complaints is: 1-800-985-3059.

Visit the CMS No Surprises Act website (https://www.cms.gov/nosurprises/consumers) for more information about your rights under federal law.

Visit the Colorado Medical Board (https://dpo.colorado.gov/Medical) website for more information about your rights under section 12-30-112, C.R.S.

CONNECTICUT GENERAL STATUTES

§ 20-7f Unfair billing practices

Connecticut General Statutes Title 20. Professional and Occupational Licensing, Certification, Title Protection and Registration. Examining Boards § 20-7f.

(a) For purposes of this section:
 (1) "Request payment" includes, but is not limited to, submitting a bill for services not actually owed or submitting for such services an invoice or other communication detailing the cost of the services that is not clearly marked with the phrase "This is not a bill".
 (2) "Health care provider" means a person licensed to provide health care services under chapters 370 to 373, 1 inclusive, chapters 375 to 383b, 2 inclusive, chapters 384a to 384c, 3 inclusive, or chapter 400j. 4
 (3) "Enrollee" means a person who has contracted for or who participates in a health care plan for such enrollee or such enrollee's eligible dependents.
 (4) "Coinsurance, copayment, deductible or other out-of-pocket expense" means the portion of a charge for services covered by a health care plan that, under the plan's terms, it is the obligation of the enrollee to pay.
 (5) "Health care plan" has the same meaning as provided in subsection (a) of section 38a-477aa.
 (6) "Health carrier" has the same meaning as provided in subsection (a) of section 38a-477aa.
 (7) "Emergency services" has the same meaning as provided in subsection (a) of section 38a-477aa.

(b) It shall be an unfair trade practice in violation of chapter 735a for any health care provider to request payment from an enrollee, other than a coinsurance, copayment, deductible or other out-of-pocket expense, for (1) health care services or a facility fee, as defined in section 19a-508c, covered under a health care plan, (2) emergency services covered under a health care plan and rendered by an out-of-network health care provider, or (3) a surprise bill, as defined in section 38a-477aa.

(c) It shall be an unfair trade practice in violation of chapter 735a for any health care provider to report to a credit reporting agency an enrollee's failure to pay a bill for the services, facility fee or surprise bill as set forth in subsection (b) of this section, when a health carrier has primary responsibility for payment of such services, fees or bills.

§ 38a-477aa Cost-sharing and health care provider reimbursements for emergency services, urgent crisis center services and surprise bills

(a) As used in this section:
 (1) "Emergency condition" has the same meaning as "emergency medical condition", as provided in section 38a-591a.

(2) "Emergency services" means, with respect to an emergency condition, (A) a medical screening examination as required under Section 1867 of the Social Security Act, as amended from time to time, that is within the capability of a hospital emergency department, including ancillary services routinely available to such department to evaluate such condition, and (B) such further medical examinations and treatment required under said Section 1867 to stabilize such individual that are within the capability of the hospital staff and facilities.

(3) "Health care plan" means an individual or a group health insurance policy or health benefit plan that provides coverage of the type specified in subdivisions (1), (2), (4), (11) and (12) of section 38a-469.

(4) "Health care provider" means an individual licensed to provide health care services under chapters 370 to 373, inclusive, chapters 375 to 383b, inclusive, and chapters 384a to 384c, inclusive.

(5) "Health carrier" means an insurance company, health care center, hospital service corporation, medical service corporation, fraternal benefit society or other entity that delivers, issues for delivery, renews, amends or continues a health care plan in this state.

(6)

(A) "Surprise bill" means a bill for health care services, other than emergency services or urgent crisis center services, received by an insured for services rendered by an out-of-network health care provider, where such services were rendered by (i) such out-of-network provider at an in-network facility, during a service or procedure performed by an in-network provider or during a service or procedure previously approved or authorized by the health carrier and the insured did not knowingly elect to obtain such services from such out-of-network provider, or (ii) a clinical laboratory, as defined in section 19a-490, as amended by this act, that is an out-of-network provider, upon the referral of an in-network provider.

(B) "Surprise bill" does not include a bill for health care services received by an insured when an in-network health care provider was available to render such services and the insured knowingly elected to obtain such services from another health care provider who was out-of-network.

(7) "Urgent crisis center" means a center that is certified as an urgent crisis center by the Department of Children and Families that is dedicated to treating children's urgent mental or behavioral health needs.

(8) "Urgent crisis center services" means pediatric mental and behavioral health services provided at an urgent crisis center.

(b)

(1) No health carrier shall require prior authorization for rendering emergency services or urgent crisis center services to an insured.

(2) No health carrier shall impose, for emergency services rendered to an insured by an out-of-network health care provider or urgent crisis center

services rendered to an insured at an out-of-network urgent crisis center, a coinsurance, copayment, deductible or other out-of-pocket expense that is greater than the coinsurance, copayment, deductible or other out-of-pocket expense that would be imposed if such emergency services were rendered by an in-network health care provider or such urgent crisis center services were rendered at an in-network urgent crisis center.

(3)

(A) If emergency services were rendered to an insured by an out-of-network health care provider, such health care provider may bill the health carrier directly and the health carrier shall reimburse such health care provider the greatest of the following amounts: (i) The amount the insured's health care plan would pay for such services if rendered by an in-network health care provider; (ii) the usual, customary and reasonable rate for such services; or (iii) the amount Medicare would reimburse for such services. As used in this subparagraph, "usual, customary and reasonable rate" means the eightieth percentile of all charges for the particular health care service performed by a health care provider in the same or similar specialty and provided in the same geographical area, as reported in a benchmarking database maintained by a nonprofit organization specified by the Insurance Commissioner. Such organization shall not be affiliated with any health carrier.

(B) If urgent crisis center services were rendered to an insured at an out-of-network urgent crisis center, such urgent crisis center may bill the health carrier directly for such urgent crisis center services. The health carrier shall reimburse such out-of-network urgent crisis center or insured, as applicable, for such urgent crisis center services at the in-network rate under the insured's health care plan as payment in full, unless such health carrier and urgent crisis center agree otherwise.

(C) Nothing in subparagraph (A) or (B) of this subdivision shall be construed to prohibit a health carrier and out-of-network health care provider or urgent crisis center from agreeing to a reimbursement amount that is greater than the minimum reimbursement amount established in subparagraph (A) or (B) of this subdivision, as applicable.

(c) With respect to a surprise bill:

(1) An insured shall only be required to pay the applicable coinsurance, copayment, deductible or other out-of-pocket expense that would be imposed for such health care services if such services were rendered by an in-network health care provider; and

(2) A health carrier shall reimburse the out-of-network health care provider or insured, as applicable, for health care services rendered at the in-network rate under the insured's health care plan as payment in full, unless such health carrier and health care provider agree otherwise.

(d) If health care services were rendered to an insured by an out-of-network health care provider and the health carrier failed to inform such insured, if such insured was required to be informed, of the network status of such health care provider pursuant to subdivision (3) of subsection (d) of section 38a-591b, the health carrier shall not impose a coinsurance, copayment, deductible or other out-of-pocket expense that is greater than the coinsurance, copayment, deductible or other out-of-pocket expense that would be imposed if such services were rendered by an in-network health care provider.

(e) The provisions of this section shall apply to a high deductible health plan, as that term is used in subsection (f) of section 38a-493 or subsection (f) of section 38a-520, as applicable, to the maximum extent permitted by federal law, except if such plan is used to establish a medical savings account or an Archer MSA pursuant to Section 220 of the Internal Revenue Code of 1986, or any subsequent corresponding internal revenue code of the United States, as amended from time to time, or a health savings account pursuant to Section 223 of said Internal Revenue Code, as amended from time to time, the provisions of this section shall apply to such plan to the maximum extent that (1) is permitted by federal law, and (2) does not disqualify such account for the deduction allowed under said Section 220 or 223, as applicable.

TITLE 18 DELAWARE CODE

§ 311 Rules and regulations; promulgation; violation

(a) The Commissioner may make reasonable rules and regulations necessary for, or as an aid to, the administration or effectuation of any provision of this title. No such rule or regulation shall extend, modify or conflict with any law of this State or the reasonable implications thereof.

(b) The Commissioner shall adopt and promulgate rules and regulations in accordance with the procedures set forth in the state Administrative Procedures Act, Chapter 101 of Title 29.

(c) Willful violation of any such rule or regulation shall subject the violator to such suspension or revocation of certificate of authority or license, or to such administrative fine in lieu thereof, as may be applicable under this title, for violation of the provision to which such rule or regulation relates; but no penalty shall apply to any act done or omitted in good faith in conformity with any such rule or regulation, notwithstanding that such rule or regulation, after such act or omission, may be amended or rescinded or determined by judicial or other authority to be invalid for any reason.

§ 3348 Referrals

(a) This section applies to every policy or contract of health insurance which is delivered or issued for delivery in this State, including each policy or contract issued by a health service corporation, and which designates network physicians or providers or preferred physicians or providers (hereinafter referred to collectively as "network providers"). In such circumstances, the non-network provider may not balance bill the insured.

(b) All individual and group health insurance policies shall provide that if medically necessary covered services are not available through network providers, or the network providers are not available within a reasonable period of time, the insurer, on the request of a network provider, within a reasonable period, shall allow referral to a non-network physician or provider and shall reimburse the non-network physician or provider at a previously agreed-upon or negotiated rate. In such circumstances, the non-network physician or provider may not balance bill the insured. Such a referral shall not be refused by the insurer absent a decision by a physician in the same or a similar specialty as the physician to whom a referral is sought that the referral is not reasonably related to the provision of medically necessary services.

(c) All individual and group health insurance policies which do not allow insureds to have direct access to health-care specialists shall establish and implement a procedure by which insureds can obtain a standing referral to a health-care specialist.

(d) The procedure established under subsection (c) of this section:

(1) Shall provide for a standing referral to a specialist if the insured's network provider determines that the insured needs continuing care from the specialist; and

(2) May require the insurer's approval of an initial treatment plan designed by the specialist containing (i) a limit on the number of visits to the specialist, (ii) a time limit on the duration of the referral, and (iii) mandatory updates on the insured's condition. Such approval shall not be withheld absent a decision by a qualified physician that the treatment sought in the treatment plan is not reasonably related to the appropriate treatment of the insured's condition.

Within the treatment period referred to in paragraph (d)(2) of this section, the specialist shall be permitted to treat the insured without a further referral from the insured's network provider and may authorize such further referrals, procedures, tests and other medical services as the individual's network provider would otherwise be permitted to provide or authorize, provided that such further referrals, procedures, tests and other medical services are part of treating the patient for the condition for which the patient was referred to the specialist. Referrals, procedures, tests, and other medical services referred to in this subsection shall be provided by network providers unless such services are not available through network providers, or the network providers are not available within a reasonable period of time. If services are not available through network providers, or the network providers are not available within a reasonable period of time, the out-of-network provider shall be reimbursed at an agreed-upon or negotiated rate. In such circumstances, the non-network provider may not balance bill the insured.

(e) Nothing in this section shall prevent the operation of policy provisions involving deductibles or copayments.

§ 3349 Emergency care

(a) This section applies to every policy or contract of health insurance, including each policy or contract issued by a health service corporation, which is delivered or issued for delivery in this State, and which designates network physicians or providers or preferred physicians or providers (hereinafter referred to collectively as "network providers"). However, this section applies only to conditions for which coverage is provided by those policies or contracts.

(b) All individual and group health insurance policies shall provide that persons covered under those policies will be insured for emergency care services performed by nonnetwork providers at an agreed-upon or negotiated rate, regardless of whether the physician or provider furnishing the services has a contractual or other arrangement with the insurer to provide items or services to persons covered under the policies. In the event that the provider of emergency services and the insurer cannot agree upon the appropriate rate, the provider shall be entitled to those charges and rates allowed by the Insurance Commissioner or the Commissioner's designee following an arbitration of the dispute. The Insurance Commissioner shall adopt regulations concerning the arbitration of such disputes. In such circumstances, the nonnetwork provider may not balance bill the insured.

(c) Prior to a determination by the Insurance Commissioner (or the Commissioner's designee) of those charges and rates allowed by the providers of emergency services pursuant to subsection (b) of this section, the insurer will pay directly to the non-network emergency care provider the highest allowable charge for each emergency care service allowed by the insurer for any other network or non-network emergency care provider during the full 12-month period immediately prior to the date of each emergency care service performed by the non-network provider. The Insurance Commissioner is authorized to adopt regulations concerning the provisions of this subsection (c).

(d) Plans described in subsections (a) and (b) of this section shall cover:
   (1) Any medical screening examination or other evaluation medically required to determine whether an emergency medical condition exists;
   (2) Necessary emergency care services, including treatment and stabilization of an emergency medical condition; and
   (3) Services originated in a hospital emergency facility or comparable facility following treatment or stabilization of an emergency medical condition as approved by the insurer with respect to services performed by non-network providers, provided that the insurer is required to approve or disapprove coverage of poststabilization care as requested by a treating physician or provider within the time appropriate to the circumstances relating to the delivery of services and the condition of the patient, but in no case to exceed 1 hour from the time of the request.

(e) Nothing in this section shall prevent the operation of policy provisions involving deductibles or copayments. As used in this section "emergency medical condition" means a medical or behavioral condition the onset of which is sudden, that manifests itself by symptoms of sufficient severity, including, but not limited to, severe pain, that a prudent layperson, possessing an average knowledge of medicine and health, could reasonably expect the absence of immediate medical attention to result in:
   (1) Placing the health of the person afflicted with such condition in serious jeopardy, or in the case of a behavioral condition, placing the health of such person or others in serious jeopardy;
   (2) Serious impairment to such person's bodily functions;
   (3) Serious impairment or dysfunction of any bodily organ or part of such person; or
   (4) Serious disfigurement of such person.

(f) This section shall not apply to services provided by a volunteer fire department recognized as such by the State Fire Prevention Commission.

(g) The Insurance Commissioner shall establish a schedule of fees for arbitration. The nonprevailing party at arbitration shall reimburse the Commissioner for the expenses related to the arbitration process. Funds paid to the Insurance Commissioner under this subsection shall be placed in the arbitration fund and shall be used exclusively for the payment of appointed arbitrators. The Insurance Commissioner may, in the Commissioner's discretion, impose a schedule of maximum fees that can be charged by an arbitrator for a given type of arbitration.

§ 3564 Referrals

(a) This section applies to every group or blanket policy or contract of health insurance, including each policy or contract issued by a health service corporation, which is delivered or issued for delivery in this State and which designates network physicians or providers or preferred physicians or providers (hereinafter referred to collectively as "network providers").

(b) All individual and group health insurance policies shall provide that if medically necessary covered services are not available through network providers, or the network providers are not available within a reasonable period of time, the insurer, on the request of a network provider, within a reasonable period, shall allow referral to a non-network physician or provider and shall reimburse the non-network physician or provider at a previously agreed-upon or negotiated rate. In such circumstances, the non-network physician or provider may not balance bill the insured. Such a referral shall not be refused by the insurer absent a decision by a physician in the same or a similar specialty as the physician to whom a referral is sought that the referral is not reasonably related to the provision of medically necessary services.

(c) All individual and group health insurance policies which do not allow insureds to have direct access to health-care specialists shall establish and implement a procedure by which insureds can obtain a standing referral to a health-care specialist.

(d) The procedure established under subsection (c) of this section:

 (1) Shall provide for a standing referral to a specialist if the insured's network provider determines that the insured needs continuing care from the specialist; and

 (2) May require the insurer's approval of an initial treatment plan designed by the specialist containing:

  a. A limit on the number of visits to the specialist;

  b. A time limit on the duration of the referral; and

  c. Mandatory updates on the insured's condition.

Such approval shall not be withheld absent a decision by a qualified physician that the treatment sought in the treatment plan is not reasonably related to the appropriate treatment of the insured's condition.

Within the treatment period referred to in paragraph (d)(2) of this section, the specialist shall be permitted to treat the insured without a further referral from the insured's network provider and may authorize such further referrals, procedures, tests and other medical services as the individual's network provider would otherwise be permitted to provide or authorize, provided that such further referrals, procedures, tests and other medical services are part of treating the patient for the condition for which the patient was referred to the specialist. Referrals, procedures, tests and other medical services referred to in this subsection shall be provided by network providers unless such services are not available through network providers, or the network providers are not available within a reasonable period of time. If services are not available through network providers, or the network providers are not available within a reasonable period of time, the out-of-network provider shall be reimbursed at an agreed-upon or negotiated rate. In such circumstances, the non-network provider may not balance bill the insured.

(e) Nothing in this section shall prevent the operation of policy provisions involving deductibles or copayments.

§ 3565 Emergency care

(a) This section applies to every group or blanket policy or contract of health insurance, including each policy or contract issued by a health service corporation, which is delivered or issued for delivery in this State and which designates network physicians or providers or preferred physicians or providers (hereinafter referred to collectively as "network providers"). However, this section applies only to conditions for which coverage is provided by those policies or contracts.

(b) All individual and group health insurance policies shall provide that persons covered under those policies will be insured for emergency care services performed by non-network providers at an agreed-upon or negotiated rate, regardless of whether the physician or provider furnishing the services has a contractual or other arrangement with the insurer to provide items or services to persons covered under the policies. In the event that the provider of emergency services and the insurer cannot agree upon the appropriate rate, the provider shall be entitled to those charges and rates allowed by the Insurance Commissioner or the Commissioner's designee following an arbitration of the dispute. The Insurance Commissioner shall adopt regulations concerning the arbitration of such disputes. In such circumstances, the non-network provider may not balance bill the insured.

(c) Prior to a determination by the Insurance Commissioner's (or the Commissioner's designee) of those charges and rates allowed by the providers of emergency services pursuant to subsection (b) of this section, the insurer will pay directly to the non-network emergency care provider the highest allowable charge for each emergency care service allowed by the insurer for any other network or non-network emergency care provider during the full 12-month period immediately prior to the date of each emergency care service performed by the non-network provider. The Insurance Commissioner is authorized to adopt regulations concerning the provisions of this subsection (c).

(d) Plans described in subsections (a) and (b) of this section shall cover:
 (1) Any medical screening examination or other evaluation medically required to determine whether an emergency medical condition exists;
 (2) Necessary emergency care services, including treatment and stabilization of an emergency medical condition; and
 (3) Services originated in a hospital emergency facility or comparable facility following treatment or stabilization of an emergency medical condition as approved by the insurer with respect to services performed by non-network providers, provided that the insurer is required to approve or disapprove coverage of poststabilization care as requested by a treating physician or provider within the time appropriate to the circumstances relating to the delivery of services and the condition of the patient, but in no case to exceed 1 hour from the time of the request.

(e) Nothing in this section shall prevent the operation of policy provisions involving deductibles or copayments. As used in this section "emergency medical condition" means a medical or behavioral condition the onset of which is sudden, that manifests itself by symptoms of sufficient severity, including, but not limited to, severe pain, that a prudent layperson, possessing an average knowledge of medicine and health, could reasonably expect the absence of immediate medical attention to result in:
 (1) Placing the health of the person afflicted with such condition in serious jeopardy, or in the case of a behavioral condition, placing the health of such person or others in serious jeopardy;
 (2) Serious impairment to such person's bodily functions;
 (3) Serious impairment or dysfunction of any bodily organ or part of such person; or
 (4) Serious disfigurement of such person.

(f) This section shall not apply to services provided by a volunteer fire department recognized as such by the State Fire Prevention Commission.

(g) The Insurance Commissioner shall establish a schedule of fees for arbitration. The nonprevailing party at arbitration shall reimburse the Commissioner for the expenses related to the arbitration process. Funds paid to the Insurance Commissioner under this subsection shall be placed in the arbitration fund and shall be used exclusively for the payment of appointed arbitrators. The Insurance Commissioner may, in the Commissioner's discretion, impose a schedule of maximum fees that can be charged by an arbitrator for a given type of arbitration.

§ 3571S Network disclosure and transparency

(a) This section applies to every policy or contract of health insurance which is delivered or issued for delivery in this State, including each policy or contract issued by a health-service corporation, which provides medical, major medical, or similar comprehensive-type coverage, and which designates network physicians or providers (hereinafter referred to collectively as "network providers"). However, this section applies only to items, services or conditions for which coverage is provided by those policies or contracts (hereinafter referred to as "covered services").

(b) For purposes of this section "facility-based provider" means a provider who provides health-care services to patients who are in an in-patient or ambulatory facility, including services such as pathology, anesthesiology, or radiology.

(c) For purposes of this section "health-care provider" means any provider who provides health-care services to patients who are not in a facility-based setting and includes a provider who provides health-care services to a covered person based upon a referral from another provider without the knowledge of or input from the covered person.

(d) Nonemergency out-of-network services.—

- (1) When a facility-based provider schedules a procedure or seeks prior authorization from a health carrier for the provision of nonemergency covered services to a covered person, the facility shall ensure that the covered person has received a timely written out-of-network disclosure that states the following:
  - a. That discloses whether the facility is a participating or out-of-network facility;
  - b. That certain facility-based providers may be called upon to render care to the covered person during the course of treatment;
  - c. That those facility-based providers may not have a contract with the covered person's health carrier and are therefore considered to be out-of-network;
  - d. That the services therefore will be provided on an out-of-network basis, which may result in additional charges for which the covered person may be responsible, and a statement that these charges are in addition to any coinsurance, deductibles and copayments applicable under the covered person's health insurance policy;
  - e. A listing, including name and contact information, of those facility-based providers who may be called upon to render care to the covered person during the course of treatment, and a statement that the covered person should contact their health insurer to determine the network status of those facility-based providers;
  - f. Notification that an estimate of the range of charges for any out-of-networks services charged by the out-of-network provider for

which the covered person may be responsible may be requested from, and will be timely provided by, the out-of-network provider; and

g. That the covered person may contact the covered person's health insurer for additional assistance or may rely on whatever other rights and remedies may be available under state or federal law.

h. The written out-of-network disclosure required by this paragraph (d)(1) shall include a written consent form which would enable a covered person who wishes to utilize the services of an out-of-network provider to: (i) acknowledge a provider may be a non-network provider; (ii) acknowledge that the services provided by the non-network provider may not be covered by the covered person's policy; (iii) acknowledge receipt of the notification that an estimate of the range of charges for any out-of-network services for which the covered person may be responsible may be obtained from the out-of-network providers; and (iv) affirmatively elect to obtain the services and agree to accept and pay the charges for the out-of-network services.

i. If a covered person requests from an out-of-network provider an estimate of the range of charges for any out-of-network services for which the covered person may be responsible, the out-of-network provider shall provide the estimate in writing to the covered person within 3 business days of the request.

j. If the facility and all facility-based providers participate in the covered person's network, this disclosure shall not be required.

(2) Prior to the delivery of nonemergency covered services to a covered person, an out-of-network health-care provider shall provide the covered person with a timely, written out-of-network disclosure that states the following:

a. That the health-care provider is an out-of-network provider and the services therefore will be provided on an out-of-network basis;

b. That out-of-network services may result in additional charges for which the covered person may be responsible, and a statement that these charges are in addition to any coinsurance, deductibles and copayments applicable under the person's health insurance policy;

c. Identification of the range of charges for any out-of-network services charged by the out-of-network provider for which the covered person may be responsible; and

d. That the covered person may contact the covered person's health insurer for additional assistance or may rely on whatever other rights and remedies may be available under state or federal law.

e. The written out-of-network disclosure required by this paragraph (d)(2) shall contain a written consent form which would enable a covered person who wishes to utilize the services of an out-of-network provider to: (i) acknowledge a provider may be a non-network provider; (ii) acknowledge that the services provided by the non-network provider may not be covered by the insured's policy; (iii) acknowledge receipt of the identification of the range of charges for any out-of-network services for which the covered person may be responsible; and (iv) affirmatively elect to obtain the services and agree to accept and pay the charges for the out-of-network services.

(3) A facility-based provider or a health-care provider may not balance bill a covered person for health-care services not covered by an insured's health insurance contract, if the facility-based provider or health-care provider:

a. Fails to provide the covered person the written out-of-network disclosure required by paragraph (d)(1) or (2) of this section.

b. Fails to obtain from the covered person in a timely manner, before the health-care services are provided, a copy of the consent form required by paragraph (d)(3) of this section that has been signed by the covered person.

(4) Nothing in paragraph (d)(3) of this section shall prevent the operation of policy provisions involving coinsurance, deductibles and copayments payable under the covered person's health insurance policy.

(5) In the event a facility-based provider or a health-care provider fails to comply with the requirements of paragraph (d)(3)a. or (3)b. of this section, and the provider of services and insurer cannot agree on the appropriate rate of reimbursement, the provider shall be entitled to those charges and rates allowed by the Insurance Commissioner or the Commissioner's designee following arbitration of the dispute pursuant to the procedures set forth in § 333 of this title and any regulation promulgated thereunder.

(6) This section shall not apply to those out-of-network services provided pursuant to §§ 3564 and 3565 of this chapter.

(e) Health insurers shall be required to maintain accurate and complete provider directories, to update provider directories frequently, to audit the accuracy and completeness of such directories and make the directories easily accessible to the covered person in a variety of formats.

(f) The Insurance Commissioner shall adopt regulations to implement the requirements of this section, including:

(1) Regulations concerning the form and content of the written out-of-network disclosures and written consent form required by paragraphs (d)(1) and (2) of this section.

(2) Regulations requiring health insurers and out-of-network providers to inform covered persons of their rights with respect to payment of balance bills.

(3) *Regulations concerning the provisions of subsection (e) of this section.*— The regulations adopted and arbitrations authorized pursuant to this section shall reflect the objectives of protecting consumers from surprise bills and not creating incentives for providers to be out-of-network.

TITLE 18 DELAWARE ADMINISTRATIVE CODE § 1316-1.0 TO 1316-6.0

Chapter 1316: Arbitration of health insurance disputes between carriers and non-network providers of emergency care services

Section 1.0 Purpose and statutory authority

The purpose of this Regulation is to implement 18 Del.C. §§ 3349 and 3565, which require the Delaware Insurance Department to establish and administer procedures for arbitration of disputes between health insurance carriers and non-network providers of emergency care services. This Regulation is promulgated pursuant to 18 Del.C. §§ 311, 3349, and 3565; and 29 Del.C. Ch. 101. This Regulation should not be construed to create any cause of action not otherwise existing at law.

Section 2.0 Definitions

The following words and terms, when used in this regulation, have the following meaning:

"Carrier" means any entity that provides health insurance in this State. Carrier includes an insurance company, health service corporation, managed care organization and any other entity providing a plan of health insurance or health benefits subject to state insurance regulation. Carrier also includes any third-party administrator or other entity that adjusts, administers or settles claims in connection with health insurance.

"Covered person" means an individual and/or family who has entered into a contractual arrangement, or on whose behalf a contractual arrangement has been entered into, with a carrier, pursuant to which the carrier provides health insurance for such person or persons.

"Department" means the Delaware Insurance Department.

"Duration of an Emergency Medical Condition" means a period of time that begins with an Emergency Medical Condition and ends when the Emergency Medical Condition is either treated or stabilized as such stabilization is evidenced by post stabilization care, as referenced in 18 Del.C. §§ 3349(d)(3) and 3565(d)(3), in a hospital where such post stabilization care is not within the definition of emergency care services.

"Emergency care provider" means a provider of emergency care services including a provider who also provides health care services that aren't emergency care services.

"Emergency care services" means those services identified in 18 Del.C. §§ 3349(d) and 3565(d) performed at any time during the Duration of an Emergency Medical Condition, including any covered service providing for the transportation of a patient to a hospital emergency facility for an emergency medical condition including air and sea ambulances so long as medical necessity criteria are met.

"Emergency Medical Condition" shall have the meaning assigned to it by 18 Del.C. §§ 3349(e) and 3565(e).

"Health care services" means any services or supplies included in the furnishing to any individual of medical care or hospitalization, or incidental to the furnishing of such care or hospitalization, as well as the furnishing to any individual of any and all other services for the purpose of preventing, alleviating, curing or healing human illness, injury, disability or disease.

"Health insurance" means a plan or policy issued by a carrier for the payment for, provision of, or reimbursement for health care services.

"Network carrier" is a carrier that has a written participation agreement with a provider to pay for emergency care services.

"Network Emergency Care Provider" is a provider who has a written participation agreement with the carrier to provide emergency care services or governing payment of emergency care services.

"Non-Network Emergency Care Provider" is a provider who is not a Network Emergency Care Provider.

"Provider" means an individual or entity, including without limitation, a licensed physician, a licensed nurse, a licensed physician assistant and a licensed nurse practitioner, a licensed diagnostic facility, a licensed clinical facility, and a licensed hospital, who or which provides health care services in this State.

Section 3.0 Provisions applicable to arbitration pursuant to 18 Delaware Code §§ 3349 and 3565

3.1 If a carrier and a non-network emergency care provider cannot agree on payment to the provider for emergency care services, within 30 days after the carrier has received from the provider clean claims, as defined in Section 4.0 of 18 DE Admin. Code 1310, for such services, either the carrier or the non-network emergency care provider (the "Petitioner") may petition for arbitration pursuant to this Section 3.0 and 18 Del.C. §§ 3349 or 3565 and the other party (the "Respondent") shall submit to such arbitration. "Respondent") shall submit to such arbitration.

3.2 Prior to the Arbitration Hearing, the Arbitrator shall at a minimum receive the following written evidence from the parties:

3.2.1 The highest allowable charge for each emergency care service subject to arbitration allowed by the carrier for any other network or non-network emergency care provider during the full twelve month period immediately prior to the date the Petition for Arbitration was filed with the Department;

3.2.2 If subsection 3.4.1 of this regulation applies, the carrier's highest allowable charge for each emergency care service subject to arbitration pursuant to the non-network provider's most recent participation agreement with the carrier;

3.2.3 The highest allowable charge for each emergency care service subject to arbitration received by the non-network emergency care provider from any other carrier during a full twelve month period immediately prior to the date the Petition for Arbitration was filed with the Department; and

3.2.4 The highest allowable charge for each emergency care service subject to arbitration received by the non-network emergency care provider from any network carrier during a full twelve month period immediately prior to the date the Petition for Arbitration was filed with the Department.

3.2.5 Each party shall also submit in writing the allowable charge each party would accept for each emergency care service subject to arbitration and each party's history of the negotiations between the parties relating to each such emergency care service.

3.2.6 Each party shall also submit a written list of all emergency care services subject to arbitration and the date each service was delivered to the patient. The Arbitrator's decision shall apply to each such service from the date of each service and the date of all other emergency care service subject to arbitration through the date provided for in subsection 3.12.2 of this regulation.

3.2.7 A copy of all information submitted to the Arbitrator by a party pursuant to this Section 3.0 will also be given to the other party except for information submitted by the provider pursuant to subsections 3.2.3 and 3.2.4 of this regulation. Subsection 3.2.3 and subsection 3.2.4 information will be redacted by the Arbitrator and given to the carrier to ensure that the carrier cannot determine pricing information relating specifically to other carriers.

3.3 All information specified in subsection 3.2 of this regulation provided to the Arbitrator shall presumptively be considered trade secret or confidential financial information under the Delaware Freedom of Information Act and shall not be disclosed to or available at any time to any person, firm or entity not involved in the arbitration.

3.4 The Arbitrator shall follow the guidelines listed in this subsection 3.4 as a basis for determining the carrier's payment to the non-network emergency care provider for each emergency care service subject to arbitration unless the evidence adduced at arbitration supports a different payment. All payments pursuant to this section are subject to reduction based on the insured's obligation for co-payments or deductibles.

3.4.1 Payments for emergency care services to a non-network emergency care provider who was a network emergency care provider at any time prior to the date the provider delivered the emergency care services which are the subject of the arbitration. The Arbitrator shall direct the carrier to pay the non-network emergency care provider based on an allowable charge for each emergency care service subject to arbitration within the following range:

3.4.1.1 The allowable charges submitted to the Arbitrator pursuant to subsection 3.2.2 of this regulation, subject to COLA adjustments as may be published in bulletins by the Commissioner from time to time; and

3.4.1.2 The allowable charges submitted to the Arbitrator pursuant to subsection 3.2.3 of this regulation.

3.4.2 Payments for emergency care services to a provider who was never a network emergency care provider with the carrier. The Arbitrator shall direct the carrier to pay the non-network emergency care provider who was never a network emergency care provider based on an allowable charge for each emergency care service subject to arbitration within the following range:

3.4.2.1 The allowable charges submitted to the carrier pursuant to subsection 3.2.1 of this regulation; and

3.4.2.2 The allowable charges submitted to the Arbitrator pursuant to subsection 3.2.3 of this regulation.

3.5 Changes in the membership of a provider group will not affect the remaining group member or members insofar as the application of this Section 3.0. In the absence of a contract provision to the contrary, a physician's existing network status and payment rights shall not be transferable to that physician's new group or practice.

3.6 Carrier Payments Prior to Arbitration.

3.6.1 Prior to Arbitrator's decision pursuant to subsection 3.12 of this regulation, the carrier will pay directly to the non-network emergency care provider the highest amount provided for in subsection 3.2.1 of this regulation, for each emergency care service subject to arbitration.

3.6.2 All payments due the non-network provider pursuant to subsection 3.6.1 of this regulation, will be paid within 30 days after the carrier has received from the provider a clean claim, as defined in Section 4.0 of 18 DE Admin. Code 1310, for each emergency care service subject to arbitration.

3.6.3 The Arbitrator will direct the carrier and the provider to pay, in the case of the carrier, or refund in the case of the provider, the difference between payments made pursuant to this subsection 3.6 and the payments determined by the Arbitrator pursuant to subsection 3.4 of this regulation.

3.7 Procedures for Arbitration Pursuant to this Section 3.0.

3.7.1 Either the non-network emergency care provider or his authorized representative or the carrier, after the carrier pays the provider pursuant to subsection 3.6.1 of this regulation, may request arbitration by delivering to the Department an original and one copy of the Petition for Arbitration, (with all applicable information required by subsection 3.2 of this regulation attached) so that the Petition is received by the Department no later than 60 days from the date the carrier was required to pay the provider pursuant to subsection 3.6.1 of this regulation.

3.7.2 At the time of delivering the Petition for Arbitration to the Department. the Petitioner or his authorized representative must also:

3.7.2.1 Send a copy of the Petition and supporting documentation to the Respondent by certified mail, return receipt requested, except as provided by subsection 3.2.7 of this regulation;

3.7.2.2 Deliver to the Department a Proof of Service confirming that a copy of the Petition has been sent to the Respondent by certified mail, return receipt requested; and

3.7.2.3 Deliver to the Department a $75.00 filing fee.

3.7.3 The Department may refuse to accept any Petition that is not timely filed or does not otherwise meet the criteria for arbitration.

3.8 Response to Petition for Arbitration

3.8.1 Within 20 days of receipt of the Petition, the Respondent or the Respondent's authorized representative must deliver to the Department an original and one copy of a Response with all information required by subsection 3.2 of this regulation attached.

3.8.2 At the time of delivering the Response to the Department, the Respondent must also:

3.8.2.1 Send a copy of the Response and supporting documentation to the Petitioner or the Petitioner's authorized representative by certified mail, postage prepaid, except as provided by subsection 3.2.7 of this regulation; and

3.8.2.2 Deliver to the Department a Proof of Service confirming that a copy of the Response was mailed to the Petitioner or the Petitioner's authorized representative.

3.8.3 The Department may return any non-conforming Response to Respondent.

3.8.4 If the Respondent fails to deliver a Response to the Department in a timely fashion, the Department, after verifying proper service, and with written notice to the parties, may assign the matter to the next scheduled Arbitrator for summary disposition.

3.8.4.1 The Arbitrator may determine the matter in the nature of a default judgment after establishing that the Petition is properly supported and was properly served on the Respondent.

3.8.4.2 The Arbitrator may allow the re-opening of the matter to prevent a manifest injustice. A request for re-opening must be made no later than seven days after notice of the default judgment.

3.9 Summary Dismissal of Petition by the Arbitrator

3.9.1 If the Arbitrator determines that the subject of the Petition is not appropriate for arbitration, the Arbitrator may summarily dismiss the Petition and provide notice of such dismissal to the parties.

3.10 Appointment of Arbitrator

3.10.1 Upon receipt of a proper Response, the Department shall assign an Arbitrator who shall schedule the matter for a hearing so that the Arbitrator can render a written decision within 45 days of the delivery to the Department of the Petition for Arbitration.

3.10.2 The Arbitrator shall be of suitable background and experience to decide the matter in dispute and shall not be affiliated with any of the parties.

3.11 Arbitration Hearing

3.11.1 The Arbitrator shall give notice of the arbitration hearing date to the parties at least 10 days prior to the hearing. The parties are not required to appear and may rely on the papers delivered to the Department.

3.11.2 The arbitration hearing is to be limited, to the maximum extent possible, to each party being given the opportunity to explain their view of the previously submitted evidence and to answer questions by the Arbitrator.

3.11.3 If the Arbitrator allows any brief testimony, the Arbitrator shall allow brief cross-examination or other response by the opposing party.

3.11.4 The Delaware Uniform Rules of Evidence will be used for general guidance but will not be strictly applied.

3.11.5 Because the testimony may involve evidence relating to personal health information that is confidential and protected by state or federal laws from public disclosure, the arbitration hearing shall be closed.

3.11.6 The Arbitrator may contact, with the parties' consent, individuals or entities identified in the papers by telephone in or outside of the parties' presence for information to resolve the matter.

3.11.7 The Arbitrator is to consider the matter based on the submissions of the parties and information otherwise obtained by the Arbitrator in accordance with this Section 3.0. The Arbitrator shall not consider any matter not contained in the original or supplemental submissions of the parties that has not been provided to the opposing party with at least five days' notice, except claims of a continuing nature that are set out in the filed papers.

3.12 Arbitrator's Written Decision

3.12.1 The Arbitrator shall render his decision and mail a copy of the decision to the parties within 45 days of the filing of the Petition.

3.12.2 The Arbitrator's decision is binding upon the parties with respect to allowable charges and payments for each emergency care service subject to arbitration for a period that will end on the 360th day after the date of the Arbitrator's decision.

3.13 Arbitration Costs

3.13.1 The non-prevailing party at arbitration shall reimburse the Commissioner for the expenses related to the arbitration process.

3.14 Arbitrations subject to this regulation shall not be subject to the provisions of 18 DE Admin. Code 1313.

3.15 Exemption from Arbitration. 18 Del.C. §§ 3349(b) and 3565(b) shall not apply to health insurance policies exempt from state regulation under federal law or regulation.

3.16 A carrier and a non-network emergency care provider can mutually agree in writing to submit to arbitration pursuant to Section 3.0 payment disputes relating to the delivery of emergency care services to patients covered by a plan otherwise exempt from arbitration, except that such agreement will only apply to the plan and the services stated therein.

3.17 The provisions of this regulation shall not apply to Medicaid or any other health insurance program where the review of coverage determinations is otherwise regulated by the provisions of other state or federal laws or regulations.

Section 4.0 Confidentiality of health information

Nothing in this Regulation shall supersede any federal or state law or regulation governing the privacy of health information.

Section 5.0 Computation of time

In computing any period of time prescribed or allowed by this Regulation, the day of the act or event after which the designated period of time begins to run shall not be included. The last day of the period so computed shall be included, unless it is a Saturday or Sunday, or other legal holiday, or other day on which the Department is closed, in which event the period shall run until the end of the next day on which the Department is open. When the period of time prescribed or allowed is less than 11 days, intermediate Saturdays, Sundays, and other legal holidays shall be excluded in the computation. As used in this section, "legal holidays" shall be those days provided by statute or appointed by the Governor or the Chief Justice of the State of Delaware.

Section 6.0 Effective date

This Regulation became effective on April 11, 2016. The [amendments to] this regulation shall become effective 10 days after being published as a final regulation. 19 DE Reg. 926 (04/01/16); 27 DE Reg. 113 (08/01/23).

1400–1403 Health maintenance organizations

Section 1.0 Purpose and statutory authority

1.1 The purpose of this Regulation is to implement 18 Del.C. Ch. 64, as amended effective July 6, 2006, which transferred regulatory authority over Managed Care Organizations from the Department of Health and Social Services to the Department of Insurance. This Regulation is promulgated pursuant to 18 Del.C. § 6408 and 29 Del.C. Ch. 101.

Section 2.0 Definitions

The following words and terms, when used in this regulation, should have the following meaning unless the context clearly indicates otherwise:

"Adverse determination" means a decision by an MCO to deny (in whole or in part), reduce, limit or terminate benefits under a health care contract.

"Appeal" means a request for external review of an MCO's determination resulting in a denial, termination or other limitations of covered health services based on medical necessity or appropriateness of services

"Appropriateness of services" means an appeal classification for adverse determinations that are made based on identification of treatment as cosmetic, investigational, experimental or not an appropriate or preferred treatment method or setting for the condition for which treatment is sought.

"Balance billing" means a health care provider's demand that a patient pay a greater amount for a given service than the amount the individual's insurer, managed care organization, or health service corporation has paid or will pay for the service.

"Basic Health Services" means a range of health care services, including at least the following:

A. Physician services, including consultant and referral services, by a physician licensed by the State of Delaware;
B. At least 365 days of inpatient hospital services;
C. Medically necessary emergency health services;
D. Diagnostic laboratory services;
E. Diagnostic and therapeutic radiological services;
F. Preventive health services; and
G. Emergency out-of-area and out-of-network coverage.

"Carrier" means any entity that provides health insurance in this State. Carrier includes an insurance company, health service corporation, managed care organization and any other entity providing a plan of health insurance or health benefits subject to state insurance regulation. Carrier also includes any third-party administrator or other entity that adjusts, administers or settles claims in connection with health insurance.

"Certificate of Authority" means the authorization by the Department to operate the MCO. This certificate shall be deemed to be a license to operate such an organization.

"Chief Executive Officer" means the individual employed to manage and direct the activities of the MCO.

"Covered health services" means services that are included in the enrollee's health care contract with the carrier.

"Covered Person": see "Enrollee."

"Department" means the Delaware Department of Insurance.

"Emergency care" means health care items or services furnished or required to evaluate or treat an emergency medical condition.

"Emergency medical condition" means a medical or behavioral condition, the onset of which is sudden, that manifests itself by symptoms of sufficient severity including, but not limited to, severe pain, that a prudent layperson, possessing an average knowledge of health and medicine, could reasonably expect the absence of immediate medical attention to result in:

A. Placing the health of the individual afflicted with such condition (or, with respect to a pregnant woman, the health of the woman or her unborn child) in serious jeopardy, or in the case of a behavioral condition, placing the health of such person or others in serious jeopardy;
B. Serious impairment to bodily functions;

C. Serious impairment or dysfunction of any bodily organ or part; or
D. Serious disfigurement of such person.

"Enrollee" means an individual and/or family who has entered into a contractual arrangement, or on whose behalf a contractual arrangement has been entered into with the MCO, under which the MCO assumes the responsibility to provide to such person(s) coverage for basic health services and such supplemental health services as are enumerated in the health care contract.

"Geographically accessible" means a location no greater than 30 miles or 40 minutes driving time from 90% of enrollees within MCO's geographic service area.

"Geographic service area" means the stated primary geographical area served by an MCO. The primary area served shall be a radius of not more than 20 miles or more than 30 minutes driving time from a primary care office operated or contracted by the MCO.

"Grievance" means a request by an enrollee that an MCO review an adverse determination by means of the MCO's internal review process.

"Health care contract" means any agreement between an MCO and an enrollee or group plan which sets forth the services to be supplied to the enrollee in exchange for payments made by the enrollee or group plan.

"Health care professional" means an individual engaged in the delivery of health care services as licensed or certified by the State of Delaware.

"Health care services" means any services included in the furnishing to any individual of medical or dental care, or hospitalization or incidental to the furnishing of such care or hospitalization, as well as the furnishing to any person of any and all other services for the purpose of preventing, alleviating, curing or healing human illness, injury or physical disability.

"Independent Health Care Appeals Program" means a program administered by the Department which provides for a review by an Independent Utilization Review Organization.

"Independent Utilization Review Organization (IURO)" means an entity that conducts independent external reviews of a carrier's determinations resulting in a denial, termination, or other limitation of covered health care services based on medical necessity or appropriateness of services.

"Intermediary" means a person authorized to negotiate and execute provider contracts with MCOs on behalf of health care providers or on behalf of a network.

"Internal review process" means a procedure established by an MCO for internal review of an adverse determination.

"Level 1 trauma center" means a regional resource trauma center that has the capability of providing leadership and comprehensive, definitive care for every aspect of injury from prevention through rehabilitation.

"Level 2 trauma center" means a regional trauma center with the capability to provide initial care for all trauma patients. Most patients would continue to be cared for in this center; there may be some complex cases which would require transfer for the depth of services of a regional Level 1 or specialty center.

"Managed Care Organization (MCO)" means a public or private organization, organized under the laws of any state, which:

A. Provides or otherwise makes available to enrollees health care services, including at least the basic health services defined in this section;
B. Is primarily compensated (except for co-payment) for the provision of basic health services to enrollee on a predetermined periodic rate basis; and
C. Provides physician services.

An MCO may also arrange for health care services on a prepayment or other financial basis.

"Medical necessity" means providing of covered health services or products that a prudent physician would provide to a patient for the purpose of diagnosing, or treating an illness, injury, disease or its symptoms in a manner that is:

A. In accordance with generally accepted standards of medical practice;
B. Consistent with the symptoms or treatment of the condition; and
C. Not solely for anyone's convenience.

"Network" means the participating providers delivering services to enrollees.

"Office" means any facility where enrollees receive primary care or other health care services.

"Out of area coverage" means health care services provided outside the MCO's geographic service areas with appropriate limitations and guidelines acceptable to the Department. At a minimum, such coverage must include emergency care.

"Participating provider" means a provider who, under a contract with the MCO or with its contractor or sub contractor, has agreed to provide health care services to enrollees with an expectation of receiving payment, other than coinsurance, co-payments or deductibles, directly or indirectly from the MCO.

"Premium" means payment(s) called for in the health care contract which must be:

A. Paid or arranged for by, or on behalf of, the enrollee before health care services are rendered by the MCO;
B. Paid on a periodic basis without regard to the date on which health care services are rendered; and

C. With respect to an individual enrollee, are fixed without regard to frequency, extent or cost of health services actually furnished.

"Primary care physician (PCP)" means a participating physician chosen by the enrollee and designated by the MCO to supervise, coordinate, or provide initial care or continuing care to an enrollee, and who may be required by the MCO to initiate a referral for specialty care and maintain supervision of health care services rendered to the enrollee.

"Provider" means a health care professional or facility.

"Staff Model MCO" means an MCO in which physicians are employed directly by the MCO or in which the MCO directly operates facilities which provide health care services to enrollees.

"Tertiary services" means health care services provided for the intensive treatment of critically ill patients who require extraordinary care on a concentrated basis in special diagnostic categories (e.g., burns, cardiovascular, neonatal, pediatric, oncology, transplants, etc.).

"Utilization review" means a set of formal techniques designed to monitor the use of, or evaluate the clinical necessity, efficacy, and/or efficiency of, health care services, procedures or settings. Techniques may include ambulatory review, prospective review, second opinion, certification, concurrent review, case management, discharge planning, or retrospective review.

Section 3.0 Certificate of authority

3.1 Each application for a Certificate of Authority as a Managed Care Organization shall be made on Form No. H-1 entitled "Application for Certificate of Authority as a Managed Care Organization" (Exhibit A to this regulation). The application shall be accompanied by the following:

3.1.1 The information specified in 18 Del.C. § 6404(a);

3.1.2 Evidence of accreditation by a nationally-recognized managed care accrediting organization such as the National Committee for Quality Assurance (NCQA), the Joint Commission on Accreditation of Healthcare Organizations (JCAHO), or similar organization;

3.1.3 For Staff Model MCOs, evidence that the MCO satisfies the physical plant requirements of a hospital as specified by the Delaware Department of Health and Social Services;

3.1.4 Copies of management, agency or administrative contracts;

3.1.5 Equifax Reports on Officers/Directors; and/or NAIC biographical or other similar biographical forms, as directed by the Department;

3.1.6 Proof of $ 50,000 bond for each officer, director, partner, or other individual who receives, collects or invests money;

3.1.7 "Admittance Questionnaire for Certificate of Authority for Managed Care Organization," Form No. H-2 (Exhibit B to this regulation);

3.1.8 "Designation of official authorized to appoint and remove agents," Form No. H-3 (Exhibit C to this regulation);

3.1.9 "Designation of person to receive bulletins, regulations, etc.," Form No. H-4 (Exhibit D to this regulation);

3.1.10 "Designation of person to receive service of process," Form No. H-5 (Exhibit E to this regulation);

3.1.11 "Biographical Affidavit of Officers and Directors" (Exhibit F to this regulation); and

3.1.12 "Power of Attorney Form" (Exhibit G to this regulation).

3.2 Each application for a Certificate of Authority as a Managed Care Organization shall be accompanied by a $ 750 filing fee in accordance with 18 Del.C. § 6409.

3.3 Each application for a Certificate of Authority as a Managed Care Organization shall be accompanied by a deposit of $ 100,000 in accordance with 18 Del.C. § 513(f).

3.4 All of the items and information specified in the foregoing sections 3.1 through 3.3 must be submitted in order for the Department to review an application for a Certificate of Authority.

3.5 Denial of Application for Certificate of Authority

3.5.1 If, within 60 days after a complete application for a Certificate of Authority has been filed, the Department has not issued such certificate, the Department shall immediately notify the applicant, in writing, of the reasons why such certificate has not been issued, and the applicant shall be entitled to request a hearing on the application.

3.5.2 The hearing shall be held within 60 days of the Department's receipt of the applicant's written request therefor. Proceedings in regard to such hearing shall be conducted in accordance with provisions for case decisions as set forth in the Administrative Procedures Act, Chapter 101 of Title 29, and in accordance with applicable rules and regulations of the Department.

Section 4.0 Capital funds required

4.1 Each MCO that obtains a Certificate of Authority shall have and maintain unimpaired capital stock or unimpaired basic surplus of at least $ 300,000 and free surplus of at least $ 150,000 or the minimum capital and free surplus as may be required by legislative changes adopted by the General Assembly from time to time.

These capital and surplus requirements are in addition to the deposit requirements of 18 Del.C. § 513(f).

4.2 Each MCO that obtains a Certificate of Authority shall demonstrate that it has provider contracts which require that the provider agrees in the event of non-payment by the MCO that the provider will not seek compensation or have any recourse against an enrollee, as described in section 7.0 of this regulation. In the event that the MCO has not entered into such agreements with all providers, the MCO must demonstrate to the Department's satisfaction that it has made a good faith effort to enter into these agreements. In lieu of these executed provider agreements, the Department, at its discretion, may allow the MCO to engage in the business of a managed care organization if the MCO establishes reserves equal to 25% of the total projected annual incurred claims or benefits payments attributable to the provider which or who has not agreed to enter into a provider agreement.

4.3 Annually, at the time of filing the annual report on June 1, each MCO which has a current Certificate of Authority shall demonstrate that it is in compliance with the requirements of Sections 4.1 and 4.2 of this regulation.

Section 5.0 Reinsurance requirement

5.1 Each MCO shall secure insurance reinsurance protection to provide to the MCO in the event of catastrophic or unusual losses which would be in excess of the levels of loss which the MCO assumes in the basis of its calculation of premium charges.

Section 6.0 Special requirement in the event of financial impairment/insolvency

6.1 In the event of the financial impairment or insolvency of an MCO doing business in this State, each MCO doing business in this State shall permit a 60-day "open enrollment" period for existing enrollees of the impaired/insolvent MCO to enroll in a solvent MCO.

6.2 Each such solvent licensed MCO shall be required to accept within the "open enrollment" period any enrollee who wishes to enroll at the rates or costs and benefits which are then in effect at the chosen MCO for the class or grouping represented by the enrollee.

6.3 Each such solvent licensed MCO shall accept such enrollee without any waiting periods or pre-existing conditions exclusions and such acceptance both as to premium as well as delivery of service shall be retroactive to the date on which a court of competent jurisdiction has declared the predecessor MCO financially impaired.

Section 7.0 Required contractual provisions

7.1 Every contract between an MCO and a participating provider shall contain the following language:

7.1.1 "Provider agrees that in no event, including but not limited to nonpayment by the MCO or intermediary, insolvency of the MCO or intermediary, or breach of this agreement, shall the provider bill, charge, collect a deposit from, seek compensation, remuneration or reimbursement from, or have any recourse against an enrollee or a person (other than the MCO or intermediary) acting on behalf of the enrollee for services provided pursuant to this agreement. This agreement does not prohibit the provider from collecting coinsurance, deductibles or co-payments, as specifically provided in the evidence of coverage, or fees for uncovered services delivered on a fee-for-service basis to enrollees."

7.1.2 "In the event of an MCO or intermediary insolvency or other cessation of operations, covered services to enrollees will continue through the period for which a premium has been paid to the MCO on behalf of the enrollee or until the enrollee's discharge from an inpatient facility, whichever time is greater. Covered benefits to enrollees confined in an inpatient facility on the date of insolvency or other cessation of operations will continue until their continued confinement in an inpatient facility is no longer medically necessary."

7.2 The contract provisions that satisfy the requirements of Section 7.1 above shall be construed in favor of the enrollee, shall survive the termination of the contract regardless of the reason for termination, including the insolvency of the MCO, and shall supersede any oral or written contrary agreement between a participating provider and an enrollee or the representative of an enrollee if the contrary agreement is inconsistent with the hold harmless and continuation of covered services provisions required by Section 7.1 above.

7.3 A contract between an MCO and a participating provider shall not contain definitions or other provisions that conflict with the definitions or provisions contained in this regulation.

Section 8.0 Enrollee rights and responsibilities

8.1 The MCO shall establish and implement written policies and procedures regarding the rights of enrollees and the implementation of these rights.

8.2 The MCO shall disclose to each new enrollee, and any enrollee upon request, in a format and language understandable to a layperson, the following minimum information:

8.2.1 Benefits covered and exclusions or limitations, including restrictions related to preexisting conditions;

8.2.2 Out-of-pocket costs to the enrollee;

8.2.3 Lists of participating providers;

8.2.4 Policies on the use of primary care physicians, referrals, use of out of network providers, and out of area services;

8.2.5 Policies governing the provision of emergency and urgent care;

8.2.6 Written explanation of the internal and external review processes;

8.2.7 For staff model MCOs, the location and hours of its inpatient and outpatient health services;

8.2.8 A statement of enrollee's rights that includes at least the right:

8.2.8.1 To available and accessible services when medically necessary, including availability of care 24 hours a day, seven days a week for urgent or emergency conditions;

8.2.8.2 To be treated with courtesy and consideration, and with respect for the enrollee's dignity and need for privacy;

8.2.8.3 To be provided with information concerning the MCO's policies and procedures regarding products, services, providers, grievance procedures and other information about the organization and the care provided;

8.2.8.4 To choose a primary care provider within the limits of the covered benefits and plan network, including the right to refuse care of specific practitioners;

8.2.8.5 To receive from the enrollee's physician(s) or provider, in terms that the enrollee understands, an explanation of his complete medical condition, recommended treatment, risk(s) of the treatment, expected results and reasonable medical alternatives. If the enrollee is not capable of understanding the information, the explanation shall be provided to his next of kin or guardian and documented in the enrollee's medical record;

8.2.8.6 To formulate advance directives;

8.2.8.7 To all the rights afforded by law or regulation as a patient in a licensed health care facility, including the right to refuse medication and treatment after possible consequences of this decision have been explained in language the enrollee understands;

8.2.8.8 To prompt notification of termination or changes in benefits, services or provider network;

8.2.8.9 To file a grievance with the MCO and to receive a response to the grievance within a reasonable period of time; and

8.2.8.10 To file a petition for arbitration or appeal for review by an Independent Utilization Review Organization, as appropriate.

8.2.9 A complete statement of responsibilities of enrollees.

8.3 In the case of nonpayment by the MCO to a participating provider for a covered service in accordance with the enrollee's health care contract, the provider may not bill the enrollee. This does not prohibit the provider from collecting coinsurance, deductibles or co-payments as determined by the MCO. This does not prohibit the provider and enrollee from agreeing to continue services solely at the expense of the enrollee, as long as the provider clearly informs the enrollee that the MCO will not cover these services.

Section 9.0 Provider relations

9.1 An MCO shall establish a mechanism by which participating providers will be notified on an ongoing basis of the specific covered health services for which the provider will be responsible, including any limitations or conditions on services.

9.2 An MCO shall establish procedures for resolution of administrative, payment or other disputes between providers and the MCO.

9.3 The MCO shall establish a policy governing termination of providers. The policy shall include at least:

> **9.3.1** Written notification to each enrollee six weeks prior to the termination or withdrawal from the MCO's provider network of an enrollee's primary care physician except in cases where termination was due to unsafe health care practices; and
>
> **9.3.2** Except in cases where termination was due to unsafe health care practices that compromise the health or safety of enrollees, assurance of continued coverage of services at the contract price by a terminated provider for up to 120 calendar days after notification of termination in cases where it is medically necessary for the enrollee to continue treatment with the terminated provider. In cases of the pregnancy of an enrollee, medical necessity shall be deemed to have been demonstrated and coverage shall continue to completion of postpartum care.

Section 10.0 Prohibited practices

10.1 An MCO shall not offer incentives to a participating provider to provide less than medically necessary services to an enrollee.

10.2 An MCO shall not penalize a participating provider because the provider, in good faith, reports to State authorities any act or practice by the MCO that jeopardizes patient health or welfare.

10.3 An MCO shall not engage in any other practices prohibited by applicable provisions of Title 18 of the Delaware Code and regulations promulgated thereunder.

Section 11.0 Quality assurance and operations

11.1 Medical Director's Duties. The medical director shall be responsible for the direction, provision and quality of health care services provided to enrollees, including but not limited to the following:

11.1.1 Establishing policies and procedures covering all health care services provided to enrollees;

11.1.2 Coordinating, supervising and overseeing the functioning of professional services;

11.1.3 Providing clinical direction and leadership to the continuous quality improvement and utilization management programs;

11.1.4 Providing clinical direction to physicians responsible for utilization management determinations;

11.1.5 Establishing a committee responsible for delineating qualifications of participating providers and reviewing and verifying credentials of participating providers;

11.1.6 Evaluating the medical aspects of provider contracts; and

11.1.7 Overseeing the continuing in-service education of professional staff.

11.2 Health Care Professional Credentialing

11.2.1 General Responsibilities. An MCO shall:

11.2.1.1 Establish written policies and procedures for credentialing verification of all health care professionals with whom the MCO contracts and apply these standards consistently;

11.2.1.2 Verify the credentials of a health care professional before entering into a contract with that health care professional;

11.2.1.3 Make available for review by the applying health care professional upon written request all application and credentialing verification policies and procedures;

11.2.1.4 Retain all records and documents relating to a health care professional's credentialing verification process for not less than four years; and

11.2.1.5 Keep confidential all information obtained in the credentialing verification process, except as otherwise provided by law.

11.2.2 Selection standards for participating providers shall be developed for primary care professionals and each health care professional discipline. The standards shall be used in determining the selection of health care professionals by the MCO, its intermediaries and any provider networks with which it contracts. Selection criteria shall not be established in a manner:

11.2.2.1 That would allow an MCO to avoid high-risk populations by excluding providers because they are located in geographic areas that contain populations or providers presenting a risk of higher than average claims, losses or health services utilization; or

11.2.2.2 That would exclude providers because they treat or specialize in treating populations presenting a risk of higher than average claims, losses or health services utilization.

11.2.3 Nothing in these regulations shall be construed to require an MCO to select a provider as a participating provider solely because the provider meets the MCO's credentialing verification standards, or to prevent the MCO from utilizing separate or additional criteria in selecting the health care professionals with whom it contracts.

11.2.4 Verification Responsibilities. An MCO shall:

11.2.4.1 Obtain primary verification of at least the following information about the applicant:

11.2.4.1.1 current license, certification, or registration to render health care in Delaware and history of same;

11.2.4.1.2 current level of professional liability coverage, if applicable;

11.2.4.1.3 status of hospital privileges, if applicable;

11.2.4.1.4 specialty board certification status, if applicable; and

11.2.4.1.5 current Drug Enforcement Agency (DEA) registration certificate, if applicable.

11.2.4.2 Obtain, subject to either primary or secondary verification:

11.2.4.2.1 the health care professional's record from the National Practitioner Data Bank; and

11.2.4.2.2 the health care professional's malpractice history.

11.2.4.3 Not less than every three years obtain primary verification of a participating health care professional's:

11.2.4.3.1 current license or certification to render health care in Delaware;

11.2.4.3.2 current level of professional liability coverage, if applicable;

11.2.4.3.3 status of hospital privileges, if applicable;

11.2.4.3.4 current DEA registration certificate, if applicable; and

11.2.4.3.5 specialty board certification status, if applicable.

11.2.4.4 Require all participating providers to notify the MCO of changes in the status of any of the items listed in this section 11.2.4 at any time and identify for participating providers the individual to whom they should report changes in the status of an item listed in this section 11.2.4.

11.2.5 Health Care Professional's Right to Review Credentialing Verification Information. An MCO shall provide a health care professional the opportunity to review and correct information submitted in support of that health care professional's credentialing verification application.

11.3 Provider Network Adequacy

11.3.1 Primary, Specialty and Ancillary Providers

11.3.1.1 The MCO shall maintain an adequate network of primary care providers, specialists, and other ancillary health care resources to serve enrollees at all times.

11.3.1.2 If a plan has an insufficient number of providers that are geographically accessible and available within a reasonable period of time to provide covered health services to enrollees, the MCO shall cover non-network providers, and shall prohibit balance billing.

11.3.1.3 The MCO shall allow referral to a non-network provider, upon the request of a network provider, when medically necessary covered health services are not available through network providers, or the network providers are not available within a reasonable period of time. The MCO shall make acceptable service arrangements with the provider and enrollee, and shall prohibit balance billing.

11.3.2 Facility and Ancillary Health Care Services

11.3.2.1 The MCO shall maintain contracts or other arrangements acceptable to the Department with institutional providers which have the capability to provide covered health services to enrollees and are geographically accessible.

11.3.2.2 The MCO shall make acceptable service arrangements with the provider and enrollee, and shall prohibit balance billing, if the appropriate level of service is not geographically accessible. These services will not be limited to the State of Delaware. These services could include but are not limited to tertiary services, burn units and transplant services.

11.3.3 Emergency and Urgent Care Services

11.3.3.1 The MCO shall establish written policies and procedures governing the provision of emergency and urgent care which shall be distributed to each enrollee at the time of initial enrollment and after any revisions are made. These policies shall be easily understood by a layperson.

11.3.3.2 When emergency care services are performed by non-network providers, the MCO shall make acceptable service arrangements with the provider and enrollee, and shall prohibit balance billing. In those cases where the MCO and the provider cannot agree upon the appropriate charge, the provider may petition the Department for arbitration.

11.3.3.3 Enrollees shall have access to emergency care 24 hours per day, seven days per week. The MCO shall cover emergency care necessary to screen and stabilize an enrollee and shall not require prior authorization of such services if a prudent lay person acting reasonably would have believed that an emergency medical condition existed.

11.3.3.4 Emergency and urgent care services shall include but are not limited to:

11.3.3.4.1 medical and psychiatric care, which shall be available 24 hours a day, seven days a week;

11.3.3.4.2 trauma services at any designated Level I or II trauma center as medically necessary. Such coverage shall continue at least until the enrollee is medically stable, no longer requires critical care, and can be safely transferred to another facility, in the judgment of the treating physician. If the MCO requests transfer to a hospital participating in the MCO network, the patient must be stabilized and the transfer effected in accordance with federal regulations at 42 CFR 489.20 and 42 CFR 489.24;

11.3.3.4.3 out of area health care for urgent or emergency conditions where the enrollee cannot reasonably access in-network services;

11.3.3.4.4 hospital services for emergency care; and

11.3.3.4.5 upon arrival in a hospital, a medical screening examination, as required under federal law, as necessary to determine whether an emergency medical condition exists.

11.3.3.5 When an enrollee has received emergency care from a non-network provider and is stabilized, the enrollee or the provider must request approval from the MCO for continued post-stabilization care by a non-network provider. The MCO is required to approve or disapprove coverage of post-stabilization care as requested by a treating physician or provider within the time appropriate to the circumstances relating to the delivery of services and the condition of the enrollee, but in no case to exceed one hour from the time of the request.

11.3.4 The MCO shall submit evidence of network adequacy to the Department upon request. If the Department receives a complaint regarding an MCO's network adequacy, the burden shall be on the MCO to prove network adequacy to the satisfaction of the Department.

11.4 Utilization Management

11.4.1 The MCO shall establish and implement a comprehensive utilization management program to monitor access to and appropriate utilization of health care and services. The program shall be under the direction of a designated physician and shall be based on a written plan that is reviewed at least annually.

11.4.2 Utilization management determinations shall be based on written clinical criteria and protocols reviewed and approved by practicing physicians and other licensed health care providers within the network. These criteria and protocols shall be periodically reviewed and updated, and shall, with the exception of internal or proprietary quantitative thresholds for utilization management, be readily available, upon request, to affected providers and enrollees.

11.4.3 All materials including internal or proprietary materials for utilization management shall be available to the Department upon request.

11.4.4 Compensation to persons providing utilization review services for an MCO shall not contain incentives, direct or indirect, for these persons to make inappropriate review decisions. Compensation to any such persons may not be based, directly or indirectly, on the quantity or type of adverse determinations rendered.

11.4.5 Utilization Management Staff Availability

11.4.5.1 At a minimum, appropriately qualified staff shall be immediately available by telephone, during routine provider work hours, to render utilization management determinations for providers.

11.4.5.2 The MCO shall provide enrollees with a toll free telephone number by which to contact customer service staff on at least a five day, 40 hours a week basis.

11.4.5.3 The MCO shall supply providers with a toll free telephone number by which to contact utilization management staff on at least a five day, 40 hours a week basis.

11.4.5.4 The MCO must have policies and procedures addressing response to inquiries concerning emergency or urgent care when a PCP or his authorized on call back up provider is unavailable.

11.4.6 Utilization Management Determinations

11.4.6.1 All determinations to authorize services shall be rendered by appropriately qualified staff.

11.4.6.2 All determinations to deny or limit an admission, service, procedure or extension of stay shall be rendered by a physician. The physician shall be under the clinical direction of the medical director responsible for medical services provided to the MCO's Delaware enrollees. Such determinations shall be made in accordance with clinical and medical criteria and standards and shall take into account the individualized needs of the enrollee for whom the service, admission, procedure or extension is requested.

11.4.6.3 All determinations shall be made on a timely basis as required by the exigencies of the situation.

11.4.6.4 An MCO may not retroactively deny reimbursement for a covered health service provided to an enrollee by a provider who relied upon the written or verbal authorization of the MCO or its agents prior to providing the service to the enrollee, except in cases where the MCO can show that there was material misrepresentation, fraud or the patient was found not to have coverage.

11.4.6.5 An enrollee must receive written notice of all determinations to deny coverage or authorization for services required and the basis for the denial.

11.5 Quality Assessment and Improvement

11.5.1 Continuous Quality Improvement

11.5.1.1 Under the direction of the Medical Director or his designated physician, the MCO shall have a system-wide continuous quality improvement program to monitor the quality and appropriateness of care and services provided to enrollees. This program shall be based on a written plan which is reviewed at least semi-annually and revised as necessary.

11.5.1.2 The MCO shall assure that participating providers have the opportunity to participate in developing, implementing and evaluating the quality improvement system.

11.5.1.3 The MCO shall provide enrollees the opportunity to comment on the quality improvement process.

11.5.1.4 The MCO shall follow up on findings from the program to assure that effective corrective actions have been taken, including at least policy revisions, procedural changes and implementation of educational activities for enrollees and providers.

11.5.1.5 The MCO shall make documentation regarding the quality improvement program available to the Department upon request.

11.5.2 External Quality Audit

11.5.2.1 Each MCO shall submit, as a part of its annual report due June 1, evidence of its most recent external quality audit that has been conducted or of acceptable accreditation status.

11.5.2.2 The report of the external quality audit must describe in detail the MCO's conformance to performance standards and the rules within this regulation. The report shall also describe in detail any corrective actions proposed and/or undertaken by the MCO.

11.5.2.3 External quality audits must be completed no less frequently than once every three years. Such audit shall be performed by a nationally known accreditation organization or an independent quality review organization acceptable to the Department.

11.5.2.4 In lieu of the external quality audit, the Department may accept evidence that an MCO has received and has maintained the appropriate accreditation from a nationally known accreditation organization or independent quality review organization.

11.5.3 Reporting and Disclosure Requirements

11.5.3.1 An MCO shall document and communicate information about its quality assessment program and its quality improvement program, and shall:

11.5.3.1.1 include a summary of its quality assessment and quality improvement programs in marketing materials;

11.5.3.1.2 include a description of its quality assessment and quality improvement programs and a statement of enrollee rights and responsibilities with respect to those programs in the materials or handbook provided to enrollees; and

11.5.3.1.3 make available annually to participating providers and enrollees findings from its quality assessment and quality improvement programs and information about its progress in meeting internal goals and external standards, where available. The reports shall include a description of the methods used to assess each specific area and an explanation of how any assumptions affect the findings.

11.5.3.2 An MCO shall submit to the Department such performance and outcome data as the Department may request.

Section 12.0 Recordkeeping and reporting requirements

12.1 Medical Records Retention

12.1.1 The MCO must maintain or provide for the maintenance of a medical records system which meets the accepted standards of the health care industry and State and federal regulations.

12.1.1.1 The MCO shall provide sufficient space and equipment for the processing and the safe storage of records.

12.1.1.2 Medical records shall be protected from loss, damage and unauthorized use.

12.1.2 Retention and Destruction

12.1.2.1 With the exception of medical records of minors (individuals under the age of 18 years), medical records shall be preserved as original records, on microfilm or electronically stored for no less than five years after the most recent patient care usage, after which time records may be destroyed at the discretion of the MCO.

12.1.2.2 Medical records of minors shall be preserved for the period of minority plus five years (i.e., 23 years) or as otherwise required by State law.

12.1.2.3 An MCO shall establish procedures for notification to patients whose records are to be destroyed prior to the destruction of such records.

12.1.3 The Department shall have access to medical records for purposes of monitoring and review of MCO practices.

12.2 Reporting Requirements and Statistics

12.2.1 Annual reports. In addition to the information required to be included in an MCO's annual report as specified in 18 Del.C. § 6406 or elsewhere in this regulation, an MCO shall submit the following information to the Department on an annual basis:

12.2.1.1 A statistical summary evaluating the network adequacy and accessibility to the enrolled population;

12.2.1.2 Annual appeal report of all grievances, petitions for arbitration and appeals under the Independent Health Care Appeals Program as required under Department Regulation 1301.

12.2.1.3 Evidence of compliance with the capital funds requirements of section 4.0 of this regulation.

12.2.2 An MCO shall submit the following information to the Department whenever there is a change:

12.2.2.1 Substantial changes in organization, bylaws, or governing board

12.2.2.2 Full name of the Chief Executive Officer

12.2.2.3 Full name of the Medical Director

12.2.2.4 Substantial changes in marketing materials, grievance procedures or the utilization management program

12.2.2.5 Any significant amendment to or revision relating to the text or subtext of an approved provider contract shall be submitted to and approved by the Department prior to the execution of an amended or revised contract with the providers of an MCO.

Section 13.0 Compliance with regulation

13.1 The MCO is responsible for meeting each requirement of this regulation. If the MCO chooses to utilize contract support or to contract functions under this regulation, the MCO retains responsibility for ensuring that the requirements of this regulation are met.

13.2 The Department may require a corrective action plan from an MCO when the Department determines that the MCO is not in compliance with applicable provisions of Title 18 of the Delaware Code or regulations promulgated thereunder.

Section 14.0 Separability provisions

14.1 If any provision of this regulation shall be held invalid, the remainder of the regulation shall not be affected thereby.

11 DE Reg. 73 (07/01/07)

FLORIDA ADMINISTRATIVE CODE

Rule 59A-12.030 Statewide provider and health plan claim dispute resolution program

(1) Definitions.
- (a) "Contracted provider" means a provider who is under a contractual agreement with a health plan.
- (b) "Disputed Claim" means a claim that has been submitted by a provider to the health plan or by a health plan to a provider for payment and has been denied in full or in part, or is presumed to have been underpaid or overpaid.
- (c) "Disputed Claim Amount" means the difference between the expected reimbursement amount and the reimbursement received.
- (d) "Health Plan" as defined in Section 408.7057(1)(b), F.S., or a managed care or long term care plan procured pursuant to Section 409.966, F.S.
- (e) "Non-contracted provider" means a provider that does not have a contractual agreement with a health plan.
- (f) "Provider" as defined in Section 641.19(15), F.S., means any physician, hospital, institution, organization, or person that furnishes health care services and is licensed or otherwise authorized to practice in the state. Includes both contracted and non-contracted providers.
- (g) "Professional services" means occupations that require special training or holding a professional license not classified as hospital inpatient or outpatient services.
- (h) "Resolution organization" means a qualified independent third-party claim-dispute resolution entity selected by and contracted with the Agency for Health Care Administration.

(2) Purpose.
- (a) To establish a program to provide assistance to providers and health plans for resolution of claim disputes that are not resolved by the provider and the health plans.
- (b) The following claim disputes can be submitted by providers or health plans:
  1. Claims disputed for services rendered after October 1, 2000.
  2. Claims disputes related to payment amounts only, provider disputes payment amount received, or health plan disputes regarding payback amount.
  3. Providers are required to aggregate claims by type of service to meet certain minimum thresholds in accordance with paragraph 59A-12.030(5)(c), F.A.C.
- (c) The resolution organization shall provide assistance to providers and health plans for resolution of claim disputes within the parameters of Section 408.7057, F.S.

(d) The resolution organization shall hear submitted claims disputes in accordance with the provisions of Section 408.7057, F.S., and this rule.

(3) Resolution Organization.

(a) The resolution organization shall determine, based on a desk review, whether the claim disputes submitted by the health plans or providers meet the statutory requirements of Section 408.7057(2), F.S.

(b) The resolution organization shall inform the Agency on the status of all claim disputes.

(4) Claim Dispute Review.

(a) The entity that does not prevail in the agency's final order must pay the review costs.

(b) In the event that both parties prevail in part, the review fee shall be apportioned in proportion to the final judgement. The apportionment shall be based on the disputed claim amount.

(c) If the non-prevailing party or parties fail to pay the ordered review costs within 35 days after the agency's final order, the non-paying party or parties are subject to a penalty of $500 per day.

(5) Jurisdictional Amounts and Methods of Aggregation for Claim Disputes.

(a) Claims submitted for dispute resolution shall be submitted separately by the following claim categories:

1. Hospital inpatient services claims.
2. Hospital outpatient services claims.
3. Professional services claims.

(b) Either the provider or the health plan may make an offer to settle the claim dispute.

(c) Entities filing a request for dispute resolution shall be permitted to aggregate claims. The minimum disputed claim amounts for claims submitted to the resolution organization shall be as follows:

1. Hospital inpatient services. Disputed individual claim amounts must be aggregated to a total amount of $25,000 for health plan contracted hospitals and $10,000 for non-contracted hospitals.
2. Hospital outpatient services. Disputed individual claim amounts must be aggregated to a total amount of $10,000 for health plan contracted hospitals, and $3,000 for non-contracted hospitals.
3. Professional services. Disputed individual claim amounts shall be aggregated to a minimum amount of $500.

(d) Rural hospitals as defined in Section 395.602(2)(e), F.S., filing requests for claim dispute resolution, are exempt from the minimum disputed claim amounts specified in subparagraphs (5)(c)1. and 2., of this rule.

(e) The offer to settle the claim dispute must state the total amount and the party to whom it is directed has 15 days to accept the offer once it is received.

(f) If the party receiving the offer does not accept the offer and the final order amount is more than 90 percent or less than 110 percent of the offer amount, the party receiving the offer must pay the final order amount to the offering party and is deemed a non-prevailing party for purposes of this section.

(g) The amount of an offer made by a provider to settle an alleged underpayment by the health plan must be greater than 110 percent of the reimbursement amount the provider received.

(h) The amount of an offer made by a health plan to settle an alleged overpayment to the provider must be less than 90 percent of the alleged overpayment amount by the health plan.

(i) Both parties may agree to settle the disputed claim at any time, for any amount, regardless of whether an offer to settle was made or rejected.

(6) Application Process.

(a) The resolution organization shall review claim disputes filed by either the providers or health plans. A request for dispute resolution and supporting documentation must be submitted in hard copy or electronically to the resolution organization in a format prescribed by the resolution organization.

(b) A complete copy of the request, including all supporting documentation, must be submitted to the adverse party at the same time.

(c) The resolution organization must review all requests for claim dispute resolution within 10 days after receipt to determine whether the request meets the statutory and rule criteria for submission to the resolution organization as specified in Sections 408.7057(2)(b)1.-7. and (d), F.S.

(d) If the resolution organization determines that the dispute resolution request does not meet the statutory and rule criteria, the request shall be returned to the entity filing the request.

(7) Hearing Process.

(a) Either party may request that the resolution organization conduct an evidentiary hearing in which both sides can present evidence and examine witnesses, and for which the cost of hearing is equally shared by the parties.

(b) In the event witnesses are called to testify, it is the responsibility of both parties to pay for its own witnesses.

(8) Resolution Organization Review and Decision Process.

(a) The resolution organization must review and consider all documentation submitted by both the health plan and the provider. The resolution organization must notify the entity requesting the dispute resolution and the adverse party electronically or by mail that the request for dispute resolution has been accepted for review.

(b) If the resolution organization determines that the documentation provided with the initial application is not sufficient, it may request additional documents from the entity filing the request for dispute resolution. The resolution organization shall require the health plan or provider submitting the claim dispute to submit any supporting documentation to the resolution organization within 15 days after receipt by the health plan or provider of a request from the resolution organization for documentation in support of the claim dispute. Failure to submit the supporting documentation within such time period shall result in the dismissal of the submitted claim dispute. Any additional documentation submitted to the resolution organization must be submitted to the adverse party at the same time.

(c) The resolution organization shall require the respondent in the claim dispute to submit all documentation in support of its position within 15 days after receiving a request from the resolution organization for supporting documentation. The resolution organization may extend the time. Failure to submit the supporting documentation within such time period shall result in a default against the health plan or provider. In the event of such a default, the resolution organization shall issue its written recommendation to the Agency that a default be entered against the defaulting entity. The written recommendation shall include a recommendation to the Agency that the defaulting entity shall pay the entity submitting the claim dispute the full amount of the claim dispute, plus all accrued interest, and shall be considered a nonprevailing party for the purposes of this section. Any additional information submitted by the adverse party to the resolution organization must be submitted to the entity filing the request for dispute resolution at the same time.

(d) The resolution organization may not communicate ex parte either with the health plan or the provider during the dispute resolution.

(e) The resolution organization shall issue a written recommendation, including findings of fact relating to the calculation under Section 641.513 (5), F.S., for the recommended amount due for the disputed claim, including any evidence relied upon.

(f) The resolution organization shall issue a written recommendation, which includes findings of fact, to the Agency within 60 days after the requested information is received by the resolution organization within the timeframes specified by the resolution organization. In no event shall the review time exceed 90 days following receipt of the initial claim dispute submission by the resolution organization.

(g) Within 30 days after receipt of the recommendations issued by the resolution organization the Agency shall adopt the recommendation as a final order.

(h) The final order is subject to judicial review pursuant to Section 120.68, F.S.

FLORIDA STATUTES

§ 408.7057 Statewide provider and health plan claim dispute resolution program

(1) As used in this section, the term:

(a) "Agency" means the Agency for Health Care Administration.

(b) "Health plan" means a health maintenance organization or a prepaid health clinic certified under chapter 641, a prepaid health plan authorized under s. 409.912, an exclusive provider organization certified under s. 627.6472, or a major medical expense health insurance policy, as defined in s. 627.643(2)(e), offered by a group or an individual health insurer licensed pursuant to chapter 624, including a preferred provider organization under s. 627.6471.

(c) "Resolution organization" means a qualified independent third-party claim-dispute-resolution entity selected by and contracted with the Agency for Health Care Administration.

(2)

(a) The agency shall establish a program to provide assistance to contracted and noncontracted providers and health plans for resolution of claim disputes that are not resolved by the provider and the health plan. The agency shall contract with a resolution organization to timely review and consider claim disputes submitted by providers and health plans and recommend to the agency an appropriate resolution of those disputes. The agency shall establish by rule jurisdictional amounts and methods of aggregation for claim disputes that may be considered by the resolution organization.

(b) The resolution organization shall review claim disputes filed by contracted and noncontracted providers and health plans unless the disputed claim:

1. Is related to interest payment;
2. Does not meet the jurisdictional amounts or the methods of aggregation established by agency rule, as provided in paragraph (a);
3. Is part of an internal grievance in a Medicare managed care organization or a reconsideration appeal through the Medicare appeals process;
4. Is related to a health plan that is not regulated by the state;
5. Is part of a Medicaid fair hearing pursued under 42 C.F.R. ss. 431.220 et seq.;
6. Is the basis for an action pending in state or federal court; or
7. Is subject to a binding claim-dispute-resolution process provided by contract entered into prior to October 1, 2000, between the provider and the managed care organization.

(c) Contracts entered into or renewed on or after October 1, 2000, may require exhaustion of an internal dispute-resolution process as a prerequisite to the submission of a claim by a provider or a health plan to the resolution organization.

(d) A contracted or noncontracted provider or health plan may not file a claim dispute with the resolution organization more than 12 months after a final determination has been made on a claim by a health plan or provider.

(e) The resolution organization shall require the health plan or provider submitting the claim dispute to submit any supporting documentation to the resolution organization within 15 days after receipt by the health plan or provider of a request from the resolution organization for documentation in support of the claim dispute. The resolution organization may extend the time if appropriate. Failure to submit the supporting documentation within such time period shall result in the dismissal of the submitted claim dispute.

(f) The resolution organization shall require the respondent in the claim dispute to submit all documentation in support of its position within 15 days after receiving a request from the resolution organization for supporting documentation. The resolution organization may extend the time if appropriate. Failure to submit the supporting documentation within such time period shall result in a default against the health plan or provider. In the event of such a default, the resolution organization shall issue its written recommendation to the agency that a default be entered against the defaulting entity. The written recommendation shall include a recommendation to the agency that the defaulting entity shall pay the entity submitting the claim dispute the full amount of the claim dispute, plus all accrued interest, and shall be considered a nonprevailing party for the purposes of this section.

(g)

1. If on an ongoing basis during the preceding 12 months, the agency has reason to believe that a pattern of noncompliance with s. 627.6131 and s. 641.3155 exists on the part of a particular health plan or provider, the agency shall evaluate the information contained in these cases to determine whether the information evidences a pattern and report its findings, together with substantiating evidence, to the appropriate licensure or certification entity for the health plan or provider.
2. In addition, the agency shall prepare a report to the Governor and the Legislature by February 1 of each year, enumerating: claims dismissed; defaults issued; and failures to comply with agency final orders issued under this section.

(h) Either the contracted or noncontracted provider or the health plan may make an offer to settle the claim dispute when it submits a request for a claim dispute and supporting documentation. The offer to settle the claim dispute must state its total amount, and the party to whom it is directed has 15 days to accept the offer once it is received. If the party receiving the offer does not accept the offer and the final order amount is more than 90 percent or less than 110 percent of the offer amount, the party receiving the offer must pay the final order amount to the offering party and is deemed a nonprevailing party for purposes of this section. The amount of an offer made by a contracted or noncontracted provider to settle an alleged underpayment by the health plan must be greater than 110 percent of the reimbursement amount the provider received. The amount of an offer made by a health plan to settle an alleged overpayment to the provider must be less than 90 percent of the alleged overpayment amount by the health plan. Both parties may agree to settle the disputed claim at any time, for any amount, regardless of whether an offer to settle was made or rejected.

(3) The agency shall adopt rules to establish a process to be used by the resolution organization in considering claim disputes submitted by a provider or health plan which must include:
  (a) That the resolution organization review and consider all documentation submitted by both the health plan and the provider;
  (b) That the resolution organization's recommendation make findings of fact;
  (c) That either party may request that the resolution organization conduct an evidentiary hearing in which both sides can present evidence and examine witnesses, and for which the cost of the hearing is equally shared by the parties;
  (d) That the resolution organization may not communicate ex parte with either the health plan or the provider during the dispute resolution;
  (e) That the resolution organization's written recommendation, including findings of fact relating to the calculation under s. 641.513(5) for the recommended amount due for the disputed claim, include any evidence relied upon; and
  (f) That the resolution organization issue a written recommendation to the agency within 60 days after the requested information is received by the resolution organization within the timeframes specified by the resolution organization. In no event shall the review time exceed 90 days following receipt of the initial claim dispute submission by the resolution organization.

(4) Within 30 days after receipt of the recommendation of the resolution organization, the agency shall adopt the recommendation as a final order. The final order is subject to judicial review pursuant to s. 120.68.

(5) The agency shall notify within 7 days the appropriate licensure or certification entity whenever there is a violation of a final order issued by the agency pursuant to this section.

(6) The entity that does not prevail in the agency's order must pay a review cost to the review organization, as determined by agency rule. Such rule must provide for an apportionment of the review fee in any case in which both parties prevail in part. If the nonprevailing party fails to pay the ordered review cost within 35 days after the agency's order, the nonpaying party is subject to a penalty of not more than $500 per day until the penalty is paid.

(7) The agency may adopt rules to administer this section.

§ 627.64194 Coverage requirements for services provided by nonparticipating providers; payment collection limitations

(1) As used in this section, the term:

(a) "Emergency services" means emergency services and care, as defined in s. 641.47(8), which are provided in a facility.

(b) "Facility" means a licensed facility as defined in s. 395.002(17) and an urgent care center as defined in s. 395.002.

(c) "Insured" means a person who is covered under an individual or group health insurance policy delivered or issued for delivery in this state by an insurer authorized to transact business in this state.

(d) "Nonemergency services" means the services and care that are not emergency services.

(e) "Nonparticipating provider" means a provider who is not a preferred provider as defined in s. 627.6471 or a provider who is not an exclusive provider as defined in s. 627.6472. For purposes of covered emergency services under this section, a facility licensed under chapter 395 or an urgent care center defined in s. 395.002 is a nonparticipating provider if the facility has not contracted with an insurer to provide emergency services to its insureds at a specified rate.

(f) "Participating provider" means, for purposes of this section, a preferred provider as defined in s. 627.6471 or an exclusive provider as defined in s. 627.6472.

(2) An insurer is solely liable for payment of fees to a nonparticipating provider of covered emergency services provided to an insured in accordance with the coverage terms of the health insurance policy, and such insured is not liable for payment of fees for covered services to a nonparticipating provider of emergency services, other than applicable copayments, coinsurance, and deductibles. An insurer must provide coverage for emergency services that:

(a) May not require prior authorization.

(b) Must be provided regardless of whether the services are furnished by a participating provider or a nonparticipating provider.

(c) May impose a coinsurance amount, copayment, or limitation of benefits requirement for a nonparticipating provider only if the same requirement applies to a participating provider.

The provisions of s. 627.638 apply to this subsection.

(3) An insurer is solely liable for payment of fees to a nonparticipating provider of covered nonemergency services provided to an insured in accordance with the coverage terms of the health insurance policy, and such insured is not liable for payment of fees to a nonparticipating provider, other than applicable copayments, coinsurance, and deductibles, for covered nonemergency services that are:

(a) Provided in a facility that has a contract for the nonemergency services with the insurer which the facility would be otherwise obligated to provide under contract with the insurer; and

(b) Provided when the insured does not have the ability and opportunity to choose a participating provider at the facility who is available to treat the insured.

The provisions of s. 627.638 apply to this subsection.

(4) An insurer must reimburse a nonparticipating provider of services under subsections (2) and (3) as specified in s. 641.513(5), reduced only by insured cost share responsibilities as specified in the health insurance policy, within the applicable timeframe provided in s. 627.6131.

(5) A nonparticipating provider of emergency services as provided in subsection (2) or a nonparticipating provider of nonemergency services as provided in subsection (3) may not be reimbursed an amount greater than the amount provided in subsection (4) and may not collect or attempt to collect from the insured, directly or indirectly, any excess amount, other than copayments, coinsurance, and deductibles. This section does not prohibit a nonparticipating provider from collecting or attempting to collect from the insured an amount due for the provision of noncovered services.

(6) Any dispute with regard to the reimbursement to the nonparticipating provider of emergency or nonemergency services as provided in subsection (4) shall be resolved in a court of competent jurisdiction or through the voluntary dispute resolution process in s. 408.7057.

§ 641.3154 Organization liability; provider billing prohibited

(1) If a health maintenance organization is liable for services rendered to a subscriber by a provider, regardless of whether a contract exists between the organization and the provider, the organization is liable for payment of fees to the provider and the subscriber is not liable for payment of fees to the provider.

(2) For purposes of this section, a health maintenance organization is liable for services rendered to an eligible subscriber by a provider if the provider follows the health maintenance organization's authorization procedures and receives authorization for a covered service for an eligible subscriber, unless the provider provided information to the health maintenance organization with the willful intention to misinform the health maintenance organization.

(3) The liability of an organization for payment of fees for services is not affected by any contract the organization has with a third party for the functions of authorizing, processing, or paying claims.

(4) A provider or any representative of a provider, regardless of whether the provider is under contract with the health maintenance organization, may not collect or attempt to collect money from, maintain any action at law against, or report to a credit agency a subscriber of an organization for payment of services for which the organization is liable, if the provider in good faith knows or should know that the organization is liable. This prohibition applies during the pendency of any claim for payment made by the provider to the organization for payment of the services and any legal proceedings or dispute resolution process to determine whether the organization is liable for the services if the provider is informed that such proceedings are taking place. It is presumed that a provider does not know and should not know that an organization is liable unless:

   (a) The provider is informed by the organization that it accepts liability;
   (b) A court of competent jurisdiction determines that the organization is liable; or
   (c) The agency issues a final order that the organization is required to pay for such services subsequent to a recommendation made by a resolution organization pursuant to s. 408.7057.

(5) An organization, the office, and the department shall report any suspected violation of this section by a health care practitioner to the Department of Health and by a facility to the agency, which shall take such action as authorized by law.

§ 641.513 Requirements for providing emergency services and care

(1) In providing for emergency services and care as a covered service, a health maintenance organization may not:

   (a) Require prior authorization for the receipt of prehospital transport or treatment or for emergency services and care.
   (b) Indicate that emergencies are covered only if care is secured within a certain period of time.
   (c) Use terms such as "life threatening" or "bona fide" to qualify the kind of emergency that is covered.
   (d) Deny payment based on the subscriber's failure to notify the health maintenance organization in advance of seeking treatment or within a certain period of time after the care is given.

(2) Prehospital and hospital-based trauma services and emergency services and care must be provided to a subscriber of a health maintenance organization as required under ss. 395.1041, 395.4045, and 401.45.

(3)

(a) When a subscriber is present at a hospital seeking emergency services and care, the determination as to whether an emergency medical condition, as defined in s. 641.47 exists shall be made, for the purposes of treatment, by a physician of the hospital or, to the extent permitted by applicable law, by other appropriate licensed professional hospital personnel under the supervision of the hospital physician. The physician or the appropriate personnel shall indicate in the patient's chart the results of the screening, examination, and evaluation. The health maintenance organization shall compensate the provider for the screening, evaluation, and examination that is reasonably calculated to assist the health care provider in arriving at a determination as to whether the patient's condition is an emergency medical condition. The health maintenance organization shall compensate the provider for emergency services and care. If a determination is made that an emergency medical condition does not exist, payment for services rendered subsequent to that determination is governed by the contract under which the subscriber is covered.

(b) If a determination has been made that an emergency medical condition exists and the subscriber has notified the hospital, or the hospital emergency personnel otherwise have knowledge that the patient is a subscriber of the health maintenance organization, the hospital must make a reasonable attempt to notify the subscriber's primary care physician, if known, or the health maintenance organization, if the health maintenance organization had previously requested in writing that the notification be made directly to the health maintenance organization, of the existence of the emergency medical condition. If the primary care physician is not known, or has not been contacted, the hospital must:

1. Notify the health maintenance organization as soon as possible prior to discharge of the subscriber from the emergency care area; or
2. Notify the health maintenance organization within 24 hours or on the next business day after admission of the subscriber as an inpatient to the hospital.

If notification required by this paragraph is not accomplished, the hospital must document its attempts to notify the health maintenance organization of the circumstances that precluded attempts to notify the health maintenance organization. A health maintenance organization may not deny payment for emergency services and care based on a hospital's failure to comply with the notification requirements of this paragraph. Nothing in this paragraph shall alter any contractual responsibility of a subscriber to make contact with the health maintenance organization, subsequent to receiving treatment for the emergency medical condition.

(c) If the subscriber's primary care physician responds to the notification, the hospital physician and the primary care physician may discuss the appropriate care and treatment of the subscriber. The health maintenance organization may have a member of the hospital staff with whom it has a contract participate in the treatment of the subscriber within the scope of the physician's hospital staff privileges. The subscriber may be transferred, in accordance with state and federal law, to a hospital that has a contract with the health maintenance organization and has the service capability to treat the subscriber's emergency medical condition. Notwithstanding any other state law, a hospital may request and collect insurance or financial information from a patient in accordance with federal law, which is necessary to determine if the patient is a subscriber of a health maintenance organization, if emergency services and care are not delayed.

(4) A subscriber may be charged a reasonable copayment, as provided in s. 641.31(12), for the use of an emergency room.

(5) Reimbursement for services pursuant to this section by a provider who does not have a contract with the health maintenance organization shall be the lesser of:

(a) The provider's charges;

(b) The usual and customary provider charges for similar services in the community where the services were provided; or

(c) The charge mutually agreed to by the health maintenance organization and the provider within 60 days of the submittal of the claim.

Such reimbursement shall be net of any applicable copayment authorized pursuant to subsection (4).

(6) Reimbursement for services under this section provided to subscribers who are Medicaid recipients by a provider for whom no contract exists between the provider and the health maintenance organization shall be determined under chapter 409.

(7) Reimbursement for services under this section provided to subscribers who are enrolled in a health maintenance organization pursuant to s. 624.91 by a provider for whom no contract exists between the provider and the health maintenance organization shall be the lesser of:

(a) The provider's charges;

(b) The usual and customary provider charges for similar services in the community where the services were provided;

(c) The charge mutually agreed to by the entity and the provider within 60 days after submittal of the claim; or

(d) The Medicaid rate.

§ 641.514 Coverage for air ambulance services

(1) As used in this section, the term:

(a) "Air ambulance service" has the same meaning as provided in s. 401.23.

(b) "Health maintenance organization" has the same meaning as provided in s. 641.19(12).

(c) "Reasonable reimbursement" means reimbursement that considers the direct cost to provide the air ambulance transportation service to the subscriber, the operation of an air ambulance service by a county which operates entirely within a designated area of critical state concern as determined by the Department of Commerce, and in-network reimbursement established by the health maintenance organization for the specific contract. The term does not include the amount of billed charges for the cost of services rendered.

(2) A health maintenance contract must require a health maintenance organization to provide reasonable reimbursement to an air ambulance service for covered nonemergency and emergency services provided to a subscriber in accordance with the coverage terms of the contract. Such reasonable reimbursement may be reduced only by applicable copayments, coinsurance, and deductibles. Payment in full by the subscriber of his or her applicable copayment, coinsurance, or deductible constitutes an accord and satisfaction of, and constitutes a release of, any claim for additional moneys owed by the subscriber to the health maintenance organization or to any person or entity in connection with the air ambulance service.

GEORGIA COMPILATION RULES AND REGULATIONS

Rule 120-2-106-.02 Scope and purpose

This Regulation is made pursuant to the "Surprise Billing Consumer Protection Act," which was passed to provide a mechanism to resolve billing and payment disputes between insurers and out-of-network providers. It will also establish a fair and equitable arbitration process to handle such disputes. This Regulation applies only to "healthcare plans" and "state healthcare plans," as defined in this Regulation. Nothing in this Regulation shall reduce a covered person's financial responsibilities concerning ground ambulance transportation. Failure of an insurer to comply with the provisions of Chapter 20E of Title 33 shall be deemed an unfair trade practice as defined in 33-6-4.

Rule 120-2-106-.03 Definitions

For the purposes of this Regulation, the following definitions apply:

(1) "Balance bill" means the amount that a non-participating provider charges for services provided to a covered person. Such amount equals the difference between the amount paid or offered by the insurer and the amount of the non-participating provider's bill charge but shall not include any amount for coinsurance, copayments, or deductibles due by the covered person.

(2) "Contracted amount" means the median in-network amount paid during the 2017 calendar year by an insurer for the emergency or non-emergency services provided by in-network providers engaged in the same or similar specialties and provided in the same or nearest geographical area. The Department shall annually adjust such amount for inflation, which may be based on the Consumer Price Index, and shall not include Medicare or Medicaid rates.

(3) "Covered person" means an individual who is insured under a healthcare plan.

(4) "Emergency medical provider" means any physician licensed by the Georgia Composite Medical Board who provides emergency medical services and any other healthcare provider licensed or otherwise authorized in this state to render emergency medical services.

(5) "Emergency medical services" means medical services rendered after the recent onset of a medical or traumatic condition, sickness, or injury exhibiting acute symptoms of sufficient severity, including, but not limited to, severe pain, that would lead a prudent layperson possessing an average knowledge of medicine and health to believe that his or her condition, sickness, or injury is of such a nature that failure to obtain immediate medical care could result in:
   - (a) Placing the patient's health in serious jeopardy;
   - (b) Serious impairment to bodily functions;
   - (c) Serious dysfunction of any bodily organ or part.

(6) "Facility" means a hospital, an ambulatory surgical treatment center, birthing center, diagnostic and treatment center, hospice, or similar institution.

(7) "Geographic area" is defined as one of 16 Geo Rating Areas established for ACA purposes by use of Georgia Standardized Metropolitan Statistical Areas, expanded by contiguous counties and which has been in required use by Georgia insurers since 2014.

(8) "Healthcare plan" means any hospital or medical insurance policy or certificate, healthcare plan contract or certificate, qualified higher deductible health plan, health maintenance organization or other managed care subscriber contract, or state healthcare plan. This term shall not include limited benefit insurance policies or plans listed under paragraph (3) of Code Section 33-1-2, air ambulance insurance, or policies issued in accordance with Chapter 21A or 31 of this title or Chapter 9 of Title 34, relating to workers' compensation, Part A, B, C, or D of Title XVIII of the Social Security Act (Medicare), or any plan or program not described in this paragraph over which the Commissioner does not have regulatory authority. Notwithstanding paragraph (3) of Code Section 33-1-2 and any other provision of this title, this chapter this term shall include stand-alone dental insurance and stand-alone vision insurance for purposes of this chapter.

(9) "Healthcare provider" or "provider" means any physician, other individual, or facility other than a hospital licensed or otherwise authorized in this state to furnish healthcare services, including, but not limited to, any dentist, podiatrist, optometrist, psychologist, clinical social worker, advanced practice registered nurse, registered optician, licensed professional counselor, physical therapist, marriage and family therapist, chiropractor, athletic trainer qualified pursuant to Code Section 43-5-8, occupational therapist, speech-language pathologist, audiologist, dietitian, or physician assistant.

(10) "Healthcare services" means emergency or non-emergency medical services.

(11) "Insurer" means an entity subject to the insurance laws and regulations of this state, or subject to the jurisdiction of the Commissioner, that contracts, offers to contract, or enters into an agreement to provide, deliver, arrange for, pay for, or reimburse any of the costs of healthcare services, including those of an accident and sickness insurance company, a health maintenance organization, a healthcare plan, a managed care plan, or any other entity providing a health insurance plan, a health benefit plan, or healthcare services.

(12) "Median" means the middle number of a sorted list of reimbursement amounts paid to in-network providers or facilities with respect to a specific emergency or non-emergency medical service, with each paid claim amount separately represented on the list, arranged in order from least to greatest. If there is an even number of items in the sorted list of paid claim amounts, the median is found by taking the average of the two middlemost numbers. The calculated median paid amount shall include copayment, coinsurance, and deductible as applicable and shall exclude claims in which the insurer is not the primary payer.

(13) "Non-emergency medical services" means the examination or treatment of persons for the prevention of illness or the correction or treatment of any physical or mental condition resulting from an illness, injury, or other human physical problem which does not qualify as an emergency medical service and includes, but is not limited to:
(a) Hospital services which include the general and usual care, services, supplies, and equipment furnished by hospitals;
(b) Medical services which include the general and usual care and services rendered and administered by doctors of medicine, dentistry, optometry, and other providers; and
(c) Other medical services which, by way of illustration only and without limiting the scope of this chapter, include the provision of appliances and supplies; nursing care by a registered nurse; institutional services, including the general and usual care, services, supplies, and equipment furnished by healthcare institutions and agencies or entities other than hospitals; physiotherapy; drugs and medications; therapeutic services and equipment, including oxygen and the rental of oxygen equipment; hospital beds; iron lungs; orthopedic services and appliances, including wheelchairs, trusses, braces, crutches, and prosthetic devices, including artificial limbs and eyes; and any other appliance, supply, or service related to healthcare which does not qualify as an emergency medical service.

(14) "Out-of-network" refers to healthcare services provided to a covered person by providers or facilities who do not belong to the provider network in the healthcare plan.

(15) "Non-participating provider" means a healthcare provider who has not entered into a contract with a healthcare plan for the delivery of medical services.

(16) "Participating provider" means a healthcare provider that has entered into a contract with an insurer for the delivery of healthcare services to covered persons under a healthcare plan.

(17) "Resolution organization" means a qualified, independent, third-party claim dispute resolution entity selected by and contracted with the Department.

(18) "State healthcare plan" means:
(a) The state employees' health insurance plan established pursuant to Article 1 of Chapter 18 of Title 45;
(b) The health insurance plan for public school teachers established pursuant to Subpart 2 of Part 6 of Article 17 of Chapter 2 of Title 20;
(c) The health insurance plan for public school employees established pursuant to Subpart 3 of Part 6 of Article 17 of Chapter 2 of Title 20; and
(d) The Regents Health Plan established pursuant to authority granted to the board pursuant to Code Sections 20-3-31, 20-3-51, and 31-2-4.

(19) "Surprise bill" means a bill resulting from an occurrence in which charges arise from a covered person receiving healthcare services from an out-of-network provider at an in-network facility.

Rule 120-2-106-.04 ERISA exempt plans

ERISA Exempt Plans subject to the exclusive jurisdiction of federal law and rules are not eligible for review under the "Surprise Billing Consumer Protection Act."

Rule 120-2-106-.05 Emergency services

(1) Insurers shall pay covered emergency medical services for covered persons regardless of whether the provider or facility is participating or non-participating in their network according to this Regulation. Such an insurer shall make such payment without prior authorization and without retrospective payment denial for emergency medical services deemed to be medically necessary.

(2) If a covered person receives emergency medical services from a non-participating provider, such person shall not be liable to the non-participating provider or facility for any amount exceeding such person's deductible, coinsurance, copayment, or other cost-sharing amount as determined by such person's policy. The amount payable by an insurer for emergency medical services paid directly to the provider shall be the greater of:

   (a) The verifiable median contracted amount paid by all eligible insurers for similar services calculated by a vendor utilized and chosen by the Commissioner;

   (b) The most recent verifiable amount agreed to by the insurer and the non-participating emergency medical provider for the same services during which time the provider was in-network with the insurer; (if applicable)

   (c) A higher amount as the insurer may deem appropriate given the complexity and circumstances of the services provided.

   Any amount payable by an insurer under this section for emergency medical services shall not include any amount of coinsurance, copayment, or deductible owed by the covered person or already paid by such person.

(3) Insurers shall not deny benefits or emergency medical services rendered based on a covered person's failure to provide subsequent notification where the insured's medical condition prevented timely notification.

(4) Emergency medical services received from non-participating providers and/or facilities shall count toward the deductible and any maximum out of pocket policy provisions as if the services were obtained from a participating provider.

(5) In cases of emergency medical services received from a non-participating facility, the facility shall bill the covered person no more than deductible, coinsurance, copayment, or other cost-sharing as determined by such person's policy.

(6) Insurer payments made to providers in this Code section shall be in accord with prompt payment requirements under 33-24-59.14. Notification should reflect whether coverage is subject to the exclusive jurisdiction of ERISA (1974), U.S.C. Sec. 1001.

Rule 120-2-106-.06 Non-emergency medical services

(1) If the provisions of 120-2-106.08 are met, an insurer that provides any benefits to covered persons with respect to non-emergency medical services shall pay for such services in the event that such services resulted in a surprise bill regardless of whether the healthcare provider furnishing non-emergency medical services is a participating provider with respect to non-emergency medical services.

(2) In the event a covered person receives care in a facility that generates a surprise bill for non-emergency medical services from a non-participating medical provider, the non-participating provider shall collect or bill the covered person no more than such person's deductible, coinsurance, copayment, or other cost-sharing amount as determined by such person's policy. The insurer shall directly pay such provider the greater of:

   (a) The verifiable median contracted amount paid by all eligible insurers for similar services calculated by a vendor utilized and chosen by the Commissioner;

   (b) The most recent verifiable amount agreed to by the insurer and the non-participating emergency medical provider for the same services during which time the provider was in-network with the insurer (if applicable);

   (c) A higher amount as the insurer may deem appropriate given the complexity and circumstances of the services provided.

   Any amount that the insurer pays the non-participating provider under this subsection shall not be required to include any amount of coinsurance, copayment, or deductible owed by the covered person or already paid by such person.

(3) Non-emergency medical services received from non-participating providers and/or facilities shall count toward the deductible and any maximum out of pocket policy provisions as if the services were obtained from a participating provider.

(4) In cases of non-emergency medical services received from a non-participating facility, the facility shall bill the covered person no more than deductible, coinsurance, copayment, or other cost-sharing as determined by such person's policy.

(5) All insurer payments made to providers pursuant to this Code section shall be in accord with Code Section 33-24-59.14. Such payments shall accompany notification to the provider from the insurer disclosing whether the healthcare plan is subject to the exclusive jurisdiction of the Employee Retirement Income Security Act of 1974, 29 U.S.C. 202 Sec. 1001, et seq.

Rule 120-2-106-.07 Balance billing provision for covered benefits from non-participating providers

No healthcare plan shall deny or restrict covered benefits from a participating provider to a covered person solely because the covered person obtained treatment from a non-participating provider leading to a balance bill. Notice of such protection shall be provided in writing to the covered person by the insurer.

Rule 120-2-106-.08 Covered person choosing to receive non-emergency medical services from a non-participating provider, referrals and procedures

(1) Nothing in this chapter shall reduce a covered person's financial responsibilities in the event that such covered person chose to receive non-emergency medical services from an out-of-network provider. Such services shall not be considered a surprise bill for the purpose of this chapter.

(2) The covered person's choice described in subsection (1) of this Code section must:

- (a) Be documented through such covered person's written and oral consent in advance of the provision of such services; and
- (b) Occur only after such person has been provided with an estimate of the potential charges.

(3) If during the provision of non-emergency medical services, a covered person requests that the attending provider refer such covered person to another provider for the immediate provision of additional non-emergency medical services, such referred provider shall be exempt from the requirements in subsection (b) of this Code section if the following requirements are satisfied:

- (a) The referring provider advises the covered person that the referred provider may be a non-participating provider and may charge higher fees than a participating provider;
- (b) The covered person orally and in writing acknowledges that he or she is aware that the referred provider may be a non-participating provider and may charge higher fees than a participating provider;
- (c) The written acknowledgment referenced in paragraph (2) of this subsection shall be on a document separate from other documents provided by the referring provider and shall include language to be determined by the Commissioner (Appendix A) and Regulation; and
- (d) The referring provider records the satisfaction of the requirements in paragraphs (1), (2), and (3) of this subsection in the covered person's medical file.

Rule 120-2-106-.09 Claims database

Pursuant to O.C.G.A. 33-20E-8(a) appropriations for an all claims database were not provided, and subsection (b) of O.C.G.A. 33-20E-8 will be triggered. The Department will utilize a verifiable median contracted amount paid by all eligible insurers for similar services calculated by a vendor utilized and chosen by the Commissioner.

Rule 120-2-106-.10 Arbitration

(1) If an out-of-network provider concludes that payment received from an insurer pursuant to regulation 120-2-106-.05 or 120-2-106-.06 is not sufficient given the complexity and circumstances of the services provided. Or, if an out-of-network facility concludes that payment received from an insurer pursuant to Regulation 120-2-106-.05 concludes the same, a request for arbitration with the Commissioner may be initiated. A request for arbitration must be submitted within 30 days of receipt of payment for the claim and concurrently provide the insurer with a copy of such request.

(2) All arbitration requests must be submitted to the Administrative Procedure Division of the Office of Insurance and Safety Fire Commissioner.

(3) Within 30 days of the insurer's receipt of a provider's or facility's request for arbitration, the insurer must submit to the Administrative Procedure Division all data necessary to determine whether the insurer's payment to such provider or facility complied with regulations 120-2-106-.05 or 120-2-106-.06.

(4) The Commissioner will dismiss specific arbitration requests if the disputed claim meets certain criteria laid out in O.C.G.A. § 33-20E-10 or in Rule 120-2-106-.08. Should an insurer believe one of these criteria is present, they should submit the appropriate data they believe supports this contention. Should the Commissioner dismiss a claim for meeting one of the criteria in O.C.G.A. § 33-20E-10, the provider or facility may request a hearing under the rules contained in Regulation 120-2-2.

(5) Before proceeding with arbitration, the parties will be permitted 30 days from the date the request was received to negotiate a settlement. The parties must notify the Administrative Procedure Division of the result of such negotiation. If the Administrative Procedure Division has not been notified within 30 days of the settlement negotiation's result, the claim will be sent to arbitration. The parties may still reach a negotiated settlement after the claim is referred but before arbitration begins. However, they will be responsible for splitting any costs incurred by the resolution organization due to the referral.

(6) Disputes are to be reviewed by independent resolution organizations with whom the Department will contract. The disputes will be decided pursuant to the rules as laid out in O.C.G.A. 33-20E *et seq.*

(7) A list of the selected organizations and their approved fee schedules will be kept by the Administrative Procedure Division and available for review upon request. In contracting with each dispute resolution organization, the Department will ensure that appropriate safeguards are put in place so that information subject to trade secret protection laws is duly protected.

(8) Upon the Commissioner's referral of a dispute to a resolution organization, the parties will have five days to select an arbitrator by mutual agreement. If the parties have not notified the resolution organization of their mutual

selection before the fifth day, the resolution organization shall select an arbitrator from among its members. Should the parties not agree to the resolution organization's choice of arbitrator, the Commissioner will select one for the parties; this decision will be final.

(9) Arbitrators should possess training and experience in health care billing, reimbursement, and usual and customary charges in consultation with a licensed doctor in active practice in the same or similar specialty as the doctor providing the service that is the subject of the dispute.

(10) In addition to the factors found in O.C.G.A. § 33-20E-15, in deciding a claim, arbitrators should also consider the following factors:
  (a) Whether there is a gross disparity between the fee charged by the provider and (1) fees paid to the provider for the same services provided to other patients in health care plans in which the provider is non-participating, and (2) the fees paid by the health plan to reimburse similarly qualified out-of-network providers for the same services in the same region;
  (b) The provider's training, education, experience, and the usual charge for comparable services when the provider does not participate with the patient's health plan;
  (c) In the case of a hospital, the teaching status, scope of services, and case-mix;
  (d) The circumstances and complexity of the case;
  (e) Patient characteristics; and
  (f) For physician services, the usual and customary cost of the service.

(11) Following the resolution of arbitration, the Commissioner is permitted to refer the decision of the arbitrator to the appropriate state agency or the governing entity with governing authority over such provider or facility if the Commissioner concludes that a provider or facility has either displayed a pattern of acting in violation of this chapter or has failed to comply with a lawful order of the Commissioner or the arbitrator. However, if the provider or facility's violations or actions fall under the Commissioner's jurisdiction, the Commissioner may investigate and proceed under the provisions of Title 33.

(12) Each resolution organization contracted with by the Department should submit its quarterly reports to the Administrative Procedure. In addition to the information required by O.C.G.A. § 33-20E-19, each resolution organization will also submit in its quarterly report: the name of each arbitrator who settled a dispute and the number of disputes they settled in favor of either the insurer or the provider or facility.

(13) The Surprise Billing Consumer Protection Act becomes effective on January 1, 2020. The Department has until July 1, 2021, to contract with one or more arbitration organizations. Any arbitration requests received after January 1, 2020, and before the Department has contracted with an arbitration organization will be held until such contract is executed.

Rule 120-2-106-.11 Hospital surprise bill rating

Insurers shall make available online and in print a health benefit plan surprise bill rating for hospitals as required in Chapter 20C of Title 33. For each hospital, health benefit plans shall clearly display a rating denoting the health benefit plan surprise bill rating factor. This factor shall range from 0, denoting no specialties are in-network, to 4, which means all specialty groups are in-network. For any rating less than 4, the health benefit plan shall display which specialty group is not in-network by marking the specialty with a red X and any specialty group that is included by a green checkmark X. If a hospital does not provide one of the qualified hospital-based specialties, the absence of that specialty shall be designated by a green N/A. The factor and markings shall be clearly displayed for the covered person or potential covered person to easily understand. Qualified hospital-based specialty groups are medical groups that include anesthesiologists, pathologists, radiologists, or emergency medicine physicians. Any changes in the hospital rating factor shall be changed by the health benefit plan within 30 days.

OFFICIAL CODE OF GEORGIA ANNOTATED

§ 33-20E-2 Application to insurers; definitions

(a) This chapter shall apply to all insurers providing a healthcare plan that pays for the provision of healthcare services to covered persons.

(b) As used in this chapter, the term:

(1) "Balance bill" means the amount that a nonparticipating provider charges for services provided to a covered person. Such amount equals the difference between the amount paid or offered by the insurer and the amount of the nonparticipating provider's bill charge, but shall not include any amount for coinsurance, copayments, or deductibles due by the covered person.

(2) "Contracted amount" means the median in-network amount paid during the 2017 calendar year by an insurer for the emergency or nonemergency services provided by in-network providers engaged in the same or similar specialties and provided in the same or nearest geographical area. Such amount shall be annually adjusted by the department for inflation which may be based on the Consumer Price Index, and shall not include Medicare or Medicaid rates.

(3) "Covered person" means an individual who is insured under a healthcare plan.

(4) "Emergency medical provider" means any physician licensed by the Georgia Composite Medical Board who provides emergency medical services and any other healthcare provider licensed or otherwise authorized in this state to render emergency medical services.

(5) "Emergency medical services" means physical or mental health care services rendered for a medical or traumatic condition, sickness, or

injury, including a mental health condition or substance use disorder, in which a person is exhibiting acute symptoms of sufficient severity, including, but not limited to, severe pain, regardless of the initial, interim, final, or other diagnoses that are given, that would lead a prudent layperson possessing an average knowledge of medicine and health to believe that his or her condition, sickness, or injury is of such a nature that failure to obtain immediate medical care could result in:

(A) Placing the patient's health in serious jeopardy;
(B) Serious impairment to bodily functions; or
(C) Serious dysfunction of any bodily organ or part.

"Emergency medical services" includes medical services rendered after such person is stabilized and as part of outpatient observation or an inpatient or outpatient stay with respect to the visit in which such services are furnished, unless each of the conditions of subdivision (a)(3)(C)(ii)(II) of the federal Public Health Service Act, 42 U.S.C. Section 300gg-111 are met.

(6) "Facility" means a hospital, an ambulatory surgical treatment center, birthing center, diagnostic and treatment center, hospice, or similar institution.

(7) "Geographic area" means a specific portion of this state which shall consist of one or more zip codes as defined by the Commissioner pursuant to department rule and regulation.

(8) "Healthcare plan" means any hospital or medical insurance policy or certificate, healthcare plan contract or certificate, qualified higher deductible health plan, health maintenance organization or other managed care subscriber contract, or state healthcare plan. This term shall not include limited benefit insurance policies or plans listed under paragraph (3) of Code Section 33-1-2, air ambulance insurance, or policies issued in accordance with Chapter 21A or 31 of this title or Chapter 9 of Title 34, relating to workers' compensation, Part A, B, C, or D of Title XVIII of the Social Security Act (Medicare), or any plan or program not described in this paragraph over which the Commissioner does not have regulatory authority. Notwithstanding paragraph (3) of Code Section 33-1-2 and any other provision of this title, for purposes of this chapter this term shall include stand-alone dental insurance and stand-alone vision insurance.

(9) "Healthcare provider" or "provider" means any physician, other individual, or facility other than a hospital licensed or otherwise authorized in this state to furnish healthcare services, including, but not limited to, any dentist, podiatrist, optometrist, psychologist, clinical social worker, advanced practice registered nurse, registered optician, licensed professional counselor, physical therapist, marriage and family therapist, chiropractor, athletic trainer qualified pursuant to Code Section 43-5-8,

occupational therapist, speech-language pathologist, audiologist, dietitian, or physician assistant.

(10) "Healthcare services" means emergency or nonemergency medical services.

(11) "Insurer" means an entity subject to the insurance laws and regulations of this state, or subject to the jurisdiction of the Commissioner, that contracts, offers to contract, or enters into an agreement to provide, deliver, arrange for, pay for, or reimburse any of the costs of healthcare services, including those of an accident and sickness insurance company, a health maintenance organization, a healthcare plan, a managed care plan, or any other entity providing a health insurance plan, a health benefit plan, or healthcare services.

(12) "Nonemergency medical services" means the examination or treatment of persons for the prevention of illness or the correction or treatment of any physical or mental condition resulting from an illness, injury, or other human physical problem which does not qualify as an emergency medical service and includes, but is not limited to:

 (A) Hospital services which include the general and usual care, services, supplies, and equipment furnished by hospitals;

 (B) Medical services which include the general and usual care and services rendered and administered by doctors of medicine, dentistry, optometry, and other providers; and

 (C) Other medical services which, by way of illustration only and without limiting the scope of this chapter, include the provision of appliances and supplies; nursing care by a registered nurse; institutional services, including the general and usual care, services, supplies, and equipment furnished by healthcare institutions and agencies or entities other than hospitals; physiotherapy; drugs and medications; therapeutic services and equipment, including oxygen and the rental of oxygen equipment; hospital beds; iron lungs; orthopedic services and appliances, including wheelchairs, trusses, braces, crutches, and prosthetic devices, including artificial limbs and eyes; and any other appliance, supply, or service related to healthcare which does not qualify as an emergency medical service.

(13) "Out-of-network" refers to healthcare services provided to a covered person by providers or facilities who do not belong to the provider network in the healthcare plan.

(14) "Nonparticipating provider" means a healthcare provider who has not entered into a contract with a healthcare plan for the delivery of medical services.

(15) "Participating provider" means a healthcare provider that has entered into a contract with an insurer for the delivery of healthcare services to covered persons under a healthcare plan.

(16) "Resolution organization" means a qualified, independent, third-party claim dispute resolution entity selected by and contracted with the department.

(17) "State healthcare plan" means:
   (A) The state employees' health insurance plan established pursuant to Article 1 of Chapter 18 of Title 45;
   (B) The health insurance plan for public school teachers established pursuant to Subpart 2 of Part 6 of Article 17 of Chapter 2 of Title 20;
   (C) The health insurance plan for public school employees established pursuant to Subpart 3 of Part 6 of Article 17 of Chapter 2 of Title 20; and
   (D) The Regents Health Plan established pursuant to authority granted to the board pursuant to Code Sections 20-3-31, 20-3-51, and 31-2-4.

(18) "Surprise bill" means a bill resulting from an occurrence in which charges arise from a covered person receiving healthcare services from an out-of-network provider at an in-network facility.

§ 33-20E-3 Exemption

(a) Nothing in this chapter shall be applicable to healthcare plans which are subject to the exclusive jurisdiction of the Employee Retirement Income Security Act of 1974, 29 U.S.C. Sec. 1001, et seq.

(b) This chapter shall be applicable only to healthcare plans and state healthcare plans as defined in this chapter.

§ 33-20E-4 Payment for emergency medical services

(a) An insurer that provides any benefits to covered persons with respect to emergency medical services shall pay for such emergency medical services regardless of whether the healthcare provider or facility furnishing emergency medical services is a participating provider or facility with respect to emergency medical services, in accordance with this chapter:
   (1) Without need for any prior authorization determination and without any retrospective payment denial for medically necessary services; and
   (2) Regardless of whether the healthcare provider or facility furnishing emergency medical services is a participating provider or facility with respect to emergency medical services.

(b) In the event a covered person receives the provision of emergency medical services from a nonparticipating emergency medical provider, the nonparticipating provider shall collect or bill no more than such person's deductible, coinsurance, copayment, or other cost-sharing amount as determined by such person's policy directly and such insurer shall directly pay such provider the greater of:

(1) The verifiable contracted amount paid by all eligible insurers subject to the provisions of this chapter for the provision of the same or similar services as determined by the department;

(2) The most recent verifiable amount agreed to by the insurer and the nonparticipating emergency medical provider for the provision of the same services during such time as such provider was in-network with such insurer; or

(3) Such higher amount as the insurer may deem appropriate given the complexity and circumstances of the services provided.

Any amount that the insurer pays the nonparticipating provider under this subsection shall not be required to include any amount of coinsurance, copayment, or deductible owed by the covered person or already paid by such person.

(c) A healthcare plan shall not deny benefits for emergency medical services previously rendered based upon a covered person's failure to provide subsequent notification in accordance with plan provisions, where the covered person's medical condition prevented timely notification.

(d) For purposes of the covered person's financial responsibilities, the healthcare plan shall treat the emergency medical services received by the covered person from a nonparticipating provider or nonparticipating facility pursuant to this Code section as if such services were provided by a participating provider or participating facility, and shall include applying the covered person's cost-sharing for such services toward the covered person's deductible and maximum out-of-pocket limit applicable to services obtained from a participating provider or a participating facility under the healthcare plan.

(e) In the event a covered person receives emergency medical services from a nonparticipating facility, the nonparticipating facility shall bill the covered person no more than such covered person's deductible, coinsurance, copayment, or other cost-sharing amount as determined by such person's policy directly.

(f) All insurer payments made to providers pursuant to this Code section shall be in accord with Code Section 33-24-59.14. Such payments shall accompany notification to the provider from the insurer disclosing whether the healthcare plan is subject to the exclusive jurisdiction of the Employee Retirement Income Security Act of 1974, 29 U.S.C. Sec. 1001, et seq.

§ 33-20E-5 Payment for nonemergency medical services

(a) In accordance with Code Section 33-20E-7 and this chapter, an insurer that provides any benefits to covered persons with respect to nonemergency medical services shall pay for such services in the event that such services resulted in a surprise bill regardless of whether the healthcare provider furnishing nonemergency medical services is a participating provider with respect to nonemergency medical services.

(b) In the event a covered person receives a surprise bill for the provision of nonemergency medical services from a nonparticipating medical provider, the nonparticipating provider shall collect or bill the covered person no more than such person's deductible, coinsurance, copayment, or other cost-sharing amount as determined by such person's policy directly and such insurer shall directly pay such provider the greater of:

  (1) The verifiable contracted amount paid by all eligible insurers subject to the provisions of this chapter for the provision of the same or similar services as determined by the department;

  (2) The most recent verifiable amount agreed to by the insurer and the nonparticipating provider for the provision of the same services during such time as such provider was in-network with such insurer; or

  (3) Such higher amount as the insurer may deem appropriate given the complexity and circumstances of the services provided.

  Any amount that the insurer pays the nonparticipating provider under this subsection shall not be required to include any amount of coinsurance, copayment, or deductible owed by the covered person or already paid by such person.

(c) For purposes of the covered person's financial responsibilities, the healthcare plan shall treat the nonemergency medical services received by the covered person from a nonparticipating provider pursuant to this Code section as if such services were provided by a participating provider, and shall include applying the covered person's cost-sharing for such services toward the covered person's deductible and maximum out-of-pocket limit applicable to services obtained from a participating provider under the healthcare plan.

(d) All insurer payments made to providers pursuant to this Code section shall be in accord with Code Section 33-24-59.14. Such payments shall accompany notification to the provider from the insurer disclosing whether the healthcare plan is subject to the exclusive jurisdiction of the Employee Retirement Income Security Act of 1974, 29 U.S.C. Sec. 1001, et seq.

(e) Notwithstanding any other law or regulation to the contrary, nothing in this Code section shall affect a covered person's financial responsibilities or a nonparticipating facility's rights with respect to nonemergency medical services received from a nonparticipating facility.

§ 33-20E-6 Denying or restricting benefits based on balance billing; notice to insured

No healthcare plan shall deny or restrict the provision of covered benefits from a participating provider to a covered person solely because the covered person obtained treatment from a nonparticipating provider leading to a balance bill. Notice of such protection shall be provided in writing to the covered person by the insurer.

§ 33-20E-7 Surprise bill exclusion; requirements

(a) Nothing in this chapter shall reduce a covered person's financial responsibilities in the event that such covered person chose to receive nonemergency medical services from an out-of-network provider. Such services shall not be considered a surprise bill for purposes of this chapter.

(b) The covered person's choice described in subsection (a) of this Code section must:

  (1) Be documented through such covered person's written and oral consent in advance of the provision of such services; and

  (2) Occur only after such person has been provided with an estimate of the potential charges.

(c) If during the provision of nonemergency medical services, a covered person requests that the attending provider refer such covered person to another provider for the immediate provision of additional nonemergency medical services, such referred provider shall be exempt from the requirements in subsection (b) of this Code section if the following requirements are satisfied:

  (1) The referring provider advises the covered person that the referred provider may be a nonparticipating provider and may charge higher fees than a participating provider;

  (2) The covered person orally and in writing acknowledges that he or she is aware that the referred provider may be a nonparticipating provider and may charge higher fees than a participating provider;

  (3) The written acknowledgment referenced in paragraph (2) of this subsection shall be on a document separate from other documents provided by the referring provider and shall include language to be determined by the Commissioner through rule and regulation; and

  (4) The referring provider records the satisfaction of the requirements in paragraphs (1), (2), and (3) of this subsection in the covered person's medical file.

§ 33-20E-8 Payer health claims data base; annual updating of website

(a) Subject to appropriation, the department shall provide for the maintenance of an all-payer health claims data base and maintain records of insurer payments which shall track such payments by a wide variety of healthcare services and by geographic areas of this state. Such appropriation must specifically reference the Surprise Billing Consumer Protection Act. The department shall update information in the all-payer health claims data base on no less than an annual basis and shall maintain such information on the department's website.

(b) In the event that the appropriation described in subsection (a) of this Code section is not made, the department shall update information from such other verifiable data as the Commissioner shall determine appropriate on no less than an annual basis and shall maintain such information on the department's website.

§ 33-20E-9 Arbitration of payment issues

(a) If an out-of-network provider concludes that payment received from an insurer pursuant to Code Section 33-20E-4 or 33-20E-5 or if an out-of-network facility concludes that payment received from an insurer pursuant to Code Section 33-20E-4 is not sufficient given the complexity and circumstances of the services provided, the provider or facility may initiate a request for arbitration with the Commissioner. Such provider or facility shall submit such request within 60 days of receipt of such payment for the claim and concurrently provide the insurer with a copy of such request. Such payment shall be indicated by the insurer on the first page of the insurer's remittance to the out-of-network provider in a manner to be determined by the Commissioner through the promulgation of rules and regulations. Such rules and regulations shall specify when the time period to request arbitration commences.

(b) A request for arbitration may involve a single patient and a single type of healthcare service, a single patient and multiple types of healthcare services, multiple patients and a single type of healthcare service, or multiple substantially similar healthcare services in the same specialty on multiple patients.

§ 33-20E-10 Dismissal of arbitration requests

(a) The Commissioner shall dismiss certain requests for arbitration if the disputed claim is:
   (1) Related to a healthcare plan that is not regulated by the state;
   (2) The basis for an action pending in state or federal court at the time of the request for arbitration;
   (3) Subject to a binding claims resolution process entered into prior to July 1, 2021;
   (4) Made against a healthcare plan subject to the exclusive jurisdiction of the Employee Retirement Income Security Act of 1974, 29 U.S.C. Sec. 1001, et seq.; or
   (5) In accord with other circumstances as may be determined by department rule.

(b) The Commissioner may dismiss certain requests for arbitration in the following circumstances:
   (1) The provider or facility has engaged in a pattern or practice of any of the following:
      (A) Failing to respond to the department's requests for data under Code Section 33-20E-11.1;

(B) Failing to respond to the department's other inquires after filing requests for arbitration; or

(C) Failing to pay resolution organizations as required under Code Section 33-20E-16;

(2) The provider or facility failed to file its request for arbitration within 60 days of receipt of payment for the claim and concurrently provide the insurer with a copy of such request; or

(3) The provider or facility failed to explain in detail the reasons arbitration is needed. Such explanation shall include a representation as to whether the insurer's payment was in accord with the relevant provisions of Code Sections 33-20E-4 or 33-20E-5 if the party requesting arbitration is an out-of-network provider, and Code Section 33-20E-4 if the requesting party is out-of-network facility. If such payment was in such accord, the explanation shall provide in detail the complexity and circumstances of the services provided which necessitate additional payment.

§ 33-20E-11 Submission to commissioner by insurer of data pending arbitration

Within 60 days of the insurer's receipt of the provider's or facility's request for arbitration, the insurer shall submit to the Commissioner all data necessary for the Commissioner to determine whether such insurer's payment to such provider or facility was in compliance with Code Section 33-20E-4 or 33-20E-5. The Commissioner shall not be required to make such a determination prior to referring the dispute to a resolution organization for arbitration. When an insurer fails to submit such data within such 60 day period, the Commissioner may assess penalties against such insurer in accord with Code Section 33-2-24 or declare a default judgment against such insurer.

§ 33-20E-12 Regulation; contracting with resolution organizations

The Commissioner shall promulgate rules implementing an arbitration process requiring the Commissioner to select one or more resolution organizations to arbitrate certain claim disputes between insurers and out-of-network providers or facilities. The Commissioner may promulgate such other rules as reasonably necessary to facilitate the arbitration process. Prior to proceeding with such arbitration, the Commissioner shall allow the parties 60 days from the date the Commissioner received the request for arbitration to negotiate a settlement. The parties shall timely notify the Commissioner of the result of such negotiation. If within 60 days of the date that the Commissioner received the request for arbitration, the parties have neither agreed upon a settlement nor agreed that more time is needed to negotiate a settlement, or both, or either party has failed to notify the Commissioner of such settlement or need for additional time to negotiate, the Commissioner shall within five days, refer the dispute to a resolution organization. The department shall contract with one or more resolution organizations by July 1, 2021, to review and consider claim disputes between insurers and out-of-network providers or facilities as such disputes are referred by the Commissioner.

§ 33-20E-13 Selection of arbitrator

Upon the Commissioner's referral of a dispute to a resolution organization, the parties shall have five days to select an arbitrator by mutual agreement. If the parties have not notified the resolution organization of their mutual selection before the fifth day, the resolution organization shall select an arbitrator from among its members. Any selected arbitrator shall be independent of the parties and shall not have a personal, professional, or financial conflict with any party to the arbitration. The arbitrator shall have experience or knowledge in healthcare billing and reimbursement rates. He or she shall not communicate ex parte with either party.

§ 33-20E-14 Submission of final offers; supporting documentation

The parties shall have ten days after the selection of the arbitrator to submit in writing to the resolution organization each party's final offer and each party's argument in support of such offer. The parties' initial arguments shall be limited to written form and shall consist of no more than 20 pages per party. The parties may submit documents in support of their arguments. The arbitrator may require the parties to submit such additional written argument and documentation as the arbitrator determines necessary, but the arbitrator may require such additional filing no more than once. Such additional written argument shall be limited to no more than ten pages per party. The arbitrator may set filing times and extend such filing times as appropriate. Failure of either party to timely submit the supportive documentation described herein may result in a default against the party failing to make such timely submission.

§ 33-20E-15 Proposed payment amounts

Each party shall submit one proposed payment amount to the arbitrator. The arbitrator shall pick one of the two amounts submitted and shall reveal that amount in the arbitrator's final decision. The arbitrator may not modify such selected amount. In making such a decision, the arbitrator shall consider the complexity and circumstances of each case, including, but not limited to, the level of training, education, and experience of the relevant physicians or other individuals at the facility who are licensed or otherwise authorized in this state to furnish healthcare services and other factors as determined by the Commissioner through rule. The arbitrator's final decision shall be in writing and shall describe the basis for such decision, including citations to any documents relied upon. Notwithstanding Code Section 33-20E-14, such decision shall be made within 60 days of the Commissioner's referral. Any default or final decision issued by the arbitrator shall be binding upon the parties and is not appealable through the court system.

§ 33-20E-16 Payment of expenses and fees

The party whose final offer amount is not selected by the arbitrator shall pay the amount of the verdict, the arbitrator's expenses and fees, and any other fees assessed by the resolution organization, directly to such resolution organization. In the event of default, the defaulting party shall also pay such moneys due directly to such organization. In the event that both parties default, the parties shall each be responsible for paying such organization one-half of all moneys due. Moneys due under this Code section shall be paid in full to the resolution organization within 15 days of arbitrator's final decision. Within three days of such organization's receipt of moneys due to the party whose final offer was selected, such moneys shall be distributed to such party.

§ 33-20E-17 Referral of parties for violations

Following the resolution of arbitration, the Commissioner may refer the decision of the arbitrator to the appropriate state agency or the governing entity with governing authority over such provider or facility if the Commissioner concludes that a provider or facility has either displayed a pattern of acting in violation of this chapter or has failed to comply with a lawful order of the Commissioner or the arbitrator. Such referral shall include a description of such violations and the Commissioner's recommendation for enforcement action. Such state agency or governing entity shall initiate an investigation regarding such referral within 30 days of receiving such referral and shall conclude the investigation within 90 days of receiving such referral.

§ 33-20E-18 Limitation on litigation when arbitration sought

Once a request for arbitration has been filed with the Commissioner by a provider or facility under this chapter, neither such provider nor such facility nor the insurer in such dispute shall file a lawsuit in court regarding the same out-of-network claim.

§ 33-20E-19 Quarterly reporting by resolution organizations

Each resolution organization contracted with by the department shall report to the department on a quarterly basis the results of all disputes referred to such organization as follows: the number of arbitrations filed, settled, arbitrated, defaulted, or dismissed during the previous calendar year and whether the arbitrators' decisions were in favor of the insurer or the provider or facility.

§ 33-20E-20 Annual reporting by commissioner

On or before July 1, 2022, and each July 1 thereafter, the Commissioner shall provide a written report to the House Committee on Insurance and the Senate Insurance and Labor Committee, or their successor committees, and shall post the report on the department's website summarizing the number of arbitrations filed, settled, arbitrated, defaulted, and dismissed during the previous calendar year; and a description of whether the arbitration decisions were in favor of the insurer or the provider or facility.

§ 33-20E-21 Exclusion from other statutory provisions

The arbitration conducted under this chapter shall be subject to neither Chapter 13 of Title 50, the "Georgia Administrative Procedure Act," nor Chapter 11 of Title 9, the "Georgia Civil Practice Act."

§ 33-20E-22 Reporting to credit reporting agencies

No nonparticipating provider shall report to any credit reporting agency any covered person who receives a surprise bill for the receipt of healthcare services from such provider and does not pay such provider any copay, coinsurance, deductible, or other cost-sharing amount beyond what such covered person would pay if such nonparticipating provider had been a participating provider.

§ 33-20E-23 Financial responsibilities for ground ambulance transportation

Nothing in this chapter shall reduce a covered person's financial responsibilities with regard to ground ambulance transportation.

HAWAII REVISED STATUTES

§ 431:26-104 Requirements for health carriers and participating providers

(a) A health carrier shall establish a mechanism by which participating providers shall be notified on an ongoing basis of the specific covered health care services for which the providers will be responsible, including any limitations or conditions on services.

(b) Every contract between a health carrier and a participating provider shall contain the following hold harmless statement, specifying protection for covered persons, or a substantially similar statement:

Provider agrees that in no event, including but not limited to nonpayment by the health carrier or intermediary, insolvency of the health carrier or intermediary, or breach of this agreement, shall the provider bill, charge, collect a deposit from, seek compensation, remuneration, or reimbursement from, or have any recourse against a covered person or a person other than the health carrier or intermediary, as applicable, acting on behalf of the covered person for services provided pursuant to this agreement. This agreement does not prohibit the provider from collecting coinsurance, deductibles, or copayments, as specifically provided in the evidence of coverage, or fees for uncovered services delivered on a fee-for-service basis to covered persons; provided that a provider shall not bill or collect from a covered person or a person acting on behalf of a covered person any charges for non-covered services or services that do not meet the criteria in section 432E-1.4, Hawaii Revised Statutes, unless an agreement of financial responsibility specific to the service is signed by the covered person or a person acting on behalf of the covered person and is obtained prior to the time services are rendered. This agreement does not prohibit a provider, except for a health care professional who is employed full-time on the staff of a health carrier and has agreed to provide services exclusively to that health carrier's covered persons and no others, and a covered person from agreeing to continue services solely at the expense of the covered person; provided that the provider has clearly informed the covered person that the health carrier may not cover or continue to cover a specific service or services. Except as provided herein, this agreement does not prohibit the provider from pursuing any available legal remedy.

(c) Every contract between a health carrier and a participating provider shall provide that in the event of a health carrier or intermediary insolvency or other cessation of operations, the provider's obligation to deliver covered services to covered persons without balance billing shall continue until the earlier of:

(1) The termination of the covered person's coverage under the network plan, including any extension of coverage provided under the contract

terms or applicable state or federal law for covered persons who are in an active course of treatment or totally disabled; or

(2) The date the contract between the carrier and the provider, including any required extension for covered persons in an active course of treatment, would have terminated if the carrier or intermediary had remained in operation.

(d) Contract provisions required by subsections (b) and (c) shall be construed in favor of the covered person, shall survive the termination of the contract regardless of the reason for termination, including the insolvency of the health carrier, and shall supersede any oral or written contrary agreement between a provider and a covered person or the representative of a covered person if the contrary agreement is inconsistent with the hold harmless and continuation-of-covered services requirements under subsections (b) and (c).

(e) In no event shall a participating provider collect or attempt to collect from a covered person any money owed to the provider by the health carrier.

(f) Selection standards shall be developed pursuant to the following:

(1) Health carrier selection standards for selecting and tiering, as applicable, participating providers shall be developed for providers and each health care professional specialty;

(2) [Effective until July 1, 2024] The standards shall be used in determining the selection of participating providers by the health carrier and the intermediaries with which the health carrier contracts. The standards shall meet requirements relating to health care professional credentialing verification developed by the commissioner by order or through rules adopted pursuant to chapter 91;

(2) [Effective July 1, 2024] The standards shall be used in determining the selection of participating providers by the health carrier and the intermediaries with which the health carrier contracts. The standards shall meet requirements relating to health care professional credentialing verification developed by the commissioner or through rules adopted pursuant to chapter 91;

(3) Selection criteria shall not be established in a manner:

(A) That would allow a health carrier to discriminate against high risk populations by excluding providers because the providers are located in geographic areas that contain populations or providers presenting a risk of higher than average claims, losses, or health care services utilization;

(B) That would exclude providers because the providers treat or specialize in treating populations presenting a risk of higher than average claims, losses, or health care services utilization; or

(C) That would discriminate with respect to participation under the health benefit plan against any provider who is acting within the scope of the provider's license or certification under applicable state law or regulations; provided that this subparagraph shall not be construed to require a health carrier to contract with any provider who is willing to abide by the terms and conditions for participation established by the carrier;

(4) Notwithstanding paragraph (3), a carrier shall not be prohibited from declining to select a provider who fails to meet the other legitimate selection criteria of the carrier developed in compliance with this article; and

(5) This article does not require a health carrier, its intermediaries, or the provider networks with which the carrier and its intermediaries contract, to employ specific providers acting within the scope of the providers' license or certification under applicable state law that may meet the selection criteria of the carrier, or to contract with or retain more providers acting within the scope of the providers' license or certification under applicable state law than are necessary to maintain a sufficient provider network.

(g) A health carrier shall make its standards for selecting participating providers available for review and approval by the commissioner. A description in plain language of the selection standards of the health carrier shall be made available to the public.

(h) A health carrier shall notify participating providers of the providers' responsibilities with respect to the health carrier's applicable administrative policies and programs, including but not limited to:

(1) Payment terms;
(2) Utilization review;
(3) Quality assessment and improvement programs;
(4) Credentialing procedures;
(5) Grievance and appeals procedures;
(6) Data reporting requirements including requirements for timely notice of changes in practice, such as discontinuance of accepting new patients;
(7) Confidentiality requirements; and
(8) Any applicable federal or state programs.

(i) A health carrier shall not offer an inducement to a provider that would encourage or otherwise motivate the provider not to provide medically necessary services to a covered person.

(j) A health carrier shall not prohibit a participating provider from discussing any specific or all treatment options with covered persons irrespective of the health carrier's position on the treatment options, or from advocating on behalf of covered persons within the utilization review or grievance or appeals processes established by the carrier or a person contracting with the carrier or in accordance with any rights or remedies available under applicable state or federal law.

(k) Every contract between a health carrier and a participating provider shall require the provider to make health records available to appropriate state and federal authorities involved in assessing the quality of care or investigating the grievances or complaints of covered persons and to comply with the applicable state and federal laws related to the confidentiality of medical and health records and the covered person's right to see, obtain copies of, or amend the person's medical and health records.

(l) The departure of a provider from a network shall be subject to the following requirements:

(1) A health carrier and participating provider shall provide at least sixty days' written notice to each other before the provider is removed or leaves the network without cause;

(2) The health carrier shall make a good faith effort to provide written notice of a provider's removal or leaving the network within thirty days of receipt or issuance of a notice provided in accordance with paragraph (1) to all covered persons who are patients seen on a regular basis by the provider who is being removed or leaving the network, irrespective of whether the removal or leaving the network is for cause or without cause;

(3) When the provider being removed or leaving the network is a primary care professional, all covered persons who are patients of that primary care professional shall also be notified. When the provider either gives or receives the notice in accordance with paragraph (1), the provider shall supply the health carrier with a list of those patients of the provider that are covered by a plan of the health carrier;

(4) When a provider leaves or is removed from the network, a health carrier shall establish reasonable procedures to transition all covered persons who are in an active course of treatment to a participating provider in a manner that provides for continuity of care;

(5) The health carrier shall provide the notice required under paragraph (1) and shall make available to all covered persons a list of available participating providers in the same geographic area who are of the same provider type and information about how the covered persons may request continuity of care as provided under paragraph (6);

(6) The continuity of care procedures shall provide that:

(A) Any request for continuity of care shall be made to the health carrier by the covered person or the covered person's authorized representative;

(B) Requests for continuity of care shall be reviewed by the health carrier's medical director after consultation with the treating provider for patients who are under the care of a provider who has not been removed or left the network for cause and who meet the criteria specified under the definition of:

(i) Active course of treatment;

(ii) Life-threatening health condition; or

(iii) Serious acute condition;

(C) Any decisions made with respect to a request for continuity of care shall be subject to the health benefit plan's internal and external grievance and appeal processes in accordance with applicable state or federal law or regulations;

(D) The continuity of care period for covered persons who are in their second or third trimester of pregnancy shall extend through the postpartum period; and

(E) The continuity of care period for covered persons who are undergoing an active course of treatment shall extend through the earliest of:

(i) The termination of the course of treatment by the covered person or the treating provider;

(ii) Ninety days, unless the medical director determines that a longer period is necessary;

(iii) The date that care is successfully transitioned to a participating provider;

(iv) The date that benefit limitations under the plan are met or exceeded; or

(v) The date that care is not medically necessary; and

(7) A continuity of care request shall only be granted when:

(A) The provider agrees in writing to accept the same payment from and abide by the same terms and conditions with respect to the health carrier for that patient as provided in the original provider contract; and

(B) The provider agrees in writing not to seek any payment from the covered person for any amount for which the covered person would not have been responsible if the physician or provider were still a participating provider.

(m) The rights and responsibilities under a contract between a health carrier and a participating provider shall not be assigned or delegated by either party without the prior written consent of the other party.

(n) A health carrier shall be responsible for ensuring that a participating provider furnishes covered benefits to all covered persons without regard to the covered person's enrollment in the plan as a private purchaser of the plan or as a participant in publicly financed programs of health care services. This subsection shall not apply to circumstances when the provider should not render services due to limitations arising from lack of training, experience, skill, or licensing restrictions.

(o) A health carrier shall notify participating providers of their obligations, if any, to collect applicable coinsurance, copayments, or deductibles from covered persons pursuant to the evidence of coverage, or of the providers' obligations, if any, to notify covered persons of their personal financial obligations for noncovered services.

(p) A health carrier shall not penalize a provider because the provider, in good faith, reports to state or federal authorities any act or practice by the health carrier that jeopardizes patient health or welfare.

(q) A health carrier shall establish procedures for resolution of administrative, payment, or other disputes between providers and the health carrier.

(r) A contract between a health carrier and a provider shall not contain provisions that conflict with the network plan or this article.

(s) A contract between a health carrier and a provider shall be subject to the following requirements:

(1) At the time the contract is signed, the health carrier and, if appropriate, the intermediary shall timely notify the participating provider of all provisions and other documents incorporated by reference in the contract;

(2) While the contract is in force, the carrier shall timely notify the participating provider of any changes to those provisions or documents that would result in material changes in the contract;

(3) The health carrier shall timely inform the provider of the provider's network participation status on any health benefit plan in which the carrier has included the provider as a participating provider; and

(4) For purposes of this subsection, the contract shall define what is considered timely notice and what is considered a material change.

IDAHO CODE

§ 48-302 Legislative intent

The Idaho legislature finds that medical billing practices have little visibility to Idaho citizens. As a result, consumers often find themselves in collection actions for debts they were unaware of, from health care providers whom they do not recognize. Once in collections, current Idaho law enables excessive attorney's fees and fails to provide judges with clear guidance to combat abuses of the collections process. This chapter shall govern the fair collection of debts owed to health care providers.

§ 48-303 Definitions

For the purposes of this chapter:

(1)

(a) "Consolidated summary of services" means a written notice that contains, at a minimum, the following:

(i) The name and contact information, including telephone number, of the patient;

(ii) The name and contact information, including telephone number, of the health care facility that the patient visited to receive goods or services;

(iii) The date and duration of the visit to the health care facility by the patient;

(iv) A general description of goods and services provided to the patient during the visit to the health care facility, including the name, address, and telephone number of each billing entity whose health care providers provided the services and goods to the patient; and

(v) A clear and conspicuous notification at the top of the notice that states: "This is Not a Bill. This is a Summary of Medical Services You Received. Retain This Summary for Your Records. Please Contact Your Insurance Company and the Health Care Providers Listed on this Summary to Determine the Final Amount You May Be Obligated to Pay."

(b) For the purpose of calculating timeline requirements in this chapter in the event of multiple notices, a "consolidated summary of services" means the notice that first supplied the information required by paragraph (a) of this subsection if such information did not change in any subsequent notices.

(2) "Contested judgment" means a court judgment sought by one (1) party that is challenged by another party through a filing with the court or by presenting evidence or argument at a hearing before the court.

(3)

(a) "Extraordinary collection action" means any of the following actions done in connection with a patient's debt:

(i) Prior to sixty (60) days from the patient's receipt of the final notice before extraordinary collection action, selling, transferring, or assigning any amount of a patient's debt to any third party or otherwise authorizing any third party to collect the debt in a name other than the name of the health care provider;

(ii) Reporting adverse information about the patient to a consumer reporting agency; or

(iii) Except as provided in paragraph (c) of this subsection, commencing any judicial or legal action or filing or recording any document in relation thereto, including but not limited to:

1. Placing a lien on a person's property or assets;
2. Attaching or seizing a person's bank account or any other personal property;
3. Initiating a civil action against any person; or
4. Garnishing an individual's wages.

(b) "Extraordinary collection action" does not include an action pursuant to and in compliance with section 28-22-105, Idaho Code.

(c) A provider authorized to file a lien to secure payment of the reasonable value of services provided to an injured patient pursuant to section 45-701, Idaho Code, is not prevented from filing such a lien by the provisions of this chapter, but must do so pursuant to the timeline and provisions of chapter 7, title 45, Idaho Code.

(4)

(a) "Final notice before extraordinary collection action" means a written notice that contains, at a minimum, the following:

(i) The name and contact information, including telephone number, of the patient;

(ii) The name and contact information, including telephone number, of the health care facility where the health care provider provided goods and services to the patient;

(iii) A list of the goods and services that the health care provider provided to the patient during the patient's visit to the health care facility, including the initial charges for the goods and services and the date the goods and services were provided, in reasonable detail;

(iv) A statement that a full itemized list of goods and services provided to the patient is available upon the patient's request;

(v) The name of the third-party payors to which the charges for health care services were submitted by the health care provider;

(vi) A detailed description of all reductions, adjustments, offsets, and third-party payor payments, including payments already received from the patient, that adjust the initial charges for the goods and services provided to the patient during the visit; and

(vii) The final amount that the patient is liable to pay after taking into account all applicable reductions, including but not limited to the items identified in subparagraph (vi) of this paragraph.

(b) For the purpose of calculating timeline requirements in this chapter in the event of multiple notices, the "final notice before extraordinary collection action" means the notice that first supplied the information required by paragraph (a) of this subsection if such information did not change in any subsequent notices.

(5) "Health care facility" means any person, entity, or institution operating a physical or virtual location that holds itself out to the public as providing health care services through itself, through its employees, or through third-party health care providers. Health care facilities include but are not limited to hospitals and other licensed inpatient centers; ambulatory surgical or treatment centers; skilled nursing centers; residential treatment centers; urgent care centers; diagnostic, laboratory, and imaging centers; and rehabilitation and other therapeutic health settings, as well as medical transportation providers.

(6) "Health care provider" means:

(a) A physician or other health care practitioner licensed, accredited, or certified to perform health care services consistent with state law, or any agent or third-party representative thereof; or

(b) A health care facility or its agent.

(7) "Health care services" means services for the diagnosis, prevention, treatment, cure, or relief of a health condition, illness, injury, or disease.

(8) "Patient" means a person who seeks or receives services from a health care provider. For the purposes of this chapter, "patient" includes a parent if the patient is a minor, a legal guardian if the patient is an adult under guardianship, or any person contractually or otherwise liable for the financial obligations of the person receiving goods or services from the health care provider.

(9) "Third-party payor" means a health carrier as defined in section 41-5903, Idaho Code, or a self-funded plan as defined in section 41-4002 or 41-4102, Idaho Code, and includes multiple third-party payors when applicable.

(10) "Uncontested judgment" means a court judgment sought by one (1) party that is not contested by another party by filing with the court or by presenting evidence or argument at a hearing before the court.

§ 48-304 Requirements for extraordinary collection action

(1) No person shall engage, directly or indirectly, in any extraordinary collection action against a patient unless:

(a) A health care provider submits its charges related to the provision of goods or delivery of services to the third-party payor of the patient, identified by the patient to the health care provider in connection with the services or, in the event no third-party payor was identified, to the patient, which submission of charges in either case shall be within forty-five (45) days from the latest of:

(i) The date of the provision of goods or the delivery of services to the patient;

(ii) The date of discharge of the patient from a health care facility; or

(iii) The first date permitted by the applicable billing code or codes and the applicable policies and procedures in connection with the patient's care in each case as published by the relevant national association;

(b) The patient receives a consolidated summary of services, free of charge, from the health care facility that the patient visited, unless the health care facility is exempted from providing a consolidated summary of services pursuant to section 48-309, Idaho Code, within sixty (60) days from the latest of:

(i) The date of the provision of goods or delivery of services to the patient;

(ii) The date of discharge of the patient from the health care facility; or

(iii) The first date permitted by the applicable billing code or codes and the applicable policies and procedures in connection with the patient's care in each case as published by the relevant national association.

(c) The patient receives, free of charge, a final notice before extraordinary collection action from the billing entity of the health care provider;

(d) The health care provider does not charge or cause to accrue any interest, fees, or other ancillary charges until at least sixty (60) days have passed from the date of receipt of the final notice before extraordinary collection action or the consolidated summary of services, whichever is received later by the patient; and

(e) At least ninety (90) days have passed from receipt of the final notice before extraordinary collection action or the consolidated summary of services, whichever is received later by the patient, and final resolution of all internal reviews, good faith disputes, and appeals of any charges or third-party payor obligations or payments; provided, however, that the ninety (90) days required by this paragraph may be shortened to forty-five (45) days for an extraordinary collection action as defined in section 48-303(3)(a)(ii), Idaho Code, if at least thirty (30) days prior to such action, the patient receives written notice that the health care provider may take an extraordinary collection action as defined in section 48-303(3)(a)(ii), Idaho Code, and that, as a consequence of taking such action, the health care provider will be prohibited from taking any extraordinary collection action as defined in section 48-303(3)(a)(iii), Idaho Code.

(2) Any person taking an extraordinary collection action as defined in section 48-303(3)(a)(ii), Idaho Code, prior to ninety (90) days from the patient's receipt of the final notice before extraordinary collection action shall be prohibited from pursuing an extraordinary collection action as defined in section 48-303(3)(a)(iii), Idaho Code.

(3) No person shall engage, directly or indirectly, in any type of extraordinary collection action against a patient unless the final notice before extraordinary collection action includes both the name of the third-party payor to which the health care provider submitted charges related to the provision of goods or delivery of services to the patient and the patient's group number and last four (4) digits of the patient's membership number; provided, however, such requirement does not apply if the health care provider has submitted all charges in connection with the patient's care to the patient's correct third-party payor. Nothing in this subsection shall be construed to exempt a person from the requirements of subsection (1) of this section or section 48-306, Idaho Code.

§ 48-305 Fees and costs for extraordinary collection action

(1) Notwithstanding any provision of law or agreement to the contrary, a patient shall have no liability to any party taking extraordinary collection action for costs, expenses, and fees, including attorney's fees, unless the party has complied with section 48-304, Idaho Code, and then subject to the following limitations:

(a) In the case of an uncontested judgment against the patient, the court may award, in addition to the outstanding principal, up to three hundred fifty dollars ($350) or an amount equal to one hundred percent (100%) of the outstanding principal amount, whichever is less, plus any prejudgment interest accrued in accordance with section 48-304(1)(d), Idaho Code, and any postjudgment interest awarded by the court;

(b) In the case of a contested judgment against the patient, the court may award, in addition to the outstanding principal, up to seven hundred fifty dollars ($750) or an amount equal to one hundred percent (100%) of the outstanding principal amount, whichever is less, plus any prejudgment interest accrued in accordance with section 48-304(1)(d), Idaho Code, and any postjudgment interest awarded by the court;

(c) In the case of postjudgment motions and writs, the court may award up to seventy-five dollars ($75.00) for any successful motion or application for a writ of attachment to any particular garnishee and twenty-five dollars ($25.00) for any subsequent application for a writ to the same garnishee. In the case of garnishments, the court may also award service fees as prescribed by the applicable board of county commissioners pursuant to section 11-729, Idaho Code.

(2) In the case of a contested judgment, if a party taking extraordinary collection action against a patient prevails against a patient and incurs costs, expenses, and fees, including attorney's fees, that are grossly disproportionate to the award amounts set forth in subsection (1)(b) of this section, then the party may petition the court for a supplemental award for costs, expenses, and fees. Upon an affirmative showing that the incurred costs, expenses, and fees are grossly disproportionate to the award amounts set forth in subsection (1)(b) of this section, and that fees were incurred because of the patient's willful attempt to avoid paying a bona fide debt, then the court may take into account the factors outlined in rule 54(e)(3) of the Idaho rules of civil procedure and may, in its discretion, award supplemental costs, expenses, and reasonable attorney's fees.

(3) Notwithstanding any provision of law or agreement to the contrary, if a patient in a contested judgment is a prevailing party, then the patient shall be entitled to recover from a nonprevailing party all costs, expenses, and fees, including attorney's fees, incurred by the patient in contesting the action, and the patient shall have no liability to any nonprevailing parties for any costs, expenses, and fees, including attorney's fees and prejudgment interest incurred by a nonprevailing party.

§ 48-306 Extraordinary collection after untimely notice—limitation

If a party is unable to engage in an extraordinary collection action because the health care provider or health care facility failed to meet the timing requirements of section 48-304(1)(a) or (b), Idaho Code, but complies with such timing requirements within either an additional forty-five (45) days for failure to meet the timing requirements of section 48-304(1)(a), Idaho Code, or an additional one hundred eighty (180) days for failure to meet the timing requirements of section 48-304(1)(b), Idaho Code, then as long as all other requirements of section 48-304, Idaho Code, have been satisfied, such party may commence an extraordinary collection action. Notwithstanding any provision of law or agreement to the contrary, in any such collection action, the patient shall have no liability for costs, expenses, and fees, including attorney's fees.

§ 48-307 Burden of proof

Any person seeking to engage in an extraordinary collection action bears the burden of establishing that the requirements of sections 48-304 and 48-306, Idaho Code, if applicable, have been satisfied prior to engaging in any extraordinary collection action. Any party commencing a judicial action against a patient must plead with particularity its compliance with each requirement of sections 48-304 and 48-306, Idaho Code, as the case may be, and must specifically identify the name, group, and policy numbers of the third-party payor to which the health care provider submitted the charges in connection with the provision of goods or delivery of services, along with the date of each submission.

§ 48-308 Rebuttable presumption of receipt

A patient shall be presumed to have received a consolidated summary of services or a final notice before extraordinary collection action three (3) days after the document has been sent by first class mail to the patient's address confirmed by the patient during the patient's last visit to the health care provider or as updated by the patient in subsequent written or electronic communications. Nothing in this section shall be interpreted as precluding the patient from agreeing in writing to receive consolidated summaries of services or final notices before extraordinary collection action via email or other electronic means.

§ 48-309 Delivery of consolidated summary of services

Notwithstanding any provision of law to the contrary in this chapter, a health care facility is not required to send a consolidated summary of services to a patient prior to engaging in extraordinary collection action if:

(1) The patient will receive a final notice before extraordinary collection action from a single billing entity for all goods and services provided to the patient at that health care facility;
(2) The patient was clearly informed in writing of the name, phone number, and address of the billing entity; and
(3) The health care facility otherwise complies with all other provisions of section 48-304, Idaho Code.

§ 48-310 Contracted service

Nothing in this chapter prohibits a health care facility from authorizing a health care provider by contract to provide the consolidated summary of services required by section 48-304(1)(b), Idaho Code, on its behalf.

§ 48-311 Enforcement and civil penalties

If any party takes any extraordinary collection action other than in accordance with section 48-304 or 48-306, Idaho Code, then:

(1) Notwithstanding any provision of law or agreement to the contrary, a patient shall have no liability to any party for any collection costs, expenses, and fees, including attorney's fees and prejudgment and postjudgment interest;
(2) The party is liable to the patient in an amount equal to any actual damages sustained by the patient as a result of any failure to comply, or one thousand dollars ($1,000), whichever is greater; and
(3) Where a court finds a party has willfully or knowingly violated section 48-304 or 48-306, Idaho Code, the court may award up to three (3) times the amount

of actual damages, or three thousand dollars ($3,000), whichever is greater. In any successful action to enforce the liability set forth in this section, the patient shall be entitled to the costs of the action, together with reasonable attorney's fees, as determined by the court.

§ 48-312 Non-extraordinary collection actions

Nothing in this chapter shall be interpreted to restrict the ability of any person to demand and collect payment for the principal amount of any medical goods or services by means other than extraordinary collection action, as defined in section 48-303, Idaho Code.

§ 72-102 Definitions

Words and terms used in the worker's compensation law, unless the context otherwise requires, are defined in the subsections which follow:

(1) "Alien" means a person who is not a citizen, a national or a resident of the United States or Canada. Any person not a citizen or national of the United States who relinquishes or is about to relinquish his residence in the United States shall be regarded as an alien.

(2) "Balance billing" means charging, billing, or otherwise attempting to collect directly from an injured employee payment for medical services in excess of amounts allowable in compensable claims as provided by rules promulgated by the commission pursuant to section 72-508, Idaho Code.

(3) "Beneficiary" means any person who is entitled to income benefits or medical and related benefits under this law.

(4) "Commission" means the industrial commission.

(5) "Community service worker" means:

    (a) Any person who has been convicted of a criminal offense, any juvenile who has been found to be within the purview of chapter 5, title 20, Idaho Code, and who has been informally diverted under the provisions of section 20-511, Idaho Code, or any person or youth who has been diverted from the criminal or juvenile justice system and who performs a public service for any department, institution, office, college, university, authority, division, board, bureau, commission, council, or other entity of the state, or any city, county, school district, irrigation district or other taxing district authorized to levy a tax or an assessment or any other political subdivision or any private not-for-profit agency which has elected worker's compensation insurance coverage for such person; or

    (b) Parolees under department of correction supervision, probationers under court order or department of correction supervision and offender residents of community work centers under the direction or order of the board of correction who are performing public service or community service work for any of the entities specified in paragraph (a) of this subsection other than the department of correction.

(6) "Compensation" used collectively means any or all of the income benefits and the medical and related benefits and medical services.

(7) "Custom farmer" means a person who contracts to supply operated equipment to a proprietor of a farm for the purpose of performing part or all of the activities related to raising or harvesting agricultural or horticultural commodities.

(8) "Death" means death resulting from an injury or occupational disease.

(9) Dependency limitations.

(a) "Adopted" and "adoption" include cases where persons are treated as adopted as well as those of legal adoption unless legal adoption is specifically provided.

(b) "Brother" and "sister" include stepbrothers and stepsisters, half brothers and half sisters, and brothers and sisters by adoption.

(c) "Child" includes adopted children, posthumous children, and acknowledged illegitimate children, but does not include stepchildren unless actually dependent.

(d) "Grandchild" includes children of legally adopted children and children of stepchildren, but does not include stepchildren of children, stepchildren of stepchildren, or stepchildren of adopted children unless actually dependent.

(e) "Parent" includes stepparents and parents by adoption.

(f) "Grandparent" includes parents of parents by adoption, but does not include parents of stepparents, stepparents of parents, or stepparents of stepparents.

(10) "Disability," for purposes of determining total or partial temporary disability income benefits, means a decrease in wage-earning capacity due to injury or occupational disease, as such capacity is affected by the medical factor of physical impairment, and by pertinent nonmedical factors as provided in section 72-430, Idaho Code.

(11) "Employee" is synonymous with "workman" and means any person who has entered into the employment of, or who works under contract of service or apprenticeship with, an employer. It does not include any person engaged in any of the excepted employments enumerated in section 72-212, Idaho Code, unless an election as provided in section 72-213, Idaho Code, has been filed. It does, however, include a volunteer firefighter for purposes of section 72-438(12) and (14), Idaho Code. Any reference to an employee who has been injured shall, where the employee is dead, include a reference to his dependents as herein defined, if the context so requires, or, where the employee is a minor or incompetent, to his committee or guardian or next friend.

(12)
- (a) "Employer" means any person who has expressly or impliedly hired or contracted the services of another. It includes contractors and subcontractors. It includes the owner or lessee of premises, or other person who is virtually the proprietor or operator of the business there carried on, but who, by reason of there being an independent contractor or for any other reason, is not the direct employer of the workers there employed. It also includes, for purposes of section 72-438(12) and (14), Idaho Code, a municipality, village, county or fire district that utilizes the services of volunteer firefighters. If the employer is secured, it means his surety so far as applicable.
- (b) "Professional employer" means a professional employer as defined in chapter 24, title 44, Idaho Code.
- (c) "Temporary employer" means the employer of temporary employees as defined in section 44-2403(7), Idaho Code.
- (d) "Work site employer" means the client of the temporary or professional employer with whom a worker has been placed.

(13) "Farm labor contractor" means any person or his agent or subcontractor who, for a fee, recruits and employs farmworkers and performs any farm labor contracting activity.

(14) "Gender and number." The masculine gender includes the feminine and neuter; "husband" or "wife" includes "spouse"; the singular number includes plural and the plural the singular.

(15) "Income benefits" means payments provided for or made under the provisions of this law to the injured employee disabled by an injury or occupational disease, or his dependents in case of death, excluding medical and related benefits.

(16) "Independent contractor" means any person who renders service for a specified recompense for a specified result, under the right to control or actual control of his principal as to the result of his work only and not as to the means by which such result is accomplished. For the purposes of worker's compensation law, a custom farmer is considered to be an independent contractor.

(17) "Injury" and "accident."
- (a) "Injury" means a personal injury caused by an accident arising out of and in the course of any employment covered by the worker's compensation law.
- (b) "Accident" means an unexpected, undesigned, and unlooked for mishap, or untoward event, connected with the industry in which it occurs, and which can be reasonably located as to time when and place where it occurred, causing an injury.
- (c) "Injury" and "personal injury" shall be construed to include only an injury caused by an accident, which results in violence to the physical structure of the body. The terms shall in no case be construed to include

an occupational disease and only such nonoccupational diseases as result directly from an injury.

(18) "Manifestation" means the time when an employee knows that he has an occupational disease, or whenever a qualified physician shall inform the injured worker that he has an occupational disease.

(19) "Medical and related benefits" means payments provided for or made for medical, hospital, burial and other services as provided in this law other than income benefits.

(20) "Medical services" means medical, surgical, dental or other attendance or treatment, nurse and hospital service, medicines, apparatus, appliances, prostheses, and related services, facilities and supplies.

(21) "Occupational diseases."

(a) "Occupational disease" means a disease due to the nature of an employment in which the hazards of such disease actually exist, are characteristic of, and peculiar to the trade, occupation, process, or employment, but shall not include psychological injuries, disorders or conditions unless the conditions set forth in section 72-451, Idaho Code, are met.

(b) "Contracted" and "incurred," when referring to an occupational disease, shall be deemed the equivalent of the term "arising out of and in the course of" employment.

(c) "Disablement," except in the case of silicosis, means the event of an employee's becoming actually and totally incapacitated because of an occupational disease from performing his work in the last occupation in which injuriously exposed to the hazards of such disease; and "disability" means the state of being so incapacitated.

(d) "Disablement," in the case of silicosis, means the event of first becoming actually incapacitated, because of such disease, from performing any work in any remunerative employment; and "disability" means the state of being so incapacitated.

(e) "Silicosis" means the characteristic fibrotic condition of the lungs caused by the inhalation of silicon dioxide (SiO_2) dust.

(22) "Outworker" means a person to whom articles or materials are furnished to be treated in any way on premises not under the control or management of the person who furnished them.

(23) "Person" means the state or any political subdivision thereof, or any individual, partnership, firm, association, trust, corporation, including the state insurance fund, or any representative thereof.

(24) "Physician" means medical physicians and surgeons, ophthalmologists, otorhinolaryngologists, dentists, osteopaths, osteopathic physicians and surgeons, optometrists, podiatrists, chiropractic physicians, and members of any other healing profession licensed or authorized by the statutes of this state to practice such profession within the scope of their practice as defined by the statutes of this state and as authorized by their licenses.

(25) "Provider" means any person, firm, corporation, partnership, association, agency, institution, or other legal entity providing any kind of medical services related to the treatment of an injured employee which are compensable under Idaho's worker's compensation law.

(26) "Secretary" means the secretary of the commission.

(27) "Self-insurer" means an employer who has been authorized under the provisions of this law to carry his own liability to his employees covered by this law.

(28) "State" includes any state, district, commonwealth, zone or territory of the United States or any province of Canada.

(29) "Surety" means any insurer authorized to insure or guarantee payment of worker's compensation liability of employers in any state; it also includes the state insurance fund, a self-insurer and an inter-insurance exchange.

(30) "United States," when used in a geographic sense, means the several states, the District of Columbia, the Commonwealth of Puerto Rico and the territories of the United States.

(31) "Volunteer emergency responder" means a firefighter or peace officer, or publicly employed certified personnel who is a bona fide member of a legally organized law enforcement agency, a legally organized fire department or a licensed emergency medical service provider organization who contributes services.

(32) "Wages" and "wage-earning capacity" prior to the injury or disablement from occupational disease mean the employee's money payments for services as calculated under section 72-419, Idaho Code, and shall additionally include the reasonable market value of board, rent, housing, lodging, fuel, and other advantages which can be estimated in money which the employee receives from the employer as part of his remuneration, and gratuities received in the course of employment from others than the employer. "Wages" shall not include sums which the employer has paid to the employee to cover any special expenses entailed on him by the nature of his employment.

(33) "Wages" and "wage-earning capacity" after the injury or disablement from occupational disease shall be presumed to be the actual earnings after the injury or disablement, which presumption may be overcome by showing that those earnings do not fairly and reasonably represent wage-earning capacity; in such a case, wage-earning capacity shall be determined in the light of all factors and circumstances which may affect the worker's capacity to earn wages.

(34) "Work experience student" means any person enrolled in the public school districts or public institutions of higher education of this state and who, as part of his instruction, is enrolled in a class or program for academic credit and for which the student is employed by, or works for, a private or governmental entity. The student need not receive wages from the private or governmental entity in order to be classified as a work experience student.

(35) "Worker's compensation law" or "workmen's compensation law" means and includes the worker's compensation law of this state and any like or similar law of any state, United States, territory, or province of Canada.

§ 72-432 Medical services, appliances and supplies—reports

(1) Subject to the provisions of section 72-706, Idaho Code, the employer shall provide for an injured employee such reasonable medical, surgical or other attendance or treatment, nurse and hospital services, medicines, crutches and apparatus, as may be reasonably required by the employee's physician or needed immediately after an injury or manifestation of an occupational disease, and for a reasonable time thereafter. If the employer fails to provide the same, the injured employee may do so at the expense of the employer.

(2) The employer shall also furnish necessary replacements or repairs of appliances and prostheses, unless the need therefor is due to lack of proper care by the employee. If the appliance or prosthesis is damaged or destroyed in an industrial accident, the employer, for whom the employee was working at the time of accident, will be liable for replacement or repair, but not for any subsequent replacement or repair not directly resulting from the accident.

(3) In addition to the income benefits otherwise payable, the employee who is entitled to income benefits shall be paid an additional sum in an amount as may be determined by the commission as by it deemed necessary, as a medical service, when the constant service of an attendant is necessary by reason of total blindness of the employee or the loss of both hands or both feet or the loss of use thereof, or by reason of being paralyzed and unable to walk, or by reason of other disability resulting from the injury or disease actually rendering him so helpless as to require constant attendance. The commission shall have authority to determine the necessity, character and sufficiency of any medical services furnished or to be furnished and shall have authority to order a change of physician, hospital or rehabilitation facility when in its judgment such change is desirable or necessary.

(4)

(a) The employee upon reasonable grounds, may petition the commission for a change of physician to be provided by the employer; however, the employee must give written notice to the employer or surety of the employee's request for a change of physicians to afford the employer the opportunity to fulfill its obligations under this section. If proper notice is not given, the employer shall not be obligated to pay for the services obtained. Nothing in this section shall limit the attending physician from arranging for consultation, referral or specialized care without permission of the employer. Upon receiving such written notice, the employer shall render its written decision on the claimant's request within fourteen (14) days. If any dispute arises over the issue of a request for change of physician, the industrial commission shall conduct an expedited hearing to determine whether or not the request for change of physician should be granted, and shall render a decision within fourteen (14) days after the filing of the response by the employer.

(b) The industrial commission shall, no later than December 31, 1997, promulgate a rule for the expeditious handling of a petition for change of physician pursuant to this section. Nothing herein shall prevent the commission from making periodic amendments, as may become necessary, to any rule for a petition for change of physician.

(5) Any employee who seeks medical care in a manner not provided for in this section, or as ordered by the industrial commission pursuant to this section, shall not be entitled to reimbursement for costs of such care.

(6) No provider shall engage in balance billing as defined in section 72-102, Idaho Code.

(7) An employee shall not be responsible for charges of physicians, hospitals or other providers of medical services to whom he has been referred for treatment of his injury or occupational disease by an employer designated physician or by the commission, except for charges for personal items or extended services which the employee has requested for his convenience and which are not required for treatment of his injury or occupational disease.

(8) The employer or surety shall not be subject to tort liability to any health care provider for complying with the provisions of this law.

(9) Nothing in this chapter shall be construed to require a workman who in good faith relies on Christian Science treatment by a duly accredited Christian Science practitioner to undergo any medical or surgical treatment, providing that neither he nor his dependents shall be entitled to income benefits of any kind beyond those reasonably expected to have been paid had he undergone medical or surgical treatment, and the employer or insurance carrier may pay for such spiritual treatment.

(10) The commission shall promulgate rules requiring physicians and other practitioners providing treatment to make regular reports to the commission containing such information as may be required by the commission. The commission shall promulgate such rules with the counsel, advice, cooperation and expertise of representatives of industry, labor, sureties and the legal and medical professions as well as institutions, hospitals and clinics having physical rehabilitation facilities.

(11) All medical information relevant to or bearing upon a particular injury or occupational disease shall be provided to the employer, surety, manager of the industrial special indemnity fund, or their attorneys or authorized representatives, the claimant, the claimant's attorneys or authorized representatives, or the commission without liability on the part of the physician, hospital or other provider of medical services and information developed in connection with treatment or examination for an injury or disease for which compensation is sought shall not be privileged communication. When a physician or hospital

willfully fails to make a report required under this section, after written notice by the commission that such report is due, the commission may order forfeiture of all or part of payments due for services rendered in connection with the particular case. An attorney representing the employer, surety, claimant or industrial special indemnity fund shall have the right to confer with any health care provider without the presence of the opposing attorney, representative or party, except for a health care provider who is retained only as an expert witness.

(12) Physicians or others providing services under this section shall assist in the rehabilitation program provided in section 72-501A, Idaho Code. They shall cooperate with specialists from the commission's rehabilitation staff and with employer rehabilitation personnel in furthering the physical or vocational rehabilitation of the employee. The extension of total temporary disability benefits during retraining as authorized by section 72-450, Idaho Code, shall be the responsibility of the commission, however, the physician shall inform the commission as soon as it is medically apparent that the employee may be unable to return to the job in which he sustained injury or occupational disease following treatment and maximum recovery.

(13) An injured employee shall be reimbursed for his expenses of necessary travel in obtaining medical care under this section. Reimbursement for transportation expenses, if the employee utilizes a private vehicle, shall be at the mileage rate allowed by the state board of examiners for state employees; provided however, that the employee shall not be reimbursed for the first fifteen (15) miles of any round trip, nor for traveling any round trip of fifteen (15) miles or less. Such distance shall be calculated by the shortest practical route of travel.

(14) An employee who leaves the locality where employed at the time of the industrial accident, or manifestation of an occupational disease, or the locality in which the employee is currently receiving medical treatment for the injury, shall give timely notice to the employer and surety of the employee's leaving the locality. The employer or surety may require the claimant to report to the treating physician for examination prior to leaving the locality, if practical. If an examination by the treating physician is not practical prior to leaving the locality, the employer or surety may assist in arranging an examination by an appropriate physician in the new locality. After receiving notice of relocation, the employer or surety shall have the same responsibility to furnish care as set forth in subsection (1) of this section.

ILLINOIS COMPILED STATUTES

210 ILCS 88/50 Notification concerning out-of-network providers

During the admission or as soon as practicable thereafter, the hospital must provide an insured patient with written notice that:

(1) the patient may receive separate bills for services provided by health care professionals affiliated with the hospital;
(2) if applicable, some hospital staff members may not be participating providers in the same insurance plans and networks as the hospital;
(3) if applicable, the patient may have a greater financial responsibility for services provided by health care professionals at the hospital who are not under contract with the patient's health care plan; and
(4) questions about coverage or benefit levels should be directed to the patient's health care plan and the patient's certificate of coverage.

215 ILCS 5/356z.3 Disclosure of limited benefit

An insurer that issues, delivers, amends, or renews an individual or group policy of accident and health insurance in this State after the effective date of this amendatory Act of the 92nd General Assembly and arranges, contracts with, or administers contracts with a provider whereby beneficiaries are provided an incentive to use the services of such provider must include the following disclosure on its contracts and evidences of coverage: "WARNING, LIMITED BENEFITS WILL BE PAID WHEN NON-PARTICIPATING PROVIDERS ARE USED. You should be aware that when you elect to utilize the services of a non-participating provider for a covered service in non-emergency situations, benefit payments to such non-participating provider are not based upon the amount billed. The basis of your benefit payment will be determined according to your policy's fee schedule, usual and customary charge (which is determined by comparing charges for similar services adjusted to the geographical area where the services are performed), or other method as defined by the policy. YOU CAN EXPECT TO PAY MORE THAN THE COINSURANCE AMOUNT DEFINED IN THE POLICY AFTER THE PLAN HAS PAID ITS REQUIRED PORTION. Non-participating providers may bill members for any amount up to the billed charge after the plan has paid its portion of the bill, except as provided in Section 356z.3a of the Illinois Insurance Code [215 ILCS 5/356z.3a] for covered services received at a participating health care facility from a nonparticipating provider that are: (a) ancillary services, (b) items or services furnished as a result of unforeseen, urgent medical needs that arise at the time the item or service is furnished, or (c) items or services received when the facility or the non-participating provider fails to satisfy the notice and consent criteria specified under Section 356z.3a. Participating providers have agreed to accept discounted payments for services with no additional billing to the member other than co-insurance and deductible amounts. You may obtain further information about the participating status of professional providers and information on out-of-pocket expenses by calling the toll free telephone number on your identification card."

215 ILCS 5/356z.3a Billing; emergency services; nonparticipating providers

(a) As used in this Section:

"Ancillary services" means:

(1) items and services related to emergency medicine, anesthesiology, pathology, radiology, and neonatology that are provided by any health care provider;
(2) items and services provided by assistant surgeons, hospitalists, and intensivists;
(3) diagnostic services, including radiology and laboratory services, except for advanced diagnostic laboratory tests identified on the most current list published by the United States Secretary of Health and Human Services under 42 U.S.C. 300gg-132(b)(3);
(4) items and services provided by other specialty practitioners as the United States Secretary of Health and Human Services specifies through rulemaking under 42 U.S.C. 300gg-132(b)(3);
(5) items and services provided by a nonparticipating provider if there is no participating provider who can furnish the item or service at the facility; and
(6) items and services provided by a nonparticipating provider if there is no participating provider who will furnish the item or service because a participating provider has asserted the participating provider's rights under the Health Care Right of Conscience Act [745 ILCS 70/1 et seq.].

"Cost sharing" means the amount an insured, beneficiary, or enrollee is responsible for paying for a covered item or service under the terms of the policy or certificate. "Cost sharing" includes copayments, coinsurance, and amounts paid toward deductibles, but does not include amounts paid towards premiums, balance billing by out-of-network providers, or the cost of items or services that are not covered under the policy or certificate.

"Emergency department of a hospital" means any hospital department that provides emergency services, including a hospital outpatient department.

"Emergency medical condition" has the meaning ascribed to that term in Section 10 of the Managed Care Reform and Patient Rights Act [215 ILCS 134/10].

"Emergency medical screening examination" has the meaning ascribed to that term in Section 10 of the Managed Care Reform and Patient Rights Act.

"Emergency services" means, with respect to an emergency medical condition:

(1) in general, an emergency medical screening examination, including ancillary services routinely available to the emergency department to evaluate such emergency medical condition, and such further medical examination and treatment as would be required to stabilize the patient regardless of the department of the hospital or other facility in which such further examination or treatment is furnished; or

(2) additional items and services for which benefits are provided or covered under the coverage and that are furnished by a nonparticipating provider or nonparticipating emergency facility regardless of the department of the hospital or other facility in which such items are furnished after the insured, beneficiary, or enrollee is stabilized and as part of outpatient observation or an inpatient or outpatient stay with respect to the visit in which the services described in paragraph (1) are furnished. Services after stabilization cease to be emergency services only when all the conditions of 42 U.S.C. 300gg-111(a)(3)(C)(ii)(II) and regulations thereunder are met.

"Freestanding Emergency Center" means a facility licensed under Section 32.5 of the Emergency Medical Services (EMS) Systems Act [210 ILCS 50/32.5].

"Health care facility" means, in the context of non-emergency services, any of the following:

(1) a hospital as defined in 42 U.S.C. 1395x(e);

(2) a hospital outpatient department;

(3) a critical access hospital certified under 42 U.S.C. 1395i-4(e);

(4) an ambulatory surgical treatment center as defined in the Ambulatory Surgical Treatment Center Act [210 ILCS 5/1 et seq.]; or

(5) any recipient of a license under the Hospital Licensing Act [210 ILCS 85/1 et seq.] that is not otherwise described in this definition.

"Health care provider" means a provider as defined in subsection (d) of Section 370g. "Health care provider" does not include a provider of air ambulance or ground ambulance services.

"Health care services" has the meaning ascribed to that term in subsection (a) of Section 370g [215 ILCS 5/370g].

"Health insurance issuer" has the meaning ascribed to that term in Section 5 of the Illinois Health Insurance Portability and Accountability Act [215 ILCS 97/5].

"Nonparticipating emergency facility" means, with respect to the furnishing of an item or service under a policy of group or individual health insurance coverage, any of the following facilities that does not have a contractual relationship directly or indirectly with a health insurance issuer in relation to the coverage:

(1) an emergency department of a hospital;
(2) a Freestanding Emergency Center;
(3) an ambulatory surgical treatment center as defined in the Ambulatory Surgical Treatment Center Act; or
(4) with respect to emergency services described in paragraph (2) of the definition of "emergency services", a hospital.

"Nonparticipating provider" means, with respect to the furnishing of an item or service under a policy of group or individual health insurance coverage, any health care provider who does not have a contractual relationship directly or indirectly with a health insurance issuer in relation to the coverage.

"Participating emergency facility" means any of the following facilities that has a contractual relationship directly or indirectly with a health insurance issuer offering group or individual health insurance coverage setting forth the terms and conditions on which a relevant health care service is provided to an insured, beneficiary, or enrollee under the coverage:

(1) an emergency department of a hospital;
(2) a Freestanding Emergency Center;
(3) an ambulatory surgical treatment center as defined in the Ambulatory Surgical Treatment Center Act; or
(4) with respect to emergency services described in paragraph (2) of the definition of "emergency services", a hospital.

For purposes of this definition, a single case agreement between an emergency facility and an issuer that is used to address unique situations in which an insured, beneficiary, or enrollee requires services that typically occur out-of-network constitutes a contractual relationship and is limited to the parties to the agreement.

"Participating health care facility" means any health care facility that has a contractual relationship directly or indirectly with a health insurance issuer offering group or individual health insurance coverage setting forth the terms and conditions on which a relevant health care service is provided to an insured, beneficiary, or enrollee under the coverage. A single case agreement between an emergency facility and an issuer that is used to address unique situations in which an insured, beneficiary, or enrollee requires services that typically occur out-of-network constitutes a contractual relationship for purposes of this definition and is limited to the parties to the agreement.

"Participating provider" means any health care provider that has a contractual relationship directly or indirectly with a health insurance issuer offering group or individual health insurance coverage setting forth the terms and conditions on which a relevant health care service is provided to an insured, beneficiary, or enrollee under the coverage.

"Qualifying payment amount" has the meaning given to that term in 42 U.S.C. 300gg-111(a)(3)(E) and the regulations promulgated thereunder.

"Recognized amount" means the lesser of the amount initially billed by the provider or the qualifying payment amount.

"Stabilize" means "stabilization" as defined in Section 10 of the Managed Care Reform and Patient Rights Act [215 ILCS 134/10].

"Treating provider" means a health care provider who has evaluated the individual.

"Visit" means, with respect to health care services furnished to an individual at a health care facility, health care services furnished by a provider at the facility, as well as equipment, devices, telehealth services, imaging services, laboratory services, and preoperative and postoperative services regardless of whether the provider furnishing such services is at the facility.

(b) Emergency services. When a beneficiary, insured, or enrollee receives emergency services from a nonparticipating provider or a nonparticipating emergency facility, the health insurance issuer shall ensure that the beneficiary, insured, or enrollee shall incur no greater out-of-pocket costs than the beneficiary, insured, or enrollee would have incurred with a participating provider or a participating emergency facility. Any cost-sharing requirements shall be applied as though the emergency services had been received from a participating provider or a participating facility. Cost sharing shall be calculated based on the recognized amount for the emergency services. If the cost sharing for the same item or service furnished by a participating provider would have been a flat-dollar copayment, that amount shall be the cost-sharing amount unless the provider has billed a lesser total amount. In no event shall the beneficiary, insured, enrollee, or any group policyholder or plan sponsor be liable to or billed by the health insurance issuer, the nonparticipating provider, or the nonparticipating emergency facility for any amount beyond the cost sharing calculated in accordance with this subsection with respect to the emergency services delivered. Administrative requirements or limitations shall be no greater than those applicable to emergency services received from a participating provider or a participating emergency facility.

(b-5) Non-emergency services at participating health care facilities.

(1) When a beneficiary, insured, or enrollee utilizes a participating health care facility and, due to any reason, covered ancillary services are provided by a nonparticipating provider during or resulting from the visit, the health insurance issuer shall ensure that the beneficiary, insured, or enrollee shall incur no greater out-of-pocket costs than the beneficiary, insured, or enrollee would have incurred with a participating provider for the ancillary services. Any cost-sharing requirements shall be applied as though the ancillary services had been received from a participating

provider. Cost sharing shall be calculated based on the recognized amount for the ancillary services. If the cost sharing for the same item or service furnished by a participating provider would have been a flat-dollar copayment, that amount shall be the cost-sharing amount unless the provider has billed a lesser total amount. In no event shall the beneficiary, insured, enrollee, or any group policyholder or plan sponsor be liable to or billed by the health insurance issuer, the non-participating provider, or the participating health care facility for any amount beyond the cost sharing calculated in accordance with this subsection with respect to the ancillary services delivered. In addition to ancillary services, the requirements of this paragraph shall also apply with respect to covered items or services furnished as a result of unforeseen, urgent medical needs that arise at the time an item or service is furnished, regardless of whether the nonparticipating provider satisfied the notice and consent criteria under paragraph (2) of this subsection.

(2) When a beneficiary, insured, or enrollee utilizes a participating health care facility and receives non-emergency covered health care services other than those described in paragraph (1) of this subsection from a nonparticipating provider during or resulting from the visit, the health insurance issuer shall ensure that the beneficiary, insured, or enrollee incurs no greater out-of-pocket costs than the beneficiary, insured, or enrollee would have incurred with a participating provider unless the nonparticipating provider or the participating health care facility on behalf of the nonparticipating provider satisfies the notice and consent criteria provided in 42 U.S.C. 300gg-132 and regulations promulgated thereunder. If the notice and consent criteria are not satisfied, then:

(A) any cost-sharing requirements shall be applied as though the health care services had been received from a participating provider;

(B) cost sharing shall be calculated based on the recognized amount for the health care services; and

(C) in no event shall the beneficiary, insured, enrollee, or any group policyholder or plan sponsor be liable to or billed by the health insurance issuer, the nonparticipating provider, or the participating health care facility for any amount beyond the cost sharing calculated in accordance with this subsection with respect to the health care services delivered.

(c) Notwithstanding any other provision of this Code, except when the notice and consent criteria are satisfied for the situation in paragraph (2) of subsection (b-5), any benefits a beneficiary, insured, or enrollee receives for services under the situations in subsection (b) or (b-5) are assigned to the nonparticipating providers or the facility acting on their behalf. Upon receipt of the provider's bill or facility's bill, the health insurance issuer shall provide the nonparticipating provider or the facility with a written explanation of benefits that specifies the proposed reimbursement and the applicable deductible, copayment, or coinsurance amounts owed by the insured, beneficiary, or enrollee. The health insurance issuer shall pay any reimbursement subject to this Section directly to the nonparticipating provider or the facility.

(d) For bills assigned under subsection (c), the nonparticipating provider or the facility may bill the health insurance issuer for the services rendered, and the health insurance issuer may pay the billed amount or attempt to negotiate reimbursement with the nonparticipating provider or the facility. Within 30 calendar days after the provider or facility transmits the bill to the health insurance issuer, the issuer shall send an initial payment or notice of denial of payment with the written explanation of benefits to the provider or facility. If attempts to negotiate reimbursement for services provided by a nonparticipating provider do not result in a resolution of the payment dispute within 30 days after receipt of written explanation of benefits by the health insurance issuer, then the health insurance issuer or nonparticipating provider or the facility may initiate binding arbitration to determine payment for services provided on a per-bill or batched-bill basis, in accordance with Section 300gg-111 of the Public Health Service Act (42 U.S.C. 300 gg-91) and the regulations promulgated thereunder. The party requesting arbitration shall notify the other party arbitration has been initiated and state its final offer before arbitration. In response to this notice, the nonrequesting party shall inform the requesting party of its final offer before the arbitration occurs. Arbitration shall be initiated by filing a request with the Department of Insurance.

(e) The Department of Insurance shall publish a list of approved arbitrators or entities that shall provide binding arbitration. These arbitrators shall be American Arbitration Association or American Health Lawyers Association trained arbitrators. Both parties must agree on an arbitrator from the Department of Insurance's or its approved entity's list of arbitrators. If no agreement can be reached, then a list of 5 arbitrators shall be provided by the Department of Insurance or the approved entity. From the list of 5 arbitrators, the health insurance issuer can veto 2 arbitrators and the provider or facility can veto 2 arbitrators. The remaining arbitrator shall be the chosen arbitrator. This arbitration shall consist of a review of the written submissions by both parties. The arbitrator shall not establish a rebuttable presumption that the qualifying payment amount should be the total amount owed to the provider or facility by the combination of the issuer and the insured, beneficiary, or enrollee. Binding arbitration shall provide for a written decision within 45 days after the request is filed with the Department of Insurance. Both parties shall be bound by the arbitrator's decision. The arbitrator's expenses and fees, together with other expenses, not including attorney's fees, incurred in the conduct of the arbitration, shall be paid as provided in the decision.

(f) (Blank).

(g) Section 368a of this Act [215 ILCS 5/368a] shall not apply during the pendency of a decision under subsection (d). Upon the issuance of the arbitrator's decision, Section 368a applies with respect to the amount, if any, by which the arbitrator's determination exceeds the issuer's initial payment under subsection (c), or the entire amount of the arbitrator's determination if initial payment was denied. Any interest required to be paid to a provider under Section 368a shall not accrue until after 30 days of an arbitrator's decision as provided in subsection (d), but in no circumstances longer than 150 days from the date the nonparticipating facility-based provider billed for services rendered.

(h) Nothing in this Section shall be interpreted to change the prudent layperson provisions with respect to emergency services under the Managed Care Reform and Patient Rights Act [215 ILCS 134/1 et seq.].

(i) Nothing in this Section shall preclude a health care provider from billing a beneficiary, insured, or enrollee for reasonable administrative fees, such as service fees for checks returned for nonsufficient funds and missed appointments.

(j) Nothing in this Section shall preclude a beneficiary, insured, or enrollee from assigning benefits to a nonparticipating provider when the notice and consent criteria are satisfied under paragraph (2) of subsection (b-5) or in any other situation not described in subsection (b) or (b-5).

(k) Except when the notice and consent criteria are satisfied under paragraph (2) of subsection (b-5), if an individual receives health care services under the situations described in subsection (b) or (b-5), no referral requirement or any other provision contained in the policy or certificate of coverage shall deny coverage, reduce benefits, or otherwise defeat the requirements of this Section for services that would have been covered with a participating provider. However, this subsection shall not be construed to preclude a provider contract with a health insurance issuer, or with an administrator or similar entity acting on the issuer's behalf, from imposing requirements on the participating provider, participating emergency facility, or participating health care facility relating to the referral of covered individuals to nonparticipating providers.

(l) Except if the notice and consent criteria are satisfied under paragraph (2) of subsection (b-5), cost-sharing amounts calculated in conformity with this Section shall count toward any deductible or out-of-pocket maximum applicable to in-network coverage.

(m) The Department has the authority to enforce the requirements of this Section in the situations described in subsections (b) and (b-5), and in any other situation for which 42 U.S.C. Chapter 6A, Subchapter XXV, Parts D or E and regulations promulgated thereunder would prohibit an individual from being billed or liable for emergency services furnished by a nonparticipating provider or nonparticipating emergency facility or for non-emergency health care services furnished by a nonparticipating provider at a participating health care facility.

(n) This Section does not apply with respect to air ambulance or ground ambulance services. This Section does not apply to any policy of excepted benefits or to short-term, limited-duration health insurance coverage.

215 ILCS 125/4-15 [Emergency transportation by ambulance]

(a) No contract or evidence of coverage for basic health care services delivered, issued for delivery, renewed or amended by a Health Maintenance Organization shall exclude coverage for emergency transportation by ambulance. For the purposes of this Section, the term "emergency" means a need for immediate medical attention resulting from a life threatening condition or situation or a need for immediate medical attention as otherwise reasonably determined by a physician, public safety official or other emergency medical personnel.

(b) Upon reasonable demand by a provider of emergency transportation by ambulance, a Health Maintenance Organization shall promptly pay to the provider, subject to coverage limitations stated in the contract or evidence of coverage, the charges for emergency transportation by ambulance provided to an enrollee in a health care plan arranged for by the Health Maintenance Organization. By accepting any such payment from the Health Maintenance Organization, the provider of emergency transportation by ambulance agrees not to seek any payment from the enrollee for services provided to the enrollee.

INDIANA STATUTES ANNOTATED

§ 27-1-45-8 Reimbursement of out of network practitioner

(a) An out of network practitioner who provides health care services at an in network facility to a covered individual may not be reimbursed more for the health care services than allowed according to the rate or amount of compensation established by the covered individual's network plan as described in subsection (b) unless all of the following conditions are met:

(1) At least five (5) business days before the health care service is scheduled to be provided to the covered individual, the facility or practitioner provides to the covered individual, on a form separate from any other form provided to the covered individual by the facility or practitioner, a statement in conspicuous type that meets the following requirements:

(A) Includes a notice reading substantially as follows: "[Name of facility or practitioner] is an out of network practitioner providing [type of care], with [name of in network facility], which is an in network provider facility within your health carrier's plan. [Name of facility or practitioner] will not be allowed to bill you the difference between the price charged for the services and the rate your health carrier will reimburse for the services during your care at [name of in network facility] unless you give your written consent to the charge."

(B) Sets forth the facility's or practitioner's good faith estimate of the established fee for the health care services provided to the covered individual.

(C) Includes a notice reading substantially as follows concerning the good faith estimate set forth under clause (B):

"The estimate of our intended charge for [name or description of health care services] set forth in this statement is provided in good faith and is our best estimate of the amount we will charge. If the actual charge for [name or description of health care services] exceeds our estimate by the greater of:

(i) one hundred dollars ($100); or

(ii) five percent (5%); we will explain to you why the charge exceeds the estimate."

(2) The covered individual signs the statement provided under subdivision (1), signifying the covered individual's consent to the charge for the health care services being greater than allowed according to the rate or amount of compensation established by the network plan.

(b) If an out of network practitioner does not meet the requirements of subsection (a), the out of network practitioner shall include on any bill remitted to a covered individual a written statement in conspicuous type stating that the covered individual is not responsible for more than the rate or amount of compensation established by the covered individual's network plan plus any required copayment, deductible, or coinsurance.

(c) If a covered individual's network plan remits reimbursement to the covered individual for health care services that did not meet the requirements of subsection (a), the network plan shall provide with the reimbursement a written statement in conspicuous type that states that the covered individual is not responsible for more than the rate or amount of compensation established by the covered individual's network plan and that is included in the reimbursement plus any required copayment, deductible, or coinsurance.

(d) If the charge of a facility or practitioner for health care services provided to a covered individual exceeds the estimate provided to the covered individual under subsection (a)(1)(B) by an amount greater than:

(1) one hundred dollars ($100); or
(2) five percent (5%);

the facility or practitioner shall explain in a writing provided to the covered individual why the charge exceeds the estimate.

(e) The department shall adopt rules under IC 4-22-2 to specify the requirements of the notifications set forth in:

(1) subsections (b) and (c); and
(2) IC 25-1-9-23(j) and IC 25-1-9-23(k).

IOWA CODE

§ 514C.16 Emergency room services

1. A carrier, as defined in section 513B.2, or a plan established pursuant to chapter 509A for public employees, which provides coverage for emergency services, is responsible for charges for emergency services provided to a covered individual, including services furnished outside any contractual provider network or preferred provider network. Coverage for emergency services is subject to the terms and conditions of the health benefit plan or contract.
2. Prior authorization for emergency services shall not be required. All services necessary to evaluate and stabilize an emergency medical condition shall be considered covered emergency services.
3. For purposes of this section, unless the context otherwise requires:
   a. "Emergency medical condition" means a medical condition that manifests itself by symptoms of sufficient severity, including but not limited to severe pain, that an ordinarily prudent person, possessing average knowledge of medicine and health, could reasonably expect the absence of immediate medical attention to result in one of the following:
      (1) Placing the health of the individual, or with respect to a pregnant woman, the health of the woman or her unborn child, in serious jeopardy.
      (2) Serious impairment to bodily function.
      (3) Serious dysfunction of a bodily organ or part.
   b. "Emergency services" means covered inpatient and outpatient health care services that are furnished by a health care provider who is qualified to provide the services that are needed to evaluate or stabilize an emergency medical condition.

LOUISIANA STATUTES ANNOTATED

§ 22:1874 Billing by contracted health care providers

A.

(1) A contracted health care provider shall be prohibited from discount billing, dual billing, attempting to collect from, or collecting from an enrollee or insured a health insurance issuer liability or any amount in excess of the contracted reimbursement rate for covered health care services.

(2) No contracted health care provider shall bill, attempt to collect from, or collect from an enrollee or insured any amounts other than those representing coinsurance, copayments, deductibles, noncovered or noncontracted health care services, or other amounts identified by the health insurance issuer on an explanation of benefits as an amount for which the enrollee or insured is liable.

(3) However, in the event that any billing, attempt to collect from, or the collection from an enrollee or insured of any amount other than those representing copayment, deductible, coinsurance, payment for noncovered or noncontracted health care services, or other amounts identified by the health insurance issuer as the liability of the enrollee or insured is based on information received from a health insurance issuer, the contracted health care provider shall not be in violation of this Subpart.

(4) A health insurance issuer contracting with a network of providers is obligated to pay to a contracted health care provider the contracted reimbursement rate of the network identified on the member identification card of the enrollee or insured, pursuant to R.S. 40:2203.1, and established by the contract between the network of providers and the contracted health care provider. The payor must comply with all provisions of the specific network contract. To the extent that a health insurance issuer does not pay to the health care provider an amount equal to the health insurance issuer liability, the contracted health care provider may collect the difference between the amount paid by the health insurance issuer and the health insurance issuer liability from the enrollee or insured. Any such collection efforts shall not constitute a violation of this Subpart.

(5)

(a) Under certain circumstances and when the provisions of Subparagraph (b) of this Paragraph are met, a health insurance issuer contracting with a group of healthcare providers that bills a health insurance issuer utilizing a group identification number, such as the group federal tax identification number or the group National Provider Identifier as set forth in 45 CFR 162.402 et seq., shall pay the contracted reimbursement rate of the provider group for covered healthcare services rendered by a new provider to the group, without healthcare provider credentialing as described in R.S. 22:1009. In addition, the health insurance issuer shall consider the new provider to be an in-network or participating provider for the purposes of any utilization management or prior authorization processes required by the health insurance issuer for that provider group. This provision shall apply in either of the following circumstances:

(i) When the new provider has already been credentialed by the health insurance issuer and the provider's credentialing is still active with the issuer.

(ii) When the health insurance issuer has received the required credentialing application, including proof of membership on a hospital medical staff, from the new provider and the issuer has not notified the provider group that credentialing of the new provider has been denied.

(iii) If the new provider is an advanced practice registered nurse or a physician assistant licensed in Louisiana, proof of membership on a hospital medical staff shall not be required if the provider provides a written attestation identifying the collaborating or supervising physician, if a physician relationship is required by law.

(b) A health insurance issuer shall comply with the provisions of Subparagraph (a) of this Paragraph no later than thirty days after receipt of a written request from the provider group. The written request shall include a statement that the provider group agrees that all contract provisions, including the provision holding covered persons harmless for charges beyond reimbursement by the issuer and deductible, coinsurance and copayments, apply to the new provider. Such compliance shall apply to any claims for covered services rendered by the new provider to covered persons on dates of service no earlier than the date of the written request from the provider group.

(c) Compliance by a health insurance issuer with the provisions of Subparagraph (a) of this Paragraph shall not be construed to mean that a provider has been credentialed by an issuer or that the issuer is required to list the provider in a directory of contracted healthcare providers.

(d) If, upon compliance with Subparagraph (a) of this Paragraph, a health insurance issuer completes the credentialing process on the new provider and determines that the provider does not meet the issuer's credentialing requirements, the following actions shall be permitted:

(i) The health insurance issuer may recover from the provider or the provider group an amount equal to the difference between appropriate payments for in-network benefits and out-of-network benefits if the health insurance issuer has notified the applicant provider of the adverse determination and has initiated action regarding the recovery within thirty days of the adverse determination.

(ii) The provider or the provider group may retain any deductible, coinsurance, or copayment collected or in the process of being collected as of the date of receipt of the issuer's determination, so long as the amount is not in excess of the amount owed by the insured or enrollee for out-of-network services.

B. No contracted health care provider may maintain any action at law against an enrollee or insured for a health insurance issuer liability or for payment of any amount in excess of the contracted reimbursement rate for such services. In the event of such an action, the prevailing party shall be entitled to recover all costs incurred, including reasonable attorney fees and court costs. However, nothing in this Subsection shall be construed to prohibit a contracted health care provider from maintaining any action at law against an enrollee or insured after a health insurance issuer determines that the health insurance issuer is not liable for the health care services rendered.

TITLE 22 MAINE REVISED STATUTES

§ 1718-D Prohibition on balance billing for surprise bills and bills for out-of-network emergency services; disputes of bills for uninsured patients and persons covered under self-insured health benefit plans; disclosure related to referrals

1. Definitions. As used in this section, unless the context otherwise indicates, the following terms have the following meanings.
   - A. "Enrollee" has the same meaning as in Title 24-A, section 4301-A, subsection 5.
   - B. "Health plan" has the same meaning as in Title 24-A, section 4301-A, subsection 7.
   - B-1. "Knowingly elected to obtain the services from an out-of-network provider" means that an enrollee chose the services of a specific provider, with full knowledge that the provider is an out-of-network provider with respect to the enrollee's health plan, under circumstances that indicate that the enrollee had and was informed of the opportunity to receive services from a network provider but instead selected the out-of-network provider. The disclosure by a provider of network status does not render an enrollee's decision to proceed with treatment from that provider a choice made knowingly pursuant to this paragraph.
   - C. "Provider" has the same meaning as in Title 24-A, section 4301-A, subsection 16.
   - D. "Surprise bill" has the same meaning as in Title 24-A, section 4303-C, subsection 1.
   - E. "Visit" means any interaction between an enrollee and one or more providers for the purpose of assessing the health status of an enrollee or providing one or more health care services between the time an enrollee enters a facility and the time an enrollee is discharged.
2. Prohibition on balance billing. An out-of-network provider reimbursed for a surprise bill or a bill for covered emergency services under Title 24-A, section 4303-C or, if there is a dispute, under Title 24-A, section 4303-E or a bill for COVID-19 screening and testing under Title 24-A, section 4320-P may not bill an enrollee for health care services beyond the applicable coinsurance, copayment, deductible or other out-of-pocket cost expense that would be imposed for the health care services if the services were rendered by a network provider under the enrollee's health plan. For an enrollee subject to coinsurance, the out-of-network provider shall calculate the coinsurance amount based on the median network rate for that health care service under the enrollee's health plan. An out-of-network provider is also subject to the following with respect to any overpayment made by an enrollee.

A. If an out-of-network provider provides health care services covered under an enrollee's health plan and the out-of-network provider receives payment from the enrollee for health care services for which the enrollee is not responsible pursuant to this subsection, the out-of-network provider shall reimburse the enrollee within 30 calendar days after the earlier of the date that the provider received notice of the overpayment and the date the provider became aware of the overpayment.

B. An out-of-network provider that fails to reimburse an enrollee for an overpayment as required by paragraph A shall pay interest on the overpayment at the rate of 10% per annum beginning on the earlier of the date the provider received notice of the overpayment and the date the provider became aware of the overpayment. An enrollee is not required to request the accrued interest from the out-of-network provider in order to receive interest with the reimbursement amount.

3. Uninsured patients; disputes of bills. An uninsured patient who has received a bill for emergency services from a provider for one or more emergency health care services rendered during a single visit totaling $750 or more may dispute the bill and request resolution of the dispute using the process under Title 24-A, section 4303-E. The independent dispute resolution entity contracted to resolve the dispute over the surprise bill shall select either the out-of-network provider's fee or the uninsured patient's proposed payment amount in accordance with Title 24-A, section 4303-E. An uninsured patient may not be charged by a provider more than the amounts generally billed to a patient who has insurance covering emergency services as determined using the method described in 26 Code of Federal Regulations, Section 1.501(r)-5, paragraph (b)(3) or (b)(4). A provider shall hold the uninsured patient harmless for the duration of the independent dispute resolution process and may not seek payment until the independent dispute resolution process is completed. Notwithstanding Title 24-A, section 4303-E, subsection 1, paragraph F, payment for the independent dispute resolution process is the responsibility of the provider. In the event a claim includes more than one emergency health care service rendered during a single visit, the independent dispute resolution entity may allocate the prorated independent dispute resolution costs at its discretion among providers.

4. Person covered under self-insured health benefit plan; disputes of surprise bills or bills for covered emergency services rendered by an out-of-network provider. A person covered under a self-insured health benefit plan that is not subject to the provisions of Title 24-A, section 4303-E pursuant to Title 24-A, section 4303-E, subsection 2 and who has received a surprise bill for emergency services or a bill for covered emergency services rendered by an out-of-network provider may dispute the bill and request resolution of the dispute using the process under Title 24-A, section 4303-E, subsection 1. The independent dispute resolution entity contracted to resolve the dispute over the bill shall select either the out-of-network provider's fee or the covered person's

proposed payment amount in accordance with Title 24-A, section 4303-E, subsection 1. This subsection does not apply to a person covered under a self-insured health benefit plan who knowingly elected to obtain the services from an out-of-network provider.

5. Referral to an out-of-network provider. A provider receiving a nonemergency referral or self-referral for any in-person health care service or procedure shall disclose to the enrollee whether that provider to whom the enrollee is being referred is a member of the provider network under the enrollee's health plan before the enrollee schedules the appointment for that service or procedure.

MAINE REVISED STATUTES TITLE 24-A

§ 4303-C Protection from surprise bills and bills for out-of-network emergency services

1. Surprise bill defined. As used in this section, unless the context otherwise indicates, "surprise bill" means a bill for health care services, including, but not limited to, emergency services, received by an enrollee for covered services rendered by an out-of-network provider, when such services were rendered by that out-of-network provider at a network provider, during a service or procedure performed by a network provider or during a service or procedure previously approved or authorized by the carrier and the enrollee did not knowingly elect to obtain such services from that out-of-network provider. "Surprise bill" does not include a bill for health care services received by an enrollee when a network provider was available to render the services and the enrollee knowingly elected to obtain the services from another provider who was an out-of-network provider.

1-A. "Knowingly elected to obtain such services from that out-of-network provider" defined. As used in this section, unless the context otherwise indicates, "knowingly elected to obtain such services from that out-of-network provider" means that an enrollee chose the services of a specific provider, with full knowledge that the provider is an out-of-network provider with respect to the enrollee's health plan, under circumstances that indicate that the enrollee had and was informed of the opportunity to receive services from a network provider but instead selected the out-of-network provider. The disclosure by a provider of network status does not render an enrollee's decision to proceed with treatment from that provider a choice made knowingly pursuant to this subsection.

2. Requirements. With respect to a surprise bill or a bill for covered emergency services rendered by an out-of-network provider:
   A. A carrier shall require an enrollee to pay only the applicable coinsurance, copayment, deductible or other out-of-pocket expense that would be

imposed for health care services if the services were rendered by a network provider. For an enrollee subject to coinsurance, the carrier shall calculate the coinsurance amount based on the median network rate for that health care service [PL 2019, c. 668, §2 (AMD).];

B. Except as provided for ambulance services in paragraph D, unless the carrier and out-of-network provider agree otherwise, a carrier shall reimburse the out-of-network provider or enrollee, as applicable, for health care services rendered at the greater of:
   (1) The carrier's median network rate paid for that health care service by a similar provider in the geographic area where the service was provided; and
   (2) The median network rate paid by all carriers for that health care service by a similar provider in the geographic area where the service was provided as determined by the all-payer claims database maintained by the Maine Health Data Organization or, if Maine Health Data Organization claims data is insufficient or otherwise inapplicable, another independent medical claims database specified by the superintendent. [PL 2021, c. 222, §1 (AMD).]

C. Notwithstanding paragraph B, if a carrier has an inadequate network, as determined by the superintendent, the carrier shall ensure that the enrollee obtains the covered service at no greater cost to the enrollee than if the service were obtained from a network provider or shall make other arrangements acceptable to the superintendent [PL 2019, c. 668, §2 (AMD).].

D-1. Unless the carrier and out-of-network provider agree otherwise, a carrier shall reimburse an out-of-network provider for ambulance services that are covered emergency services at the rate applicable to the out-of-network provider pursuant to section 4303-F.

E. If an out-of-network provider disagrees with a carrier's payment amount for a surprise bill for emergency services or for covered emergency services as determined in accordance with paragraph B or paragraph D, the carrier and the out-of-network provider have 30 calendar days to negotiate an agreement on the payment amount in good faith. If the carrier and the out-of-network provider do not reach agreement on the payment amount within 30 calendar days, the out-of-network provider may submit a dispute regarding the payment and receive another payment from the carrier determined in accordance with the dispute resolution process in section 4303-E, including any payment made pursuant to section 4303-E, subsection 1, paragraph G [PL 2021, c. 241, §2 (AMD).]; and

F. The enrollee's responsibility for payment for covered out-of-network emergency services must be limited so that if the enrollee has paid the enrollee's share of the charge as specified in the plan for in-network services, the carrier shall hold the enrollee harmless from any additional amount owed to an out-of-network provider for covered emergency services and make payment to the out-of-network provider in accordance with this section or, if there is a dispute, in accordance with section 4303-E. [PL 2019, c. 668, §2 (NEW).]

3. Payment after resolution of disputes. Following an independent dispute resolution determination pursuant to section 4303-E, the determination by the independent dispute resolution entity of a reasonable payment for a specific health care service or treatment rendered by an out-of-network provider is binding on a carrier, out-of-network provider and enrollee for 90 days. During that 90-day period, a carrier shall reimburse an out-of-network provider at that same rate for that specific health care service or treatment, and an out-of-network provider may not dispute any bill for that service under section 4303-E.

§ 4303-E Dispute resolution process for surprise bills and bills for out-of-network emergency services

1. Independent dispute resolution process. The superintendent shall establish an independent dispute resolution process by which a dispute for a surprise bill for emergency services or a bill for covered emergency services rendered by an out-of-network provider in accordance with section 4303-C, subsection 2 may be resolved as provided in this subsection beginning no later than October 1, 2020.
   - A. The superintendent may select an independent dispute resolution entity to conduct the dispute resolution process. The superintendent shall adopt rules to implement a dispute resolution process that uses a standard arbitration form and includes the selection of an arbitrator from a list of qualified arbitrators developed pursuant to the rules. A qualified arbitrator must be independent; may not be affiliated with a carrier, health care facility or provider or any professional association of carriers, health care facilities or providers; may not have a personal, professional or financial conflict with any parties to the arbitration; and must have experience in health care billing and reimbursement rates. Rules adopted pursuant to this paragraph are routine technical rules as defined in Title 5, chapter 375, subchapter 2-A. [PL 2019, c. 668, §3 (NEW).]
   - B. An independent dispute resolution entity shall make a decision within 30 days of receipt of the dispute for review. [PL 2019, c. 668, §3 (NEW).]
   - C. In determining a reasonable fee for the health care services rendered, an independent dispute resolution entity shall select either the carrier's payment or the out-of-network provider's fee. The independent dispute resolution entity shall determine which amount to select based upon the conditions and factors set forth in this paragraph. In determining

the reasonable fee for a health care service, an independent dispute resolution entity shall consider all relevant factors, including:

(1) The out-of-network provider's level of training, education, specialization, quality and experience and, in the case of a hospital, the teaching staff, scope of services and case mix;

(2) The out-of-network provider's previously contracted rate with the carrier, if the provider had a contract with the carrier that was terminated or expired within one year prior to the dispute; and

(3) The median network rate for the particular health care service performed by a provider in the same or similar specialty, as determined by the all-payer claims database maintained by the Maine Health Data Organization or, if Maine Health Data Organization claims data is insufficient or otherwise inapplicable, another independent medical claims database. If authorized by rule, the superintendent may enter into an agreement to obtain data from an independent medical claims database to carry out the functions of this subparagraph. [PL 2019, c. 668, §3 (NEW).]

D. If an independent dispute resolution entity determines, based on the carrier's payment and the out-of-network provider's fee, that a settlement between the carrier and out-of-network provider is reasonably likely, or that both the carrier's payment and the out-of-network provider's fee represent unreasonable extremes, the independent dispute resolution entity may direct both parties to attempt a good faith negotiation for settlement. The carrier and out-of-network provider may be granted up to 10 business days for this negotiation, which runs concurrently with the 30-day period for dispute resolution. [PL 2019, c. 668, §3 (NEW).]

E. The determination of an independent dispute resolution entity is binding on the carrier, out-of-network provider and enrollee and is admissible in any court proceeding between the carrier, out-of-network provider and enrollee or in any administrative proceeding between this State and the provider. [PL 2019, c. 668, §3 (NEW).]

F. When an independent dispute resolution entity determines the carrier's payment is reasonable, payment for the dispute resolution process is the responsibility of the out-of-network provider. When the independent dispute resolution entity determines the out-of-network provider's fee is reasonable, payment for the dispute resolution process is the responsibility of the carrier. When a good faith negotiation directed by the independent dispute resolution entity results in a settlement between the carrier and the out-of-network provider, the carrier and the out-of-network provider shall evenly divide and share the prorated cost for dispute resolution. [PL 2019, c. 668, §3 (NEW).]

G. [PL 2021, c. 222, §2 (RP).]

H. The superintendent shall enforce the determination of an independent dispute resolution entity pursuant to this subsection or any agreement made by a carrier and an out-of-network provider after the conclusion of the independent dispute resolution process pursuant to this subsection. The superintendent may use any powers provided to the superintendent under this Title. [PL 2019, c. 668, §3 (NEW).]

I. Following a determination by an independent dispute resolution entity of a reasonable fee for a particular health care service, an out-of-network provider may not initiate the dispute resolution process under this subsection for that same health care service for a period of 90 days. [PL 2021, c. 222, §3 (NEW).]

2. Self-insured health benefit plans. An entity providing or administering a self-insured health benefit plan exempted from the applicability of this section under the federal Employee Retirement Income Security Act of 1974, 29 United States Code, Sections 1001 to 1461 (1988) may elect to be subject to the provisions of this section to resolve disputes with respect to a surprise bill for emergency services or a bill for covered emergency services from an out-of-network provider. In the event an entity providing or administering a self-insured health benefit plan elects to be subject to the provisions of this section, the provisions of this section apply to a self-insured health benefit plan and its members in the same manner as the provisions of this section apply to a carrier and its enrollees. To elect to be subject to the provisions of this section, the entity shall provide notice, on an annual basis, to the superintendent, on a form and in a manner prescribed by the superintendent, attesting to the entity's participation and agreeing to be bound by the provisions of this section. The entity shall amend the health benefit plan, coverage policies, contracts and any other plan documents to reflect that the provisions of this section apply to the plan's members. [PL 2019, c. 668, §3 (NEW).]

3. Information required from carriers. As part of the carrier's annual public regulatory filings made to the superintendent, a carrier shall submit in a form and manner determined by the superintendent information related to:

A. The use of out-of-network providers by enrollees and the impact on premium affordability and benefit design [PL 2019, c. 668, §3 (NEW).]; and

B. The number of claims submitted by a provider to the carrier that are denied or down coded by the carrier and the reason for the denial or down coding determination. [PL 2019, c. 668, §3 (NEW).]

4. Report from superintendent. On or before January 31st annually, beginning January 1, 2022, the superintendent shall report the following information received from all carriers in the aggregate:

A. The number of requests for independent dispute resolution filed pursuant to this section between January 1st and December 31st of the previous calendar year, including the percentage of all claims that were subject to dispute. For each independent dispute resolution determination, the carrier shall provide aggregate information that does not identify any provider, carrier, enrollee or uninsured patient involved in each determination about:
   (1) Whether the determination was in favor of the carrier, out-of-network provider or uninsured patient;
   (2) The payment amount offered by each side of the independent dispute resolution process and the award amount from the independent dispute resolution determination;
   (3) The category and practice specialty of each out-of-network provider involved, as applicable; and
   (4) A description of the health care service that was subject to dispute. [PL 2019, c. 668, §3 (NEW).];

B. The percentage of facilities and hospital-based professionals, by specialty, that are in network for each carrier in this State as reported in access plans submitted to the superintendent [PL 2019, c. 668, §3 (NEW).];

C. The number of complaints the superintendent receives relating to out-of-network health care charges [PL 2019, c. 668, §3 (NEW).];

D. Annual trends on health benefit plan premium rates, the total annual amount of spending on inadvertent and emergency out-of-network costs by carriers and medical loss ratios in the State to the extent that the information is available [PL 2019, c. 668, §3 (NEW).];

E. The number of physician specialists practicing in the State in a particular specialty and whether they are in network or out of network with respect to the carriers that administer the state employee group health plan under Title 5, section 285, the Maine Education Association benefits trust health plan, the qualified health plans offered pursuant to the federal Affordable Care Act and other health benefit plans offered in the State [PL 2019, c. 668, §3 (NEW).];

F. A summary of the information submitted to the superintendent pursuant to subsection 3 concerning the number of claims submitted by health care providers to carriers that are denied or down coded by the carrier and the reasons for the denials or down coding determinations [PL 2019, c. 668, §3 (NEW).];

G. An analysis of the impact of this section, with respect to both emergency services and other health care services, on premium affordability and the breadth of provider networks [PL 2019, c. 668, §3 (NEW).]; and

H. Any other benchmarks or information that the superintendent considers appropriate to make publicly available to further the goals of this section. [PL 2019, c. 668, §3 (NEW).]
The superintendent shall submit the report to the joint standing committee of the Legislature having jurisdiction over health insurance matters and shall post the report on the bureau's publicly accessible website.

[PL 2019, c. 668, §3 (NEW).]
SECTION HISTORY
PL 2019, c. 668, §3 (NEW). PL 2021, c. 222, §§2, 3 (AMD).

CODE OF MAINE RULES

02-031-365 Standards for independent dispute resolution of emergency medical service bills

Section 1. Authority and purpose

This rule is adopted pursuant to 24-A M.R.S. §§ 212. and 4303-E, to implement the Independent Dispute Resolution (IDR) process established by PL 2019, chapter 668, *An Act To Protect Consumers from Surprise Emergency Medical Bills.*

Section 2. Applicability and scope

1. This rule shall apply to the following entities:
   A. A carrier, including a participating self-insured health plan.
   B. A patient who is eligible to initiate IDR under 22 M.R.S. § 1718-.D.
   C. A provider that has rendered emergency services to an eligible patient, or that has rendered emergency services on an out-of-network basis to a patient covered by a carrier's health plan and is unable in good faith to negotiate agreement with the carrier on the payment amount within 30 calendar days after the carrier has given the provider notice as required in paragraph 6(1)(C).
2. This rule shall apply to the following types of bills, except in cases where the patient knowingly elected to obtain the services from an out-of-network provider:
   A. A surprise bill for emergency services;
   B. Any other bill for covered emergency services rendered by an out-of-network provider to a person covered by an insured or self-insured health plan; and
   C. A bill totaling $750 or more received by an uninsured person for emergency health services if the total bill for the single visit is $750 or more regardless of the number of providers included in the bill.

Section 3. Definitions

The following definitions apply for purposes of this rule:

1. "Carrier" has the same meaning as in 24-A M.R.S. § 4301-A(3). Unless the context otherwise indicates, "carrier" also includes a participating self-insured health benefit plan.
2. "Control" has the same meaning as in 24-A M.R.S. § 222(2)(B).
3. "Eligible patient" means:
   A. an uninsured person who has received a bill for emergency services totaling $750 from one or more providers for a single visit; or
   B. a person covered under a nonparticipating self-insured health plan who has received a surprise bill for emergency services or a bill for covered emergency services rendered by an out-of-network provider, and did not knowingly elect to obtain the services from an out-of-network provider.
4. "Emergency services" has the same meaning as 24-A M.R.S. § 4301-A(4-B).
5. "Enrollee" means a person covered by a carrier under a policy, certificate, or benefit plan.
6. "Geographic rating area" means an area designated by the Superintendent for health insurance rating purposes under 24-A M.R.S. §§ 2736-C(2)(C-1) & 2808-B(2)(C-1).
7. "Independent dispute resolution entity" or "IDRE" means an entity selected by the Superintendent pursuant to this rule to conduct the independent dispute resolution process.
8. "Material financial affiliation" means any financial interest of more than five percent of total annual revenue or total annual income of an IDRE or officer, director, or managers thereof; or arbitrator employed or engaged thereby to conduct any independent dispute review in the dispute resolution process. Revenue received from a carrier or physician by an IDRE to conduct a dispute resolution pursuant to this rule is not a material financial affiliation.
9. "Material personal affiliation" means any relationship as a spouse or domestic partner; as a child, parent, or sibling; as the child, parent, or sibling of a spouse or domestic partner; or as the spouse or domestic partner of a child, parent, or sibling.
10. "Material professional affiliation" means any physician-patient relationship, any partnership or employment relationship, a shareholder or similar ownership interest in a professional corporation, or any independent contractor arrangement that constitutes a material financial affiliation with any expert or any officer or director of the IDRE.
11. "Out-of-network provider" means a physician, hospital, or other provider that does not have a contract with the carrier to provide services to an enrollee.

12. "Participating self-insured health benefit plan" means a self-insured health benefit plan that has elected to participate in the IDR system pursuant to 24 A M.R.S. § 4303-E(2) and subsection 6(7) of this rule.
13. "Surprise bill" has the same meaning as in 24-A M.R.S § 4303-C(1).

Section 4. Application for selection as an IDRE

An entity applying for selection as an IDRE shall submit to the Superintendent an application on the form prescribed by the Superintendent. The application must describe the proposed IDRE's organizational structure and capability to operate a statewide IDR process, including:

1. copies of its certificate of incorporation or articles of organization, bylaws or operating agreement, and, as applicable, those of its holding company or parent company;
2. its organizational chart;
3. the names and biographical information relevant to the business of independent dispute resolution services for all members of its board of directors, its officers, and its executives, including their respective roles, and responsibilities;
4. the names of all corporations and organizations that it controls, is controlled by, or is under common control with, and the nature and extent of that control;
5. its policies and procedures governing all aspects of the IDR process, including at a minimum:
   - A. a description and a chart or diagram of the sequence of steps through which a dispute will move from receipt through notification of the dispute determination to interested parties;
   - B. procedures for ensuring that the arbitrator assigned to a dispute has no prohibited material financial, material personal, or material professional affiliation. These procedures must include a requirement for a signed attestation by each arbitrator assigned to review a dispute;
   - C. procedures to ensure that each dispute is reviewed by a neutral and impartial arbitrator with training and experience in healthcare billing, reimbursement, and usual and customary charges;
   - D. procedures for reporting and reviewing an arbitrator's conflicts of interest, for determining whether there is a conflict of interest, and for assigning or reassigning an IDR where a conflict is identified;
   - E. procedures to ensure that reviews are conducted within the time frames specified in this rule and any required notices are provided in a timely manner;
   - F. procedures to ensure the confidentiality of personal health information, personally identifiable information, and review materials;

G. procedures to ensure adherence to the requirements of this rule by any contractor, subcontractor, agent, or employee;

H. a description of the following:
   (1) its ability to provide review services statewide;
   (2) the qualifications the arbitrators retained to review payment disputes, including current and past employment history, as applicable;
   (3) the procedures employed to ensure that arbitrators reviewing payment disputes are:
      (a) trained in the principles of dispute resolution and the procedures and standards of the proposed IDRE;
      (b) knowledgeable about the health care service which is the subject of the payment dispute under review; and
      (c) trained and experienced in health care billing, reimbursement and usual and customary charges;
   (4) the methods of recruiting and selecting neutral and impartial arbitrators and matching such reviewers to specific cases;

I. its organizational arrangements and ongoing procedures for the identification, evaluation, resolution, and follow-up of potential and actual problems in payment dispute reviews; and the maintenance of program standards pursuant to this subdivision;

J. written procedures documenting that:
   (1) appropriate personnel are reasonably accessible at least 40 hours per week during normal business hours to discuss the dispute resolution process and to allow response to telephone requests; and
   (2) a response to an answered call or recorded message shall be made no later than the next business day after the call was received;

K. its fees, which must include disclosure of:
   (1) the total amount that it will charge for reviews, inclusive of indirect costs, administrative fees and incidental expenses;
   (2) the pro-rated fee that will be charged when a good faith negotiation directed by the proposed IDRE results in a settlement between a carrier and a provider;
   (3) an application processing fee if the dispute is determined by the proposed IDRE to be ineligible for review;
   (4) the fee that will be charged to the provider when an eligible patient requests an IDR;
   (5) the methodology used to calculate all fees; and
   (6) any fee charged for the configuration of a portal to receive IDR applications from out-of-network providers and eligible patients;

L. how it provides requisite notifications, screens for material affiliations, responds during normal business hours to inquiries from the State and from interested persons regarding the dispute resolution process; and

M. such other information as the Superintendent may require.

Section 5. Conflict of interest

1. No person may be selected as an IDRE if it owns or controls, is owned or controlled by, or is under common control with:
   A. any national, state, or local illness, health benefit, or public advocacy group;
   B. any national, state, or local society or association of hospitals, physicians, or other providers of health care services; or
   C. any national, state, or local association of insurance carriers.
2. If an IDRE acquires control of, becomes controlled by, or comes under common control with any entity described in subsection 1, the IDRE shall notify the Superintendent in writing within three business days of the acquisition or exercise of control and shall consult with the Superintendent as to how to mitigate the conflict of interest.
3. Before accepting an IDR, an IDRE shall submit a sworn statement setting forth that the proposed arbitrator has no material financial, personal, or professional affiliation with:
   A. any officer, director, or manager of the carrier;
   B. any health care provider, physician's medical group, independent practice association, or provider of pharmaceutical products or services or durable medical equipment that provided or supplied the health care service that is the subject of the IDR;
   C. the facility at which the health service was provided;
   D. any officer, director, partner, or manager of the physician's medical group, independent practice association, or facility that provided the heath care service;
   E. the developer or manufacturer of the principal health service that is the subject of the IDR;
   F. the patient whose health care service is the subject of the IDR; or
   G. any organization described in subsection 1.

Section 6. Responsibilities of carriers

1. Upon receipt of a claim for covered emergency services rendered by an out-of-network provider, a carrier shall:
   A. pay the claim based on an allowable charge calculated in accordance with paragraph B, unless the carrier and provider negotiate a different amount or the patient knowingly elected to obtain the services from an out-of-network provider. The carrier shall pay the allowable charge to the provider, subject to the following adjustments:
      (1) Payment shall be made net of the coinsurance, copayment, deductible, and any other out-of-pocket expense for which the enrollee is responsible under subsection 3;
      (2) To the extent that the enrollee has paid the provider more than the cost sharing required by subparagraph (1), the carrier shall

pay the excess to the enrollee and deduct that amount from the payment otherwise due to the provider;

(3) Payment shall be made net of any amounts already paid by the carrier; and

(4) If the carrier is a secondary payer, the enrollee's and carrier's responsibility shall be reduced as called for by applicable coordination of benefits procedures;

B. determine the total amount the provider is entitled to receive for health care services rendered. The carrier's determination of median network rates shall be based on the CPT code for the claim and the geographic rating area in which the service was rendered, unless the carrier determines that the available data are insufficient or otherwise inapplicable, in which case the carrier, subject to the process of negotiation and IDR review, may use a broader geographic area or bundle of CPT codes. The provider's allowable charge shall be the greatest of:

(1) the carrier's median network rate paid for the service by a similar provider in the geographic area in which the service was rendered;

(2) the median network rate paid by all carriers for that health care service by a similar provider in the geographic area in which the service was rendered as determined by the all-payer claims database maintained by the Maine Health Data Organization or, if Maine Health Data Organization claims data is insufficient or otherwise inapplicable, another independent medical claims database; or

C. give notice to the provider, in a form and manner prescribed by the Superintendent, specifying the carrier's allowable charge for the service, and describing how the provider may initiate the IDR process if the carrier and provider are unable to reach agreement within 30 days;

D. if the carrier pays an amount less than the provider's charge, provide the enrollee with notice which shall explain that the enrollee shall incur no greater out-of-pocket costs for the services than the enrollee would have incurred with a network provider. The carrier may provide this notice on or with the explanation of benefits required under 24-A M.R.S. § 3404.(13); and

E. direct the enrollee to contact the carrier if the provider bills the enrollee for the out-of-network service for more than the amount indicated as the enrollee's responsibility on the carrier's explanation of benefits.

2. A carrier shall prominently post on its website the following information regarding surprise bills and bills for emergency services rendered by out-of-network providers, and include the same information in disclosure materials provided to enrollees:

A. a description of what constitutes a surprise bill;

B. an explanation of which surprise bills are eligible for the IDR process;

C. a description of the IDR process;

D. information on how an out-of-network provider may submit a dispute for resolution by an IDRE.

3. A carrier shall ensure that the enrollee does not incur any greater out-of-pocket costs for the services than the enrollee would have incurred with a provider charging the carrier's median network rate. The carrier may not increase the enrollee's coinsurance if negotiation or IDR results in an increase in the applicable network rate.
4. If an IDRE directs a carrier to engage in negotiations with an out-of-network provider, the IDRE shall specify a time period for negotiation, not to exceed ten business days, and the parties shall negotiate in good faith. If a settlement is reached, the carrier shall notify the IDRE of the settlement within two business days and shall make any additional payment to the provider within thirty days. If a settlement is not reached or the parties agree that a settlement is not attainable, the carrier shall promptly notify the IDRE within the period granted by the IDRE for negotiation.
5. If the IDRE issues a determination in favor of the provider, the carrier shall pay the provider any additional amount owed within 30 days after the date of the determination.
6. A carrier shall designate, and identify to the Superintendent, someone knowledgeable about the IDR process who shall be responsible for oversight of the carrier's compliance with the process. The carrier shall make at least one staff member available full time during normal business hours. The carrier shall respond to all inquiries from the Superintendent relating to the IDR process within five business days.
7. A self-insured employer or the administrator of a self-insured health benefit plan may elect to be treated as a carrier under this rule by filing a notice in a form and manner prescribed by the Superintendent as provided in this subsection. The plan's rights and responsibilities as a carrier apply to all services provided to enrollees after the notice of participation is received by the Superintendent, unless the plan requests a different effective date. In order for the plan's participating status to remain in effect without interruption, a renewal notice must be received before the expiration of the plan year. The initial and renewal notices must include the following:
   A. the identity and contact information of the self-insured employer and the plan administrator;
   B. an agreement to submit to the jurisdiction of the Superintendent and to be bound by the requirements of this rule, the applicable provisions of the Maine Insurance Code, and any order or decision made by an IDRE pursuant to this rule; and
   C. evidence that the plan documents have been amended to reflect the applicability of the IDR process to the plan's enrollees.

Section 7. Process to submit and resolve disputes

1. The out-of-network provider or eligible patient requesting IDR (the "applicant") shall submit an application in a form and manner prescribed by the Superintendent.

2. The applicant shall provide the following information, to the extent known to the applicant:
   A. the name and contact information of the patient, the provider or providers, and, unless the applicant is an uninsured patient, the carrier or self-insured health benefit plan;
   B. the fee that is the subject of the dispute and a copy of the bill;
   C. the claim number or numbers and date or dates of service;
   D. if the application is submitted by a provider, the following additional information:
      (1) the provider's level of training, education, and experience;
      (2) an explanation of the circumstances and complexity of the particular case, including time and place of the service;
      (3) individual patient characteristics, if relevant; and
      (4) the provider's usual charge for comparable services rendered to uninsured patients, patients treated on an out-of-network basis, patients treated under contracts with other carriers or self-insured plans, and, if applicable, patients treated under a contract with the carrier or plan involved in the dispute that was terminated or that expired within one year before the date the service was rendered;
   E. an agreement to be bound by the outcome of the IDR, to submit to the jurisdiction of the Superintendent and the courts of this State, and if the applicant is an out-of-network provider, to refrain from billing the enrollee more than the applicable out-of-pocket costs permitted by 22 M.R.S. § 1718.(D)(2);
   F. any other information the applicant deems relevant; and
   G. an attestation affirming that the information provided by the applicant is true and accurate.
3. An eligible patient shall not be required to pay the provider's fee in order to be eligible to submit the dispute for review by an IDRE.
4. If the Superintendent chooses to screen applications for eligibility, the Superintendent shall promptly notify all parties upon determining that an application is ineligible for IDR, and shall assign each eligible application to an IDRE and promptly forward the application materials to the assigned IDRE. Otherwise, the Superintendent shall assign each application to an IDRE, which shall screen the application for eligibility within three business days. The IDRE shall contact the applicant, and any other party that might have the necessary information, if additional information is needed to determine eligibility of the request for IDR. The IDRE shall allow a reasonable time, not less than three business days, to submit the information and provide an explanation of where the information should be sent. If the information is not submitted, the IDRE shall make a second request and allow one business day to submit the information.
5. Within three business days after an application has been determined to be eligible, the IDRE shall assign an arbitrator and notify the patient, the provider

or providers, and, if applicable, the carrier or self-insured plan. The notification shall include:

A. the name and contact information of the IDRE and the assigned arbitrator;

B. a brief description of the process, and the parties' rights and responsibilities, including:

(1) if the IDR was initiated by the provider, an explanation that the disputed bill is the carrier's responsibility and the patient's cost-sharing obligation cannot be increased as a result of the IDR; and

(2) if the patient is enrolled in a nonparticipating self-insured plan, an explanation that any participation by the plan in the IDR process, including the provision of any requested information, is voluntary; and

C. an explanation of how and where each party may send the arbitrator any additional information it considers important to a clear understanding and fair resolution of the dispute, and the deadline for submitting such information.

6. The arbitrator may request information at any time from the patient, the provider or providers, and the carrier or self-insured plan, and shall advise the requested party that if a partial response or no response is received, the dispute will be decided based on the available information. Any party shall provide the information requested within the time requested, which shall be no less than five business days after the request is received, and shall attest that the information provided is true and complete.

7. In resolving a dispute, the IDRE must consider all relevant factors, including but not limited to the factors identified in 24-A M.R.S. § 4303-.E(1)(C)(1)-(3).

8. The IDRE shall issue its decision within thirty days after its receipt of a completed application.

9. The party responsible for payment of the IDRE's fee, or its share of the fee in the case of a negotiated settlement, shall pay the IDRE within 90 days after the issuance of the decision or submission of the settlement agreement.

Section 8. Severability

If any section, term, or provision of this rule shall be deemed invalid for any reason, any remaining section, provision, or definition shall remain in full force and effect.

Section 9. Effective date

This rule is effective October 24, 2020. This rule applies to all IDR applications relating to services rendered on or after October 1, 2020.

MARYLAND CODE ANNOTATED, HEALTH–GENERAL

§ 19-710 Basic requirements to operate as a health maintenance organization [effective until July 1, 2025]

(a) To qualify for a certificate of authority to operate as a health maintenance organization, an applicant shall satisfy the Commissioner that the applicant will meet the requirements of this section.

(b) The applicant shall conform to the definition of a health maintenance organization.

(c) The applicant shall establish and operate a bona fide health maintenance organization that can provide health care services in the proposed geographic area.

(d)

(1) The health maintenance organization shall be actuarially sound.

(2)

(i) Except as otherwise provided in this paragraph, the surplus that the health maintenance organization is required to have shall be paid in full.

(ii) The health maintenance organization licensed on or after July 1, 1989 shall have an initial surplus that exceeds the liabilities of the health maintenance organization by at least $1,500,000.

(iii) All health maintenance organizations shall maintain a surplus that exceeds the liabilities of the health maintenance organization in the amount that is at least equal to the greater of $750,000 or 5 percent of the subscription charges earned during the prior calendar year as recorded in the annual report filed by the health maintenance organization with the Commissioner.

(iv) No health maintenance organization shall be required to maintain a surplus in excess of a value of $3,000,000.

(3)

(i) For the protection of the health maintenance organization's members and creditors, the applicant shall deposit and maintain in trust with the State Treasurer $100,000 in cash or government securities of the type described in § 5-701(b) of the Insurance Article.

(ii)

1. The deposits shall be accepted and held in trust by the State Treasurer in accordance with Title 5, Subtitle 7 of the Insurance Article.

2. For the purpose of applying this subparagraph, a health maintenance organization shall be treated as an insurer.

(4) The Commissioner may waive the surplus and deposit requirements contained in this subsection if the Commissioner is satisfied that:

(i) The health maintenance organization has sufficient net worth and an adequate history of generating net income to assure financial viability for the next year;

(ii) The health maintenance organization's performance and obligations are guaranteed by another person with sufficient net worth and an adequate history of generating net income; or

(iii) The assets of the health maintenance organization or contracts with insurers, governments, providers, or other persons are sufficient to reasonably assure the performance of the health maintenance organization's obligations.

(e) The provisions of Title 4, Subtitle 3 (Risk Based Capital Standards for Insurers) and § 15-604 (Rates for Payments to Hospitals) of the Insurance Article apply to health maintenance organizations in the same manner as they apply to insurers.

(f) The terms of contracts, including any medical assistance program contracts under Title XVIII or Title XIX of the Social Security Act or Title III of the Public Health Service Act, proposed to be made or made with government or private agencies that cover all or part of the cost of subscriptions to provide health care services, facilities, appliances, medicines, or supplies shall be financially sound, based on reasonable actuarial assumptions that the health maintenance organization can meet its obligations to the agencies and their beneficiaries by reason of the health maintenance organization's net worth position, stop loss, reinsurance arrangements with authorized insurers, or other arrangements that are satisfactory to the Commissioner.

(g)

(1) The terms of the contracts to be offered to subscribers shall provide that the health care services provided to members of the health maintenance organization will meet reasonable standards of quality of care that are applicable to the geographic area to be served, as approved by the Department.

(2) If a health maintenance organization offers services that are within the scope of practice of a physician and another health care practitioner who is licensed under the Health Occupations Article, the health maintenance organization shall offer those services through other licensed health care practitioners, where appropriate, as determined by the health maintenance organization.

(h) The procedures for offering health care services and offering and terminating contracts to subscribers may not discriminate unfairly on the basis of age, sex, race, health, or economic status. This requirement does not prohibit:

(1) Reasonable underwriting classifications for establishing contract rates; or
(2) Experience rating.

(i)
(1) The terms of the agreements between a health maintenance organization and providers of health services shall contain a "hold harmless" clause.
(2) The hold harmless clause shall provide that the provider may not, under any circumstances, including nonpayment of money due the providers by the health maintenance organization, insolvency of the health maintenance organization, or breach of the provider contract, bill, charge, collect a deposit, seek compensation, remuneration, or reimbursement from, or have any recourse against the subscriber, member, enrollee, patient, or any persons other than the health maintenance organization acting on their behalf, for services provided in accordance with the provider contract.
(3) Collection from the subscriber or member of copayments or supplemental charges in accordance with the terms of the subscriber's contract with the health maintenance organization, or charges for services not covered under the subscriber's contract, may be excluded from the hold harmless clause.
(4) Each provider contract shall state that the hold harmless clause will survive the termination of the provider contract, regardless of the cause of termination.

(j) The health maintenance organization shall provide evidence of adequate insurance coverage or an adequate plan for self-insurance to satisfy claims for injuries that may occur from providing health care.

(k) The health maintenance organization shall provide for having its health and medical facilities and services audited and reviewed periodically:
(1) By personnel outside the health maintenance organization who:
(i) Act in a manner that is approved by the Department; and
(ii) Use methods that will assure objective evaluation and keep the identity of patients as confidential as possible;
(2) By the health maintenance organization's own internal quality of care committee audit procedures, if the Department approves the procedures; or
(3) By a professional standards review organization, as described in Title XI of the Social Security Act, that is certified by the Department of Health and Human Services as capable of serving individuals in the area where the health maintenance organization operates who are receiving benefits under Title XVIII or Title XIX of the Social Security Act or Title III of the Public Health Service Act, if the professional standards review organization is acting consistently with its certification.

(l)

(1) With the approval of the Department, the health maintenance organization shall provide continuous internal peer review for monitoring and evaluating patient records for:

(i) Quality of care; and

(ii) Overuse and underuse of provider care; and

(2) The health maintenance organization shall meet the requirements of Subtitle 13 of this title and all regulations for the performance of utilization review.

(m) The health maintenance organization shall provide an internal grievance system to resolve adequately any grievances initiated by any of its members, in a manner approved by the Department on matters concerning quality of care and by the Commissioner on all other matters covered by this subtitle, under rules and regulations adopted under this subtitle.

(n) The health maintenance organization shall establish procedures to offer each member an opportunity to participate in matters of policy and operation.

(o) The health maintenance organization shall maintain a health and medical records system that:

(1) Under procedures assuring maximum confidentiality, is readily accessible to authorized persons;

(2) Can accurately document use by each member; and

(3) At a minimum:

(i) Identifies clearly each patient by:

1. Name;
2. Number;
3. Age; and
4. Sex; and

(ii) Shows clearly:

1. The services provided;
2. When the services are provided;
3. Where the services are provided;
4. By whom the services are provided;
5. The diagnosis and prognosis, if appropriate;
6. The treatment;
7. Any drug therapy; and
8. The health status of the patient, if appropriate.

(p)

(1) Except as provided in paragraph (3) of this subsection, individual enrollees and subscribers of health maintenance organizations issued certificates of authority to operate in this State may not be liable to any health care provider for any covered services provided to the enrollee or subscriber.

(2)

(i) A health care provider or any representative of a health care provider may not collect or attempt to collect from any subscriber or enrollee any money owed to the health care provider by a health maintenance organization issued a certificate of authority to operate in this State.

(ii) A health care provider or any representative of a health care provider may not maintain any action against any subscriber or enrollee to collect or attempt to collect any money owed to the health care provider by a health maintenance organization issued a certificate of authority to operate in this State.

(3) Notwithstanding any other provision of this subsection, a health care provider or representative of a health care provider may collect or attempt to collect from a subscriber or enrollee:

(i) Any copayment or coinsurance sums owed by the subscriber or enrollee to a health maintenance organization issued a certificate of authority to operate in this State for covered services provided by the health care provider;

(ii) If Medicare is the primary insurer and a health maintenance organization is the secondary insurer, any amount up to the Medicare approved or limiting amount, as specified under the Social Security Act, that is not owed to the health care provider by Medicare or the health maintenance organization after coordination of benefits has been completed, for Medicare covered services provided to the subscriber or enrollee by the health care provider; or

(iii) Any payment or charges for services that are not covered services.

(q)

(1) The Commissioner shall require each health maintenance organization to have an insolvency plan by January 1, 1990 which provides for:

(i) Continuation of benefits to subscribers and enrollees for the duration of the contract period for which premiums have been paid; and

(ii) Continuation of benefits to subscribers or enrollees who are admitted to an inpatient health care facility on the date of insolvency until, the earlier of:

1. The subscriber or enrollee is discharged from the inpatient health care facility; or
2. 365 days.

(2) In determining the adequacy of any insolvency plan, the Commissioner may consider:

(i) The existence of insurance to cover expenses incurred in continuing benefits after an insolvency;

(ii) Provisions in provider contracts obligating providers to continue to provide services to enrollees or subscribers:

1. For the duration of the contract period for which premiums have been made; and

2. If admitted to an inpatient health care facility, until the enrollee or subscriber is discharged or 365 days, whichever occurs first;

(iii) Reserves;

(iv) Letters of credit;

(v) Guarantees; or

(vi) Any other arrangement to assure that benefits are continued in accordance with the provisions of paragraph (1) of this subsection.

(r) Repealed by Acts 1996, ch. 503, § 1, effective July 1, 1996.

(s)

(1) In this subsection, "practice profile" means a profile, summary, economic analysis, or other analysis of data concerning services rendered or utilized by a provider under contract with or employed by a health maintenance organization for the provision of health care services by the provider to enrollees or subscribers of the health maintenance organization.

(2) If a health maintenance organization uses a practice profile as a factor in its contract review to evaluate a provider's status on a provider panel, the health maintenance organization shall disclose at the commencement and renewal of the contract and, not more often than annually, upon the request of the provider:

(i) A description of the criteria used to compile the practice profile concerning the provider; and

(ii) The manner in which the practice profile is used to evaluate the provider.

(3) The information provided under this subsection may not be used to create a cause of action.

(4) A health maintenance organization may not terminate a provider contract or provider's employment with the health maintenance organization on the basis of a practice profile without first informing the provider of the findings of the practice profile and the provider specific data underlying those findings.

(t) A health maintenance organization may not by contract, or in any other manner, require a provider to indemnify the health maintenance organization or hold the health maintenance organization harmless from a coverage decision or negligent act of the health maintenance organization.

§ 19-710.1 Payment to health care provider not under written contract

(a)

(1) In this section the following words have the meanings indicated.

(2) "Adjunct claims documentation" means an abstract of an enrollee's medical record which describes and summarizes the diagnosis and treatment of, and services rendered to, the enrollee, including, in the case of trauma rendered in a trauma center, an operative report, a discharge summary, a Maryland Ambulance Information Systems form, or a medical record.

(3) "Berenson-Eggers Type of Service Code" means a code in a classification system developed by the Centers for Medicare and Medicaid Services that groups Current Procedural Terminology codes together based on clinical consistency.

(4) "Enrollee" means a subscriber or member of a health maintenance organization.

(5) "Evaluation and management service" means any service with a Berenson-Eggers Type of Service Code in the category of evaluation and management.

(6) "Institute" means the Maryland Institute for Emergency Medical Services Systems.

(7) "Medicare Economic Index" means the fixed-weight input price index that:

(i) Measures the weighted average annual price change for various inputs needed to produce physician services; and

(ii) Is used by the Centers for Medicare and Medicaid Services in the calculation of reimbursement of physician services under Title XVIII of the federal Social Security Act.

(8) "Similarly licensed provider" means:

(i) For a physician:

1. A physician who is board certified or eligible in the same practice specialty; or

2. A group physician practice that contains board certified or eligible physicians in the same practice specialty;

(ii) For a health care provider that is not a physician, a health care provider that holds the same type of license.

(9)

(i) "Trauma center" means a primary adult resource center, level I trauma center, level II trauma center, level III trauma center, or pediatric trauma center that has been designated by the institute to provide care to trauma patients.

(ii) "Trauma center" includes an out-of-state pediatric facility that has entered into an agreement with the institute to provide care to trauma patients.

(10) "Trauma patient" means a patient that is evaluated or treated in a trauma center and is entered into the State trauma registry as a trauma patient.
(11) "Trauma physician" means a licensed physician who has been credentialed or designated by a trauma center to provide care to a trauma patient at a trauma center.

(b) In addition to any other provisions of this subtitle, for a covered service rendered to an enrollee of a health maintenance organization by a health care provider not under written contract with the health maintenance organization, the health maintenance organization or its agent:
(1) Shall pay the health care provider within 30 days after the receipt of a claim in accordance with the applicable provisions of this subtitle; and
(2) Shall pay the claim submitted by:
(i) A hospital at the rate approved by the Health Services Cost Review Commission;
(ii) A trauma physician for trauma care rendered to a trauma patient in a trauma center, at the greater of:
1. 140% of the rate paid by the Medicare program, as published by the Centers for Medicare and Medicaid Services, for the same covered service, to a similarly licensed provider; or
2. The rate as of January 1, 2001 that the health maintenance organization paid in the same geographic area, as published by the Centers for Medicare and Medicaid Services, for the same covered service, to a similarly licensed provider; and
(iii) Any other health care provider:
1. For an evaluation and management service, no less than the greater of:
A. 125% of the average rate the health maintenance organization paid as of January 1 of the previous calendar year in the same geographic area, as defined by the Centers for Medicare and Medicaid Services, for the same covered service, to similarly licensed providers under written contract with the health maintenance organization; or
B. 140% of the rate paid by Medicare, as published by the Centers for Medicare and Medicaid Services, for the same covered service to a similarly licensed provider in the same geographic area as of August 1, 2008, inflated by the change in the Medicare Economic Index from 2008 to the current year; and
2. For a service that is not an evaluation and management service, no less than 125% of the average rate the health maintenance organization paid as of January 1 of the previous calendar year in the same geographic area, as defined

by the Centers for Medicare and Medicaid Services, to a similarly licensed provider under written contract with the health maintenance organization for the same covered service.

(c) For the purposes of subsection (b)(2)(iii) of this section, a health maintenance organization shall calculate the average rate paid to similarly licensed providers under written contract with the health maintenance organization for the same covered service by summing the contracted rate for all occurrences of the Current Procedural Terminology Code for that service and then dividing by the total number of occurrences of the Current Procedural Terminology Code.

(d) A health maintenance organization shall disclose, on request of a health care provider not under written contract with the health maintenance organization, the reimbursement rate required under subsection (b)(2)(ii) and (iii) of this section.

(e)

(1) Subject to paragraph (2) of this subsection, a health maintenance organization may require a trauma physician not under contract with the health maintenance organization to submit appropriate adjunct claims documentation and to include on the uniform claim form a provider number assigned to the trauma physician by the health maintenance organization.

(2) If a health maintenance organization requires a trauma physician to include a provider number on the uniform claim form in accordance with paragraph (1) of this subsection, the health maintenance organization shall assign a provider number to a trauma physician not under contract with the health maintenance organization at the request of the physician.

(3) A trauma center, on request from a health maintenance organization, shall verify that a licensed physician is credentialed or otherwise designated by the trauma center to provide trauma care.

(4) Notwithstanding the provisions of § 19-701(d) of this subtitle, for trauma care rendered to a trauma patient in a trauma center by a trauma physician, a health maintenance organization may not require a referral or preauthorization for a service to be covered.

(f)

(1) A health maintenance organization may seek reimbursement from an enrollee for any payment under subsection (b) of this section for a claim or portion of a claim submitted by a health care provider and paid by the health maintenance organization that the health maintenance organization determines is the responsibility of the enrollee.

(2) The health maintenance organization may request and the health care provider shall provide adjunct claims documentation to assist in making the determination under paragraph (1) of this subsection or under subsection (b) of this section.

(g)

(1) A health care provider may enforce the provisions of this section by filing a complaint against a health maintenance organization with the Maryland Insurance Administration or by filing a civil action in a court of competent jurisdiction under § 1-501 or § 4-201 of the Courts Article.

(2) The Maryland Insurance Administration or a court shall award reasonable attorney fees if the complaint of the health care provider is sustained.

(h) The Maryland Health Care Commission annually shall review payments to health care providers to determine the compliance of health maintenance organizations with the requirements of this section and report its findings to the Maryland Insurance Administration.

(i) The Maryland Insurance Administration may take any action authorized under this subtitle or the Insurance Article, including conducting an examination under Title 2, Subtitle 2 of the Insurance Article, to investigate and enforce a violation of the provisions of this section.

(j) In addition to any other penalties under this subtitle, the Commissioner may impose a penalty not to exceed $5,000 on any health maintenance organization which violates the provisions of this section if the violation is committed with such frequency as to indicate a general business practice of the health maintenance organization.

(k) The Maryland Insurance Administration, in consultation with the Maryland Health Care Commission, shall adopt regulations to implement this section.

MARYLAND CODE ANNOTATED, INSURANCE

§ 14-205.2 Collection of money for services rendered by on-call physician or hospital-based physician

(a) Except as otherwise provided, this section applies to both on-call physicians and hospital-based physicians who:

(1) are nonpreferred providers;

(2) obtain an assignment of benefits from an insured; and

(3) notify the insurer of an insured in a manner specified by the Commissioner that the on-call physician or hospital-based physician has obtained and accepted the assignment of benefits from the insured.

(b)

(1) Except as provided in paragraph (3) of this subsection, an insured may not be liable to an on-call physician or a hospital-based physician subject to this section for covered services rendered by the on-call physician or hospital-based physician.

(2) An on-call physician or hospital-based physician subject to this section or a representative of an on-call physician or hospital-based physician subject to this section may not:

(i) collect or attempt to collect from an insured of an insurer any money owed to the on-call physician or hospital-based physician by the insurer for covered services rendered to the insured by the on-call physician or hospital-based physician; or

(ii) maintain any action against an insured of an insurer to collect or attempt to collect any money owed to the on-call physician or hospital-based physician by the insurer for covered services rendered to the insured by the on-call physician or hospital-based physician.

(3) An on-call physician or hospital-based physician subject to this section or a representative of an on-call physician or hospital-based physician subject to this section may collect or attempt to collect from an insured of an insurer:

(i) any deductible, copayment, or coinsurance amount owed by the insured for covered services rendered to the insured by the on-call physician or hospital-based physician;

(ii) if Medicare is the primary insurer and the insurer is the secondary insurer, any amount up to the Medicare approved or limiting amount, as specified under the federal Social Security Act, that is not owed to the on-call physician or hospital-based physician by Medicare or the insurer after coordination of benefits has been completed, for Medicare covered services rendered to the insured by the on-call physician or hospital-based physician; and

(iii) any payment or charges for services that are not covered services.

(c)

(1) This subsection applies only to on-call physicians subject to this section.

(2) For a covered service rendered to an insured of an insurer by an on-call physician subject to this section, the insurer or its agent:

(i) shall pay the on-call physician within 30 days after the receipt of a claim in accordance with the applicable provisions of this title; and

(ii) shall pay a claim submitted by the on-call physician for a covered service rendered to an insured in a hospital, no less than the greater of:

1. 140% of the average rate the insurer paid for the 12-month period that ends on January 1 of the previous calendar year in the same geographic area, as defined by the Centers for Medicare and Medicaid Services, for the same covered

service, to similarly licensed providers under written contract with the insurer; or

2. the average rate the insurer paid for the 12-month period that ended on January 1, 2010, in the same geographic area, as defined by the Centers for Medicare and Medicaid Services, for the same covered service to a similarly licensed provider not under written contract with the insurer, inflated by the change in the Medicare Economic Index from 2010 to the current year.

(d)

(1) This subsection applies only to hospital-based physicians subject to this section.

(2) For a covered service rendered to an insured of an insurer by a hospital-based physician subject to this section, the insurer or its agent:

(i) shall pay the hospital-based physician within 30 days after the receipt of the claim in accordance with the applicable provisions of this title; and

(ii) shall pay a claim submitted by the hospital-based physician for a covered service rendered to an insured no less than the greater of:

1. 140% of the average rate the insurer paid for the 12-month period that ends on January 1 of the previous calendar year in the same geographic area, as defined by the Centers for Medicare and Medicaid Services, for the same covered service, to similarly licensed providers, who are hospital-based physicians, under written contract with the insurer; or

2. the final allowed amount of the insurer for the same covered service for the 12-month period that ended on January 1, 2010, inflated by the change in the Medicare Economic Index to the current year, to the hospital-based physician billing under the same federal tax identification number the hospital-based physician used in calendar year 2009.

(e)

(1) For the purposes of subsections (c)(2)(ii)1 and (d)(2)(ii)1 of this section, an insurer shall calculate the average rate paid to similarly licensed providers under written contract with the insurer for the same covered service by summing the contracted rate for all occurrences of the Current Procedural Terminology Code for that covered service and then dividing by the total number of occurrences of the Current Procedural Terminology Code.

(2) For the purposes of subsection (c)(2)(ii)2 of this section, an insurer shall calculate the average rate paid to similarly licensed providers not under written contract with the insurer for the same covered service

by summing the rates paid to similarly licensed providers not under written contract with the insurer for all occurrences of the Current Procedural Terminology Code for that covered service and then dividing by the total number of occurrences of the Current Procedural Terminology Code.

(f) An insurer shall disclose, on request of an on-call physician or hospital-based physician subject to this section, the reimbursement rate required under subsection (c)(2)(ii) or (d)(2)(ii) of this section.

(g)

(1) An insurer may seek reimbursement from an insured for any payment under subsection (c)(2)(ii) or (d)(2)(ii) of this section for a claim or portion of a claim submitted by an on-call physician or hospital-based physician subject to this section and paid by the insurer that the insurer determines is the responsibility of the insured based on the insurance contract.

(2) The insurer may request and the on-call physician or hospital-based physician shall provide adjunct claims documentation to assist in making the determination under paragraph (1) of this subsection or under subsection (c) of this section.

(h)

(1) An on-call physician or hospital-based physician subject to this section may enforce the provisions of this section by filing a complaint against an insurer with the Administration or by filing a civil action in a court of competent jurisdiction under § 1-501 or § 4-201 of the Courts Article.

(2) The Administration or a court shall award reasonable attorney's fees if the Administration or court finds that:

(i) the insurer's conduct in maintaining or defending the proceeding was in bad faith; or

(ii) the insurer acted willfully in the absence of a bona fide dispute.

(i) The Administration may take any action authorized under this article, including conducting an examination under Title 2, Subtitle 2 of this article, to investigate and enforce a violation of the provisions of this section.

(j) In addition to any other penalties under this article, the Commissioner may impose a penalty not to exceed $5,000 on an insurer for each violation of this section.

(k) The Administration, in consultation with the Maryland Health Care Commission, shall adopt regulations to implement this section.

MINNESOTA STATUTES

§ 62J.811 Provider balance billing requirements

Subdivision 1. Billing requirements.

(a) Each health care provider and health facility shall comply with the federal Consolidated Appropriations Act, 2021, Division BB also known as the "No Surprises Act," including any federal regulations adopted under that act.

(b) For the purposes of this section, "provider" or "facility" means any health care provider or facility pursuant to section 62A.63, subdivision 2, or 62J.03, subdivision 8, that is subject to relevant provisions of the No Surprises Act.

Subdivision 2. Investigations and compliance.

(a) The commissioner shall, to the extent practicable, seek the cooperation of health care providers and facilities, and may provide any support and assistance as available, in obtaining compliance with this section.

(b) The commissioner shall determine the manner and processes for fulfilling any responsibilities and taking any of the actions in paragraphs (c) to (f).

(c) A person who believes a health care provider or facility has not complied with the requirements of the No Surprises Act or this section may file a complaint with the commissioner in the manner determined by the commissioner.

(d) The commissioner shall conduct compliance reviews and investigate complaints filed under this section in the manner determined by the commissioner to ascertain whether health care providers and facilities are complying with this section.

(e) The commissioner may report violations under this section to other relevant federal and state departments and jurisdictions as appropriate, including the attorney general and relevant licensing boards, and may also coordinate on investigations and enforcement of this section with other relevant federal and state departments and jurisdictions as appropriate, including the attorney general and relevant licensing boards.

(f) A health care provider or facility may contest whether the finding of facts constitute a violation of this section according to the contested case proceeding in sections 14.57 to 14.62, subject to appeal according to sections 14.63 to 14.68.

(g) Any data collected by the commissioner as part of an active investigation or active compliance review under this section are classified (1) if the data is not on individuals, it is classified as protected nonpublic data pursuant to section 13.02 subdivision 13; or (2) if the data is on individuals, it is classified as confidential pursuant to sections 13.02, subdivision 3. Data describing the final disposition of an investigative or compliance review are classified as public.

Subdivision 3. Civil penalty.

(a) The commissioner, in monitoring and enforcing this section, may levy a civil monetary penalty against each health care provider or facility found to be in violation of up to $100 for each violation, but may not exceed $25,000 for identical violations during a calendar year.

(b) No civil monetary penalty shall be imposed under this section for violations that occur prior to January 1, 2024.

§ 62K.11 Balance billing prohibited

(a) A network provider is prohibited from billing an enrollee for any amount in excess of the allowable amount the health carrier has contracted for with the provider as total payment for the health care service. A network provider is permitted to bill an enrollee the approved co-payment, deductible, or coinsurance.

(b) A network provider is permitted to bill an enrollee for services not covered by the enrollee's health plan as long as the enrollee agrees in writing in advance before the service is performed to pay for the noncovered service.

§ 62Q.556 Consumer protections against balance billing

Subdivision 1. Nonparticipating provider balance billing prohibition.

(a) Except as provided in paragraph (b), balance billing is prohibited when an enrollee receives services from:

(1) a nonparticipating provider at a participating hospital or ambulatory surgical center, as described by the No Surprises Act, including any federal regulations adopted under that act;

(2) a participating provider that sends a specimen taken from the enrollee in the participating provider's practice setting to a nonparticipating laboratory, pathologist, or other medical testing facility; or

(3) a nonparticipating provider or facility providing emergency services as defined in section 62Q.55, subdivision 3, and other services as described in the requirements of the No Surprises Act.

(b) The services described in paragraph (a), clauses (1), (2), and (3), as defined in the No Surprises Act, and any federal regulations adopted under that act, are subject to balance billing if the enrollee provides informed consent prior to receiving services from the nonparticipating provider acknowledging that the use of a provider, or the services to be rendered, may result in costs not covered by the health plan. The informed consent must comply with all requirements of the No Surprises Act, including any federal regulations adopted under that act.

Subdivision 2. Cost-sharing requirements and independent dispute resolution.

(a) An enrollee's financial responsibility for the nonparticipating provider services described in subdivision 1, paragraph (a), shall be the same cost-sharing requirements, including co-payments, deductibles, coinsurance, coverage restrictions, and coverage limitations, as those applicable to services received by the enrollee from a participating provider. A health plan company must apply any enrollee cost sharing requirements, including co-payments, deductibles, and coinsurance, for nonparticipating provider services to the enrollee's annual out-of-pocket limit to the same extent payments to a participating provider would be applied.

(b) A health plan company must attempt to negotiate the reimbursement, less any applicable enrollee cost sharing under paragraph (a), for the nonparticipating provider services with the nonparticipating provider. If the attempt to negotiate reimbursement for the nonparticipating provider services does not result in a resolution, either party may initiate the federal independent dispute resolution process pursuant to the No Surprises Act, including any federal regulations adopted under that act.

Subdivision 3. Annual data reporting.

(a) Beginning April 1, 2024, a health plan company must report annually to the commissioner of health:
   (1) the total number of claims and total billed and paid amounts for nonparticipating provider services, by service and provider type, submitted to the health plan in the prior calendar year; and
   (2) the total number of enrollee complaints received regarding the rights and protections established by the No Surprises Act in the prior calendar year.

(b) The commissioners of commerce and health shall develop the form and manner for health plan companies to comply with paragraph (a).

Subdivision 4. Enforcement

(a) Any provider or facility, including a health care provider or facility pursuant to section 62A.63, subdivision 2, or 62J.03, subdivision 8, that is subject to the relevant provisions of the No Surprises Act is subject to the requirements of this section and section 62J.811.

(b) The commissioner of commerce or health shall enforce this section.

(c) If a health-related licensing board has cause to believe that a provider has violated this section, it may further investigate and enforce the provisions of this section pursuant to chapter 214.

MISSOURI CODE REGULATIONS TITLE 20

§ 400-14.100 External Arbitration

(1) When a health carrier or a health care professional provides written notification to the director and the other party of its intent to initiate arbitration proceedings pursuant to section 376.690.2(5), RSMo, the health carrier or health care professional shall provide the following information to the director:
   (A) The name and contact information for the health carrier;
   (B) The name and contact information for the out-of-network health care professional;
   (C) The billed amount charged by the out-of-network health care professional for the service that is the subject of the dispute;
   (D) The amount of the final offer made by each party, and the date the final offer was made;
   (E) An attestation affirming that the information provided by the health carrier or health care professional is true and accurate; and
   (F) Any additional information requested by the director.

(2) Prior to commencing arbitration proceedings pursuant to section 376.690.2(5), RSMo, a health care professional and a health carrier must demonstrate they have completed the negotiation period described in section 376.690.2(1)-(3), RSMo.

(3) The director shall publish on the department's website (www.insurance.mo.gov) a list of entities providing arbitration services.

(4) In order to qualify as a provider of arbitration services as described in section 376.690, RSMo, an entity or arbitrator must—
   (A) Be currently engaged in arbitrating disputes between health carriers and health care professionals;
   (B) Adhere to procedural rules outlined by the American Arbitration Association, the American Health Lawyers Association, or another entity with similar procedural rules, as determined by the director; and
   (C) Have in place policies and procedures to avoid conflicts of interest.

(5) An arbitrator or entity seeking to be included on the list published by the department may submit such a request in writing to the director, outlining its qualifications. The director has sole discretion to determine whether or not to include an arbitrator or arbitration entity on the list published by the department, and may amend or revise the list from time-to-time as he or she deems necessary.

MISSOURI CODE REGULATIONS TITLE 22

§ 10-2.010 Definitions

(1) Accident. An unforeseen and unavoidable event resulting in an injury.

(2) Active employee. A benefit-eligible person employed by the state or agency of the state who meets the plan eligibility requirements. An eligible

variable-hour employee is considered an active employee for the purposes of this chapter.

(3) Activities of daily living. Bathing, dressing, toileting, and associated personal hygiene; transferring (being moved in and out of a bed, chair, wheelchair, tub, or shower); mobility, eating (getting nourishment into the body by any means other than intravenous), and continence (voluntarily maintaining control of bowel and/or bladder function; in the event of incontinence, maintaining a reasonable level of personal hygiene).

(4) Administrative appeal. A written request submitted by or on behalf of a member involving plan-related administrative issues such as eligibility, effective dates of coverage, and plan changes.

(5) Adverse benefit determination. An adverse benefit determination means any of the following:

  (A) A denial, reduction, or termination of, or a failure to provide or make payment (in whole or in part) for a benefit based on a determination of an individual's eligibility to participate in the plan;

  (B) A denial, reduction, or termination of, or a failure to provide or make payment (in whole or in part) for a benefit resulting from the application of any utilization review, or a failure to cover an item or service for which benefits are otherwise provided because it is determined to be experimental, investigational, or not medically necessary or appropriate; or

  (C) Rescission of coverage after an individual has been covered under the plan.

(6) Allowed amount. Maximum amount on which payment is based for covered health care services. This may be called eligible expense, payment allowance, or negotiated rate. If the provider charges more than the allowed amount, the member may be balance-billed (see balance billing, section (8)).

(7) Applied behavior analysis. The design, implementation, and evaluation of environmental modifications, using behavior stimuli and consequences, to produce socially-significant improvement in human behavior, including the use of observation, measurement, and functional analysis of the relationship between environment and behavior.

(8) Balance billing. When a provider bills for the difference between the provider's charge and the allowed amount. For example, if the provider's charge is one hundred dollars ($ 100) and the allowed amount is seventy dollars ($ 70), the provider may bill the member for the remaining thirty dollars ($ 30). A network provider may not balance bill.

(9) Benefits. Health care services covered by the plan.

(10) Board. The board of trustees of the Missouri Consolidated Health Care Plan (MCHCP).

(11) Cancellation of coverage. The ending of medical, dental, or vision coverage per a subscriber's voluntary request.

(12) Claims administrator. An organization or group responsible for processing claims and associated services for a health plan.

(13) Coinsurance. The member's share of the costs of a covered health care service, calculated as a percent (for example, twenty percent (20%)) of the allowed amount for the service. The member pays coinsurance plus any deductibles owed. For example, if the health insurance or plan's allowed amount for an office visit is one hundred dollars ($ 100) and the member has met his/her deductible, the member's coinsurance payment of twenty percent (20%) would be twenty dollars ($ 20). The health insurance or plan pays the rest of the allowed amount.

(14) Congenital defect. Existing or dating from birth. Acquired through development while in the uterus.

(15) Copayment. A fixed amount, for example, fifteen dollars ($ 15), the member pays for a covered health care service, usually when the member receives the service. The amount can vary by the type of covered health care service.

(16) Date of service. Date medical services are received.

(17) Deductible. The amount the member owes for health care services that the health plan covers before the member's health plan begins to pay. For example, if the deductible is one thousand dollars ($ 1,000), the member's plan will not pay anything until s/he meets his/her one thousand dollar ($ 1,000) deductible for covered health care services subject to the deductible. The deductible may not apply to all services.

(18) Dependent. Spouse or child(ren) enrolled in the plan by a subscriber.

(19) Diabetes Self-Management Education. A program prescribed by a provider and facilitated by health care professionals with the appropriate credentials, training, and experience to educate and support members with diabetes.

(20) Doctor/physician. A licensed practitioner of the healing arts, as approved by the plan administrator, including:

- (A) Doctor of medicine;
- (B) Doctor of osteopathy;
- (C) Podiatrist;
- (D) Optometrist;
- (E) Chiropractor;
- (F) Psychologist;
- (G) Doctor of dental medicine, including dental surgery;
- (H) Doctor of dentistry; or
- (I) Qualified practitioner of spiritual healing whose organization is generally recognized for health insurance reimbursement purposes and whose principles and practices of spiritual healing are well established and recognized.

(21) Effective date. The date on which coverage takes effect.

(22) Eligible variable-hour employee. An employee of a state department or agency, whose employees are otherwise eligible for coverage, but is in a position not covered by a retirement system and the employer has notified the plan administrator that the employee has become benefit eligible due to having worked

on average for thirty (30) or more hours per week during the time period measured.

(23) Eligibility date. The first day a member is qualified to enroll for coverage.

(24) Eligibility period. The time allowed to enroll in accordance with the rules in this chapter.

(25) Emergency medical condition. The sudden and, at the time, unexpected onset of a health condition that manifests itself by symptoms of sufficient severity that would lead a prudent layperson, possessing an average knowledge of medicine and health, to believe that immediate medical care is required, which may include, but shall not be limited to:
  - (A) Placing a person's health in significant jeopardy;
  - (B) Serious impairment to a bodily function;
  - (C) Serious dysfunction of any bodily organ or part;
  - (D) Inadequately controlled pain; or
  - (E) With respect to a pregnant woman who is having contractions—
    1. That there is inadequate time to effect a safe transfer to another hospital before delivery; or
    2. That transfer to another hospital may pose a threat to the health or safety of the woman or unborn child.

(26) Emergency services. With respect to an emergency medical condition—
  - (A) A medical screening examination that is within the capability of the emergency department of a hospital, including ancillary service routinely available to the emergency department to evaluate such emergency medical condition; and
  - (B) Such further medical examination and treatment, to the extent they are within the capabilities of the staff and facilities available at the hospital, as are required to stabilize the patient. The term "to stabilize" means to provide such medical treatment of the condition as may be necessary to ensure, within reasonable medical probability, that no material deterioration of the condition is likely to result from, or occur during, the transfer of the individual from a facility.

(27) Employee. A benefit-eligible person employed by the state, including present and future retirees from state employment, who meet the plan eligibility requirements.

(28) Employer. The state department or agency that employs the eligible employee.

(29) Essential benefits. The plan covers essential benefits as required by the Patient Protection and Affordable Care Act. Essential benefits include:
  - (A) Ambulatory patient services—office visits, urgent care, outpatient diagnostic procedures, outpatient surgery, and outpatient hospice;
  - (B) Emergency services—ambulance services and emergency room services;
  - (C) Hospitalization—inpatient hospital benefits, inpatient surgery, transplants, and inpatient hospice;

(D) Maternity and newborn care—maternity coverage and newborn screenings;
(E) Mental health and substance use disorder services, including behavioral health treatment—inpatient and outpatient and mental health/substance use disorder office visits;
(F) Prescription drugs;
(G) Rehabilitative and habilitative services and devices—durable medical equipment; cardiac and pulmonary rehabilitation; outpatient physical, speech, and occupational therapy; and home health care;
(H) Laboratory services—lab and X-ray;
(I) Preventive and wellness services and chronic disease management; and
(J) Pediatric services, including oral and vision care—routine vision exam, dental care/accidental injury, vaccinations, preventive services, and newborn screenings.

(30) Excluded drug. A drug the pharmacy benefit manager (PBM) does not pay for or cover unless an exception is approved by the PBM.

(31) Excluded services. Health care services that the member's health plan does not pay for or cover.

(32) Experimental/investigational/unproven. A treatment, procedure, device, or drug that meets any of the criteria listed below and that the plan administrator determines, in the exercise of its discretion, is considered experimental/investigational/unproven and is not eligible for coverage under the plan—
(A) Has not received the approval of the U.S. Food and Drug Administration for marketing the drug or device at the time it is furnished, if such approval is required by law;
(B) Is shown by reliable evidence that the consensus of opinion among experts regarding the treatment, procedure, device, or drug is that further studies or clinical trials are necessary to determine its maximum tolerated dose, its toxicity, its safety, its efficacy, or its efficiency as compared with the standard means of treatment or diagnosis; or
(C) Reliable evidence includes anything determined to be such by the plan administrator, in the exercise of its discretion, and may include published reports and articles in the medical and scientific literature generally considered to be authoritative by the national medical professional community.

(33) Formulary. A list of U.S. Food and Drug Administration approved drugs and supplies developed by the pharmacy benefit manager (PBM) and covered by the plan administrator. The PBM categorizes each formulary drug and formulary supply as preferred or non-preferred.

(34) Foster parent. Any approved specialized foster parent as defined in section 210.543, RSMo, also referred to as Elevated Needs Level B, and licensed under Chapter 210, RSMo, who provides temporary foster care for children who have a documented history of presenting behaviors or diagnoses which render

the child unable to effectively function outside of a highly structured setting, not in anticipation of adoption, and not for children related to such Elevated Needs Level B foster parent.

(35) Generic drug. The chemical equivalent of a brand-name drug with an expired patent. The color or shape may be different, but the active ingredients must be the same for both.

(36) Health assessment (HA). An online questionnaire about a member's health and lifestyle habits required for participation the *Strive for Wellness*(R) Partnership Incentive.

(37) Health Education Quiz. A series of questions administered by MCHCP designed to measure understanding of MCHCP benefits and/or general health knowledge.

(38) Health Savings Account (HSA). A tax-advantaged savings account that may be used to pay for current or future qualified medical expenses. Enrollment in the plan's qualified High Deductible Health Plan is required for participation in an HSA.

(39) High Deductible Health Plan. A health plan with a higher deductible than a traditional health plan that, when combined with an HSA, provides a tax-advantaged way to help save for future medical expenses.

(40) Illness. Any bodily sickness, disease, or mental/nervous disorder. For purposes of this plan, pregnancy is considered an illness.

(41) Incident. A definite and separate occurrence of a condition.

(42) Injury. A condition that results independently of an illness and all other causes and is a result of an external force or accident.

(43) Lifetime maximum. The amount payable by a medical plan during a covered member's life for specific non-essential benefits.

(44) Long-term disability subscriber. A subscriber eligible for long-term disability coverage from Missouri State Employees' Retirement System (MOSERS), Missouri Department of Transportation and Highway Patrol Employees' Retirement System (MPERS), or another retirement system whose members are grandfathered for coverage under the plan by law.

(45) MCHCPid. An individual MCHCP subscriber identifier used for member verification and validation.

(46) myMCHCP. A secure MCHCP member website that allows members to review coverage selections, verify covered dependents, make coverage changes, add/change email address, retrieve and send secure messages, upload documents, and access health plan websites.

(47) Medically necessary. The fact that a provider has performed, prescribed, recommended, ordered, or approved a treatment, procedure, service, or supply; or that it is the only available treatment, procedure, service, or supply for a condition, does not, in itself, determine medical necessity. Medically necessary treatments, procedures, services, or supplies that the plan administrator or its designee determines, in the exercise of its discretion are—

(A) Expected to be of clear clinical benefit to the member;

(B) Clinically appropriate, in terms of type, frequency, extent, site and duration, and considered effective for a member's illness, injury, mental illness, substance use disorder, disease, or its symptoms;

(C) In accordance with generally accepted standards of medical practice that are based on credible scientific evidence published in peer-reviewed medical literature generally recognized by the relevant medical community;

(D) Not primarily for member or provider convenience; and

(E) Not more costly than an alternative service(s) or supply that is at least as likely to produce equivalent therapeutic or diagnostic results as to the diagnosis or treatment of member's illness, injury, disease, or symptoms.

(48) Medicare-allowed amount. The fee Medicare sets as reasonable for a covered medical service. This is the amount a provider is paid by the member and Medicare for a service or supply. It may be less than the actual amount charged by a health care provider.

(49) Medicare Prescription Drug Plan (PDP). The Medicare Prescription Drug Plan, administered by Express Scripts Medicare PDP, is a Medicare Part D Plan with additional coverage to ensure Medicare members have similar benefits to non-Medicare members.

(50) Member. Any person covered as either a subscriber or a dependent in accordance with the terms and conditions of the plan.

(51) Network. The providers, the health insurer, or plan has contracted with to provide health care services to members.

(52) Non-network. The providers, the health insurer, or plan does not contract with to provide health care services to members. Some providers may be a part of secondary provider networks recognized by the vendor for non-network benefits.

(53) Out-of-pocket maximum. The most the member will pay during a plan year before the plan begins to pay one hundred percent (100%) of the allowed amount. This limit never includes the member's premium, balance-billed charges, or health care services the plan does not cover.

(54) Participant. Shall have the same meaning as the term member defined herein (see member, section (50)).

(55) Plan. The program of health care benefits established by the board of trustees of the Missouri Consolidated Health Care Plan as authorized by state law.

(56) Plan administrator. The board of trustees of the Missouri Consolidated Health Care Plan, which is the sole fiduciary of the plan. The board has all discretionary authority to interpret its provisions and to control the operation and administration of the plan and whose decisions are final and binding on all parties.

(57) Plan year. The period of January 1 through December 31.

(58) Preferred provider organization (PPO). An arrangement with providers whereby discounted rates are given to plan members. Benefits are paid at a higher level when network providers are used.

(59) Premium. The monthly amount that must be paid for health insurance.

(60) Primary care provider (PCP). An internist, family/general practitioner, pediatrician, or physician assistant or nurse practitioner in any of the practice areas listed in this definition.

(61) Preauthorization. A decision by the plan that a health care service, treatment plan, prescription drug, or durable medical equipment is medically necessary. Sometimes called prior authorization, prior approval, or precertification. The plan may require preauthorization for certain services before the member receives them, except in an emergency. Preauthorization is not a promise the plan will cover the cost. The provider must contact the appropriate plan administrator to request preauthorization.

(62) Provider. A physician, hospital, medical agency, specialist, or other duly licensed health care facility or practitioner certified or otherwise authorized to furnish health care services pursuant to the law of the jurisdiction in which care or treatment is received. A doctor/physician as defined in 22 CSR 10-2.010(22). Other providers include, but are not limited to:

- (A) Audiologist (AUD or Ph.D.);
- (B) Certified Addiction Counselor for Substance Abuse (CAC);
- (C) Certified Nurse Midwife (CNM)—when acting within the scope of his/her license in the state in which s/he practices and performing a service which would be payable under this plan when performed by a physician;
- (D) Certified Social Worker or Masters in Social Work (MSW);
- (E) Chiropractor;
- (F) Licensed Clinical Social Worker (LCSW);
- (G) Licensed Professional Counselor (LPC);
- (H) Licensed Psychologist (LP);
- (I) Nurse Practitioner (NP);
- (J) Physician Assistant (PA);
- (K) Occupational Therapist;
- (L) Physical Therapist;
- (M) Speech Therapist;
- (N) Registered Nurse Anesthetist (CRNA);
- (O) Registered Nurse Practitioner (ARNP); or
- (P) Therapist with a Ph.D. or Master's Degree in Psychology or Counseling.

(63) Prudent layperson. An individual possessing an average knowledge of health and medicine.

(64) Qualified Medical Child Support Order (QMCSO). A child support order from a court of competent jurisdiction or state child care agency, which requires the plan to provide coverage for a dependent child or member if the plan normally provides coverage for dependent children.

(65) Retiree. Notwithstanding any provision of law to the contrary, for the purposes of these regulations a "retiree" is defined as a former employee who, at the

time of retirement, is receiving an annuity benefit from a state-sponsored retirement system.

(66) Sound, natural teeth. Teeth and/or tissue that is viable, functional, and free of disease. A sound, natural tooth has no decay, fillings on no more than two (2) surfaces, no gum disease associated with bone loss, no history of root canal therapy, is not a dental implant, and functions normally in chewing and speech.

(67) Specialty care physician/specialist. A physician who is not a primary care physician and provides medical services to members concentrated in a specific medical area of expertise.

(68) Specialty medications. High-cost drugs, as determined by the pharmacy benefit manager and/or third party administrator, which treat chronic or complex conditions such as hepatitis C, multiple sclerosis, and rheumatoid arthritis.

(69) State. Missouri.

(70) Step therapy. Therapy designed to encourage use of therapeutically equivalent, lower-cost alternatives before using more expensive therapy. It is especially for people who take prescription drugs regularly to treat ongoing medical conditions and is developed under the guidance and direction of independent, licensed doctors, pharmacists, and other medical experts.

(71) Subrogation. The substitution of one (1) "party" for another. Subrogation entitles the insurer to the rights and remedies that would otherwise belong to the insured (the subscriber) for a loss covered by the insurance policy. Subrogation allows the plan to stand in the place of the member and recover the money directly from the other insurer.

(72) Subscriber. The person who elects coverage under the plan.

(73) Survivor. A dependent of a deceased vested active employee, terminated vested subscriber, vested long-term disability subscriber, or retiree.

(74) Termination of coverage. The termination of medical, dental, or vision coverage initiated by the employer or required by MCHCP eligibility policies.

(75) Tobacco. Cigarettes, cigarette papers, clove cigarettes, cigars, smokeless tobacco, smoking tobacco, other form of tobacco products, or products made with tobacco substitute containing nicotine.

(76) Tobacco-free. A member has not used a tobacco product in at least the previous three (3) months and plans to remain tobacco-free in the future.

(77) Usual, customary, and reasonable. The amount paid for a medical service in a geographic area based on what providers in the area usually charge for the same or similar medical service.

(78) Vendor. The current applicable third-party administrators of MCHCP benefits or other services.

(79) Vested subscriber. An active employee eligible for coverage under the plan and eligible for future benefits from MOSERS, MPERS, or grandfathered for coverage under the plan by law.

MISSOURI REVISED STATUTES

§ 376.690 Unanticipated out-of-network care, claim procedure—definitions—limitation on amount billed to patient—external arbitration process—rulemaking authority

1. As used in this section, the following terms shall mean:
   (1) "Emergency medical condition", the same meaning given to such term in section 376.1350;
   (2) "Facility", the same meaning given to such term in section 376.1350;
   (3) "Health care professional", the same meaning given to such term in section 376.1350;
   (4) "Health carrier", the same meaning given to such term in section 376.1350;
   (5) "Unanticipated out-of-network care", health care services received by a patient in an in-network facility from an out-of-network health care professional from the time the patient presents with an emergency medical condition until the time the patient is discharged.

2.
   (1) Health care professionals shall send any claim for charges incurred for unanticipated out-of-network care to the patient's health carrier within one hundred eighty days of the delivery of the unanticipated out-of-network care on a U.S. Centers of Medicare and Medicaid Services Form 1500, or its successor form, or electronically using the 837 HIPAA format, or its successor.
   (2) Within forty-five processing days, as defined in section 376.383, of receiving the health care professional's claim, the health carrier shall offer to pay the health care professional a reasonable reimbursement for unanticipated out-of-network care based on the health care professional's services. If the health care professional participates in one or more of the carrier's commercial networks, the offer of reimbursement for unanticipated out-of-network care shall be the amount from the network which has the highest reimbursement.
   (3) If the health care professional declines the health carrier's initial offer of reimbursement, the health carrier and health care professional shall have sixty days from the date of the initial offer of reimbursement to negotiate in good faith to attempt to determine the reimbursement for the unanticipated out-of-network care.
   (4) If the health carrier and health care professional do not agree to a reimbursement amount by the end of the sixty-day negotiation period, the dispute shall be resolved through an arbitration process as specified in subsection 4 of this section.

(5) To initiate arbitration proceedings, either the health carrier or health care professional must provide written notification to the director and the other party within one hundred twenty days of the end of the negotiation period, indicating their intent to arbitrate the matter and notifying the director of the billed amount and the date and amount of the final offer by each party. A claim for unanticipated out-of-network care may be resolved between the parties at any point prior to the commencement of the arbitration proceedings. Claims may be combined for purposes of arbitration, but only to the extent the claims represent similar circumstances and services provided by the same health care professional, and the parties attempted to resolve the dispute in accordance with subdivisions (3) to (5) of this subsection.

(6) No health care professional who sends a claim to a health carrier under subsection 2 of this section shall send a bill to the patient for any difference between the reimbursement rate as determined under this subsection and the health care professional's billed charge.

3.

(1) When unanticipated out-of-network care is provided, the health care professional who sends a claim to a health carrier under subsection 2 of this section may bill a patient for no more than the cost-sharing requirements described under this section.

(2) Cost-sharing requirements shall be based on the reimbursement amount as determined under subsection 2 of this section.

(3) The patient's health carrier shall inform the health care professional of its enrollee's cost-sharing requirements within forty-five processing days of receiving a claim from the health care professional for services provided.

(4) The in-network deductible and out-of-pocket maximum cost-sharing requirements shall apply to the claim for the unanticipated out-of-network care.

4. The director shall ensure access to an external arbitration process when a health care professional and health carrier cannot agree to a reimbursement under subdivision (3) of subsection 2 of this section. In order to ensure access, when notified of a parties' intent to arbitrate, the director shall randomly select an arbitrator for each case from the department's approved list of arbitrators or entities that provide binding arbitration. The director shall specify the criteria for an approved arbitrator or entity by rule. The costs of arbitration shall be shared equally between and will be directly billed to the health care professional and health carrier. These costs will include, but are not limited to, reasonable time necessary for the arbitrator to review materials in preparation for the arbitration, travel expenses and reasonable time following the arbitration for drafting of the final decision.

5. At the conclusion of such arbitration process, the arbitrator shall issue a final decision, which shall be binding on all parties. The arbitrator shall provide a copy of the final decision to the director. The initial request for arbitration, all correspondence and documents received by the department and the final arbitration decision shall be considered a closed record under section 374.071. However, the director may release aggregated summary data regarding the arbitration process. The decision of the arbitrator shall not be considered an agency decision nor shall it be considered a contested case within the meaning of section 536.010.
6. The arbitrator shall determine a dollar amount due under subsection 2 of this section between one hundred twenty percent of the Medicare-allowed amount and the seventieth percentile of the usual and customary rate for the unanticipated out-of-network care, as determined by benchmarks from independent nonprofit organizations that are not affiliated with insurance carriers or provider organizations.
7. When determining a reasonable reimbursement rate, the arbitrator shall consider the following factors if the health care professional believes the payment offered for the unanticipated out-of-network care does not properly recognize:
   (1) The health care professional's training, education, or experience;
   (2) The nature of the service provided;
   (3) The health care professional's usual charge for comparable services provided;
   (4) The circumstances and complexity of the particular case, including the time and place the services were provided; and
   (5) The average contracted rate for comparable services provided in the same geographic area.
8. The enrollee shall not be required to participate in the arbitration process. The health care professional and health carrier shall execute a nondisclosure agreement prior to engaging in an arbitration under this section.
9. The department of insurance, financial institutions and professional registration may promulgate rules and fees as necessary to implement the provisions of this section, including but not limited to procedural requirements for arbitration. Any rule or portion of a rule, as that term is defined in section 536.010, that is created under the authority delegated in this section shall become effective only if it complies with and is subject to all of the provisions of chapter 536 and, if applicable, section 536.028. This section and chapter 536 are nonseverable and if any of the powers vested with the general assembly pursuant to chapter 536 to review, to delay the effective date, or to disapprove and annul a rule are subsequently held unconstitutional, then the grant of rulemaking authority and any rule proposed or adopted after August 28, 2018, shall be invalid and void.

§ 376.1367 Emergency services benefit determination, coverage required, when

When conducting utilization review or making a benefit determination for emergency services:

(1) A health carrier shall cover emergency services necessary to screen and stabilize an enrollee, as determined by the treating emergency department health care provider, and shall not require prior authorization of such services;

(2) Coverage of emergency services shall be subject to applicable co-payments, coinsurance and deductibles;

(3) Before a health carrier denies payment for an emergency medical service based on the absence of an emergency medical condition, it shall review the enrollee's medical record regarding the emergency medical condition at issue. If a health carrier requests records for a potential denial where emergency services were rendered, the health care provider shall submit the record of the emergency services to the carrier within forty-five processing days, or the claim shall be subject to section 376.383. The health carrier's review of emergency services shall be completed by a board-certified physician licensed under chapter 334 to practice medicine in this state;

(4) When an enrollee receives an emergency service that requires immediate post evaluation or post stabilization services, a health carrier shall provide an authorization decision within sixty minutes of receiving a request; if the authorization decision is not made within sixty minutes, such services shall be deemed approved;

(5) When a patient's health benefit plan does not include or require payment to out-of-network health care providers for emergency services including but not limited to health maintenance organization plans, as defined in section 354.400, or a health benefit plan offered by a health carrier consistent with subdivision (19) of section 376.426, payment for all emergency services as defined in section 376.1350 necessary to screen and stabilize an enrollee shall be paid directly to the health care provider by the health carrier. Additionally, any services authorized by the health carrier for the enrollee once the enrollee is stabilized shall also be paid by the health carrier directly to the health care provider.

MONTANA CODE ANNOTATED

§ 30-14-2602 Balance billing information—notification to ambulance companies

(2)An ambulance service that transfers a bill to a collection agency shall state that the collection agency may not report as delinquent to a consumer reporting agency a bill covered by subsection (1).

§ 39-71-704 Payment of medical, hospital, and related services—fee schedules and hospital rates—fee limitation

(1) In addition to the compensation provided under this chapter and as an additional benefit separate and apart from compensation benefits actually provided, the following must be furnished:
   (a) After the happening of a compensable injury or occupational disease and subject to other provisions of this chapter, the insurer shall furnish reasonable primary medical services, including prescription drugs for conditions that are a direct result of the compensable injury or occupational disease, for those periods specified in this section.
   (b) Subject to the limitations in this chapter, the insurer shall furnish secondary medical services only upon a clear demonstration of cost-effectiveness of the services in returning the injured worker to actual employment.
   (c) The insurer shall replace or repair prescription eyeglasses, prescription contact lenses, prescription hearing aids, and dentures that are damaged or lost as a result of an injury, as defined in 39-71-119, arising out of and in the course of employment.
   (d)
      (i) The insurer shall reimburse a worker for reasonable travel, lodging, meals, and miscellaneous expenses incurred in travel to a health care provider for treatment of an injury pursuant to rules adopted by the department. Reimbursement must be at the rates allowed for reimbursement for state employees.
      (ii) Rules adopted under subsection (1)(d)(i) must provide for submission of claims, within 90 days from the date of travel, following notification to the claimant of reimbursement rules, must provide procedures for reimbursement receipts, and must require the use of the least costly form of travel unless the travel is not suitable for the worker's medical condition. The rules must exclude from reimbursement:
         (A) 100 miles of automobile travel for each calendar month unless the travel is requested or required by the insurer pursuant to 39-71-605;

(B) travel to a health care provider within the community in which the worker resides;

(C) travel outside the community in which the worker resides if comparable medical treatment is available within the community in which the worker resides, unless the travel is requested by the insurer; and

(D) travel for unauthorized treatment or disallowed procedures.

(iii) An insurer is not liable for injuries or conditions that result from an accident that occurs during travel or treatment, except that the insurer retains liability for the compensable injuries and conditions for which the travel and treatment were required.

(e) Pursuant to rules adopted by the department, an insurer shall reimburse a catastrophically injured worker's family or, if a family member is unavailable, a person designated by the injured worker or approved by the insurer for travel assistance expenditures in an amount not to exceed $2,500 to be used as a match to those funds raised by community service organizations to help defray the costs of travel and lodging expenses incurred by the family member or designated person when traveling to be with the injured worker. These funds must be paid in addition to any travel expenses paid by an insurer for a travel companion when it is medically necessary for a travel companion to accompany the catastrophically injured worker.

(f)

(i) The benefits provided for in this section terminate 60 months from the date of injury or diagnosis of an occupational disease. A worker may request reopening of medical benefits that were terminated under this subsection (1)(f) as provided in 39-71-717.

(ii) Subsection (1)(f)(i) does not apply to a worker who is permanently totally disabled as a result of a compensable injury or occupational disease or for the repair or replacement of a prosthesis furnished as a direct result of a compensable injury or occupational disease.

(g) Notwithstanding subsection (1)(a), the insurer may not be required to furnish, after the worker has achieved medical stability, palliative or maintenance care except:

(i) when provided to a worker who has been determined to be permanently totally disabled and for whom it is medically necessary to monitor administration of prescription medication to maintain the worker in a medically stationary condition;

(ii) when necessary to monitor the status of a prosthetic device; or

(iii) when the worker's treating physician believes that the care that would otherwise not be compensable under this subsection (1)(g) is appropriate to enable the worker to continue current employment or that there is a clear probability of returning the worker to employment. A dispute regarding the compensability of palliative or maintenance care is considered a dispute over which, after mediation pursuant to department rule, the workers' compensation court has jurisdiction.

(h) Notwithstanding any other provisions of this chapter, the department, by rule and upon the advice of the professional licensing boards of practitioners affected by the rule, may exclude from compensability any medical treatment that the department finds to be unscientific, unproved, outmoded, or experimental.

(2)

(a) The department shall annually establish a schedule of fees for medical services that are necessary for the treatment of injured workers. Regardless of the date of injury, payment for medical services is based on the fee schedule rates in this section in effect on the date on which the medical service is provided. Charges submitted by providers must be the usual and customary charges for nonworkers' compensation patients. The department may require insurers to submit information to be used in establishing the schedule.

(b)

(i) The department may not set the rate for medical services at a rate greater than 10% above the average of the conversion factors used by up to the top five insurers or third-party administrators providing group health insurance coverage within this state who use the resource-based relative value scale to determine fees for covered services. To be included in the rate determination, the insurer or third-party administrator must occupy at least 1% of the market share for group health insurance policies as reported annually to the state auditor.

(ii) The insurers or third-party administrators included under subsection (2)(b)(i) shall provide their standard conversion rates to the department.

(iii) The department may use the conversion rates only for the purpose of determining average conversion rates under this subsection (2).

(iv) The department shall maintain the confidentiality of the conversion rates.

(c) The fee schedule rates established in subsection (2)(b), when adopted, must be based on the following standards as adopted by the centers for Medicare and Medicaid services, regardless of where services are provided:

(i) the American medical association current procedural terminology codes, as those codes exist on January 1 of each year;

(ii) the healthcare common procedure coding system, as those codes and their relative weights exist on January 1 of each year;
(iii) the Medicare severity diagnosis-related groups, as those codes and their relative weights exist on January 1 of each year;
(iv) the ambulatory payment classifications, as those codes and their relative weights exist on January 1 of each year;
(v) the ratio of costs to charges for each hospital, as those codes exist on January 1 of each year;
(vi) the national correct coding initiative edits, as those codes exist on January 1 of each year; and
(vii) the relative value units in the published resource-based relative value scale, as those codes exist on January 1 of each year.

(d) The department may establish additional codes and coding standards for use by providers when billing for medical services under this section.

(3)

(a) The department shall establish by rule evidence-based utilization and treatment guidelines for primary and secondary medical services. There is a rebuttable presumption that the adopted utilization and treatment guidelines establish compensable medical treatment for an injured worker.

(b)

(i) The department may adopt a drug formulary as part of its utilization and treatment guidelines. To implement this section, the department may annually adopt by rule an evidence-based commercial or other evidence-based drug formulary as part of its utilization and treatment guidelines.
(ii) If the department adopts a commercial drug formulary, the formulary automatically includes all of the changes and updates furnished by the commercial vendor that are made during the year. This process is independent of the provisions of 2-4-307.
(iii) If the department adopts a drug formulary, the department shall, by rule, provide for:
(A) an appropriate transition of treatment, if the treatment began prior to the adoption of a drug formulary, to treatment that is consistent with the application of the formulary; and
(B) a timely and responsive dispute resolution process for disputes related to use of the formulary.

(c) An insurer is not responsible for treatment or services that do not fall within the utilization and treatment guidelines adopted by the department unless the provider obtains prior authorization from the insurer.

If prior authorization is not requested or obtained from the insurer, an injured worker is not responsible for payment of the medical treatment or services.

(d) The department, in consultation with health care providers with relevant experience and education, shall provide for an annual review of the evidence-based utilization and treatment guidelines to consider amendments or changes to the guidelines.

(4) The department shall hire a medical director. The department may establish by rule an independent medical review process for treatment or services denied by an insurer pursuant to subsection (3) prior to mediation under 39-71-2401.

(5) For services available in Montana, insurers may pay facilities located outside Montana according to the workers' compensation fee schedule of the state where the medical service is performed.

(6)

(a) An insurer shall make payments at the fee schedule rate within 30 days of receipt of medical bills for which a claim has been accepted and for which no other disputes exist. Disputes must be defined by the department by rule.

(b) Any unpaid balance under this subsection (6) accrues interest at 12% a year or 1% a month or a fraction of a month. If the charge is not paid within 30 days, interest on the unpaid balance accrues from the date of receipt of the original billing.

(7) Once a determination has been made regarding the correct reimbursement amount, any overpayment made to a health care provider must be reimbursed to the insurer within 30 days of the determination. Any reimbursement amount remaining unpaid after 30 days accrues interest at 12% a year or 1% a month or a fraction of a month. Interest on the reimbursement amount remaining unpaid accrues from the date of receipt of the determination of the correct reimbursement amount.

(8) For a critical access hospital licensed pursuant to Title 50, chapter 5, the rate for services is the usual and customary charge.

(9) Payment pursuant to reimbursement agreements between managed care organizations or preferred provider organizations and insurers is not bound by the provisions of this section.

(10) After mediation pursuant to department rules, an unresolved dispute between an insurer and a health care provider regarding the amount of a fee for medical services may be brought before the workers' compensation court.

(11)

(a) After the initial visit, the worker is responsible for $25 of the cost of each subsequent visit to a hospital emergency department for treatment relating to a compensable injury or occupational disease.

(b) "Visit", as used in this subsection (11), means each time that the worker obtains services relating to a compensable injury or occupational disease from:
   (i) a treating physician;
   (ii) a physical therapist;
   (iii) a psychologist; or
   (iv) hospital outpatient services available in a nonhospital setting.

(c) A worker is not responsible for the cost of a subsequent visit pursuant to subsection (11)(a) if the visit is for treatment requested by an insurer.

NEBRASKA REVISED STATUTES

§ 44-6834 Act, how cited

Sections 44-6834 to 44-6850 shall be known and may be cited as the Out-of-Network Emergency Medical Care Act.

§ 44-6835 Definitions, where found

For purposes of the Out-of-Network Emergency Medical Care Act, the definitions found in sections 44-6836 to 44-6846 apply.

§ 44-6836 Covered person, defined

Covered person means a person on whose behalf an insurer is obligated to pay health care expense benefits or provide health care services.

§ 44-6837 Emergency medical condition, defined

Emergency medical condition means a medical or behavioral condition, the onset of which is sudden, that manifests itself by symptoms of sufficient severity, including, but not limited to, severe pain, that a prudent layperson, possessing an average knowledge of medicine and health, could reasonably expect the absence of immediate medical attention to result in (1) placing the health of the person afflicted with such condition in serious jeopardy or, in the case of a behavioral condition, placing the health of such persons or others in serious jeopardy, (2) serious impairment to such person's bodily functions, (3) serious impairment of any bodily organ or part of such person, or (4) serious disfigurement of such person.

§ 44-6838 Emergency services, defined

Emergency services means health care services medically necessary to screen and stabilize a covered person in connection with an emergency medical condition.

§ 44-6839 Health benefits plan, defined

(1) Health benefits plan means a benefits plan which pays or provides hospital and medical expense benefits for covered services and is delivered or issued for delivery in this state by or through an insurer.

(2) Health benefits plan does not include the medical assistance program, Medicare, Medicare advantage, accident-only, credit, disability, or long-term care coverage, TRICARE supplement coverage, coverage arising out of a workers' compensation or similar law, automobile medical payment insurance, personal injury protection insurance, and hospital confinement indemnity coverage.

§ 44-6840 Health care facility, defined

Health care facility means a general acute hospital, satellite emergency department, or ambulatory surgical center licensed pursuant to the Health Care Facility Licensure Act.

§ 44-6841 Health care professional, defined

Health care professional means an individual who is credentialed pursuant to the Uniform Credentialing Act, who is acting within the scope of his or her credential, and who provides a covered service defined by the health benefits plan.

§ 44-6842 Health care provider, defined

Health care provider means a health care professional or health care facility.

§ 44-6843 Insurer, defined

Insurer means an entity that contracts to provide, deliver, arrange for, pay for, or reimburse any of the costs of health care services under a health benefits plan, including (1) any individual or group sickness and accident insurance policy or subscriber contract delivered, issued for delivery, or renewed in this state and any hospital, medical, or surgical expense-incurred policy, except for a policy that provides coverage for a specified disease or other limited-benefit coverage, and (2) any self-funded employee benefit plan to the extent not preempted by federal law.

§ 44-6844 Medical assistance program, defined

Medical assistance program means the medical assistance program established pursuant to the Medical Assistance Act.

§ 44-6845 Medically necessary, defined

Medically necessary means a health care service that a health care provider, exercising his or her prudent clinical judgment, would provide to a covered person for the purpose of evaluating, diagnosing, or treating an illness, an injury, or a disease, or its symptoms, and that is in accordance with the generally accepted standards of medical practice; that is clinically appropriate, in terms of type, frequency, extent, site, and duration, and considered effective for the covered person's illness, injury, or disease; that is not primarily for the convenience of the covered person or the health care provider; and that is not more costly than an alternative service or sequence of services at least as likely to produce equivalent therapeutic or diagnostic results as to the diagnosis or treatment of that covered person's illness, injury, or disease.

§ 44-6846 TRICARE, defined

TRICARE means a health care program of the United States Department of Defense Military Health System.

§ 44-6847 Emergency services; facility, bill; limitation

If a covered person receives emergency services at any health care facility, the facility shall not bill the covered person in excess of any deductible, copayment, or coinsurance amount applicable to in-network services pursuant to the covered person's health benefits plan.

§ 44-6848 Emergency services; health care provider, bill; limitation

If a covered person receives emergency services at an in-network or out-of-network health care facility, the health care provider performing those services shall not bill the covered person in excess of any deductible, copayment, or coinsurance amount applicable to in-network services pursuant to the covered person's health benefits plan.

§ 44-6849 Emergency services; insurer; duties; payment; presumed reasonable; dispute resolution procedure

(1) If a covered person receives emergency services at an in-network or out-of-network health care facility, the insurer shall ensure that the covered person incurs no greater out-of-pocket costs than the covered person would have incurred with an in-network health care provider for covered services.

(2) With respect to emergency services at an in-network or out-of-network health care facility, if the out-of-network health care provider bills an insurer directly, any reimbursement paid by the insurer shall be paid directly to the out-of-network health care provider. The insurer shall provide the out-of-network health care provider with a written remittance of payment that specifies the proposed reimbursement and the applicable deductible, copayment, or coinsurance amounts owed by the covered person.

(3) If emergency services provided at an in-network or out-of-network health care facility are performed, the out-of-network health care provider may bill the insurer for the services rendered. The insurer may pay the billed amount. A claim or a payment shall be presumed reasonable if it is based on the higher of (a) the contracted rate under any then-existing in-network contractual relationship between the insurer and the out-of-network health care provider for the same or similar services or (b) one hundred seventy-five percent of the payment rate for Medicare services received from the federal Centers for Medicare and Medicaid Services for the same or similar services in the same geographic area. If the out-of-network health care provider deems the payment

made by the insurer unreasonable, the out-of-network health care provider shall return payment to the insurer and utilize the dispute resolution procedure under section 44-6850.

§ 44-6850 Settlement, negotiation; mediation, when

(1) If an insurer or an out-of-network health care provider provides notification that it considers a claim or payment to be not reasonable, the insurer and the health care provider shall have thirty days after the date of such notification to negotiate a settlement. If a settlement has not been reached after such thirty-day period, the insurer and the health care provider shall engage in mediation in accordance with the Uniform Mediation Act. The insurer may attempt to negotiate a final reimbursement amount with the out-of-network health care provider which differs from the amount paid by the insurer pursuant to this section.

(2) Following completion of the mediation process, the cost of mediation shall be split evenly and paid by the insurer and the health care provider.

(3) Mediation shall not be used when the insurer and the health care provider agree to a separate payment arrangement.

NEVADA REVISED STATUTES ANNOTATED

§ 439B.745 Limitation on amount out-of-network provider may collect from covered person; duties of out-of-network emergency facility upon providing services

1. An out-of-network provider shall not collect from a covered person for medically necessary emergency services, and a covered person is not responsible for paying, an amount that exceeds the copayment, coinsurance or deductible required for such services provided by an in-network provider by the coverage for that person.
2. An out-of-network emergency facility that provides medically necessary emergency services to a covered person shall:

   (a) When possible, notify the third party that provides coverage for the covered person not later than 8 hours after the covered person presents at the out-of-network emergency facility to receive medically necessary emergency services; and
   (b) Notify the third party that the condition of the covered person has stabilized to such a degree that the person may be transferred to an in-network emergency facility not later than 24 hours after the person's emergency medical condition is stabilized. Not later than 24 hours after the third party receives such notice, the third party shall arrange for the transfer of the person to such a facility.

§ 439B.754 Determination of amount owed when no recent contract exists between out-of-network provider and third party; arbitration to resolve dispute; no interest pending resolution of dispute; confidentiality of arbitration

1. An out-of-network provider shall accept or reject an amount paid pursuant to subsection 2 of NRS 439B.748 or paragraph (c) of subsection 1 or subsection 2 of NRS 439B.751 as payment in full for the medically necessary emergency services for which the payment was offered within 30 days after receiving the payment. If an out-of-network provider fails to comply with the requirements of this section, the amount paid shall be deemed accepted as payment in full for the medically necessary emergency services for which the payment was offered 30 days after the out-of-network provider received the payment.
2. If an out-of-network provider rejects the amount paid as payment in full, the out-of-network provider must request from the third party an additional amount which, when combined with the amount previously paid, the out-of-network provider is willing to accept as payment in full for the medically necessary emergency services.

3. If the third party refuses to pay the additional amount requested by the out-of-network provider pursuant to subsection 2 or fails to pay that amount within 30 days after receiving the request for the additional amount, the out-of-network provider must request a list of five randomly selected arbitrators from an entity authorized by regulations of the Director of the Department to provide such arbitrators. Such regulations must require:
   (a) For claims of less than $5,000, the use of arbitrators who will conduct the arbitration in an economically efficient manner. Such arbitrators may include, without limitation, qualified employees of the State and arbitrators from the voluntary program for the use of binding arbitration established in the judicial district pursuant to NRS 38.255 or, if no such program has been established in the judicial district, from the program established in the nearest judicial district that has established such a program.
   (b) For claims of $5,000 or more, the use of arbitrators from nationally recognized providers of arbitration services, which may include, without limitation, the American Arbitration Association, JAMS or their successor organizations.
4. Upon receiving the list of randomly selected arbitrators pursuant to subsection 3, the out-of-network provider and the third party shall each strike two arbitrators from the list. If one arbitrator remains, that arbitrator must arbitrate the dispute concerning the amount to be paid for the medically necessary emergency services. If more than one arbitrator remains, an arbitrator randomly selected from the remaining arbitrators by the entity that provided the list of arbitrators pursuant to subsection 3 must arbitrate that dispute.
5. The out-of-network provider and the third party shall participate in binding arbitration of the dispute concerning the amount to be paid for the medically necessary emergency services conducted by the arbitrator selected pursuant to subsection 4. The out-of-network provider or third party may provide the arbitrator with any relevant information to assist the arbitrator in making a determination.
6. The arbitrator shall require:
   (a) The out-of-network provider to accept as payment in full for the provision of the medically necessary emergency services, except for any copayment, coinsurance or deductible that the coverage requires the covered person to pay for the services when provided by an in-network provider, the amount paid by the third party pursuant to subsection 2 of NRS 439B.748 or paragraph (c) of subsection 1 or subsection 2 of NRS 439B.751, as applicable; or
   (b) The third party to pay the additional amount requested by the out-of-network provider pursuant to subsection 2.
7. If the arbitrator requires:
   (a) The out-of-network provider to accept the amount paid by the third party pursuant to subsection 2 of NRS 439B.748 or paragraph (c) of

subsection 1 or subsection 2 of NRS 439B.751, as applicable, as payment in full for the provision of the medically necessary emergency services, except for any copayment, coinsurance or deductible that the coverage requires the covered person to pay for the services when provided by an in-network provider, the out-of-network provider must pay the costs of the arbitrator.

(b) The third party to pay the additional amount requested by the out-of-network provider pursuant to subsection 2, the third party must pay the costs of the arbitrator.

8. If a qualified employee of the State serves as an arbitrator pursuant to paragraph (a) of subsection 3, the state agency that employs the arbitrator may retain money paid by the out-of-network provider or third party pursuant to subsection 7 for the costs of the arbitrator.

9. An out-of-network provider or a third party must pay its own attorney's fees incurred during the process prescribed by this section.

10. Interest does not accrue on any claim for which an offer of payment is rejected pursuant to subsection 1 for the period beginning on the date of the rejection and ending 30 days after the arbitrator renders a decision.

11. Except as otherwise provided in this subsection and NRS 439B.760, any decision of an arbitrator pursuant to this section and any documents associated with such a decision are confidential and are not admissible as evidence during a legal proceeding, including, without limitation, a legal proceeding between the third party and the out-of-network provider. The decision of an arbitrator and any documents associated with such a decision may be disclosed and are admissible as evidence during a legal proceeding to enforce the decision.

NEW HAMPSHIRE REVISED STATUTES

§ 329:31-b Prohibition on balance billing; payment for reasonable value of services

I. When a commercially insured patient is covered by a managed care plan as defined under RSA 420-J:3, XXV, a health care provider performing anesthesiology, radiology, emergency medicine, or pathology services shall not balance bill the patient for fees or amounts other than copayments, deductibles, or coinsurance, if the service is performed in a hospital or ambulatory surgical center that is in-network under the patient's health insurance plan. This prohibition shall apply whether or not the health care provider is contracted with the patient's insurance carrier.

II. Pursuant to paragraph I, fees for health care services submitted to an insurance carrier for payment shall be limited to a commercially reasonable value, based on payments for similar services from New Hampshire insurance carriers to New Hampshire health care providers.

III. In the event of a dispute between a provider and an insurance carrier relative to the reasonable value of a service under this section, the insurance commissioner shall have exclusive jurisdiction under RSA 420-J:8-e to determine if the fee is commercially reasonable. The provider and the insurance carrier shall each make best efforts to resolve any dispute prior to applying to the insurance commissioner for resolution, which shall include presenting to the other party evidence supporting its contention that the fee level it is proposing is commercially reasonable. The department of insurance may require the parties to engage in mediation prior to rendering a decision.

NEW JERSEY STATUTES

§ 26:2S-6.1 Managed care plan to pay full contractual rate to out-of-network provider, direct payments, certain circumstances

a. With respect to a carrier which offers a managed care plan that provides for both in-network and out-of-network benefits, in the event that:
   (1) a covered person is admitted by an out-of-network health care provider to an in-network health care facility for covered, medically necessary health care services; or
   (2) the covered person receives covered, medically necessary health care services from an out-of-network health care provider while the covered person is a patient at an in-network health care facility and was admitted to the health care facility by an in-network provider, the carrier shall reimburse the health care facility for the services provided by the facility at the carrier's full contracted rate without any penalty for the patient's selection of an out-of-network provider, in accordance with the in-network policies and in-network copayment, coinsurance or deductible requirements of the managed care plan.

b. The provisions of subsection a. of this section shall apply only if the covered person complies with the preauthorization or review requirements of the health benefits plan regarding the determination of medical necessity to access in-network inpatient benefits, as set forth in writing pursuant to section 5 of P.L.1997, c.192 (C.26:2S-5).

c. With respect to a carrier which offers a managed care plan that provides for both in-network and out-of-network benefits, in the event that the covered person assigns, through an assignment of benefits, his right to receive reimbursement for medically necessary health care services to an out-of-network health care provider, the carrier shall remit payment for the reimbursement directly to the health care provider in the form of a check payable to the health care provider, or in the alternative, to the health care provider and the covered person as joint payees, with a signature line for each of the payees. Payment shall be made in accordance with the provisions of this section and P.L.1999, c.154 (C.17B:30-23 et al.). Any payment made only to the covered person rather than the health care provider under these circumstances shall be considered unpaid, and unless remitted to the health care provider within the time frames established by P.L.1999, c.154 (C.17B:30-23 et al.), shall be considered overdue and subject to an interest charge as provided in that act.

NEW MEXICO ADMINISTRATIVE CODE

§ 13.10.16.10 Appeals

At the request of a provider, the superintendent shall conduct an external review of a provider grievance as authorized by this section.

A. Types of grievances subject to appeal. The superintendent shall only review a provider grievance that pertains to:
   (1) an alleged violation of a law enforceable by the superintendent;
   (2) alleged noncompliance with an order of the superintendent; or
   (3) a termination based on a provider's alleged failure to comply with a law or order enforceable by the superintendent.

B. Disposition. In the disposition of an appeal, the superintendent may only impose a remedy, penalty, or corrective action authorized by the Insurance Code.

C. Exhaustion of internal remedies required. The superintendent shall not review a provider grievance appeal unless the provider has exhausted the carrier's internal grievance process.

D. Timeline for filing appeal. A provider appeal of a grievance shall be filed no later than 30 days after the provider receives a response to the grievance, or the deadline for the response, whichever is earlier.

E. Appeal content. The superintendent shall not review a provider grievance appeal that does not contain the following information:
   (1) the provider's name, license number, address, daytime telephone number, email address, and any relevant claim number(s);
   (2) the name and phone number of the carrier;
   (3) certification that the grievance did not pertain to Medicaid or Medicare coverage, excluding Medicare supplement;
   (4) a copy of the carrier's written disposition of the grievance, or certification by the provider that the carrier did not issue a written disposition within the time allowed by law;
   (5) the date the provider received the carrier's written disposition of the grievance, or the date by which the carrier was required to provide a written disposition if no disposition was received; and
   (6) a clear and concise statement of the issue on appeal, and the remedy requested on appeal.

F. Additional documentation. Within 45 days of receipt of a provider grievance appeal, the superintendent shall determine whether the appeal is authorized by this section and otherwise reviewable. The superintendent may request supplemental information from the provider or carrier to so determine. The time between any such request and the delivery of the requested information by the superintendent shall be excluded from the 45-day deadline imposed by this section.

(1) If the superintendent determines that an appeal is not authorized or reviewable, the superintendent shall issue an order dismissing the appeal and stating the reason for dismissal.

(2) If the superintendent determines that an appeal is authorized and reviewable, the superintendent shall schedule either a formal or an informal hearing pursuant to the superintendent's rules, as appropriate to the issues, facts and circumstances presented in the appeal. The order setting the hearing shall authorize a designated hearing officer to take or authorize any action authorized by law to resolve the appeal.

G. Settlement. The superintendent may order the parties to an appeal to participate in formal or informal settlement discussions focused on resolving the issue on appeal. If all parties to an appeal consent, the assigned hearing officer may facilitate the settlement discussions without being disqualified from issuing a recommended decision on appeal.

H. Waiver. Upon an express finding of good cause, the superintendent may waive any deadline, format or process requirement imposed by this section.

§ 13.10.33.9 Covered person rights

A carrier shall afford a covered person these rights:

A. Out of state care. A carrier shall reimburse a surprise medical bill as required by law regardless of the situs of delivery of the medical care, including medical care rendered out-of-state.

B. Specific consent. For purposes of Subparagraph (b) of Paragraph (1) of Subsection Y of Section 59A-57A-2 NMSA 1978, "specific consent" shall only be valid if the covered person has a meaningful choice between a participating provider and a nonparticipating provider; the covered person was not encouraged or coerced by a network provider or the carrier into selecting the out-of-network provider; and the covered person signs a notice and disclosure statement, at least five days before the service or supply is received, acknowledging that the covered person may be liable for a balance bill and chooses to receive the service or supply.

C. Notice of Rights. A carrier shall provide each covered person with notice of surprise billing protection act rights in the plan's evidence of coverage and as directed by the superintendent in a bulletin.

§ 13.10.33.12 Provider complaints

A provider may dispute the denial, or reimbursement amount, of a surprise bill pursuant to the applicable procedures in 13.10.16 NMAC.

NEW MEXICO STATUTES ANNOTATED

§ 59A-57A-3 Emergency care; reimbursement; limitation on charges

A. A health insurance carrier shall reimburse a nonparticipating provider for emergency care necessary to evaluate and stabilize a covered person if a prudent layperson would reasonably believe that emergency care is necessary, regardless of eventual diagnosis.

B. A health insurance carrier shall not require that prior authorization for emergency care be obtained by, or on behalf of, a covered person prior to the point of stabilization of that covered person if a prudent layperson would reasonably believe that the covered person requires emergency care.

C. A health insurance carrier may impose a cost-sharing or limitation of benefits requirement for emergency care performed by a nonparticipating provider only to the same extent that the copayment, co-insurance or limitation of benefits requirement applies for participating providers and is documented in the policy.

D. A health insurance carrier may require an emergency care provider to notify a health insurance carrier of a covered person's admission to the hospital within a reasonable time period after the covered person has been stabilized.

§ 59A-57A-4 Non-emergency care; limitation on charges

A. Other than applicable cost sharing that would apply if a participating provider had rendered the same services, a health insurance carrier shall provide reimbursement for and a covered person shall not be liable for charges and fees for covered non-emergency care rendered by a nonparticipating provider that are delivered when:

(1) the covered person at an in-network facility does not have the ability or opportunity to choose a participating provider who is available to provide the covered services; or

(2) medically necessary care is unavailable within a health benefits plan's network; provided that "medical necessity" shall be determined by a covered person's provider in conjunction with the covered person's health benefits plan and health insurance carrier.

B. Except as set forth in Subsection A of this section, nothing in this section shall preclude a nonparticipating provider from balance billing for non- emergency care provided by a nonparticipating provider to an individual who has knowingly chosen to receive services from that nonparticipating provider.

§ 59A-57A-8 Health care provider reimbursement rates; surprise billing

A. The superintendent shall convene appropriate stakeholders, including rural providers, insurers and consumer advocates, and review the reimbursement rate for surprise bills annually to ensure fairness to providers and to evaluate the impact on health insurance premiums and health benefits plan networks.

B. Calculation of the date of health insurance carrier receipt of a claim shall align with requirements for prompt payment established pursuant to Section 59A-16-21.1 NMSA 1978.

C. A health insurance carrier shall make available to providers access to claims status information.

NEW YORK FINANCIAL SERVICES LAW

§ 601 Dispute resolution process established

The superintendent shall establish a dispute resolution process by which a dispute for a bill for emergency services or a surprise bill may be resolved. The superintendent shall have the power to grant and revoke certifications of independent dispute resolution entities to conduct the dispute resolution process. The superintendent shall promulgate regulations establishing standards for the dispute resolution process, including a process for certifying and selecting independent dispute resolution entities. An independent dispute resolution entity shall use licensed physicians in active practice in the same or similar specialty as the physician providing the service that is subject to the dispute resolution process of this article for disputes that involve physician services. To the extent practicable, the physician shall be licensed in this state. Disputes shall be submitted to an independent dispute resolution entity within three years of the date the health care plan made the original payment on the claim that is the subject of the dispute.

§ 602 Applicability

(a) This article shall not apply to health care services, including emergency services, where physician fees are subject to schedules or other monetary limitations under any other law, including the workers' compensation law and article fifty-one of the insurance law, and shall not preempt any such law.

§ 603 Definitions

For the purposes of this article:

(a) "Emergency condition" means a medical or behavioral condition that manifests itself by acute symptoms of sufficient severity, including severe pain, such that a prudent layperson, possessing an average knowledge of medicine and health, could reasonably expect the absence of immediate medical attention to result in:
 (1) placing the health of the person afflicted with such condition in serious jeopardy, or in the case of a behavioral condition placing the health of such person or others in serious jeopardy;
 (2) serious impairment to such person's bodily functions;
 (3) serious dysfunction of any bodily organ or part of such person;
 (4) serious disfigurement of such person; or
 (5) a condition described in clause (i), (ii) or (iii) of section 1867(e)(1)(A) of the social security act 42 U.S.C. Section 1395dd.

(b) "Emergency services" means, with respect to an emergency condition:
 (1) a medical screening examination as required under section 1867 of the social security act, 42 U.S.C. Section 1395dd, which is within the

capability of the emergency department of a hospital, including ancillary services routinely available to the emergency department to evaluate such emergency medical condition; and

(2) within the capabilities of the staff and facilities available at the hospital, such further medical examination and treatment as are required under section 1867 of the social security act, 42 U.S.C. Section 1395dd, to stabilize the patient.

(c) "Health care plan" means an insurer licensed to write accident and health insurance pursuant to article thirty-two of the insurance law; a corporation organized pursuant to article forty-three of the insurance law; a municipal cooperative health benefit plan certified pursuant to article forty-seven of the insurance law; a health maintenance organization certified pursuant to article forty-four of the public health law; or a student health plan established or maintained pursuant to section one thousand one hundred twenty-four of the insurance law.

(d) "Insured" means a patient covered under a health care plan's policy or contract.

(e) "Non-participating" means not having a contract with a health care plan to provide health care services to an insured.

(f) "Participating" means having a contract with a health care plan to provide health care services to an insured.

(g) "Patient" means a person who receives health care services, including emergency services, in this state.

(h) "Surprise bill" means a bill for health care services, other than emergency services, with respect to:

(1) an insured for services rendered by a non-participating provider at a participating hospital or ambulatory surgical center, where a participating provider is unavailable or a non-participating provider renders services without the insured's knowledge, or unforeseen medical services arise at the time the health care services are rendered; provided, however, that a surprise bill shall not mean a bill received for health care services when a participating provider is available and the insured has elected to obtain services from a non-participating provider;

(2) an insured for services rendered by a non-participating provider, where the services were referred by a participating physician to a non-participating provider without explicit written consent of the insured acknowledging that the participating physician is referring the insured to a non-participating provider and that the referral may result in costs not covered by the health care plan; or

(3) a patient who is not an insured for services rendered by a physician at a hospital or ambulatory surgical center, where the patient has not timely received all of the disclosures required pursuant to section twenty-four of the public health law.

(i) "Usual and customary cost" means the eightieth percentile of all charges for the particular health care service performed by a provider in the same or similar specialty and provided in the same geographical area as reported in a benchmarking database maintained by a nonprofit organization specified by the superintendent. The nonprofit organization shall not be affiliated with an insurer, a corporation subject to article forty-three of the insurance law, a municipal cooperative health benefit plan certified pursuant to article forty-seven of the insurance law, or a health maintenance organization certified pursuant to article forty-four of the public health law.

§ 604 Criteria for determining a reasonable fee

In determining the appropriate amount to pay for a health care service, an independent dispute resolution entity shall consider all relevant factors, including:

(a) whether there is a gross disparity between the fee charged by the provider for services rendered as compared to:
   (1) fees paid to the involved provider for the same services rendered by the provider to other patients in health care plans in which the provider is not participating, and
   (2) in the case of a dispute involving a health care plan, fees paid by the health care plan to reimburse similarly qualified providers for the same services in the same region who are not participating with the health care plan;
(b) the level of training, education and experience of the health care professional, and in the case of a hospital, the teaching staff, scope of services and case mix;
(c) the provider's usual charge for comparable services with regard to patients in health care plans in which the provider is not participating;
(d) the circumstances and complexity of the particular case, including time and place of the service;
(e) individual patient characteristics;
(f) the median of the rate recognized by the health care plan to reimburse similarly qualified providers for the same or similar services in the same region that are participating with the health care plan; and
(g) with regard to physician services, the usual and customary cost of the service.

§ 605 Dispute resolution for emergency services[143]

(a) Emergency services for an insured.
   (1) When a health care plan receives a bill for emergency services from a non-participating provider, including a bill for inpatient services which

143 Effective January 1, 2025.

follow an emergency room visit, or a bill for services from a mobile crisis intervention services provider licensed, certified, or designated by the office of mental health or the office of addiction services and supports, the health care plan shall pay an amount that it determines is reasonable for the emergency services, including inpatient services which follow an emergency room visit or for the mobile crisis intervention services, rendered by the non-participating provider, in accordance with section three thousand two hundred twenty-four-a of the insurance law, except for the insured's co-payment, coinsurance or deductible, if any, and shall ensure that the insured shall incur no greater out-of-pocket costs for the emergency services, including inpatient services which follow an emergency room visit or for the mobile crisis intervention services, than the insured would have incurred with a participating provider. The non-participating provider may bill the health care plan for the services rendered. Upon receipt of the bill, the health care plan shall pay the non-participating provider the amount prescribed by this section and any subsequent amount determined to be owed to the provider in relation to the emergency services provided, including inpatient services which follow an emergency room visit or for the mobile crisis intervention services.

(2) A non-participating provider or a health care plan may submit a dispute regarding a fee or payment for emergency services, including inpatient services which follow an emergency room visit, or for services rendered by a mobile crisis intervention services provider licensed, certified, or designated by the office of mental health or the office of addiction services and supports, for review to an independent dispute resolution entity.

(3) The independent dispute resolution entity shall make a determination within thirty business days of receipt of the dispute for review.

(4) In determining a reasonable fee for the services rendered, an independent dispute resolution entity shall select either the health care plan's payment or the non-participating provider's fee. The independent dispute resolution entity shall determine which amount to select based upon the conditions and factors set forth in section six hundred four of this article. If an independent dispute resolution entity determines, based on the health care plan's payment and the non-participating provider's fee, that a settlement between the health care plan and non-participating provider is reasonably likely, or that both the health care plan's payment and the non-participating provider's fee represent unreasonable extremes, then the independent dispute resolution entity may direct both parties to attempt a good faith negotiation for settlement. The health care plan and non-participating provider may be granted up to ten business days for this negotiation, which shall run concurrently with the thirty business day period for dispute resolution.

(b) Emergency services for a patient that is not an insured.
   (1) A patient that is not an insured or the patient's physician may submit a dispute regarding a fee for emergency services, including inpatient services which follow an emergency room visit, for review to an independent dispute resolution entity upon approval of the superintendent.
   (2) An independent dispute resolution entity shall determine a reasonable fee for the services based upon the same conditions and factors set forth in section six hundred four of this article.
   (3) A patient that is not an insured shall not be required to pay the physician's or hospital's fee in order to be eligible to submit the dispute for review to an independent dispute resolution entity.

(c) The determination of an independent dispute resolution entity shall be binding on the health care plan, provider and patient, and shall be admissible in any court proceeding between the health care plan, provider or patient, or in any administrative proceeding between this state and the provider.

(d) For purposes of the hospital payment pursuant to subsection (a) of this section, the amount the health care plan shall pay to the hospital shall be at least twenty-five percent greater than the amount the health care plan would have paid for the claim had the hospital been in network, based on the most recent contract between the health care plan and the hospital. Provided however, the amount paid by the health care plan pursuant to this subsection shall not prejudice either party or preclude either party from submitting a dispute to the dispute resolution entity relating to the payment to the hospital or preclude the hospital from seeking additional payment from the health care plan prior to a decision by the dispute resolution entity. To the extent the prior contract between the hospital and health care plan expired greater than twelve months prior to the payment of the disputed claim, the payment amount shall be adjusted based upon the medical consumer price index. The provisions of this subsection shall only apply to the extent the health care plan and hospital had previously entered into a participating provider agreement.

§ 606 Hold harmless for insured from bills for emergency services and surprise bills[144]

(a) A non-participating provider shall not bill an insured for a surprise bill except for any applicable copayment, coinsurance or deductible that would be owed if the insured utilized a participating provider.

(b) A non-participating provider shall not bill an insured for emergency services, including inpatient services which follow an emergency room visit, or for services rendered by a mobile crisis intervention services provider licensed,

144 Effective January 1, 2025.

certified, or designated by the office of mental health or the office of addiction services and supports, except for any applicable copayment, coinsurance or deductible that would be owed if the insured utilized a participating provider.

§ 607 Dispute resolution for surprise bills

(a) Surprise bill involving an insured.

  (1) For a surprise bill involving an insured, the health care plan shall pay the non-participating provider in accordance with paragraphs two and three of this subsection.

  (2) The non-participating provider may bill the health care plan for the health care services rendered, and the health care plan shall pay the non-participating provider the billed amount or attempt to negotiate reimbursement with the non-participating provider.

  (3) If the health care plan's attempts to negotiate reimbursement for health care services provided by a non-participating provider does not result in a resolution of the payment dispute between the non-participating provider and the health care plan, the health care plan shall pay the non-participating provider an amount the health care plan determines is reasonable for the health care services rendered, except for the insured's copayment, coinsurance or deductible, in accordance with section three thousand two hundred twenty-four-a of the insurance law, and shall ensure that the insured shall incur no greater out-of-pocket costs for the surprise bill than the insured would have incurred with a participating provider.

  (4) Either the health care plan or the non-participating provider may submit the dispute regarding the surprise bill for review to an independent dispute resolution entity, provided however, the health care plan may not submit the dispute unless it has complied with the requirements of paragraphs one, two and three of this subsection.

  (5) The independent dispute resolution entity shall make a determination within thirty business days of receipt of the dispute for review.

  (6) When determining a reasonable fee for the services rendered, the independent dispute resolution entity shall select either the health care plan's payment or the non-participating provider's fee. An independent dispute resolution entity shall determine which amount to select based upon the conditions and factors set forth in section six hundred four of this article. If an independent dispute resolution entity determines, based on the health care plan's payment and the non-participating provider's fee, that a settlement between the health care plan and non-participating provider is reasonably likely, or that both the health care plan's payment and the non-participating provider's fee represent unreasonable extremes, then the independent dispute resolution entity may

direct both parties to attempt a good faith negotiation for settlement. The health care plan and non-participating provider may be granted up to ten business days for this negotiation, which shall run concurrently with the thirty business day period for dispute resolution.

(b) Surprise bill received by a patient who is not an insured.

(1) A patient who is not an insured and who receives a surprise bill may submit a dispute regarding the surprise bill for review to an independent dispute resolution entity.

(2) The independent dispute resolution entity shall determine a reasonable fee for the services rendered based upon the conditions and factors set forth in section six hundred four of this article.

(3) A patient shall not be required to pay the physician's fee to be eligible to submit the dispute for review to the independent dispute resolution entity.

(c) The determination of an independent dispute resolution entity shall be binding on the patient, provider and health care plan, and shall be admissible in any court proceeding between the patient or insured, provider or health care plan, or in any administrative proceeding between this state and the provider.

§ 608 Payment for independent dispute resolution entity

(a) For disputes involving an insured, when the independent dispute resolution entity determines the health care plan's payment is reasonable, payment for the dispute resolution process shall be the responsibility of the non-participating provider. When the independent dispute resolution entity determines the non-participating provider's fee is reasonable, payment for the dispute resolution process shall be the responsibility of the health care plan. When a good faith negotiation directed by the independent dispute resolution entity pursuant to paragraph four of subsection (a) of section six hundred five of this article, or paragraph six of subsection (a) of section six hundred seven of this article results in a settlement between the health care plan and non-participating provider, the health care plan and the non-participating provider shall evenly divide and share the prorated cost for dispute resolution.

(b) For disputes involving a patient that is not an insured, when the independent dispute resolution entity determines the physician's fee is reasonable, payment for the dispute resolution process shall be the responsibility of the patient unless payment for the dispute resolution process would pose a hardship to the patient. The superintendent shall promulgate a regulation to determine payment for the dispute resolution process in cases of hardship. When the independent dispute resolution entity determines the physician's fee is unreasonable, payment for the dispute resolution process shall be the responsibility of the physician.

NEW YORK COMPILATION OF CODES, RULES AND REGULATIONS TITLE 23

§ 400.0 Preamble

Part H of chapter 60 of the Laws of 2014 provided new rights and obligations, effective March 31, 2015, concerning disputes involving bills by health care providers. Health care plans, physicians, and when applicable, other health care providers and patients, have the right to request a review by an IDRE to resolve a payment dispute regarding a bill for certain emergency services or surprise bills. Chapters 375 and 377 of the Laws of 2019, effective January 1, 2020, provided additional rights and obligations for disputes involving hospital bills for emergency services and inpatient services that follow an emergency room visit. Part YY of chapter 56 of the Laws of 2020, effective April 3, 2020, provided new hold harmless requirements and assignment of benefits rights and obligations for emergency services, including inpatient services, that follow an emergency room visit. This Part implements the requirements of Financial Services Law article 6 by establishing a dispute resolution process and the standards for such process, including criteria and the process for certifying and selecting an IDRE.

§ 400.1 Applicability

(a) This Part shall apply to health care services provided in this State on and after March 31, 2015. This Part also shall apply to emergency services provided by non-participating hospitals and inpatient services that follow an emergency room visit provided in this State on and after January 1, 2020. The requirements relating to assignment of benefits and provider hold harmless for emergency services in subdivisions (a)(2) and (b)(2) of section 400.6 of this Part shall apply to emergency services provided in this State on and after April 3, 2020.

(b) This Part shall not apply to health care services, including emergency services, where physician fees are subject to schedules or other monetary limitations under any other law, including the Workers' Compensation Law and Insurance Law article 51, and shall not preempt any such law. This Part shall not apply to emergency services subject to Financial Services Law section 602(b).

(c) The requirements of this Part for emergency services provided by non-participating hospitals, including inpatient services that follow an emergency admission, shall not apply to hospitals that had at least 60 percent of inpatient discharges annually that consisted of Medicaid, uninsured, and dual eligible individuals as determined by the Department of Health in its determination of safety net hospitals.

§ 400.2 Definitions

As used in this Part:

(a) *Active practice* means actively treating persons in a state where the physician is licensed.
(b) *Affiliated* means controls, controlled by, or under common control.
(c) *Control* shall have the meaning ascribed by Insurance Law section 107(a)(16).
(d) *Dispute resolution process* means a process to resolve a dispute for a fee for emergency services, including inpatient services that follow an emergency room visit, or a surprise bill.
(e) *Emergency condition* means a medical or behavioral condition that manifests itself by acute symptoms of sufficient severity, including severe pain, such that a prudent layperson, possessing an average knowledge of medicine and health, could reasonably expect the absence of immediate medical attention to result in:
  (1) placing the health of the person afflicted with such condition in serious jeopardy, or in the case of a behavioral condition placing the health of such person or others in serious jeopardy;
  (2) serious impairment to such person's bodily functions;
  (3) serious dysfunction of any bodily organ or part of such person;
  (4) serious disfigurement of such person; or
  (5) a condition described in 42 U.S.C. § 1395.dd (Social Security Act section 1867(e)(1)(A)(i), (ii) or (iii)).
(f) *Emergency services* means, with respect to an emergency condition:
  (1) a medical screening examination as required under 42 U.S.C. § 1395.dd, that is within the capability of the emergency department of a hospital, including ancillary services routinely available to the emergency department to evaluate such emergency medical condition; and
  (2) within the capabilities of the staff and facilities available at the hospital, such further medical examination and treatment as are required under 42 U.S.C. § 1395.dd to stabilize the patient.
(g) *Health care plan* means an insurer licensed to write accident and health insurance pursuant to Insurance Law articles 41 and 42; a corporation organized pursuant to Insurance Law article 43; a municipal cooperative health benefit plan certified pursuant to Insurance Law article 47; a health maintenance organization certified pursuant to Public Health Law article 44; or a student health plan established or maintained pursuant to Insurance Law section 1124.
(h) *Health care provider* means a health care professional who is appropriately licensed, registered or certified pursuant to Education Law Title 8, or comparably licensed, registered or certified by another state, or a facility that is licensed or certified pursuant to Public Health Law articles 5, 28, 36, 44 or 47, or Mental Hygiene Law articles 19, 31 or 32, or comparably licensed by another state.

(i) *Hospital* means a general hospital operating pursuant to Public Health Law article 28.

(j) *Independent dispute resolution entity* or *IDRE* means an entity certified by the superintendent pursuant to section 400.3 of this Part.

(k) *Insured* means a patient covered under a policy or contract with a health care plan. A patient insured by an insurer other than a health care plan is not an insured for purposes of this Part.

(l) *Material familial affiliation* means any relationship as a spouse, child, parent, sibling, spouse's parent, spouse's child, child's parent, child's spouse, or sibling's spouse.

(m) *Material financial affiliation* means any financial interest of more than five percent of total annual revenue or total annual income of an IDRE or officer, director, or managers thereof; or reviewer or reviewing physician employed or engaged thereby to conduct any independent dispute review in the dispute resolution process. The term material financial affiliation shall not include revenue received from a health care plan or physician by:

  (1) an IDRE to conduct a dispute resolution pursuant to Financial Services Law article 6; or

  (2) a reviewing physician for health services rendered to patients in this State.

(n) *Material professional affiliation* means any physician-patient relationship, any partnership or employment relationship, a shareholder or similar ownership interest in a professional corporation, or any independent contractor arrangement that constitutes a material financial affiliation with any expert or any officer or director of the IDRE.

(o) *Non-participating* means not having a contract with a health care plan to provide health care services to an insured.

(p) *Non-participating referred health care provider* means a non-participating health care provider to which an insured was referred by a participating physician without explicit written consent of the insured acknowledging that the participating physician is referring the insured to a non-participating referred health care provider and that the referral may result in costs not covered by the health care plan.

(q) *Participating* means having a contract with a health care plan to provide health care services to an insured.

(r) *Patient* means a person who receives health care services, including emergency services, in this State.

(s) *Physician* means an individual licensed to practice medicine pursuant to Education Law article 131 or as provided under the law of the State where the individual practices medicine.

(t) *Reviewer* means a person with training and experience in health care billing, reimbursement, and usual and customary charges who renders a dispute resolution determination in consultation with a reviewing physician.

(u) *Reviewing physician* means a licensed physician in active practice in the same or similar specialty as the physician that provided the service that is subject to the dispute resolution process, who renders a dispute resolution determination in consultation with a reviewer.

(v) *Surprise bill* means a bill for health care services, other than emergency services, received by:

(1) an insured for services rendered by a non-participating physician at a participating hospital or ambulatory surgical center, where a participating physician is unavailable or a non-participating physician renders services without the insured's knowledge, or unforeseen medical services arise at the time the health care services are rendered; provided, however, that a surprise bill shall not mean a bill received for health care services when a participating physician is available and the insured has elected to obtain services from a non-participating physician;

(2) an insured for services rendered by a non-participating referred health care provider, where the services were referred by a participating physician to a non-participating referred health care provider without explicit written consent of the insured acknowledging that the participating physician is referring the insured to a non-participating referred health care provider and that the referral may result in costs not covered by the health care plan. A referral to a non-participating referred health care provider occurs when:

(i) health care services are performed by a non-participating health care provider in the participating physician's office or practice during the course of the same visit;

(ii) the participating physician sends a specimen taken from the patient in the participating physician's office to a non-participating laboratory or pathologist; or

(iii) for any other health care services performed by a non-participating health care provider, when referrals are required under the insured's contract; or

(3) a patient who is not an insured for services rendered by a physician at a hospital or ambulatory surgical center, where the patient has not timely received all of the disclosures required pursuant to Public Health Law section 24.

(w) *Usual and customary cost* means the 80th percentile of all charges for the particular health care service performed by a provider in the same or similar specialty and provided in the same geographical area as reported in a benchmarking database maintained by a nonprofit organization specified by the superintendent, which is not affiliated with a health care plan.

§ 400.3 Independent dispute resolution entity (IDRE) certification requirements

(a) An entity applying to be an IDRE certified to perform reviews regarding bills for emergency services, including inpatient services that follow an emergency room visit, and surprise bills pursuant to Financial Services Law article 6, shall submit to the superintendent:

(1) a description of the proposed IDRE's organizational structure and capability to operate a statewide IDRE, including:

(i) a certificate of incorporation, articles of organization and bylaws or operating agreement of the proposed IDRE and, as applicable, those of the proposed IDRE's holding company or parent company;

(ii) the proposed IDRE's organizational chart;

(iii) identification of management staff and a description of such management staff's responsibilities;

(iv) the name and credentials of a medical director appointed by the proposed IDRE, who is a physician in possession of a current and valid non-restricted license to practice medicine in New York;

(v) the names and biographies of all controlling employees, officers, and executives of the proposed IDRE; and information concerning the governing board of the proposed IDRE, including roles and responsibilities, identification of the board members and a description of their qualifications;

(2) a sworn statement, as described in section 400.4(b) of this Part, signed by the chief executive officer of the proposed IDRE regarding conflicts of interest;

(3) the names of all corporations and organizations that control, are controlled by, or under common control with the proposed IDRE, and the nature and extent of any such control;

(4) the proposed IDRE's policies and procedures governing all aspects of the dispute resolution process, including at a minimum:

(i) a description and a chart or diagram of the sequence of steps through which a dispute will move from receipt through notification to the health care plan, physician, superintendent, and provider, insured, or patient, if applicable, regarding the dispute determination;

(ii) procedures for ensuring that no prohibited material familial, financial or professional affiliation exists with respect to the reviewer and reviewing physician assigned to the dispute. The procedures shall include, for each reviewer and reviewing physician assigned to review a dispute, a requirement for a signed attestation affirming, under penalty of perjury, that no prohibited material familial, financial or professional affiliation exists with respect to the reviewer's or reviewing physician's participation in the review of the dispute;

(iii) procedures to ensure that the dispute is reviewed by a neutral and impartial reviewer with training and experience in healthcare billing, reimbursement, and usual and customary charges and determinations are made in consultation with a neutral and impartial licensed reviewing physician in active practice in the same or similar specialty as the physician providing the service that is subject to the dispute, who is also, to the extent practicable, licensed in New York;

(iv) procedures for the reporting and review of reviewer's and reviewing physician's conflicts of interest and for assigning or reassigning a dispute resolution where a conflict or potential conflict is identified;

(v) procedures to ensure that reviews are conducted within the time frames specified in section 400.8 of this Part and any required notices are provided in a timely manner;

(vi) procedures to ensure the confidentiality of medical and treatment records and review materials; and

(vii) procedures to ensure adherence to the requirements of this Part by any contractor, subcontractor, agent or employee affiliated by contract or otherwise with the proposed IDRE;

(5) a description of the reviewer and reviewing physician network, including:

(i) an assessment of the proposed IDRE's ability to provide review services statewide;

(ii) a description of the qualifications of the reviewers and reviewing physicians retained to review payment disputes, including current and past employment history and practice affiliations, as applicable;

(iii) a description of the procedures employed to ensure that reviewers and reviewing physicians reviewing payment disputes are:

(a) appropriately licensed, registered or certified, if applicable;

(b) trained in the principles, procedures and standards of the proposed IDRE;

(c) knowledgeable about the health care service which is the subject of the payment dispute under review; and

(d) with respect to reviewers, trained and experienced in health care billing, reimbursement and usual and customary charges;

(iv) a description of the methods of recruiting and selecting neutral and impartial reviewers and reviewing physicians and matching such reviewers and reviewing physicians to specific cases;

(v) the number of reviewers and reviewing physicians retained by the proposed IDRE, and a description of the areas of expertise available from reviewing physicians and the types of cases reviewing physicians are qualified to review;

(vi) the proposed IDRE's quality assurance program, which shall include written descriptions, to be provided to all individuals involved in such program; the organizational arrangements and ongoing procedures for the identification, evaluation, resolution and follow-up of potential and actual problems in payment dispute reviews performed by the reviewer and reviewing physician; and the maintenance of program standards pursuant to this subdivision; and

(vii) written procedures documenting that:

(a) appropriate personnel are reasonably accessible not less than 40 hours per week during normal business hours to discuss the dispute resolution process and to allow response to telephone requests;

(b) a response to an accepted or recorded message shall be made not less than one business day after the date on which the call was received; and

(viii) documentation of accreditation by a nationally recognized private accrediting organization, if accreditation is available;

(6) a list of its fees, which shall reflect the total amount that will be charged by the proposed IDRE for reviews, inclusive of indirect costs, administrative fees and incidental expenses, and a description of the methodology used to calculate the fees. The description shall include the pro-rated fee that will be charged when a good faith negotiation directed by the proposed IDRE results in a settlement between the health care plan and the non-participating physician, non-participating hospital, or non-participating referred health care provider. The description also shall include an application processing fee when the dispute is determined by the proposed IDRE to be ineligible for review. The description shall provide a waiver of the fee for disputes submitted by patients when the fee would pose a financial hardship to the patient;

(7) a description of the proposed IDRE's ability to accept requests for reviews, provide requisite notifications, screen for material affiliations, respond to calls from the State and meet other requirements during normal business hours; and

(8) such other information as the superintendent may require.

(b) An IDRE may not charge any fee unless it has been filed with the superintendent and the superintendent has determined that the fee is reasonable.

§ 400.4 Conflict of interest

(a) No proposed IDRE shall be qualified for certification as an IDRE if it owns or controls, is owned or controlled by, or is under common control with any of the following:
  (1) any national, state or local illness, health benefit or public advocacy group;
  (2) any national, state or local society or association of hospitals, physicians, or other providers of health care services; or
  (3) any national, state or local association of health care plans.

(b) An IDRE shall submit a sworn statement, as described in section 400.3(a)(2) of this Part, setting forth that none of the control affiliations proscribed in subdivision (a) of this section apply to the IDRE, and that the IDRE, its medical director and each of its owners, officers, directors and managers, either:
  (1) has no material familial, financial, or professional affiliation with any person or entity listed in subparagraphs (i) – (vi) of paragraph (2) of this subdivision; or
  (2) provides a list of those material familial, financial and professional affiliations, each of which may, upon certification, result in a prohibited conflict of interest in connection with a dispute because of such affiliation with:
    (i) any health care plan;
    (ii) any owner, officer, director, or manager of any health care plan;
    (iii) any health care provider, physician's medical group, independent practice association, or provider of pharmaceutical products or services or durable medical equipment;
    (iv) any facility at which a health service would be provided;
    (v) any officer, director, partner, or manager of a physician's medical group, independent practice association, or facility at which a health care service would be provided; or
    (vi) any developer or manufacturer of a health service or product.

(c) Following certification:
  (1) if an IDRE acquires control of, becomes controlled by, or comes under common control with any entity described in subdivision (a) of this section, the IDRE shall notify the superintendent in writing within three business days of the acquisition or exercise of control and shall no longer be eligible to review disputes; and
  (2) the sworn statement required by subdivision (b) of this section shall be amended and resubmitted to the superintendent within three business days of the addition or deletion of any material affiliation as described in subdivision (a) of this section.

(d) An IDRE or an officer, director, or manager thereof, or a reviewer or reviewing physician employed or engaged thereby to conduct any dispute resolution pursuant to Financial Services Law article 6 shall not have any material professional affiliation, material familial affiliation, or material financial affiliation with:

(1) the health care plan;

(2) any officer, director, or manager of the health care plan;

(3) any health care provider, physician's medical group, independent practice association, or provider of pharmaceutical products or services or durable medical equipment that provided or supplied the health care service;

(4) the facility at which the health service was provided;

(5) any officer, director, partner, or manager of the physician's medical group, independent practice association, or facility that provided the health care service;

(6) the developer or manufacturer of the principal health service that is the subject of the dispute resolution; or

(7) the patient whose health care service is the subject of the dispute resolution.

(e) Unavoidable conflicts; minimization.

(1)

(i) If the superintendent determines that a conflict exists to the dispute to be assigned and is unavoidable because all IDREs certified pursuant to this Part, or their medical directors, owners, officers, directors or managers, have a disqualifying material familial, financial or professional affiliation with one or more of the persons or entities listed in subdivision (b) of this section, the superintendent will make a random assignment of the dispute, provided that the IDRE assigned shall, within two business days of the assignment, certify to the superintendent by sworn statement that the reviewer and reviewing physician who will review the dispute have been assigned in accordance with paragraph (2) of this subdivision.

(ii) When a dispute must be assigned pursuant to this paragraph, the superintendent will notify the health care plan, physician, and, as applicable, the provider and patient, that all IDREs have a proscribed material familial, financial or professional affiliation; of the need to randomly assign the dispute to a certified IDRE in order that a determination of the dispute be obtained; of the nature of the affiliation involving the IDRE assigned to the dispute; and that the IDRE's reviewer and reviewing physician who review the dispute shall not have any affiliation proscribed by this section.

(2) An IDRE assigned pursuant to this Part shall not assign a dispute resolution to a reviewer or reviewing physician who has a material familial, financial or professional affiliation with any of those persons listed in subdivision (d) of this section.

§ 400.5 Responsibilities of health care plans for disputes regarding emergency services and surprise bills

(a) Upon receipt of a claim for emergency services, including inpatient services that follow an emergency room visit, rendered by a non-participating physician or a non-participating hospital, a health care plan shall:

(1)

(i) pay the claim, within the timeframes established in Insurance Law section 3224-a, in an amount that it deems reasonable for the services rendered by the non-participating physician or non-participating hospital that had not previously entered into a participating provider agreement with the health care plan, except for the insured's co-payment, coinsurance or deductible, if any; or

(ii) in disputes involving a non-participating hospital that had previously entered into a participating provider agreement with the health care plan, pay the claim, within the timeframes established in Insurance Law section 3224-a, in an initial amount that is at least 25 percent greater than the amount the health care plan would have paid for the claim had the hospital been in-network, based on the most recent participating provider agreement between the health care plan and the non-participating hospital, except for the insured's co-payment, coinsurance or deductible, if any. In the event the prior participating provider agreement between the health care plan and the non-participating hospital expired more than 12 months prior to the payment of the disputed claim, the payment amount shall be adjusted based upon the annual medical consumer price index, compounded for each year subsequent to the year the contract terminated up until the year the claim is paid. If a health care plan believes that this initial payment amount to a non-participating hospital with which it had previously entered into a participating provider agreement is not reasonable, it may submit a dispute to the superintendent for review by an IDRE, as provided in section 400.7 of this Part, and propose an amount it deems reasonable, provided that the health care plan:

(a) notifies the non-participating hospital of its intent to submit the dispute to the superintendent, together with the health care plan's best and final offer and an explanation of the calculation, including the aggregation or any other methodology used by the health care plan to develop its best and final offer;

(b) provides the non-participating hospital with 15 business days to respond to the health care plan with the non-participating hospital's best and final offer before submitting the dispute to the superintendent;

(c) includes its best and final offer and the non-participating hospital's best and final offer, if any, in its submission of the dispute to the superintendent; and

(d) notifies the non-participating hospital of the dispute at the time of the submission to the superintendent; and

(iii) not be precluded from attempting to negotiate the reimbursement amount with the non-participating physician or non-participating hospital within the timeframes established in Insurance Law section 3224-a;

(2) if the claim is submitted by the non-participating physician or non-participating hospital, or if payment is made to the non-participating physician or non-participating hospital, provide notice to the non-participating physician or non-participating hospital describing how to initiate the independent dispute resolution process;

(3) if the health care plan pays an amount less than the non-participating physician's or non-participating hospital's charge, provide the insured with notice, included on or in conjunction with, an explanation of benefits, which shall:

(i) explain that the insured shall incur no greater out-of-pocket costs for the services than the insured would have incurred with a participating physician or participating hospital;

(ii) explain that the insured's cost-sharing may increase in the event the IDRE determines that the health care plan must pay additional amounts for the services of the non-participating physician or non-participating hospital; and

(iii) direct the insured to contact the health care plan in the event that the non-participating physician or non-participating hospital bills the insured for the out-of-network service other than the insured's in-network copayment, coinsurance, or deductible; and

(4) pay the amount set forth in subparagraph (i) or (ii) of paragraph (1) of this subdivision directly to the non-participating physician or non-participating hospital if an insured assigns benefits to the non-participating physician or non-participating hospital.

(b) Upon receipt of a claim for a surprise bill that is submitted with an assignment of benefits form, or that the health care plan otherwise determines is a surprise bill, the health care plan shall:

(1) pay the non-participating physician or non-participating referred health care provider the billed amount or attempt to negotiate reimbursement with the non-participating physician or non-participating referred health care provider. If the health care plan's attempts to negotiate reimbursement for the health care services provided by the non-participating physician or non-participating referred health care provider do not result in a resolution of the payment dispute, the health care plan shall pay the non-participating physician or non-participating referred health care provider an amount the health care plan determines is reasonable for the health care services rendered, except for the insured's copayment, coinsurance or deductible, in accordance with the timeframes established in Insurance Law section 3224-a;

(2) provide notice to the non-participating physician or, as applicable, to the non-participating referred health care provider, describing how to initiate the independent dispute resolution process; and

(3) provide the insured with notice, included on or in conjunction with, an explanation of benefits, which shall:

(i) explain that the insured shall incur no greater out-of-pocket costs for the services than the insured would have incurred with a participating physician or health care provider;

(ii) explain that the insured's cost-sharing may increase in the event the IDRE determines that the health care plan must pay additional amounts for the services of the non-participating physician or non-participating referred health care provider; and

(iii) direct the insured to contact the health care plan in the event that the non-participating physician or non-participating referred health care provider bills the insured for the out-of-network service other than the insured's in-network copayment, coinsurance, or deductible.

(c) Upon receipt of a claim for the services of a non-participating physician or a non-participating referred health care provider that could be a surprise bill and that is not submitted with an assignment of benefits form, the health care plan shall provide the insured with notice, included on or in conjunction with, an explanation of benefits, which shall:

(1) advise the insured that the claim could be a surprise bill;

(2) explain that if the claim is a surprise bill and the insured submits an assignment of benefits form, the insured will incur no greater out-of-pocket costs for the services than the insured would have incurred with a participating physician or health care provider; and

(3) direct the insured to contact the health care plan or visit the health care plan's website for additional information regarding surprise bills and to obtain an assignment of benefits form for surprise bills.

(d) If the health care plan receives a claim for services of a non-participating health care provider that could be a surprise bill that is not submitted with an assignment of benefits form and the health care plan denies the claim because the health care provider is a non-participating provider, the health care plan shall, upon receipt of the assignment of benefits form, comply with the requirements of subdivision (b) of this section.

(e) If the health care plan receives a claim for services of a non-participating health care provider that is not submitted with an assignment of benefits form and pays the claim, the health care plan shall, upon receipt of the assignment of benefits form, determine whether it will attempt to negotiate additional reimbursement with the non-participating physician or non-participating referred health care provider. After receipt of the assignment of benefits form, if the health care plan attempts to negotiate additional reimbursement for the surprise bill and the attempts do not result in a resolution of the payment dispute or the health care plan does not attempt to negotiate the additional reimbursement for the surprise bill, the health care plan shall:

(1) pay the non-participating physician or non-participating referred health care provider any additional amount the health care plan determines is reasonable for the health care services rendered, except for the insured's copayment, coinsurance or deductible, in accordance with the timeframes established in Insurance Law section 3224-a; and

(2) provide the insured with notice that shall:

(i) explain that the insured will incur no greater out-of-pocket costs for the services than the insured would have incurred with a participating physician or health care provider;

(ii) explain that the insured's cost-sharing may increase in the event the IDRE determines that the health care plan must pay additional amounts for the services of the non-participating physician or non-participating referred health care provider;

(iii) explain that if the health care plan paid the insured directly, then the insured must remit that payment to the non-participating physician or non-participating referred health care provider;

(iv) direct the insured to contact the health care plan in the event that the non-participating physician or non-participating referred health care provider bills the insured for the out-of-network service other than the insured's in-network copayment, coinsurance, or deductible; and

(v) direct the insured to the health care plan's website for additional information regarding surprise bills.

(f) A health care plan shall prominently post on its website the information in paragraphs (1)–(5) of this subdivision and include in disclosure materials provided to insureds pursuant to Insurance Law sections 3217-a(a), 4324(a) and Public Health Law section 4408(1) the information in paragraphs (1)–(4) of this subdivision, as follows:

(1) a description of what constitutes a surprise bill;

(2) a description of the independent dispute resolution process;

(3) an assignment of benefits form for surprise bills;
(4) the health care plan's designated electronic and mailing address where the assignment of benefits form can be submitted; and
(5) information on how an insured, non-participating physician, non-participating hospital, or, as applicable, a non-participating referred health care provider, may submit a dispute to an IDRE.

(g) An assignment of benefits form for surprise bills shall be in a form prescribed by the superintendent.

(h) A health care plan shall ensure that the insured shall incur no greater out-of-pocket costs for the services than the insured would have incurred with a participating physician, participating hospital, or participating health care provider:
(1) for emergency services, including inpatient services that follow an emergency room visit; and
(2) for a dispute involving a surprise bill when the insured has assigned benefits to a non-participating physician or a non-participating referred health care provider.

(i) If the IDRE directs the health care plan to engage in negotiations with the non-participating physician, non-participating hospital, or non-participating referred health care provider the health care plan shall do so in good faith. If a settlement is reached, the health care plan shall notify the IDRE within two business days of the settlement and shall make any additional payment to the non-participating physician, non-participating hospital, or non-participating referred health care provider within the timeframes prescribed in Insurance Law section 3224-a. If a settlement is not reached or the parties agree that a settlement is not attainable, the health care plan shall promptly notify the IDRE no later than the end of the time period granted by the IDRE for negotiation.

(j) If the IDRE issues a determination in favor of the non-participating physician, non-participating hospital, or non-participating referred health care provider, the health care plan shall pay the non-participating physician, non-participating hospital, or, as applicable, the non-participating referred health care provider, any additional amount owed within 30 days from the date of the determination.

(k) A health care plan shall designate, and inform the superintendent of, at least one officer and one staff member knowledgeable about the independent dispute resolution process who shall be responsible for oversight of the health care plan's compliance with the independent dispute resolution process. The health care plan shall make at least one staff person available during normal business hours for not less than 40 hours per week. The health care plan shall respond to all inquiries from the superintendent relating to the dispute resolution process within three business days.

(1)

(1) If a health care plan receives an assignment of benefits form for a surprise bill and determines that the bill is not a surprise bill, the health care plan shall provide written notice of such determination. The notice shall include the procedures for filing a grievance under Insurance Law section 4802 or Public Health Law section 4408-a and information on how to file a complaint with the superintendent.

(2) If a health care plan makes a determination on a grievance disputing that a bill is a surprise bill, the health care plan shall comply with the Insurance Law section 4802 or Public Health Law section 4408-a grievance requirements.

§ 400.6 Responsibilities of physicians, hospitals, and non-participating referred health care providers for disputes regarding emergency services and surprise bills

(a)

(1) If a non-participating physician or non-participating referred health care provider bills a patient for a surprise bill, the non-participating physician or non-participating referred health care provider shall provide a claim form to the patient and an assignment of benefits form in a form prescribed by the superintendent.

(2) If a non-participating physician or a non-participating hospital bills a patient for emergency services, including inpatient services that follow an emergency room visit, the non-participating physician or non-participating hospital shall provide a claim form and an assignment of benefits form to the patient.

(b)

(1) If an insured assigns benefits for a surprise bill in writing to a non-participating physician or non-participating referred health care provider that knows the insured is insured under a health care plan, the non-participating physician or non-participating referred health care provider shall not bill or seek payment from the insured except for any applicable copayment, coinsurance or deductible that would be owed if the insured utilized a participating physician.

(2) If an insured assigns benefits for emergency services, including inpatient services that follow an emergency room visit, to a non-participating physician or non-participating hospital that knows the insured is insured under a health care plan, the non-participating physician or non-participating hospital shall not bill or seek payment from the insured except for any applicable copayment, coinsurance or deductible that would be owed if the insured utilized a participating physician or hospital.

(c) If a health care plan attempts to negotiate reimbursement with a non-participating physician, non-participating hospital that had not previously entered into a participating provider agreement with the health care plan, or non-participating referred health care provider, the non-participating physician, non-participating hospital, or non-participating referred health care provider shall have at least seven business days to respond to the health care plan's offer, except when the seven business days would exceed the timeframes established in Insurance Law section 3224-a for a health care plan to pay a claim.

(d) In disputes involving emergency services, including inpatient services that follow an emergency room visit, rendered by a non-participating hospital that had previously entered into a participating provider agreement with a health care plan, if the non-participating hospital believes that the initial payment amount paid pursuant to subparagraph (ii) of paragraph (1) of subdivision (a) of section 400.5 of this Part by the health care plan is not reasonable, the non-participating hospital may submit a dispute to the superintendent for review by an IDRE, as provided in section 400.7 of this Part, and propose an amount it deems reasonable, provided that the non-participating hospital:

(1) notifies the health care plan of its intent to submit the dispute to the superintendent, together with the non-participating hospital's best and final offer and an explanation of the calculation, including the aggregation or any other methodology used by the non-participating hospital to develop its best and final offer;

(2) provides the health care plan with 15 business days to respond to the non-participating hospital with the health care plan's best and final offer before submitting the dispute to the superintendent;

(3) includes its best and final offer and the health care plan's best and final offer, if any, in its submission of the dispute to the superintendent; and

(4) notifies the health care plan of the dispute at the time of the submission to the superintendent.

(e) If the IDRE directs the non-participating physician, non-participating hospital, or non-participating referred health care provider to engage in negotiations with the health care plan, the non-participating physician, non-participating hospital, or non-participating referred health care provider shall do so in good faith. If a settlement is reached, the non-participating physician, non-participating hospital, or non-participating referred health care provider shall notify the IDRE within two business days of the settlement. If a settlement is not reached or the parties agree that a settlement is not attainable, the non-participating physician, non-participating hospital, or non-participating referred health care provider shall promptly notify the IDRE no later than the end of the time period granted by the IDRE for negotiation.

(f) A non-participating physician, non-participating hospital, or non-participating referred health care provider shall respond to all inquiries from the superintendent relating to the dispute resolution process within three business days.

(g) If the IDRE issues a determination in favor of the health care plan in a dispute involving emergency services provided by a non-participating hospital that had previously entered into a participating provider agreement with the health care plan, including inpatient services that follow an emergency room visit, the non-participating hospital shall pay any amount owed to the health care plan within 30 days from the date of the determination.

§ 400.7 Process to submit disputes regarding emergency services or surprise bills

(a)

(1) Emergency services. A health care plan, a non-participating physician, a non-participating hospital, or a patient who is not an insured may submit a dispute regarding emergency services, including inpatient services that follow an emergency room visit, to the superintendent for review by an IDRE.

(2) Surprise bills. A health care plan, a non-participating physician, a non-participating referred health care provider, an insured who does not assign benefits, or a patient who is not an insured may submit a dispute regarding a surprise bill to the superintendent for review by an IDRE.

(b) The dispute shall be submitted by completing an application in a form and manner prescribed by the superintendent.

(c) A health care plan shall provide the following information:

(1) the name and contact information of the health care plan;

(2) the name and contact information of the non-participating physician, non-participating hospital, or non-participating referred health care provider;

(3) the fee charged by the non-participating physician, non-participating hospital, or non-participating referred health care provider for the service that is the subject of the dispute, and provide a copy of the bill;

(4) the fee paid to the non-participating physician, non-participating hospital, or non-participating referred health care provider for the service that is the subject of the dispute;

(5) at least three fees paid in the last 24 months by the health care plan to reimburse similarly qualified non-participating physicians, non-participating hospitals, or non-participating referred health care providers for the same services in the same region that reflect the final and full payment to the non-participating physician, non-participating hospital, or the non-participating referred health care provider, if available;

(6) an explanation of the circumstances and complexity of the particular case, including time and place of the service, if available;

(7) individual patient characteristics, if available;

(8) for a dispute involving a non-participating physician, the usual and customary cost for the service, when the benchmarking database contains the usual and customary cost for the service subject to the dispute;

(9) for a dispute involving a non-participating hospital that had previously entered into a participating provider agreement with the health care plan, for emergency services, including inpatient services that follow an emergency room visit, the health care plan's best and final offer, if different from the payment made pursuant to subparagraph (ii) of paragraph (1) of subdivision (a) of section 400.5 of this Part, and the non-participating hospital's best and final offer, if any;
(10) any other information the health care plan deems relevant;
(11) the patient's coverage type;
(12) an attestation affirming that the information provided by the health care plan is true and accurate; and
(13) any information requested by the IDRE.

(d) A non-participating physician, non-participating hospital, or non-participating referred health care provider shall provide the following information:
(1) the name and contact information of the physician, hospital, or non-participating referred health care provider;
(2) the name and contact information of the health care plan;
(3) the fee charged by the physician, hospital, or non-participating referred health care provider for the service that is the subject of the dispute and a copy of the bill;
(4) the fee paid to the physician, hospital, or non-participating referred health care provider for the service that is the subject of the dispute;
(5) at least three fees paid to the physician, hospital, or non-participating referred health care provider, in the last 24 months for the same services rendered by the physician, hospital, or non-participating referred health care provider to other patients in health care plans in which the physician, hospital, or non-participating referred health care provider is not participating that reflect the final and full payment to the non-participating physician, non-participating hospital, or the non-participating health care provider, if available;
(6) the physician's, hospital's, or non-participating referred health care provider's usual charge for comparable services rendered to other patients in health care plans in which the physician, hospital, or non-participating referred health care provider is not participating;
(7) the physician's or non-participating referred health care provider's level of training, education and experience;
(8) for a dispute involving a non-participating hospital, the non-participating hospital's teaching status, scope of services, and case mix;
(9) an explanation of the circumstances and complexity of the particular case, including time and place of the service;
(10) individual patient characteristics;
(11) any other information the physician, hospital, or non-participating referred health care provider deems relevant;

(12) an attestation affirming that the information provided by the physician, hospital, or non-participating referred health care provider is true and accurate; and

(13) any information requested by the IDRE.

(e) Patients submitting the dispute shall provide the following information:

(1) the name and contact information of the patient;

(2) the name and contact information of the physician, hospital, or non-participating referred health care provider;

(3) the name and contact information of the health care plan, if the patient is an insured;

(4) the fee charged by the physician, hospital, or non-participating referred health care provider for the service that is the subject of the dispute and a copy of the bill;

(5) an explanation of the circumstances and complexity of the particular case, including time and place of the service;

(6) individual patient characteristics, if available;

(7) any other information the patient deems relevant;

(8) a consent to the release of medical information;

(9) with respect to a patient who is not an insured and who requests a waiver of the fee based on hardship, information to demonstrate that the patient is eligible for a hardship exemption;

(10) with respect to a patient who is not an insured and who submits a dispute for a surprise bill, a statement that the required disclosures have not been provided;

(11) an attestation affirming that the information provided by the patient is true and accurate; and

(12) any information requested by the IDRE.

(f) A patient shall not be required to pay the physician's, hospital's, or non-participating referred health care provider's fee in order to be eligible to submit the dispute for review to an IDRE.

(g) A health care plan, physician, hospital, non-participating referred health care provider or patient shall provide any information requested by an IDRE as soon as possible, but no later than the timeframe requested by the IDRE, as provided under section 400.8 of this Part.

§ 400.8 Responsibilities of an IDRE

(a) Within three business days of receipt of an application submitted by a health care plan, non-participating physician, non-participating hospital, non-participating referred health care provider or a patient, an IDRE shall screen the application for any conflicts of interest in accordance with section 400.4 of this Part. If the IDRE determines a conflict exists, the IDRE shall reject the application and return it to the superintendent within those three business days.

(b) If the IDRE determines that a conflict does not exist, the IDRE shall, within three business days of receiving an application submitted by a health care plan, non-participating physician, non-participating hospital, or non-participating referred health care provider:
   (1) screen the application for eligibility;
   (2) contact the health care plan, physician, hospital, or non-participating referred health care provider if additional information is needed to determine eligibility of the request for dispute resolution and provide the health care plan, the physician, hospital, or non-participating referred health care provider three business days to submit the information and provide an explanation of where the information should be sent. If the information is not submitted, the IDRE shall make a second request and provide one business day to submit the information. If the information is not submitted, or if the application is not eligible, the IDRE shall promptly reject the application.

(c) Within three business days of a determination that the health care plan's, physician's, hospital's or non-participating referred health care provider's application is eligible, or within three business days of receipt of the patient's application from the superintendent, the IDRE shall send notification of the assignment to the health care plan, physician, hospital, non-participating referred health care provider and, for a patient initiated application, to the patient. The IDRE shall include in the notification:
   (1) a request for the information specified in subdivisions (c), (d), and (e) of section 400.7 of this Part;
   (2) a request for any additional information that may be available to support the appeal;
   (3) an explanation of where the information should be sent;
   (4) a statement that all information must be submitted within five business days of the notification;
   (5) a statement that if a partial response or no response is received, the dispute will be decided based on the available information; and
   (6) a statement that the IDRE shall not reconsider a dispute for which a determination has been made based upon receipt of additional information subsequent to such determination.

(d) If the requested information is not received within five business days, the IDRE shall make a determination based on the information available to the IDRE. If the requested information or additional information is received before the determination is rendered, the IDRE shall consider the information.

(e) If the IDRE determines, in a case involving a health care plan, based on the health care plan's payment or best and final offer, if applicable, and the non-participating physician's or non-participating referred health care provider's fee, or the non-participating hospital's fee or best and final offer, as applicable, that a settlement between the health care plan and the non-participating physician, non-participating hospital, or non-participating referred health care provider is reasonably likely, or that both the health care plan's payment or best and final offer, if applicable, and the non-participating physician's or non-participating referred health care provider's fee, or the non-participating hospital's fee or best and final offer, as applicable, represent unreasonable extremes, the IDRE may direct both parties to attempt a good faith negotiation for settlement. The health care plan and the non-participating physician, non-participating hospital, or non-participating referred health care provider may be granted up to ten business days for this negotiation, which shall run concurrently with the 30 day period for dispute resolution.

(f) The IDRE shall have the dispute reviewed by a neutral and impartial reviewer with training and experience in health care billing, reimbursement, and usual and customary charges. All determinations shall be made in consultation with a neutral and impartial licensed reviewing physician in active practice in the same or similar specialty as the physician providing the service that is subject to the dispute. To the extent practicable, the reviewing physician shall be licensed in this State.

(g) An IDRE shall make a determination within 30 days of receiving the request for the dispute resolution.

(h) For disputes involving a health care plan, in determining a reasonable fee for the services rendered, an IDRE shall select either the health care plan's payment, or in cases involving a non-participating hospital that had previously entered into a participating provider agreement with the health care plan, the health care plan's best and final offer, if applicable, or the non-participating physician's or non-participating referred health care provider's fee, or the non-participating hospital's fee, or, in cases involving a non-participating hospital that had previously entered into a participating provider agreement with the health care plan, the non-participating hospital's best and final offer, as applicable. For disputes that do not involve a health care plan, the IDRE shall determine a reasonable fee.

(i) An IDRE shall use the conditions and factors set forth in Financial Services Law section 604 when determining the reasonable fee and shall consider any other information submitted by the parties pursuant to subdivisions (c)(10), (d)(11), and (e)(7) of section 400.7 of this Part.

(j) An IDRE shall forward copies of the dispute resolution determination to the health care plan, the physician, hospital, or the non-participating referred health care provider, superintendent, and as applicable, patient, within two business days of rendering the determination. The notification shall include:

(1) the fee determined to be reasonable along with the reasons for the determination, including a discussion of the fee charged by the physician, hospital, or non-participating referred health care provider, or, as applicable, the non-participating hospital's best and final offer; the fee paid by the health care plan, or, in cases involving a non-participating hospital, the health care plan's best and final offer, if applicable; the usual and customary charge for disputes involving physician services; and other information provided;

(2) a statement attesting that no prohibited material affiliation existed with respect to the reviewer or reviewing physician;

(3) the biographies of the reviewer and the reviewing physician; and

(4) a request for payment to the party that does not prevail.

(k) An IDRE shall not divulge to the health care plan, physician, hospital, non-participating referred health care provider or patient the name of the reviewer or reviewing physician assigned to the dispute.

(l) For each dispute resolution determination made by the IDRE, the IDRE shall certify that:

(1) the IDRE, the reviewer and the reviewing physician assigned to review the dispute followed appropriate procedures as specified in Financial Services Law article 6 and this Part;

(2) the reviewer and reviewing physician met the criteria for conducting the dispute pursuant to Financial Services Law article 6 and this Part; and

(3) for the reviewer and reviewing physician assigned to review the dispute, the IDRE has obtained a signed attestation affirming, under penalty of perjury, that no prohibited material affiliation exists with respect to the reviewer's or reviewing physician's participation in the review of the dispute pursuant to section 400.4(d) of this Part. The attestation shall be in such form as prescribed by the superintendent.

(m) An IDRE shall not reconsider a dispute for which a determination has been made based upon receipt of additional information subsequent to the determination.

§ 400.9 IDRE record retention and compliance

(a) An IDRE shall retain case records in accordance with 11 NYCRR 243 (Insurance Regulation 152) for audit and examination for a period of six years from the date of the IDRE's determination. The IDRE shall keep and maintain all documentation relating to a case for no less than six years from the date of the IDRE's determination. The IDRE shall maintain on file each attestation required to be submitted pursuant to section 400.3(a)(4)(ii) of this Part for six years from the date of the IDRE's determination.

(b) An IDRE shall ensure the confidentiality of medical and treatment records and review materials in accordance with 11 NYCRR 420 (Insurance Regulation 169) and 11 NYCRR 421 (Insurance Regulation 173) relating to the privacy and confidentiality of health information.

(c) Every attestation required to be submitted pursuant to section 400.3(a)(4)(ii) of this Part shall be in a form prescribed by the superintendent.

(d) An IDRE shall be subject to examination by the superintendent at any time to ascertain compliance with Financial Services Law article 6 and this Part.

(e) An IDRE shall provide ready access to the superintendent to all data, records, and information collected and maintained concerning the IDRE's dispute resolution activities.

(f) An IDRE shall provide the superintendent data, information, and reports as the superintendent determines necessary to evaluate the dispute resolution process within two business days or such other period acceptable to the superintendent.

(g) An IDRE shall consent to cooperate in court proceedings relevant to its role as an IDRE.

(h) The superintendent may suspend IDRE case assignment if the IDRE fails to comply with any of the requirements of this Part and the superintendent may require all necessary corrective actions be taken by the IDRE.

§ 400.10 Payment for the independent dispute resolution

(a) Disputes involving an insured.
  (1) If an IDRE determines the health care plan's payment, or best and final offer, as applicable, is reasonable, payment for the dispute resolution process shall be the responsibility of the non-participating physician, non-participating hospital, or as applicable, non-participating referred health care provider.
  (2) If an IDRE determines the non-participating physician's or non-participating referred health care provider's fee or the non-participating hospital's fee or best and final offer, as applicable, is reasonable, payment for the dispute resolution process shall be the responsibility of the health care plan.
  (3) If good faith negotiations directed by the IDRE results in a settlement between the health care plan and the non-participating physician, non-participating hospital or non-participating referred health care provider, the health care plan and the non-participating physician, non-participating hospital or non-participating referred health care provider shall evenly divide and share the prorated cost for dispute resolution.
  (4) For disputes that are rejected as ineligible or due to the requesting non-participating physician, non-participating hospital, non-participating referred health care provider or health care plan's failure to submit information, an IDRE may charge an application processing fee, which shall be the responsibility of the requesting physician, hospital, health care provider or health care plan.
(b) Disputes involving a patient who is not an insured.
  (1) If an IDRE determines the physician's or hospital's fee is reasonable, payment for the independent dispute resolution process shall be the responsibility of the patient. If the superintendent determines that payment would pose a hardship to the patient pursuant to subdivision (c) of this section, the IDRE shall waive payment for the dispute resolution process.
  (2) If an IDRE determines the physician's or hospital's fee is not reasonable, payment for the independent dispute resolution process shall be the responsibility of the physician or hospital.
(c) A hardship shall exist if the household income of the patient who is not an insured is below 250 percent of the federal poverty level, as determined annually by the Secretary of Health and Human Services.
(d) Any payments due to an IDRE under this section shall be made to the IDRE within 30 calendar days from receipt of the IDRE's written determination and invoice.

OHIO REVISED CODE ANNOTATED

§ 3902.51 Reimbursement for unanticipated out-of-network care

(A)

(1)

(a) A health plan issuer shall reimburse an out-of-network provider for unanticipated out-of-network care when both of the following apply:

(i) The services are provided to a covered person at an in-network facility.

(ii) The services would be covered if provided by an in-network provider.

(b) A health plan issuer shall reimburse both of the following for emergency services provided to a covered person at an out-of-network emergency facility:

(i) An out-of-network provider;

(ii) The out-of-network emergency facility.

(c) A health plan issuer shall reimburse both of the following for emergency services provided to a covered person by an out-of-network ambulance:

(i) An out-of-network provider;

(ii) The out-of-network ambulance.

(2) In the case of clinical laboratory services provided in connection with care described in division (A)(1) of this section, a health plan issuer shall reimburse any out-of-network provider and any out-of-network facility that provided the clinical laboratory services.

(3) For purposes of sections 3902.50 to 3902.54 of the Revised Code:

(a) In the request for reimbursement, the provider, facility, emergency facility, or ambulance shall include the proper billing code for the service for which reimbursement is requested.

(b) The health plan issuer shall send the provider, facility, emergency facility, or ambulance its intended reimbursement as described in division (B)(1) of this section.

(c) Within the period of time specified by the superintendent of insurance in rule, the provider, facility, emergency facility, or ambulance shall either notify the health plan issuer of its acceptance of the reimbursement or seek to negotiate reimbursement under division (B)(2) of this section. Failure to timely notify the issuer of an intent to negotiate shall be considered acceptance of the issuer's reimbursement.

(B)

(1) Unless the provider, facility, emergency facility, or ambulance wishes to negotiate reimbursement under division (B)(2) of this section, the reimbursement required to be paid to the provider, facility, emergency facility, or ambulance under division (A) of this section shall be the greatest of the following amounts:

(a) The amount negotiated with in-network providers, facilities, emergency facilities, or ambulances for the service in question in that geographic region under that health benefit plan, excluding any in-network cost sharing imposed under the health benefit plan. If there is more than one such amount, the relevant amount shall be the median of those amounts, excluding any in-network cost sharing imposed under the health benefit plan. In determining the median amount, the amount negotiated with each in-network provider, facility, emergency facility, or ambulance shall be treated as a separate amount even if the same amount is paid to more than one provider. If there is no per-service amount, such as under a capitation or similar payment arrangement, the amount described in division (B)(1)(a) of this section shall be disregarded.

(b) The amount for the service calculated using the same method the health benefit plan generally uses to determine payments for out-of-network health care services, such as the usual, customary, and reasonable amount, excluding any in-network cost sharing imposed under the health benefit plan. This amount shall be determined with reduction for cost sharing that generally applies under the health benefit plan with respect to out-of-network health care services.

(c) The amount that would be paid under the Medicare program, part A or part B of Title XVIII of the Social Security Act, 42 U.S.C. 1395, as amended, for the service in question, excluding any in-network cost sharing imposed under the health benefit plan.

(2) In lieu of accepting reimbursement under division (B)(1) of this section, a provider, facility, emergency facility, or ambulance may notify the health plan issuer that the provider, facility, emergency facility, or ambulance wishes to negotiate reimbursement. Upon receipt of such notice, the health plan issuer shall attempt a good faith negotiation with the provider, facility, emergency facility, or ambulance.

(C)

(1) For unanticipated out-of-network care provided at an in-network facility in this state, a provider shall not bill a covered person for the difference between the health plan issuer's reimbursement and the provider's charge for the services.

(2) For emergency services provided at an out-of-network emergency facility in this state, neither the emergency facility nor an out-of-network provider shall bill a covered person for the difference between the health plan issuer's reimbursement and the emergency facility's or the provider's charge for the services.

(3) For emergency services provided by an out-of-network ambulance in this state, neither the ambulance nor an out-of-network provider shall bill a covered person for the difference between the health plan issuer's reimbursement and the ambulance's or provider's charge for the services.

(4) In the case of clinical laboratory services provided in this state in connection with care described in division (A)(1) of this section, no

out-of-network provider or out-of-network facility shall bill a covered person for the difference between the health plan issuer's reimbursement and the provider's or facility's charge for the clinical laboratory services.

(D) A health plan issuer shall not require cost sharing for any service described in division (A) of this section from the covered person at a rate higher than if the services were provided in network.

(E) For health care services, other than those described in division (A) of this section, that are covered under a health benefit plan but are provided to a covered person by an out-of-network provider at an in-network facility, both of the following apply:

(1) For services provided in this state, the provider shall not bill the covered person for the difference between the health plan issuer's out-of-network reimbursement and the provider's charge for the services unless all of the following conditions are met:

(a) The provider informs the covered person that the provider is not in the covered person's health benefit plan network.

(b) The provider provides to the covered person a good faith estimate of the cost of the services, including the provider's charge, the estimated reimbursement by the health plan issuer, and the covered person's responsibility. The estimate shall contain a disclaimer that the covered person is not required to obtain the health care service at that location or from that provider.

(c) The covered person affirmatively consents to receive the services.

(2) The health plan issuer may reimburse the provider at either the in-network or out-of-network rate as described in the covered person's health benefit plan.

(F) Nothing in this section is subject to section 3901.71 of the Revised Code.

§ 3902.52 Arbitration regarding claim by provider

(A)

(1) If a negotiation undertaken pursuant to division (B)(2) of section 3902.51 of the Revised Code has not successfully concluded within thirty days, or if both parties agree that they are at an impasse, the provider, facility, emergency facility, or ambulance may send a request for arbitration to the superintendent of insurance and shall notify the health plan issuer of its request. To be eligible for arbitration, both of the following must apply:

(a) The service in question was provided not more than one year prior to the request.

(b) The billed amount exceeds seven hundred fifty dollars, except as provided in division (A)(2)(b) of this section.

(2)

(a) In seeking arbitration, a provider, facility, emergency facility, or ambulance may bundle up to fifteen claims with respect to the same health benefit plan that involve the same or similar services provided under similar circumstances. Any bundled claims shall be for services using the same coding set and providers of the same license type.

(b) A claim that is bundled with other claims may be seven hundred fifty dollars or less so long as the sum of the bundled claims is greater than seven hundred fifty dollars.

(B) If arbitration is requested under division (A) of this section, each party shall submit its final offer to the arbitrator. The parties also may submit, and the arbitrator may consider, evidence that relates to the factors described in division (C) of this section if the evidence is in a form that can be verified and authenticated.

(C) An arbitrator shall consider all of the following factors in rendering a decision:

(1) The in-network rates that other health benefit plans reimburse, and have reimbursed, that particular provider, facility, emergency facility, or ambulance for the service in question, including the factors that went into those rates such as guaranteed patient volume or availability of providers in the provider's, facility's, emergency facility's, or ambulance's geographic area;

(2) The in-network rates that the health benefit plan reimburses, or has reimbursed, other providers, facilities, emergency facilities, or ambulances for the service in question in that particular geographic area, including the factors that went into those rates such as guaranteed patient volume or availability of providers in that particular geographic area;

(3) If the health plan issuer and the provider, facility, emergency facility, or ambulance have had a contractual relationship in the previous six years, any in-network reimbursement rates previously agreed upon between the issuer and the provider, facility, emergency facility, or ambulance;

(4) The results of, or any documents submitted in the course of, a previous arbitration between the parties conducted under this section that the arbitrator considers relevant in rendering a decision.

(D) After considering the evidence submitted by the parties pursuant to division (B) of this section and the criteria described in division (C) of this section, the arbitrator shall issue a decision that awards the final offer of either party that best reflects a fair reimbursement rate based upon the factors considered under division (C) of this section.

(E) The nonprevailing party shall pay seventy per cent of the arbitrator's fees, and the prevailing party shall pay thirty per cent.

(F) A final arbitration decision shall be binding except as to other remedies available at law.

(G) Documents and other evidence submitted to an arbitrator under this section are confidential, not public records for the purposes of section 149.43 of the Revised Code, and shall not be released except as authorized pursuant to this division. If release of the evidence is required pursuant to a court order, the arbitrator shall release the evidence pursuant to the court order but shall redact from the evidence released information that constitutes intellectual property, trade secrets, or information requiring redaction pursuant to a rule adopted by the superintendent of insurance.

(H) As used in this section, "provider" includes a practice of providers to the extent permitted by rules adopted by the superintendent of insurance under division (D) of section 3902.54 of the Revised Code including but not limited to rules adopted regarding the maximum number of providers in a practice.

§ 4769.02 Balance billing of Medicare beneficiaries prohibited

No health care practitioner, and no person that employs any health care practitioner, shall balance bill for any supplies or service provided to a Medicare beneficiary.

OREGON ADMINISTRATIVE RULES

§ 836-053-1605 Definitions for 836-053-1600 to 836-053-1615

(1) "Anesthesia Conversion factor" means the dollar value assigned to the following geographic rating area where the procedure is performed:
   (a) Area 1 is $ 68.00;
   (b) Area 2 is $ 70.40;
   (c) Area 3 is $ 67.85;
   (d) Area 4 is $ 75.88;
   (e) Area 5 is $ 68.00;
   (f) Area 6 is $ 66.17; and
   (g) Area 7 is $ 70.77.

(2) "Base units" means the number of units assigned to the relevant CPT code for the anesthesia-related procedure published in the American Society of Anesthesiologists (ASA), Relative Value Guide 2018. To obtain a copy of the ASA Relative Value Guide 2018, contact the American Society of Anesthesiologists, 1061 American Lane, Schaumberg, IL 60173, 847-825-5586, or www.asahq.org.

(3) "Base Rate" means the dollar amount listed on the Non-Anesthesia Base Rate Fee Schedule under Appendix A.

(4) "CMS" means the Center for Medicare and Medicaid Services.

(5) "CPT"® means Current Procedural Terminology codes and terminology under the American Medical Association's (AMA) Current Procedural Terminology (CPT® 2018), Fourth Edition Revised, 2017, for billing by medical providers.

(6) "CPI adjustment" means the annual adjustment designated by the director calculated with the Consumer Price Index for All Urban Consumers U.S. city average series for all items, not seasonally adjusted. Prior to January 1 of each year the director shall publish the adjustment figure representing the Consumer Price Index adjustment from January 2015 to July of the prior year. For 2019, the designated CPI adjustment is 107.83%.

(7) "Director" means the Director of the Department of Consumer and Business Services.

(8) "Geographic rating area" means the rating area defined under OAR 836-053-0063(6).

(9) "Modifier adjustment" means the adjustment allowed under the CMS CY 2018 Physician Fee Schedule Final Rule as of January 1, 2018, for the following modifiers, if applicable: AS, FX, FY, SA, UE, 22, 23, 25, 47, 50, 51, 52, 53, 54, 55, 56, 62, 66, 73, 78, 80, 81, 82. The CY 2018 Physician Fee Schedule Final Rule is available at https://www.cms.gov/Medicare/Medicare-Fee-for-Service-Payment/PhysicianFeeSched/PFS-Federal-Regulation-Notices-Items/CMS-1676-F.html. The adjustment for any other modifier or no modifier is 100%.

(10) "Out-of-network reimbursement" means the allowable rate paid by the insurer to the out-of-network provider for emergency services or other covered inpatient or outpatient services provided at an in-network health care facility in Oregon in accordance with ORS 743B.287(3). The amount to be paid by the insurer may include applicable coinsurance, copayment, and deductible amounts paid by the enrollee as outlined in the insurance policy.

(11) "Physical status units" means the number of units assigned based on the provider's assessment of the medical condition of the patient. Physical status units are assigned as follows:
- (a) 1 unit for P3 – A patient with severe systemic disease;
- (b) 2 units for P4 – A patient with severe systemic disease that is a constant threat to life;
- (c) 3 units for P5 – A moribund patient who is not expected to survive without the operation; and
- (d) 0 units for all others.

(12) "Q modifier adjustment" means the relevant percentage adjustment, if applicable, assigned for the following modifiers:
- (a) 50% for QK – medical direction of two, three, or four concurrent anesthesia procedures involving qualified individuals;
- (b) 50% for QX – CRNA service; with medical direction by a physician;
- (c) 50% for QY – Medical direction of one certified registered nurse anesthetist (CRNA) by an anesthesiologist; and
- (d) 100% for no modifier or any other modifier.

(13) "Time units" means the relevant amount of time for an anesthesia-related procedure expressed in 15-minute increments.

§ 836-053-1610 Non-anesthesia-related claims

(1) Out-of-network reimbursement for non-anesthesia-related claims shall be no less than:
Base rate × Modifier adjustment × CPI adjustment

(2) Out-of-network reimbursement for a non-anesthesia-related claim that does not have a base rate listed on the Non-Anesthesia Fee Schedule shall be at a rate agreed upon in good faith by the insurer and the provider to be usual and customary for in-network commercial claims, using best efforts to establish a rate within a reasonable amount of time.

§ 836-053-1615 Anesthesia-related claims

(1) Out-of-network reimbursement for anesthesia-related claims, including obstetric anesthesia claims, shall be no less than:
(Base units + Time units + Physical status units) × Anesthesia Conversion factor × Q modifier adjustment × CPI adjustment

(2) Out-of-network reimbursement for an anesthesia-related claim that does not have a number of base units published in the CY 2018 Physician Fee Schedule Final Rule shall be reimbursed at a rate calculated with a number of base units agreed upon in good faith by the insurer and provider to be usual and customary for in-network commercial claims, using best efforts to establish a rate within a reasonable amount of time.

OREGON REVISED STATUTES

§ 743B.282 Estimate of costs for out-of-network procedure or service

(1) An insurer offering a health benefit plan as defined in ORS 743B.005 must establish a procedure for providing to an enrollee in the plan a reasonable estimate of the enrollee's costs for an out-of-network procedure or service covered by the enrollee's health benefit plan, including the difference between the insurer's allowable charge and the billed charge for the procedure or service, in advance of the procedure or service, when an enrollee or an enrollee's authorized representative provides the following information to the insurer:
   (a) The type of procedure or service;
   (b) The name of the provider;
   (c) The enrollee's member number or policy number;
   (d) If requested by the insurer, the site where the procedure or service will be performed; and
   (e) The provider's billed charge amount.

(2) The estimate of costs described in subsection (1) of this section must include an itemization of:
   (a) The enrollee's deductible;
   (b) The amount of the deductible that has been met by processed claims;
   (c) Coinsurance, copayment or other cost share to be paid by the enrollee for the procedure or service;
   (d) Any applicable benefit maximum;
   (e) The difference between the insurer's allowable charge and the billed charge for the procedure or service; and
   (f) The insurer's average payment or allowable charge for the procedure or service if performed in-network.

(3) Subsections (1) and (2) of this section apply to the insurer's five most common procedures or services within each of the following categories:
   (a) Office visits;
   (b) Diagnostic radiology and imaging;
   (c) Diagnostic pathology and laboratory procedures;
   (d) Normal vaginal delivery;
   (e) Immunizations;
   (f) Orthopedic-musculoskeletal surgery; and
   (g) Digestive system endoscopy.

(4) In addition to the information specified in subsections (1) and (2) of this section, the insurer's estimate must include the following disclosures:
  (a) That other services may be provided to the enrollee that are medically necessary and appropriate as part of the common procedures, of which the insurer or enrollee may not be aware at the time of the inquiry and for which the enrollee may have additional financial responsibility;
  (b) That the enrollee may be responsible for costs of procedures or services not covered by the plan;
  (c) How an enrollee may contact the insurer for an explanation, if the estimate differs from the actual cost or if the enrollee has other questions; and
  (d) The toll-free telephone number of the consumer advocacy unit of the Department of Consumer and Business Services and the address for the department's consumer information and complaints website.

(5) An insurer must make the information required by this section available to enrollees and out-of-network providers through an interactive website and by toll-free telephone.

(6) This section does not prohibit an insurer from providing information in addition to or in more detail than the information required by this section.

§ 743B.287 Balance billing prohibited for health care facility services; rules

(1) As used in this section:
  (a) "Emergency services" has the meaning given that term in ORS 743A.012.
  (b) "Enrollee" means:
    (A) An individual who is enrolled in a health benefit plan or a covered dependent or beneficiary of the individual; or
    (B) A subscriber to a health care service contract or a covered dependent or beneficiary of the subscriber.
  (c) "Health benefit plan" has the meaning given that term in ORS 743B.005.
  (d) "Health care facility" has the meaning given that term in ORS 442.015, excluding long term care facilities.
  (e) "Health care service contractor" has the meaning given that term in ORS 750.005.
  (f) "In-network" has the meaning given that term in ORS 743B.280.
  (g) "Out-of-network" means a provider or provider group that has not contracted or has indirectly contracted with the insurer or health care service contractor.

(2) A provider who is an out-of-network provider may not bill an enrollee in the health benefit plan or health care service contract for emergency services or other inpatient or outpatient services provided at an in-network health care facility.

(3) Subsection (2) of this section does not apply:

(a) To applicable coinsurance, copayments or deductible amounts that apply to services provided by an in-network provider; or

(b) To services, other than emergency services, provided to enrollees who choose to receive services from an out-of-network provider.

(4)

(a) If labor and delivery services are provided to an individual insured under a health benefit plan or a health care service contract at an out-of-network health care facility due solely to the diversion of the individual from an in-network health care facility during a state or federally declared public health emergency, the health benefit plan or health care service contract:

(A)

(i) Shall reimburse the out-of-network provider in accordance with 42 U.S.C. 300gg-111(c) or in accordance with a method adopted by the Department of Consumer and Business Services by rule; and

(ii) May not impose a deductible, out-of-pocket maximum, copayment or coinsurance requirement that exceeds the deductible, out-of-pocket maximum, copayment or coinsurance applicable to in-network providers of labor and delivery services.

(B) Shall provide coverage, as prescribed in ORS 743A.012 (2) and (3), for emergency medical services transports of the individual between medical facilities if the individual presents with signs of labor.

(b) Paragraph (a)(A)(i) of this subsection does not apply to services provided by an in network provider at an out-of-network health care facility.

(5) If an enrollee chooses to receive services from an out-of-network provider, the provider shall inform the enrollee that the enrollee will be financially responsible for coinsurance, copayments or other out-of-pocket expenses attributable to choosing an out-of-network provider.

TEXAS INSURANCE CODE

§ 752.0002 Injunction for balance billing

(a) If the attorney general receives a referral from the appropriate regulatory agency indicating that an individual or entity, including a health benefit plan issuer or administrator, has exhibited a pattern of intentionally violating a law that prohibits the individual or entity from billing an insured, participant, or enrollee in an amount greater than an applicable copayment, coinsurance, and deductible under the insured's, participant's, or enrollee's managed care plan or that imposes a requirement related to that prohibition, the attorney general may bring a civil action in the name of the state to enjoin the individual or entity from the violation.

(b) If the attorney general prevails in an action brought under Subsection (a), the attorney general may recover reasonable attorney's fees, costs, and expenses, including court costs and witness fees, incurred in bringing the action.

§ 752.0003 Enforcement by regulatory agency

(a) An appropriate regulatory agency that licenses, certifies, or otherwise authorizes a physician, health care practitioner, health care facility, or other health care provider to practice or operate in this state may take disciplinary action against the physician, practitioner, facility, or provider if the physician, practitioner, facility, or provider violates a law that prohibits the physician, practitioner, facility, or provider from billing an insured, participant, or enrollee in an amount greater than an applicable copayment, coinsurance, and deductible under the insured's, participant's, or enrollee's managed care plan or that imposes a requirement related to that prohibition.

(b) The department may take disciplinary action against a health benefit plan issuer or administrator if the issuer or administrator violates a law requiring the issuer or administrator to provide notice of a balance billing prohibition or make a related disclosure.

(c) A regulatory agency described by Subsection (a) or the commissioner may adopt rules as necessary to implement this section. Section 2001.0045, Government Code, does not apply to rules adopted under this subsection.

§ 1275.001 Definitions[145]

In this chapter:

(1) "Enrollee" means an individual enrolled in a health benefit plan to which this chapter applies.

(2) "Usual and customary rate" means the relevant allowable amount as described by the applicable master benefit plan document.

145 Tex. Ins. Code Title 8, Subtit. C, Ch. 1275 Balance Billing Prohibitions and Out-Of-Network Claim Dispute Resolution for Certain Plans.

§ 1275.002 Applicability of chapter

This chapter applies only to:

(1) a health benefit plan offered by a nonprofit agricultural organization under Chapter 1682; and
(2) a health benefit plan:
 (A) that is a self-insured or self-funded plan established by an employer for the benefit of the employers employees in accordance with the Employee Retirement Income Security Act of 1974 (29 U.S.C. Section 1001 et seq.); and
 (B) for which the plan sponsor has made an election, submitted to the commissioner in the form and manner prescribed by the commissioner, to apply this chapter to the plan for the relevant plan year.

§ 1275.003 Balance billing prohibition notice[146]

(a) The administrator of a health benefit plan to which this chapter applies shall provide written notice in accordance with this section in an explanation of benefits provided to the enrollee and the physician or health care provider in connection with a health care or medical service or supply provided by an out-of-network provider. The notice must include:
 (1) a statement of the billing prohibition under Section 1275.051, 1275.052, or 1275.053, as applicable;
 (2) the total amount the physician or provider may bill the enrollee under the enrollee's health benefit plan and an itemization of copayments, coinsurance, deductibles, and other amounts included in that total; and
 (3) for an explanation of benefits provided to the physician or provider, information required by commissioner rule advising the physician or provider of the availability of mediation or arbitration, as applicable, under Chapter 1467.
(b) The administrator shall provide the explanation of benefits with the notice required by this section to a physician or health care provider not later than the date the administrator makes a payment under Section 1275.051, 1275.052, or 1275.053, as applicable.

§ 1275.004 Out-of-network claim dispute resolution

Chapter 1467 applies to a health benefit plan to which this chapter applies, and the administrator of a health benefit plan to which this chapter applies is an administrator for purposes of that chapter.

146 Effective September 1, 2025.

§ 1275.051 Emergency care payments

(a) In this section, "emergency care" has the meaning assigned by Section 1301.155.

(b) The administrator of a health benefit plan to which this chapter applies shall pay for covered emergency care performed by or a covered supply related to that care provided by an out-of-network provider at the usual and customary rate or at an agreed rate. The administrator shall make a payment required by this subsection directly to the provider not later than, as applicable:

  (1) the 30th day after the date the administrator receives an electronic claim for those services that includes all information necessary for the administrator to pay the claim; or

  (2) the 45th day after the date the administrator receives a nonelectronic claim for those services that includes all information necessary for the administrator to pay the claim.

(c) For emergency care subject to this section or a supply related to that care, an out-of-network provider or a person asserting a claim as an agent or assignee of the provider may not bill an enrollee in, and the enrollee does not have financial responsibility for, an amount greater than an applicable copayment, coinsurance, and deductible under the enrollee's health benefit plan that:

  (1) is based on:

    (A) the amount initially determined payable by the administrator; or

    (B) if applicable, a modified amount as determined under the administrator's internal appeal process; and

  (2) is not based on any additional amount determined to be owed to the provider under Chapter 1467.

§ 1275.052 Out-of-network facility-based provider payments

(a) In this section, "facility-based provider" means a physician or health care provider who provides health care or medical services to patients of a health care facility.

(b) Except as provided by Subsection (d), the administrator of a health benefit plan to which this chapter applies shall pay for a covered health care or medical service performed for or a covered supply related to that service provided to an enrollee by an out-of-network provider who is a facility-based provider at the usual and customary rate or at an agreed rate if the provider performed the service at a health care facility that is a participating provider. The administrator shall make a payment required by this subsection directly to the provider not later than, as applicable:

  (1) the 30th day after the date the administrator receives an electronic claim for those services that includes all information necessary for the administrator to pay the claim; or

(2) the 45th day after the date the administrator receives a nonelectronic claim for those services that includes all information necessary for the administrator to pay the claim.

(c) Except as provided by Subsection (d), an out-of-network provider who is a facility-based provider or a person asserting a claim as an agent or assignee of the provider may not bill an enrollee receiving a health care or medical service or supply described by Subsection (b) in, and the enrollee does not have financial responsibility for, an amount greater than an applicable copayment, coinsurance, and deductible under the enrollee's health benefit plan that:
  (1) is based on:
    (A) the amount initially determined payable by the administrator; or
    (B) if applicable, a modified amount as determined under the administrator's internal appeal process; and
  (2) is not based on any additional amount determined to be owed to the provider under Chapter 1467.

(d) This section does not apply to a nonemergency health care or medical service:
  (1) that an enrollee elects to receive in writing in advance of the service with respect to each out-of-network provider providing the service; and
  (2) for which an out-of-network provider, before providing the service, provides a complete written disclosure to the enrollee that:
    (A) explains that the provider does not have a contract with the enrollee's health benefit plan;
    (B) discloses projected amounts for which the enrollee may be responsible; and
    (C) discloses the circumstances under which the enrollee would be responsible for those amounts.

§ 1275.053 Out-of-network diagnostic imaging provider or laboratory service provider payments

(a) In this section, "diagnostic imaging provider" and "laboratory service provider" have the meanings assigned by Section 1467.001.

(b) Except as provided by Subsection (d), the administrator of a health benefit plan to which this chapter applies shall pay for a covered health care or medical service performed for or a covered supply related to that service provided to an enrollee by an out-of-network provider who is a diagnostic imaging provider or laboratory service provider at the usual and customary rate or at an agreed rate if the provider performed the service in connection with a health care or medical service performed by a participating provider. The administrator shall make a payment required by this subsection directly to the provider not later than, as applicable:

(1) the 30th day after the date the administrator receives an electronic claim for those services that includes all information necessary for the administrator to pay the claim; or
(2) the 45th day after the date the administrator receives a nonelectronic claim for those services that includes all information necessary for the administrator to pay the claim.

(c) Except as provided by Subsection (d), an out-of-network provider who is a diagnostic imaging provider or laboratory service provider or a person asserting a claim as an agent or assignee of the provider may not bill an enrollee receiving a health care or medical service or supply described by Subsection (b) in, and the enrollee does not have financial responsibility for, an amount greater than an applicable copayment, coinsurance, and deductible under the enrollee's health benefit plan that:
(1) is based on:
(A) the amount initially determined payable by the administrator; or
(B) if applicable, the modified amount as determined under the administrator's internal appeal process; and
(2) is not based on any additional amount determined to be owed to the provider under Chapter 1467.

(d) This section does not apply to a nonemergency health care or medical service:
(1) that an enrollee elects to receive in writing in advance of the service with respect to each out-of-network provider providing the service; and
(2) for which an out-of-network provider, before providing the service, provides a complete written disclosure to the enrollee that:
(A) explains that the provider does not have a contract with the enrollee's health benefit plan;
(B) discloses projected amounts for which the enrollee may be responsible; and
(C) discloses the circumstances under which the enrollee would be responsible for those amounts.

§ 1275.054 Out-of-network emergency medical services provider payments[147]

(a) In this section, "emergency medical services provider" has the meaning assigned by Section 773.003, Health and Safety Code, except that the term does not include an air ambulance.

(b) Except as provided by Subsection (c), the administrator of a health benefit plan to which this chapter applies shall pay for a covered health care or medical service performed for, or a covered supply or covered transport related to that

147 This section expires September 1, 2025.

service provided to, an enrollee by an out-of-network provider who is an emergency medical services provider at:

(1) if the political subdivision has submitted the rate to the department under Section 38.006, the rate set, controlled, or regulated by the political subdivision in which:
   (A) the service originated; or
   (B) the transport originated if transport is provided; or
(2) if the political subdivision has not submitted the rate to the department, the lesser of:
   (A) the provider's billed charge; or
   (B) 325 percent of the current Medicare rate, including any applicable extenders and modifiers.

(c) The administrator shall adjust a payment required by Subsection (b)(1) each plan year by increasing the payment by the lesser of the Medicare Inflation Index or 10 percent of the provider's previous calendar year rates.

(d) The administrator shall make a payment required by this section directly to the provider not later than, as applicable:
   (1) the 30th day after the date the administrator receives an electronic claim for those services that includes all information necessary for the administrator to pay the claim; or
   (2) the 45th day after the date the administrator receives a nonelectronic claim for those services that includes all information necessary for the administrator to pay the claim.

(e) An out-of-network provider who is an emergency medical services provider or a person asserting a claim as an agent or assignee of the provider may not bill an enrollee receiving a health care or medical service or supply or transport described by Subsection (b) in, and the enrollee does not have financial responsibility for, an amount greater than an applicable copayment, coinsurance, and deductible under the enrollee's health benefit plan that is based on:
   (1) the amount initially determined payable by the administrator; or
   (2) if applicable, the modified amount as determined under the administrator's internal appeal process.

(f) This section expires September 1, 2025.

§ 1467.001 Definitions[148]

In this chapter:

(1) "Administrator" means:
   (A) an administering firm for a health benefit plan providing coverage under Chapter 1551, 1575, or 1579; and
   (B) if applicable, the claims administrator for the health benefit plan.

148 Out-of-Network Claim Dispute Resolution.

(1-a) "Arbitration" means a process in which an impartial arbiter issues a binding determination in a dispute between a health benefit plan issuer or administrator and an out-of-network provider or the provider's representative to settle a health benefit claim.

(2) [Repealed.]

(2-a) "Diagnostic imaging provider" means a health care provider who performs a diagnostic imaging service on a patient for a fee or interprets imaging produced by a diagnostic imaging service.

(2-b) "Diagnostic imaging service" means magnetic resonance imaging, computed tomography, positron emission tomography, or any hybrid technology that combines any of those imaging modalities.

(2-c) "Emergency care" has the meaning assigned by Section 1301.155.

(2-d) "Emergency care provider" means a physician, health care practitioner, facility, or other health care provider who provides and bills an enrollee, administrator, or health benefit plan for emergency care.

(3) "Enrollee" means an individual who is eligible to receive benefits through a health benefit plan subject to this chapter.

(3-a) "Facility" has the meaning assigned by Section 324.001, Health and Safety Code.

(4) "Facility-based provider" means a physician, health care practitioner, or other health care provider who provides health care or medical services to patients of a facility.

(4-a) "Health care practitioner" means an individual who is licensed to provide health care services.

(4-b) "Laboratory service provider" means an accredited facility in which a specimen taken from a human body is interpreted and pathological diagnoses are made or a physician who makes an interpretation of or diagnosis based on a specimen or information provided by a laboratory based on a specimen.

(5) "Mediation" means a process in which an impartial mediator facilitates and promotes agreement between the health benefit plan issuer or the administrator and an out-of-network provider or the provider's representative to settle a health benefit claim of an enrollee.

(6) "Mediator" means an impartial person who is appointed to conduct a mediation under this chapter.

(6-a) "Out-of-network provider" means a diagnostic imaging provider, emergency care provider, facility-based provider, or laboratory service provider that is not a participating provider for a health benefit plan.

(7) "Party" means a health benefit plan issuer offering a health benefit plan, an administrator, or an out-of-network provider or the provider's representative who participates in a mediation or arbitration conducted under this chapter.

§ 1467.002 Applicability of chapter

This chapter applies to:

(1) a health benefit plan offered by a health maintenance organization operating under Chapter 843;
(2) a preferred provider benefit plan, including an exclusive provider benefit plan, offered by an insurer under Chapter 1301; and
(3) an administrator of a health benefit plan, other than a health maintenance organization plan, under Chapter 1551, 1575, or 1579.

§ 1467.003 Rules

(a) The commissioner, the Texas Medical Board, and any other appropriate regulatory agency shall adopt rules as necessary to implement their respective powers and duties under this chapter.
(b) Section 2001.0045, Government Code, does not apply to a rule adopted under this chapter.

§ 1467.004 Remedies not exclusive

The remedies provided by this chapter are in addition to any other defense, remedy, or procedure provided by law, including the common law.

§ 1467.005 Reform

This chapter may not be construed to prohibit:

(1) a health benefit plan issuer or administrator from, at any time, offering a reformed claim settlement; or
(2) an out-of-network provider from, at any time, offering a reformed charge for health care or medical services or supplies.

§ 1467.006 Benchmarking database

(a) In this section, "geozip area" means an area that includes all zip codes with identical first three digits. For purposes of this section, a health care or medical service or supply provided at a location that does not have a zip code is considered to be provided in the geozip area closest to the location at which the service or supply is provided.
(b) The commissioner shall select an organization to maintain a benchmarking database in accordance with this section. The organization may not:
    (1) be affiliated with a health benefit plan issuer or administrator or a physician, health care practitioner, or other health care provider; or
    (2) have any other conflict of interest.

(c) The benchmarking database must contain information necessary to calculate, with respect to a health care or medical service or supply, for each geozip area in this state:
  (1) the 80th percentile of billed charges of all physicians or health care providers who are not facilities; and
  (2) the 50th percentile of rates paid to participating providers who are not facilities.

(d) The commissioner may adopt rules governing the submission of information for the benchmarking database described by Subsection (c).

§ 1467.050 Applicability of subchapter[149]

(a) This subchapter applies only with respect to a health benefit claim submitted by an out-of-network provider that is a facility.

(b) This subchapter does not apply to a health benefit claim for the professional or technical component of a physician service.

§ 1467.0505 Establishment and administration of mediation program

(a) The commissioner shall establish and administer a mediation program to resolve disputes over out-of-network provider charges in accordance with this subchapter.

(b) The commissioner:
  (1) shall adopt rules, forms, and procedures necessary for the implementation and administration of the mediation program, including the establishment of a portal on the department's Internet website through which a request for mediation under Section 1467.051 may be submitted; and
  (2) shall maintain a list of qualified mediators for the program.

§ 1467.051 Availability of mandatory mediation

(a) An out-of-network provider or a health benefit plan issuer or administrator may request mediation of a settlement of an out-of-network health benefit claim through a portal on the department's Internet website if:
  (1) there is an amount billed by the provider and unpaid by the issuer or administrator after copayments, deductibles, and coinsurance for which an enrollee may not be billed; and

149 Tex. Ins. Code Title 8, Subtit. F, Ch. 1467, Subch. B Mandatory mediation for Out-of-Network Facilities

(2) the health benefit claim is for:
(A) emergency care;
(B) an out-of-network laboratory service; or
(C) an out-of-network diagnostic imaging service.

(b) If a person requests mediation under this subchapter, the out-of-network provider or the provider's representative, and the health benefit plan issuer or the administrator, as appropriate, shall participate in the mediation.

(c) [Repealed.]

(d) [Repealed.]

§ 1467.052 Mediator qualifications

(a) Except as provided by Subsection (b), to qualify for an appointment as a mediator under this subchapter a person must have completed at least 40 classroom hours of training in dispute resolution techniques in a course conducted by an alternative dispute resolution organization or other dispute resolution organization approved by the commissioner.

(b) A person not qualified under Subsection (a) may be appointed as a mediator on agreement of the parties.

(c) A person may not act as mediator for a claim settlement dispute if the person has been employed by, consulted for, or otherwise had a business relationship with a health benefit plan issuer or administrator or a physician, health care practitioner, or other health care provider during the three years immediately preceding the request for mediation.

(d) The commissioner shall immediately terminate the approval of a mediator who no longer meets the requirements under this subchapter and rules adopted under this subchapter to serve as a mediator.

§ 1467.053 Appointment of mediator; fees

(a) A mediation shall be conducted by one mediator.

(b) [Repealed.]

(b-1) If the parties do not select a mediator by mutual agreement on or before the 30th day after the date the mediation is requested, the party requesting the mediation shall notify the commissioner, and the commissioner shall select a mediator from the commissioner's list of approved mediators.

(c) [Repealed.]

(d) The mediator's fees shall be split evenly and paid by the health benefit plan issuer or administrator and the out-of-network provider.

§ 1467.054 Request and preliminary procedures for mandatory mediation

(a) An out-of-network provider or a health benefit plan issuer or administrator may request mandatory mediation under this subchapter.

(b) [Repealed.]

(b-1) The person who requests the mediation shall provide written notice on the date the mediation is requested in the form and manner provided by commissioner rule to:

(1) the department; and

(2) each other party.

(c) [Repealed.]

(d) In an effort to settle the claim before mediation, all parties must participate in an informal settlement teleconference not later than the 30th day after the date on which a person submits a request for mediation under this subchapter.

(e) A dispute to be mediated under this chapter that does not settle as a result of a teleconference conducted under Subsection (d) must be conducted in the county in which the health care or medical services were rendered.

(f) [Repealed.]

(g) [Repealed.]

§ 1467.055 Conduct of mediation; confidentiality

(a) A mediator may not impose the mediator's judgment on a party about an issue that is a subject of the mediation.

(b) A mediation session is under the control of the mediator.

(c) Except as provided by this chapter, the mediator must hold in strict confidence all information provided to the mediator by a party and all communications of the mediator with a party.

(c-1) Information submitted by the parties to the mediator is confidential and not subject to disclosure under Chapter 552, Government Code.

(d) [Repealed.]

(e) A party must have an opportunity during the mediation to speak and state the party's position.

(f) Except on the agreement of the participating parties, a mediation may not last more than four hours.

(g) A mediation shall be held not later than the 180th day after the date of the request for mediation.

(h) [Repealed.]

(i) A health care or medical service or supply provided by an out-of-network provider may not be summarily disallowed. This subsection does not require a health benefit plan issuer or administrator to pay for an uncovered service or supply.

(j) A mediator may not testify in a proceeding, other than a proceeding to enforce this chapter, related to the mediation agreement.

(k) On agreement of all parties, any deadline under this subchapter may be extended.

§ 1467.056 Matters considered in mediation; agreed resolution

(a) In a mediation under this subchapter, the parties shall evaluate whether:
  (1) the amount charged by the out-of-network provider for the health care or medical service or supply is excessive; and
  (2) the amount paid by the health benefit plan issuer or administrator represents the usual and customary rate for the health care or medical service or supply or is unreasonably low.

(b) The out-of-network provider may present information regarding the amount charged for the health care or medical service or supply. The health benefit plan issuer or administrator may present information regarding the amount paid by the issuer or administrator.

(c) Nothing in this chapter prohibits mediation of more than one claim between the parties during a mediation.

(d) The goal of the mediation is to reach an agreement between the out-of-network provider and the health benefit plan issuer or administrator, as applicable, as to the amount paid by the issuer or administrator to the out-of-network provider and the amount charged by the out-of-network provider.

§ 1467.0575 Right to file action

Not later than the 45th day after the date that the mediator's report is provided to the department under Section 1467.060, either party to a mediation for which there was no agreement may file a civil action to determine the amount due to an out-of-network provider. A party may not bring a civil action before the conclusion of the mediation process under this subchapter.

§ 1467.060 Report of mediator

Not later than the 45th day after the date the mediation concludes, the mediator shall report to the commissioner and the Texas Medical Board or other appropriate regulatory agency:

(1) the names of the parties to the mediation; and
(2) whether the parties reached an agreement.

§ 1467.081 Applicability of subchapter

This subchapter applies only with respect to a health benefit claim submitted by an out-of-network provider who is not a facility.

§ 1467.082 Establishment and administration of arbitration program

(a) The commissioner shall establish and administer an arbitration program to resolve disputes over out-of-network provider charges in accordance with this subchapter.

(b) The commissioner:
   (1) shall adopt rules, forms, and procedures necessary for the implementation and administration of the arbitration program, including the establishment of a portal on the department's Internet website through which a request for arbitration under Section 1467.084 may be submitted; and
   (2) shall maintain a list of qualified arbitrators for the program.

§ 1467.083 Issue to be addressed; basis for determination

(a) The only issue that an arbitrator may determine under this subchapter is the reasonable amount for the health care or medical services or supplies provided to the enrollee by an out-of-network provider.
(b) The determination must take into account:
   (1) whether there is a gross disparity between the fee billed by the out-of-network provider and:
      (A) fees paid to the out-of-network provider for the same services or supplies rendered by the provider to other enrollees for which the provider is an out-of-network provider; and
      (B) fees paid by the health benefit plan issuer to reimburse similarly qualified out-of-network providers for the same services or supplies in the same region;
   (2) the level of training, education, and experience of the out-of-network provider;
   (3) the out-of-network provider's usual billed charge for comparable services or supplies with regard to other enrollees for which the provider is an out-of-network provider;
   (4) the circumstances and complexity of the enrollee's particular case, including the time and place of the provision of the service or supply;
   (5) individual enrollee characteristics;
   (6) the 80th percentile of all billed charges for the service or supply performed by a health care provider in the same or similar specialty and provided in the same geozip area as reported in a benchmarking database described by Section 1467.006;
   (7) the 50th percentile of rates for the service or supply paid to participating providers in the same or similar specialty and provided in the same geozip area as reported in a benchmarking database described by Section 1467.006;
   (8) the history of network contracting between the parties;
   (9) historical data for the percentiles described by Subdivisions (6) and (7); and
   (10) an offer made during the informal settlement teleconference required under Section 1467.084(d).

§ 1467.084 Availability of mandatory arbitration

(a) Not later than the 90th day after the date an out-of-network provider receives the initial payment for a health care or medical service or supply, the out-of-network provider or the health benefit plan issuer or administrator may request arbitration of a settlement of an out-of-network health benefit claim through a portal on the department's Internet website if:
   (1) there is a charge billed by the provider and unpaid by the issuer or administrator after copayments, coinsurance, and deductibles for which an enrollee may not be billed; and
   (2) the health benefit claim is for:
      (A) emergency care;
      (B) a health care or medical service or supply provided by a facility-based provider in a facility that is a participating provider;
      (C) an out-of-network laboratory service; or
      (D) an out-of-network diagnostic imaging service.

(b) If a person requests arbitration under this subchapter, the out-of-network provider or the provider's representative, and the health benefit plan issuer or the administrator, as appropriate, shall participate in the arbitration.

(c) The person who requests the arbitration shall provide written notice on the date the arbitration is requested in the form and manner prescribed by commissioner rule to:
   (1) the department; and
   (2) each other party.

(d) In an effort to settle the claim before arbitration, all parties must participate in an informal settlement teleconference not later than the 30th day after the date on which the arbitration is requested. A health benefit plan issuer or administrator, as applicable, shall make a reasonable effort to arrange the teleconference.

(e) The commissioner shall adopt rules providing requirements for submitting multiple claims to arbitration in one proceeding. The rules must provide that:
   (1) the total amount in controversy for multiple claims in one proceeding may not exceed $5,000; and
   (2) the multiple claims in one proceeding must be limited to the same out-of-network provider.

§ 1467.085 Effect of arbitration and applicability of other law

(a) Notwithstanding Section 1467.004, an out-of-network provider or health benefit plan issuer or administrator may not file suit for an out-of-network claim subject to this chapter until the conclusion of the arbitration on the issue of the amount to be paid in the out-of-network claim dispute.

(b) An arbitration conducted under this subchapter is not subject to Title 7, Civil Practice and Remedies Code.

§ 1467.086 Selection and approval of arbitrator

(a) If the parties do not select an arbitrator by mutual agreement on or before the 30th day after the date the arbitration is requested, the party requesting the arbitration shall notify the commissioner, and the commissioner shall select an arbitrator from the commissioner's list of approved arbitrators.

(b) In selecting an arbitrator under this section, the commissioner shall give preference to an arbitrator who is knowledgeable and experienced in applicable principles of contract and insurance law and the health care industry generally.

(c) In approving an individual as an arbitrator, the commissioner shall ensure that the individual does not have a conflict of interest that would adversely impact the individual's independence and impartiality in rendering a decision in an arbitration. A conflict of interest includes current or recent ownership or employment of the individual or a close family member in any health benefit plan issuer or administrator or physician, health care practitioner, or other health care provider.

(d) The commissioner shall immediately terminate the approval of an arbitrator who no longer meets the requirements under this subchapter and rules adopted under this subchapter to serve as an arbitrator.

§ 1467.087 Procedures

(a) The arbitrator shall set a date for submission of all information to be considered by the arbitrator.

(b) A party may not engage in discovery in connection with the arbitration.

(c) On agreement of all parties, any deadline under this subchapter may be extended.

(d) Unless otherwise agreed to by the parties, an arbitrator may not determine whether a health benefit plan covers a particular health care or medical service or supply.

(e) The parties shall evenly split and pay the arbitrator's fees and expenses.

(f) Information submitted by the parties to the arbitrator is confidential and not subject to disclosure under Chapter 552, Government Code.

§ 1467.088 Decisions

(a) Not later than the 51st day after the date the arbitration is requested, an arbitrator shall provide the parties with a written decision in which the arbitrator:

(1) determines whether the billed charge or the payment made by the health benefit plan issuer or administrator, as those amounts were last modified during the issuer's or administrator's internal appeal process, if the provider elects to participate, or the informal settlement

teleconference required by Section 1467.084(d), as applicable, is the closest to the reasonable amount for the services or supplies determined in accordance with Section 1467.083(b); and

(2) selects the amount determined to be closest under Subdivision (1) as the binding award amount.

(b) An arbitrator may not modify the binding award amount selected under Subsection (a).

(c) An arbitrator shall provide written notice in the form and manner prescribed by commissioner rule of the reasonable amount for the services or supplies and the binding award amount. If the parties settle before a decision, the parties shall provide written notice in the form and manner prescribed by commissioner rule of the amount of the settlement. The department shall maintain a record of notices provided under this subsection.

§ 1467.089 Effect of decision

(a) An arbitrator's decision under Section 1467.088 is binding.

(b) Not later than the 45th day after the date of an arbitrator's decision under Section 1467.088, a party not satisfied with the decision may file an action to determine the payment due to an out-of-network provider.

(c) In an action filed under Subsection (b), the court shall determine whether the arbitrator's decision is proper based on a substantial evidence standard of review.

(d) Not later than the 30th day after the date of an arbitrator's decision under Section 1467.088, a health benefit plan issuer or administrator shall pay to an out-of-network provider any additional amount necessary to satisfy the binding award.

TEXAS ADMINISTRATIVE CODE TITLE 26

§ 509.67 Billing requirements

(a) A facility shall comply with the following balance billing requirements.

(1) A facility may not violate a law that prohibits the facility from billing a patient who is an insured, participant, or enrollee in a managed care plan an amount greater than an applicable copayment, coinsurance, and deductible under the insured's, participant's, or enrollee's managed care plan or that imposes a requirement related to that prohibition.

(2) A facility shall comply with Senate Bill 1264, 86th Legislature, Regular Session, 2019, and with related Texas Department of Insurance rules at 28 TAC Chapter 21, Subchapter OO §§ 21.4901–21.4904 (relating to Disclosures by Out-of-Network Providers) to the extent this subchapter applies to the facility.

(b) A facility shall comply with the itemized bill requirements under Texas Health and Safety Code § 185.002.

TEXAS ADMINISTRATIVE CODE TITLE 28

§ 21.5010 Qualified mediation claim criteria

(a) Required criteria. An out-of-network provider that is a facility or a health benefit plan issuer or administrator may request mandatory mediation of an out-of-network claim under § 21.5011 of this title (relating to Mediation Request Procedure) if the claim complies with the criteria specified in this subsection. An out-of-network claim that complies with those criteria is referred to as a "qualified mediation claim" in this subchapter.
   (1) The out-of-network health benefit claim must be for:
      (A) emergency care;
      (B) an out-of-network laboratory service provided in connection with a health care or medical service or supply provided by a participating provider; or
      (C) an out-of-network diagnostic imaging service provided in connection with a health care or medical service or supply provided by a participating provider.
   (2) There is an amount billed by the provider and unpaid by the health benefit plan issuer or administrator after copayments, deductibles, and coinsurance, for which an enrollee may not be billed.

(b) Submission of multiple claim forms. The use of more than one form in the submission of a claim, as defined in § 21.5003 of this title (relating to Definitions), does not prevent eligibility of a claim for mandatory mediation under this subchapter if the claim otherwise meets the requirements of this section.

(c) Ineligible claims. This division does not require a health benefit plan issuer or administrator to pay for an uncovered service or supply.

§ 21.5011 Mediation request procedure

(a) Mediation request and notice.
   (1) An out-of-network provider that is a facility or a health benefit plan issuer or administrator may request mediation. To be eligible for mediation, the party requesting mediation must complete the mediation request information required on the department's website at www.tdi.texas.gov, as specified in subsection (b) of this section.
   (2) The party who requests the mediation must provide written notice to each other party on the date the mediation is requested. The notification must contain the information as specified on the department's website, including the necessary claim information and contact information of the parties. A health benefit plan issuer or administrator requesting mediation must send the mediation notification to the mailing address or email address specified in the claim submitted by the provider. If a

provider does not specify an address to receive notice requesting mediation in the claim, a health benefit plan issuer or administrator may provide notice to the provider at the provider's last known address the issuer or administrator has on file for the provider. A provider requesting mediation must send the mediation notification to the email address specified in the explanation of benefits by the health benefit plan issuer or administrator.

(b) Submission of request. The requesting party must submit information necessary to complete the initial mediation request, including:
  (1) facility details, including identifying the facility type, facility contact information, and facility representative information;
  (2) claim information, including the claim number, type of service or supply provided, date of service, billed amount, amount paid, and balance; and
  (3) relevant information from the enrollee's health benefit plan identification card or other similar document, including plan number and group number.

(c) Notice of teleconference outcome. Parties must submit additional information on the department's website at the completion of the informal settlement teleconference period, including the date the teleconference request was received and the date of the teleconference.

(d) Mediator selection.
  (1) The parties must notify the department through the department's website on or before 30 days from the date the mediation is requested if:
    (A) the parties agree to a settlement;
    (B) the parties agree to the selection of a mediator; or
    (C) the parties agree to extend the deadline to have the department select a mediator and notify the department of new deadlines.
  (2) If the department is not given notification under paragraph (1) of this subsection, the department will assign a mediator after the 30th day from the date the mediation is requested. The parties must pay the nonrefundable mediator's fee to the mediator when the mediator is assigned. Failure to pay the mediator when the mediator is assigned constitutes bad faith participation.

(e) Submission of information. Parties must submit information, as specified on the department's website, to the department at the completion of the mediation or informal settlement, including:
  (1) the name of the mediator, the date when the mediator was selected, the date when the mediation was held, the date of the agreement, the date of the mediator report, and when payment was made; and
  (2) the agreement, including the original billed amount, payment amount, and the total agreed amount.

(f) Mediator approval and removal.
  (1) Mediators may apply to the department using a method as determined by the Commissioner, including through an application on the

department's website or through the department's procurement process. An individual or entities that employ mediators may apply for approval.

(2) A list of qualified mediators will be maintained on the department's website. A mediator must notify the department immediately if the mediator wants to voluntarily withdraw from the list.

(3) At the discretion of the department, a mediator may be removed from the list of qualified mediators in certain circumstances, including failure to comply with any requirement under Insurance Code Chapter 1467, concerning Out-of-Network Claim Dispute Resolution, or rules adopted under Insurance Code § 1467.003, concerning Rules.

(g) Mediation process.

(1) A party may request mediation after 20 days from the date an out-of-network provider receives the initial payment for a health benefit claim, during which time the out-of-network provider may attempt to resolve a claim payment dispute through the health benefit plan issuer's or administrator's internal appeal process.

(2) The parties may submit written information to a mediator concerning the amount charged by the out-of-network provider for the health care or medical service or supply and the amount paid by the health benefit plan issuer or administrator.

(3) The parties must evaluate the factors specified in Insurance Code § 1467.056, concerning Matters Considered in Mediation; Agreed Resolution.

(4) Each party is responsible for reviewing the list of mediators and notifying the department within 10 days of the request for mediation whether there is a conflict of interest with any of the mediators on the list to avoid the department assigning a mediator with a conflict of interest.

(5) The parties may agree to aggregate claims between the same facility and same health benefit plan issuer or administrator for mediation.

(h) Assistance. Assistance with submitting a request for mediation is available on the department's website at www.tdi.texas.gov.

§ 21.5012 Informal settlement teleconference

All parties subject to mandatory mediation requested by an out-of-network provider that is a facility or a health benefit plan issuer or administrator under this subchapter must use best efforts to coordinate the informal settlement teleconference required by Insurance Code § 1467.054 (concerning Request and Preliminary Procedures for Mandatory Mediation). The parties or representatives of the parties must arrange a date and time when the parties or representatives of the parties can participate in the informal settlement teleconference, which must occur not later than the 30th day after the date on which the party submitted a request for mediation, unless the parties agree to extend the deadline.

§ 21.5013 Mediation participation

Under Insurance Code § 1467.101 (concerning Bad Faith), conduct that constitutes bad faith mediation includes failing to:

(1) participate in the mediation;
(2) provide information that the mediator believes is necessary to facilitate an agreement; or
(3) designate a representative participating in the mediation with full authority to enter into any mediated agreement.

§ 21.5020 Qualified arbitration claim criteria

(a) Required criteria. An out-of-network provider that is not a facility or a health benefit plan issuer or administrator may request mandatory binding arbitration of an out-of-network claim under § 21.5021 of this title (relating to Arbitration Request Procedure) if the claim complies with the criteria specified in this section. An out-of-network claim that complies with those criteria is referred to as a "qualified arbitration claim" in this subchapter.
    (1) The health benefit claim must be for:
        (A) emergency care;
        (B) a health care or medical service or supply provided by a facility-based provider in a facility that is a participating provider;
        (C) an out-of-network laboratory service provided in connection with a health care or medical service or supply provided by a participating provider; or
        (D) an out-of-network diagnostic imaging service provided in connection with a health care or medical service or supply provided by a participating provider; and
    (2) The health benefit claim must be for a charge billed by the provider and unpaid by the health benefit plan issuer or administrator after copayments, coinsurance, and deductibles for which an enrollee may not be billed.
(b) Availability. Not later than the 90th day after the date an out-of-network provider receives the initial payment for a health care or medical service or supply, the out-of-network provider or the health benefit plan issuer or administrator may request arbitration of a settlement of an out-of-network health benefit claim. The initial payment could be zero dollars if the allowable amount was applied to an enrollee's deductible.
(c) Ineligible claims. Unless otherwise agreed to by the parties, an arbitrator may not determine whether a health benefit plan covers a particular health care or medical service or supply.

§ 21.5021 Arbitration request procedure

(a) Arbitration request and notice.

(1) An out-of-network provider or a health benefit plan issuer or administrator may request arbitration. To be eligible for arbitration, the party requesting arbitration must complete the arbitration request information required on the department's website at www.tdi.texas.gov, as specified in subsection (b) of this section.

(2) The party who requests the arbitration must provide written notice to each other party on the date the arbitration is requested. The notification must contain the information as specified on the department's website, including the necessary claim information and contact information of the parties. A health benefit plan issuer or administrator requesting arbitration must send the arbitration notification to the mailing address or email address specified in the claim submitted by the provider. If a provider does not specify an address to receive notice requesting arbitration in the claim, the health benefit plan issuer or administrator may provide notice to the provider at the provider's last known address the issuer or administrator has on file for the provider. A provider requesting arbitration must send the arbitration notification to the email address specified in the explanation of benefits by the health benefit plan issuer or administrator.

(b) Submission of request. The requesting party must submit information necessary to complete the initial arbitration request, including:

(1) provider details, including identifying the provider type, provider contact information, and provider representative information;

(2) claim information, including the claim number, type of service or supply provided, date of service, billed amount, amount paid, and balance; and

(3) relevant information from the enrollee's health benefit plan identification card or a similar document, including plan number and group number.

(c) Notice of teleconference outcome. Parties must submit additional information on the department's website at the completion of the informal settlement teleconference period, including the date the teleconference request was received, the date of the teleconference, and settlement offer amounts.

(d) Arbitrator selection.

(1) The parties must notify the department, through the department's website, on or before 30 days from the date arbitration was requested if:

(A) the parties agree to a settlement;

(B) the parties agree to the selection of an arbitrator; or

(C) the parties agree to extend the deadline to have the department select an arbitrator and notify the department of new deadlines.

(2) If the department is not given notification under paragraph (1) of this subsection, the department will assign an arbitrator after the 30th day from the date the arbitration is requested. The parties must pay the nonrefundable arbitrator's fee to the arbitrator when the arbitrator is assigned. Failure to pay the arbitrator when the arbitrator is assigned constitutes bad faith participation, and the arbitrator may award the binding amount to the other party.

(e) Submission of information.

(1) The arbitrator must submit information, as specified on the department's website, to the department at the completion of the arbitration, including:

(A) the name of the arbitrator, the date when the arbitrator was selected, the date of the decision, the date of the arbitrator report, and when payment was made; and

(B) the written decision, including any final offers made during the health benefit plan issuer's or administrator's internal appeal process or informal settlement, reasonable amount for the services or supplies, and the binding award amount.

(2) If the parties settle the dispute before the arbitrator's decision, the parties must submit information, as specified on the department's website, to the department, including:

(A) the date of the settlement; and

(B) the amount of the settlement.

(f) Arbitrator approval and removal.

(1) Arbitrators may apply to the department using a method as determined by the Commissioner, including through an application on the department's website or the department's procurement process. An individual or entities that employ arbitrators may apply for approval.

(2) A list of qualified arbitrators will be maintained on the department's website. An arbitrator must notify the department immediately if the arbitrator wants to voluntarily withdraw from the list.

(3) At the discretion of the department, an arbitrator may be removed from the list of qualified arbitrators in certain circumstances, including failure to comply with any requirement under Insurance Code Chapter 1467, concerning Out-of-Network Claim Dispute Resolution, or rules adopted under Insurance Code § 1467.003, concerning Rules.

(g) Arbitration process.

(1) A party may request arbitration after 20 days from the date an out-of-network provider receives the initial payment for a health benefit claim, during which time the out-of-network provider may attempt to resolve a claim payment dispute through the health benefit plan issuer's or administrator's internal appeal process.

(2) The parties must submit written information to an arbitrator concerning the amount charged by the out-of-network provider for the health care

or medical service or supply, and the amount paid by the health benefit plan issuer or administrator.

(3) The arbitrator must evaluate only the factors specified in Insurance Code § 1467.083, concerning Issue to Be Addressed; Basis for Determination.

(4) The arbitrator must provide the parties an opportunity to review the written information submitted by the other party, submit additional written information, and respond in writing to the arbitrator on the time line set by the arbitrator.

(5) Each party is responsible for reviewing the list of arbitrators and notifying the department within 10 days of the request for arbitration if there is a conflict of interest with any of the arbitrators on the list to avoid the department assigning an arbitrator with a conflict of interest.

(6) If a party does not respond to the arbitrator's request for information, the dispute will be decided based on the available information received by the arbitrator without an opportunity for reconsideration.

(7) The submission of multiple claims to arbitration in one proceeding must be for the same provider and the same health benefit plan issuer or administrator and the total amount in controversy may not exceed $5,000.

(h) Assistance. Assistance with submitting a request for arbitration is available on the department's website at www.tdi.texas.gov.

§ 21.5022 Informal settlement teleconference

A party subject to mandatory arbitration requested by an out-of-network provider or a health benefit plan issuer or administrator under this division must use best efforts to coordinate an informal settlement teleconference, as required by Insurance Code § 1467.084 (concerning Availability of Mandatory Arbitration). The health benefit plan issuer or administrator must make a reasonable effort to arrange the teleconference at a date and time when the parties or representatives of the parties can participate in the informal settlement teleconference. The informal settlement teleconference must occur no later than the 30th day after arbitration is requested, unless the parties agree to extend the deadline.

§ 21.5023 Arbitration participation

Under Insurance Code § 1467.101 (concerning Bad Faith), conduct that constitutes bad faith arbitration includes failing to:

(1) participate in the informal settlement teleconference under § 1467.084(d) or an arbitration;

(2) provide information that the arbitrator believes is necessary to facilitate a decision; or

(3) designate a representative participating in the arbitration with full authority to enter into any agreement.

UTAH CODE ANNOTATED

§ 31A-2-216 Office of Consumer Health Assistance

(1) The commissioner shall establish an Office of Consumer Health Assistance before July 1, 1999.
(2) The office shall:
  (a) be a resource for health insurance consumers concerning health insurance coverage or the need for such coverage;
  (b) help health insurance consumers understand:
    (i) contractual rights and responsibilities;
    (ii) statutory protections; and
    (iii) available remedies, including adverse benefit determination processes;
  (c) educate health insurance consumers:
    (i) by producing or collecting and disseminating educational materials to consumers and health insurers; and
    (ii) through outreach and other educational activities;
  (d) for health insurance consumers that have difficulty in accessing their health insurance policies because of language, disability, age, or ethnicity, provide information and services, directly or through referral;
  (e) analyze and monitor federal and state consumer health insurance statutes, rules, and regulations; and
  (f) summarize information gathered under this section and make the summaries available to the public, government agencies, and the Legislature.
(3) The office may:
  (a) obtain data from health insurance consumers as necessary to further the office's duties under this section;
  (b) investigate complaints and attempt to resolve complaints at the lowest possible level; and
  (c) assist, but not testify or represent, a consumer in an adverse benefit determination, arbitration, judicial, or related proceeding, unless the proceeding is in connection with an enforcement action under Section 31A-2-308.
(4) The commissioner may adopt rules necessary to implement the requirements of this section.

§ 31A-22-627 Coverage of emergency medical services

(1) A health insurance policy or managed care organization contract:
  (a) shall provide coverage of emergency services; and
  (b) may not:
    (i) require any form of preauthorization for treatment of an emergency medical condition until after the insured's condition has been stabilized;

(ii) deny a claim for any covered evaluation, covered diagnostic test, or other covered treatment considered medically necessary to stabilize the emergency medical condition of an insured; or

(iii) impose any cost-sharing requirement for out-of-network that exceeds the cost-sharing requirement imposed for in-network.

(2)

(a) A health insurance policy or managed care organization contract may require authorization for the continued treatment of an emergency medical condition after the insured's condition has been stabilized.

(b) If authorization described in Subsection (2)(a) is required, an insurer who does not accept or reject a request for authorization may not deny a claim for any evaluation, diagnostic testing, or other treatment considered medically necessary that occurred between the time the request was received and the time the insurer rejected the request for authorization.

(3) For purposes of this section:

(a) "Hospital emergency department" means that area of a hospital in which emergency services are provided on a 24-hour-a-day basis.

(b) "Stabilize" means the same as that term is defined in 42 U.S.C. Sec. 1395dd(e)(3).

(4) Nothing in this section may be construed as:

(a) altering the level or type of benefits that are provided under the terms of a contract or policy; or

(b) restricting a policy or contract from providing enhanced benefits for certain emergency medical conditions that are identified in the policy or contract.

(5) Notwithstanding Section 31A-2-308, if the commissioner finds an insurer has violated this section, the commissioner may:

(a) work with the insurer to improve the insurer's compliance with this section; or

(b) impose the following fines:

(i) not more than $5,000; or

(ii) twice the amount of any profit gained from violations of this section.

§ 31A-45-501 Access to health care providers

(1) As used in this section:

(a) "Class of health care provider" means a health care provider or a health care facility regulated by the state within the same professional, trade, occupational, or certification category established under Title 58, Occupations and Professions, or within the same facility licensure category established under Title 26B, Chapter 2, Part 2, Health Care Facility Licensing and Inspection.

(b) "Covered health care services" or "covered services" means health care services for which an enrollee is entitled to receive under the terms of a managed care organization contract.

(c) "Credentialed staff member" means a health care provider with active staff privileges at an independent hospital or federally qualified health center.

(d) "Federally qualified health center" means as defined in the Social Security Act, 42 U.S.C. Sec. 1395x.

(e) "Independent hospital" means a general acute hospital or a critical access hospital that:

(i) is either:

(A) located 20 miles or more from any other general acute hospital or critical access hospital; or

(B) licensed as of January 1, 2004;

(ii) is licensed pursuant to Title 26B, Chapter 2, Part 2, Health Care Facility Licensing and Inspection;

(iii) is controlled by a board of directors of which 51% or more reside in the county where the hospital is located; and

(iv)

(A) the hospital's board of directors is ultimately responsible for the policy and financial decisions of the hospital; or

(B) the hospital is licensed for 60 or fewer beds and is not owned, in whole or in part, by an entity that owns or controls a health maintenance organization if the hospital is a contracting facility of the organization.

(f) "Noncontracting provider" means an independent hospital, federally qualified health center, or credentialed staff member that has not contracted with a managed care organization to provide health care services to enrollees of the managed care organization.

(2) Except for a managed care organization that is under the common ownership or control of an entity with a hospital located within 10 paved road miles of an independent hospital, a managed care organization shall pay for covered health care services rendered to an enrollee by an independent hospital, a credentialed staff member at an independent hospital, or a credentialed staff member at his local practice location if:

(a) the enrollee:

(i) lives or resides within 30 paved road miles of the independent hospital; or

(ii) if Subsection (2)(a)(i) does not apply, lives or resides in closer proximity to the independent hospital than a contracting hospital;

(b) the independent hospital is located prior to December 31, 2000 in a county with a population density of less than 100 people per square mile, or the independent hospital is located in a county with a population density of less than 30 people per square mile; and

(c) the enrollee has complied with the prior authorization and utilization review requirements otherwise required by the managed care organization contract.

(3) A managed care organization shall pay for covered health care services rendered to an enrollee at a federally qualified health center if:

(a) the enrollee:

(i) lives or resides within 30 paved road miles of the federally qualified health center; or

(ii) if Subsection (3)(a)(i) does not apply, lives or resides in closer proximity to the federally qualified health center than a contracting provider;

(b) the federally qualified health center is located in a county with a population density of less than 30 people per square mile; and

(c) the enrollee has complied with the prior authorization and utilization review requirements otherwise required by the managed care organization contract.

(4)

(a) A managed care organization shall reimburse a noncontracting provider or the enrollee for covered services rendered pursuant to Subsection (2) a like dollar amount as the managed care organization pays to contracting providers under a noncapitated arrangement for comparable services.

(b) A managed care organization shall reimburse a federally qualified health center or the enrollee for covered services rendered pursuant to Subsection (3) a like amount as paid by the managed care organization under a noncapitated arrangement for comparable services to a contracting provider in the same class of health care providers as the provider who rendered the service.

(5)

(a) A noncontracting independent hospital may not balance bill a patient when the managed care organization reimburses a noncontracting independent hospital or an enrollee in accordance with Subsection (4)(a).

(b) A noncontracting federally qualified health center may not balance bill a patient when the federally qualified health center or the enrollee receives reimbursement in accordance with Subsection (4)(b).

(6) A noncontracting provider may only refer an enrollee to another noncontracting provider so as to obligate the enrollee's managed care organization to pay for the resulting services if:

(a) the noncontracting provider making the referral or the enrollee has received prior authorization from the organization for the referral; or

(b) the practice location of the noncontracting provider to whom the referral is made:

(i) is located in a county with a population density of less than 25 people per square mile; and

(ii) is within 30 paved road miles of:
(A) the place where the enrollee lives or resides; or
(B) the independent hospital or federally qualified health center at which the enrollee may receive covered services pursuant to Subsection (2) or (3).

(7) Notwithstanding this section, a managed care organization may contract directly with an independent hospital, federally qualified health center, or credentialed staff member.

(8)
(a) A managed care organization that violates any provision of this section is subject to sanctions as determined by the commissioner in accordance with Section 31A-2-308.
(b) Violations of this section include:
(i) failing to provide the notice required by Subsection (8)(d) by placing the notice in any managed care organization's provider list that is supplied to enrollees, including any website maintained by the managed care organization;
(ii) failing to provide notice of an enrollee's rights under this section when:
(A) an enrollee makes personal contact with the managed care organization by telephone, electronic transaction, or in person; and
(B) the enrollee inquires about the enrollee's rights to access an independent hospital or federally qualified health center; and
(iii) refusing to reprocess or reconsider a claim, initially denied by the managed care organization, when the provisions of this section apply to the claim.
(c) The commissioner shall, pursuant to Chapter 2, Part 2, Duties and Powers of Commissioner:
(i) adopt rules as necessary to implement this section;
(ii) identify in rule:
(A) the counties with a population density of less than 100 people per square mile;
(B) independent hospitals as defined in Subsection (1)(e); and
(C) federally qualified health centers as defined in Subsection (1)(d).
(d)
(i) A managed care organization shall:
(A) use the information developed by the commissioner under Subsection (8)(c) to identify the rural counties, independent hospitals, and federally qualified health centers that are located in the managed care organization's service area; and

(B) include the providers identified under Subsection (8)(d)(i)(A) in the notice required in Subsection (8)(d)(ii).

(ii) The managed care organization shall provide the following notice, in bold type, to enrollees as specified under Subsection (8)(b)(i), and shall keep the notice current:

"You may be entitled to coverage for health care services from the following noncontracted providers if you live or reside within 30 paved road miles of the listed providers, or if you live or reside in closer proximity to the listed providers than to your contracted providers:

This list may change periodically, please check on our website or call for verification. Please be advised that if you choose a non-contracted provider you will be responsible for any charges not covered by your health insurance plan.

This list may change periodically, please check on our website or call for verification. Please be advised that if you choose a non-contracted provider you will be responsible for any charges not covered by your health insurance plan.

If you have questions concerning your rights to see a provider on this list you may contact your managed care organization at __________________________. If the managed care organization does not resolve your problem, you may contact the Office of Consumer Health Assistance in the Insurance Department, toll free."

(e) A person whose interests are affected by an alleged violation of this section may contact the Office of Consumer Health Assistance and request assistance, or file a complaint as provided in Section 31A-2-216.

VIRGINIA ADMINISTRATIVE CODE TITLE 14

§ 14VAC-5-405-30 Balance billing for out-of-network services

A. Pursuant to § 38.2-3445.01 of the Code of Virginia, no out-of-network provider shall balance bill or attempt to collect payment amounts from an enrollee other than those described in subsection B of this section for:

1. Emergency services provided to an enrollee by an out-of-network provider; or
2. Nonemergency services provided to an enrollee at an in-network facility if the nonemergency services involve otherwise covered surgical or ancillary services provided by an out-of-network provider.

B. An enrollee who receives services described in subsection A of this section is obligated to pay the in-network cost-sharing requirement specified in the enrollee's or applicable group health plan contract, which shall be determined using the carrier's median in-network contracted rate for the same or similar service in the same or similar geographic area. When there is no median in-network contracted rate for the specific services provided, the enrollee's cost-sharing requirement shall be determined as provided in § 38.2-3407.3 of the Code of Virginia. An enrollee who is enrolled in a high deductible health plan associated with a Health Savings Account or other health plan for which the carrier is prohibited from providing first-dollar coverage prior to the enrollee meeting the deductible requirement under 26 USC § 223(c)(2) or any other applicable federal or state law may be responsible for any additional amounts necessary to meet deductible requirements beyond those described in this subsection, including additional amounts pursuant to subsection E of this section and owed to the out-of-network provider in 14VAC5-405-40, but only to the extent that the deductible has not yet been met and not to exceed the deductible amount.

C. When a clean claim is received pursuant to the provisions of subsection A of this section, the health carrier shall be responsible for:

1. Providing an explanation of benefits to the enrollee and the out-of-network provider that reflects the cost-sharing requirement determined under this subsection;
2. Applying the in-network cost-sharing requirement under subsection B of this section and any cost-sharing requirement paid by the enrollee for such services toward the in-network maximum out-of-pocket payment obligation;
3. Making commercially reasonable payments for services other than cost-sharing requirements directly to the out-of-network provider without requiring the completion of any assignment of benefits or other documentation by the provider or enrollee;

4. Paying any additional amounts owed to the out-of-network provider through good faith negotiation or arbitration directly to the out-of-network provider; and
5. Making available to a provider through electronic or other method of communication generally used by a provider to verify enrollee eligibility and benefits information regarding whether an enrollee's health benefit plan is subject to the requirements of this section.

D. If the enrollee pays the out-of-network provider an amount that exceeds the amount determined under subsection B of this section, the out-of-network provider shall be responsible for:
1. Refunding to the enrollee the excess amount that the enrollee paid to the provider within 30 business days of receipt of the later of payment or notice that the enrollee's managed care plan is subject to the requirements of this section; and
2. Paying the enrollee interest computed daily at the legal rate of interest stated in § 6.2-301 of the Code of Virginia beginning on the first calendar day after the 30 business days for any unrefunded payments.

E. The amount paid to an out-of-network provider for health care services described in subsection A of this section shall be a commercially reasonable amount, based on payments for the same or similar services provided in a similar geographic area. Within 30 calendar days of receipt of a clean claim from an out-of-network provider, the carrier shall offer to pay the provider a commercially reasonable amount. Disputes between the out-of-network provider and the carrier regarding the commercially reasonable amount shall be handled as follows:
1. If the out-of-network provider disputes the carrier's payment, the provider shall notify the carrier in writing and negotiate in good faith no later than 30 calendar days after the earlier of receipt of payment or payment notification from the carrier; and
2. If the carrier and provider do not agree to a commercially reasonable payment amount within the good faith negotiation period and either party acts within the required timeframes to pursue further action to resolve the dispute, the dispute shall be resolved through arbitration as provided in § 38.2-3445.02 of the Code of Virginia and 14VAC5-405-40. A carrier may not require a provider to reject or return claim payment as a condition of pursuing further arbitration.

F. A health carrier shall not be prohibited from (i) informing enrollees in a nonemergency situation of the availability of in-network facilities that employ or contract with only in-network providers that render surgical and ancillary services; or (ii) offering plan designs that encourage enrollees to utilize specific in-network health care providers.

§ 14VAC-5-405-40 Arbitration process

A. If a good faith negotiation does not result in resolution of the dispute, the health carrier or provider may initiate arbitration by providing the notice of intent to arbitrate form to the commission and the non-initiating party within 10 calendar days following completion of the good faith negotiation period. The notice shall state the initiating party's final payment offer. Failure to timely submit the notice of intent to arbitrate form shall negate the party's opportunity to seek arbitration for the claim that was the subject of the untimely notice.

B. Agreement between the parties may be reached at any time in the process. The arbitration will then be terminated. The claim shall then be paid within 10 calendar days and the matter closed upon agreement.

C. The commission shall maintain a list of qualified arbitrators and each arbitrator's fixed fee on its website.

1. Within five calendar days of the notice of intent to arbitrate, the initiating party shall notify the commission of either agreement on an arbitrator from the list or that the parties cannot agree on an arbitrator.
2. If the parties cannot agree on an arbitrator, within five calendar days the commission shall provide the parties with the names of five arbitrators from the list. Within five calendar days, each party is responsible for reviewing the list of five arbitrators and notifying the commission if there is an apparent conflict of interest with any of the arbitrators on the list. Each party may veto up to two of the named arbitrators. If one name remains, that arbitrator shall be chosen. If more than one name remains, the commission shall choose the arbitrator from the remaining names.
3. Once the arbitrator is chosen, the commission shall notify the parties and the arbitrator within five calendar days.
4. The arbitrator's fee is payable within 10 calendar days of the assignment of the arbitrator with the health carrier and the provider to divide the fee equally.

D. Both parties shall agree to and execute a nondisclosure agreement within 10 business days following receipt of the notice of intent to arbitrate.

E. Within 30 calendar days following receipt of the notice of intent to arbitrate, each party shall provide written submissions in support of its position as well as the final payment offers directly to the arbitrator. At this time, the non-initiating party also shall provide its final offer to the initiating party. Each party shall include in its written submission the evidence and methodology for asserting that the amount proposed to be paid is or is not commercially reasonable. Any party that fails to make a written submission required by this subsection without good cause shown will be in default. The arbitrator shall require the defaulting party to pay or accept the final payment offer of the non-defaulting party and may require the defaulting party to pay the entirety of the arbitrator's fee.

F. The arbitrator shall consider the following factors in reviewing the submissions of the parties and making a decision requiring payment of the final offer amount of either the initiating or non-initiating party:

1. The evidence and methodology submitted by the parties to assert that their final offer amount is reasonable;
2. Patient characteristics and the circumstances and complexity of the case, including time and place of service and type of facility, that are not already reflected in the provider's billing code for the service;
3. The arbitrator may also consider other information that a party believes is relevant as part of their original written submission, including data sets developed pursuant to § 38.2-3445.03 of the Code of Virginia. The arbitrator shall not require extrinsic evidence of authenticity for admitting such data sets.

G. Within 15 calendar days after receipt of the parties' written submissions, the arbitrator shall issue a written decision requiring payment of the final offer amount of either of the parties. The arbitrator shall notify the parties and the commission of this decision. The decision shall include an explanation by the arbitrator of the basis for the decision and factors relied upon in making the decision and copies of all written submissions by each party. The decision shall also include information required to be reported to the commission, including the name of the health carrier, the name of the provider, the provider's employer or business entity in which the provider has an ownership interest, the name of the facility where services were provided, and the type of health care service at issue. The claim shall be paid within 10 calendar days after the arbitration decision.

H. Within 30 calendar days of receipt of the arbitrator's decision, either party may appeal to the commission in accordance with the provisions of 5VAC5-20-100 B based only on one of the following grounds: (i) the decision was substantially influenced by corruption, fraud, or other undue means; (ii) there was evident partiality, corruption, or misconduct prejudicing the rights of any party; (iii) the arbitrator exceeded his powers; or (iv) the arbitrator conducted the proceeding contrary to the provisions of § 38.2-3445.02 of the Code of Virginia and commission rules, in such a way as to materially prejudice the rights of the party.

I. A single provider is permitted to bundle claims for arbitration. Multiple claims may be addressed in a single arbitration proceeding if the claims at issue (i) involve identical health carrier or administrator and provider parties; (ii) involve claims with the same or related Current Procedural Technology (CPT) codes, Healthcare Common Procedure Coding System (HCPCS) codes, or in the case of facility services, Diagnosis Related Group (DRG) codes, Revenue Codes, or other procedural codes relevant to a particular procedure, and (iii) occur within a period of two months of one another. Provider groups are not permitted to bundle claims for arbitration if the health care professional providing the service is not the same.

J. All written submissions and notifications required under this section shall be submitted electronically. Individual information related to any arbitration is confidential and not subject to disclosure.

VIRGINIA CODE ANNOTATED

§ 38.2-3445.01 Balance billing for certain services; prohibited

A. No out-of-network provider shall balance bill an enrollee for (i) emergency services provided to an enrollee or (ii) nonemergency services provided to an enrollee at an in-network facility if the nonemergency services involve surgical or ancillary services provided by an out-of-network provider.

B. An enrollee that receives services described in subsection A satisfies his obligation to pay for the services if he pays the in-network cost-sharing requirement specified in the enrollee's or applicable group health plan contract. The enrollee's obligation shall be determined using the carrier's median in-network contracted rate for the same or similar service in the same or similar geographical area. The carrier shall provide an explanation of benefits to the enrollee and the out-of-network provider that reflects the cost-sharing requirement determined under this subsection. The obligation of an enrollee in a health benefit plan that uses no median in-network contracted rate for the services provided shall be determined as provided in § 38.2-3407.3.

C. The health carrier and the out-of-network provider shall ensure that the enrollee incurs no greater cost than the amount determined under subsection B and shall not balance bill or otherwise attempt to collect from the enrollee any amount greater than such amount. Additional amounts owed to health care providers through good faith negotiations or arbitration shall be the sole responsibility of the carrier unless the carrier is prohibited from providing the additional benefits under 26 U.S.C. § 223(c)(2) or any other federal or state law. Nothing in this subsection shall preclude a provider from collecting a past due balance on a cost-sharing requirement with interest.

D. The health carrier shall treat any cost-sharing requirement determined under subsection B in the same manner as the cost-sharing requirement for health care services provided by an in-network provider and shall apply any cost-sharing amount paid by the enrollee for such services toward the in-network maximum out-of-pocket payment obligation.

E. If the enrollee pays the out-of-network provider an amount that exceeds the amount determined under subsection B, the provider shall refund the excess amount to the enrollee within 30 business days of receipt. The provider shall pay the enrollee interest computed daily at the legal rate of interest stated in § 6.2-301 beginning on the first calendar day after the 30 business days for any unrefunded payments.

F. The amount paid to an out-of-network provider for health care services described in subsection A shall be a commercially reasonable amount, based on payments for the same or similar services provided in a similar geographic area. Within 30 calendar days of receipt of a clean claim from an out-of-network provider, the carrier shall offer to pay the provider a commercially reasonable amount. If the out-of-network provider disputes the carrier's payment, the provider shall notify the carrier no later than 30 calendar days after receipt of payment or payment notification from the carrier. If the out-of-network provider disputes the carrier's initial offer, the carrier and provider shall have 30 calendar days from the initial offer to negotiate in good faith. If the carrier and provider do not agree to a commercially reasonable payment amount within 30 calendar days and either party chooses to pursue further action to resolve the dispute, the dispute shall be resolved through arbitration as provided in § 38.2-3445.02.

G. The carrier shall make payments for services described in subsection A directly to the provider.

H. Carriers shall make available through electronic and other methods of communication generally used by a provider to verify enrollee eligibility and benefits information regarding whether an enrollee's health plan is subject to the requirements of this section.

2020, cc. 1080, 1081.

§ 38.2-3445.02 Arbitration

A. If good faith negotiation, as described in § 38.2-3445.01, does not result in resolution of the dispute, and the carrier or the out-of-network provider chooses to pursue further action to resolve the dispute, the carrier or out-of-network provider shall initiate arbitration to determine a commercially reasonable payment amount. To initiate arbitration, the carrier or provider shall provide written notification to the Commission and the noninitiating party no later than 10 calendar days following completion of the period of good faith negotiation provided in § 38.2-3445.01. Such notification shall state the initiating party's final offer. No later than 30 calendar days following receipt of the notification, the noninitiating party shall provide its final offer to the initiating party. The parties may reach an agreement on reimbursement during this time and before the arbitration proceeding.

B. The parties shall be permitted to bundle claims for arbitration. Multiple claims may be addressed in a single arbitration proceeding if the claims at issue (i) involve identical carrier and provider parties, (ii) involve claims with the same or related current procedural terminology codes relevant to a particular procedure, and (iii) occur within a period of two months of one another.

C. Within seven calendar days of receipt of notification from the initiating party, the Commission shall provide the parties with a list of approved arbitrators or entities that provide arbitrations. The arbitrators on the list shall not have a conflict of interest with the parties and shall be trained and have experience and be selected by the Commission as set out in the standards established by the Commission through regulation. The parties may agree on an arbitrator from the list provided by the Commission. If the parties do not agree on an arbitrator, they shall notify the Commission, and the Commission shall provide the parties with the names of five arbitrators from the list. Each party may veto up to two of the five named arbitrators. If one arbitrator remains, that arbitrator shall be the chosen arbitrator. If more than one arbitrator remains, the Commission shall choose the arbitrator from the remaining arbitrators. The parties and the Commission shall complete this process within 20 calendar days of receipt of the original list from the Commission.

D. No later than 30 days after final selection of the arbitrator pursuant to subsection C, each party shall provide written submissions in support of its position to the arbitrator. The initiating party shall include in its written submission the evidence and methodology for asserting that the amount proposed to be paid is or is not commercially reasonable. A party that fails to make timely written submissions under this subsection without good cause shown shall be considered to be in default, and the arbitrator shall require the defaulting party to pay the final offer of the nondefaulting party and may require the defaulting party to pay the arbitrator's fixed fee. Written submissions required by this subsection may be submitted electronically.

E. No later than 30 calendar days after the receipt of the parties' written submissions, the arbitrator shall (i) issue a written decision requiring payment of the final offer amount of either the initiating or noninitiating party, (ii) notify the parties of the decision, and (iii) provide the decision and the information described in subsection I to the Commission.

F. In reviewing the submissions of the parties and making a decision requiring payment of the final offer amount of either the initiating or noninitiating party, the arbitrator shall consider the following factors:

1. The evidence and methodology submitted by the parties to assert that their final offer amount is reasonable; and
2. Patient characteristics and the circumstances and complexity of the case, including time and place of service and type of facility, that are not already reflected in the provider's billing code for the service.

The arbitrator may also consider other information that a party believes is relevant to the required factors included in this subsection or other information requested by the arbitrator and information provided by the parties that is relevant to such request, including data sets developed pursuant to § 38.2-3445.03. The arbitrator shall not require extrinsic evidence of authenticity for admitting such data sets.

G. The Commission shall establish a schedule of fixed fees for the costs of arbitration. Except as provided in subsection D, such fees shall be divided equally among the parties to the arbitration. The enrollee shall not be liable for any of the costs of arbitration and shall not be required to participate in the arbitration process as a witness or otherwise.

H. Within 10 business days of a party notifying the Commission and the noninitiating party of intent to initiate arbitrations, both parties shall agree to and execute a nondisclosure agreement. The nondisclosure agreement shall not preclude the arbitrator from submitting the arbitrator's decision to the Commission or impede the Commission's duty to prepare the annual report required by subsection I.

I. The Commission shall prepare an annual report summarizing the dispute resolution information provided by arbitrators, including information related to the matters decided through arbitration as well as the following information for each dispute resolved through arbitration: the name of the carrier, the name of the health care provider, the health care provider's employer or the business entity in which the provider has an ownership interest, the health care facility where the services were provided, and the type of health care services at issues. The Commission shall post the report on the Bureau's website and submit it to the Chairs of the House Committee on Labor and Commerce and Committee on Appropriations and the Senate Committee on Commerce and Labor and Committee on Finance and Appropriations annually by July 1. The provisions of this subsection shall expire on July 1, 2025.

J. The Commission shall establish an appeals process for a party to appeal to the Commission an arbitrator's decision on the grounds that (i) the decision was substantially influenced by corruption, fraud, or other undue means; (ii) there was evident partiality, corruption, or misconduct prejudicing the rights of any party; (iii) the arbitrator exceeded his powers; or (iv) the arbitrator conducted the proceeding contrary to the provisions of this section and Commission regulations, in such a way as to materially prejudice the rights of the party.

K. The provisions of the Uniform Arbitration Act, Article 2 (§ 8.01-581.01 et seq.) of Chapter 21 of Title 8.01, shall not apply to arbitration proceedings initiated pursuant to this section.

2020, cc. 1080, 1081.

§ 38.2-3445.03 Data sets for determining commercially reasonable payments

A. The Commission shall contract with the nonprofit data services organization to establish a data set and business process to provide health carriers, health care providers, and arbitrators with data to assist in determining commercially reasonable payments and resolving payment disputes for out-of-network medical services rendered by health care providers.

B. Such data set and business protocols shall be (i) developed in collaboration with health carriers and health care providers and (ii) reviewed by the advisory committee established pursuant to § 32.1-276.7:1.

C. The data set shall provide the amounts for the services described in subsection A of § 38.2-3445.01. The data used to calculate the median in-network and out-of-network allowed amounts and the median billed charge amounts by geographic area, for the same or similar services, shall be drawn from commercial health plan claims and shall not include claims paid under Medicare or Medicaid or other claims paid on other than a fee-for-service basis. The 2020 data set shall be based upon the most recently available full calendar year of claims data. The data set for each subsequent year shall be adjusted by applying the Consumer Price Index-Medical Component as published by the Bureau of Labor Statistics of the U.S. Department of Labor to the previous year's data set.

2020, cc. 1080, 1081.

§ 38.2-5801 General provisions

A. No person shall operate an MCHIP in this Commonwealth unless the health carrier who directly or indirectly manages, owns, contracts with, or employs the providers for the plan is licensed in accordance with provisions in this title as an insurance company, a health maintenance organization, or a nonstock corporation organized in accordance with provisions in Chapter 42 (§ 38.2-4200 et seq.) or Chapter 45 (§ 38.2-4500 et seq.) of this title. Such health carrier shall be deemed responsible for the MCHIP and its compliance with this chapter and the provisions of Title 32.1 concerning quality assurance of MCHIPs. A health carrier may be responsible for more than one MCHIP; however, no MCHIP shall have more than one responsible health carrier.

B. Except as provided in subsection C, no person shall operate an MCHIP in this Commonwealth unless the health carrier responsible for the MCHIP holds an active or temporarily suspended certificate of quality assurance issued by the Department of Health.

C.

1. A health maintenance organization applying for licensure under this title on or after July 1, 1998, or whose application for such licensure is pending before the Commission on July 1, 1998, shall request its initial certificate of quality assurance prior to licensing and a copy of its request shall be included with and made a part of the licensing application and material filed with the Commission pursuant to § 38.2-4301 and subsection B of § 38.2-5802. Until July 1, 2000, (i) issuance of a license under § 38.2-4302 shall be contingent upon receipt of notice from the State Health Commissioner that the health maintenance organization's description of its complaint system has been reviewed and approved by the State Health Commissioner and (ii) upon issuance of the license such health maintenance organization shall be deemed in compliance with subsection B provided no certificate of quality assurance has been issued to the health maintenance organization which has been revoked or not renewed by the State Health Commissioner. Effective July 1, 2000, issuance of a license under § 38.2-4302 shall be contingent upon the Department of Health's issuance of a certificate of quality assurance.
2. Until July 1, 2000, a health maintenance organization licensed under this title on and before July 1, 1998, shall be deemed in compliance with the provisions of this section if (i) a request for initial certification has been filed with the Department of Health on or before December 1, 1998, and is pending before the State Health Commissioner and (ii) no certificate has been issued to the health maintenance organization which has been revoked or not renewed by the State Health Commissioner.
3. A health carrier, other than a health maintenance organization, responsible for an MCHIP pursuant to this chapter, shall request its initial

certificate of quality assurance from the Department of Health on or before December 1, 1998, or becoming responsible for a MCHIP under this title. Until July 1, 2000, such health carrier shall be deemed in compliance with the provisions of this section if (i) a request for initial certification is pending before the Department of Health and (ii) no certificate has been issued to the health carrier which has been revoked or not renewed by the State Health Commissioner.

D. The provisions of this chapter shall apply to all health carriers and all MCHIPs operating in this Commonwealth unless an exemption is recognized in accordance with § 38.2-3420; and, except as otherwise provided in this chapter, the provisions of this chapter shall be supplemental and in addition to those otherwise applicable under this title or Title 32.1.

WASHINGTON REVISED CODE ANNOTATED

§ 48.49.003 Findings—Intent—2019

(1) The legislature finds that:
- (a) Consumers receive surprise bills or balance bills for services provided at nonparticipating facilities or by nonparticipating health care providers at in-network facilities;
- (b) Consumers must not be placed in the middle of contractual disputes between providers and health insurance carriers; and
- (c) Facilities, providers, and health insurance carriers all share responsibility to ensure consumers have transparent information on network providers and benefit coverage, and the insurance commissioner is responsible for ensuring that provider networks include sufficient numbers and types of contracted providers to reasonably ensure consumers have in-network access for covered benefits.

(2) It is the intent of the legislature to:
- (a) Ban balance billing of consumers enrolled in fully insured, regulated insurance plans and plans offered to public employees under chapter 41.05 RCW for the services described in RCW 48.49.020, and to provide self-funded group health plans with an option to elect to be subject to the provisions of this chapter;
- (b) Remove consumers from balance billing disputes and require that nonparticipating providers and carriers negotiate nonparticipating provider payments in good faith under the terms of this chapter;
- (c) Align Washington state law with the federal balance billing prohibitions and transparency protections in sections 2799A-1 et seq. of the public health service act (P.L. 116-260) and implementing federal regulations in effect on March 31, 2022, while maintaining provisions of this chapter that provide greater protection for consumers; and
- (d) Provide an environment that encourages self-funded groups to negotiate payments in good faith with nonparticipating providers and facilities in return for balance billing protections. [2022 c 263 § 6; 2019 c 427 § 1.]

§ 48.49.005 Short title

This chapter may be known and cited as the Balance Billing Protection Act.

§ 48.49.010 Definitions

The definitions in RCW 48.43.005 apply throughout this chapter unless the context clearly requires otherwise.

§ 48.49.020 Balance billing—when prohibited—carrier's duty to hold an enrollee harmless from balance billing under certain circumstances

(1) A nonparticipating provider or facility may not balance bill an enrollee for the following health care services as provided in section 2799A-1(b) of the public health service act (42 U.S.C. Sec. 300gg-111(b)) and implementing federal regulations in effect on March 31, 2022:
   (a) Emergency services provided to an enrollee;
   (b) Nonemergency health care services performed by nonparticipating providers at certain participating facilities; or
   (c) Air ambulance services.

(2) Payment for services described in subsection (1) of this section is subject to the provisions of sections 2799A-1 and 2799A-2 of the public health service act (42 U.S.C. Secs. 300gg-111 and 300gg-112) and implementing federal regulations in effect on March 31, 2022, except that:
   (a) Until July 1, 2023, or a later date determined by the commissioner, RCW 48.49.160 and 48.49.040 apply to the nonparticipating provider or facility payment standard and dispute resolution process for services described in subsection (1) of this section, other than air ambulance services;
   (b) A health care provider, health care facility, or air ambulance service provider may not request or require a patient at any time, for any procedure, service, or supply, to sign or otherwise execute by oral, written, or electronic means, any document that would attempt to avoid, waive, or alter any provision of RCW 48.49.020 and 48.49.030 or sections 2799A-1 et seq. of the public health service act (P.L. 116-260) and implementing federal regulations in effect on March 31, 2022;
   (c) If the enrollee pays a nonparticipating provider, nonparticipating facility, or nonparticipating air ambulance service provider an amount that exceeds the in-network cost-sharing amount determined under sections 2799A-1 and 2799A-2 of the public health service act (42 U.S.C. Secs. 300gg-111 and 300gg-112) and implementing federal regulations as in effect on March 31, 2022, the provider or facility must refund any amount in excess of the in-network cost- sharing amount to the enrollee within 30 business days of receipt. Interest must be paid to the enrollee for any unrefunded payments at a rate of 12 percent beginning on the first calendar day after the 30 business days; and
   (d) Carriers must make available through electronic and other methods of communication generally used by a provider to verify enrollee eligibility and benefits information regarding whether an enrollee's health plan is subject to the requirements of this chapter or section 2799A-1 et seq. of the public health service act (42 U.S.C. Sec. 300gg-111 et seq.) and implementing federal regulations in effect on March 31, 2022.

(3) A behavioral health emergency services provider may not balance bill an enrollee for emergency services provided to an enrollee.

(4) Payment for emergency services provided by behavioral health emergency services providers under subsection (3) of this section is subject to RCW 48.49.030, 48.49.160, and 48.49.040.

(5) This section applies to health care providers, facilities, or behavioral health emergency services providers providing services to members of entities administering a self-funded group health plan and its plan members only if the entity has elected to participate in this section and RCW 48.49.030, 48.49.160, and 48.49.040 as provided in RCW 48.49.130. [2022 c 263 § 7; 2019 c 427 § 6.]

Effective date—2022 c 263: See note following RCW 43.371.100.

WASHINGTON REVISED CODE

§ 48.49.030 Enrollee's obligation to pay for services

(1) If an enrollee receives emergency services from a behavioral health emergency services provider under the circumstances described in RCW 48.49.020(3):

   (a) The enrollee satisfies his or her obligation to pay for the health care services if he or she pays the in-network cost-sharing amount specified in the enrollee's or applicable group's health plan contract. The enrollee's obligation must be determined using the methodology for calculating the qualifying payment amount as described in 45 C.F.R. Sec. 149.140 as in effect on March 31, 2022. The carrier must provide an explanation of benefits to the enrollee and the nonparticipating provider that reflects the cost-sharing amount determined under this subsection.

   (b) The carrier, nonparticipating behavioral health emergency services provider, and an agent, trustee, or assignee of the carrier or nonparticipating behavioral health emergency services provider must ensure that the enrollee incurs no greater cost than the amount determined under (a) of this subsection.

   (c) The nonparticipating behavioral health emergency services provider and an agent, trustee, or assignee of the nonparticipating behavioral health emergency services provider may not balance bill or otherwise attempt to collect from the enrollee any amount greater than the amount determined under (a) of this subsection. This does not impact the behavioral health emergency services provider's ability to collect a past due balance for that cost-sharing amount with interest.

   (d) The carrier must treat any cost-sharing amounts determined under (a) of this subsection paid by the enrollee for a nonparticipating behavioral health emergency services provider's services in the same manner as cost-sharing for health care services provided by an in-network behavioral health emergency services provider and must apply any cost-sharing amounts paid by the enrollee for such services toward the enrollee's maximum out-of-pocket payment obligation.

(e) If the enrollee pays the nonparticipating behavioral health emergency services provider an amount that exceeds the in-network cost-sharing amount determined under (a) of this subsection, the behavioral health emergency services provider must refund any amount in excess of the in-network cost-sharing amount to the enrollee within thirty business days of receipt. Interest must be paid to the enrollee for any unrefunded payments at a rate of twelve percent beginning on the first calendar day after the thirty business days.

(2) This section shall only apply to health care providers, facilities, or behavioral health emergency services providers providing services to members of entities administering a self-funded group health plan and its plan members if the entity has elected to participate in this section and RCW 48.49.020, 48.49.160, and 48.49.040 as provided in RCW 48.49.130. [2022 c 263 § 8; 2019 c 427 § 7.]

Effective date—2022 c 263: See note following RCW 43.371.100.

§ 48.49.040 Dispute resolution process—determination of commercially reasonable payment amount

(1) Effective July 1, 2023, or a later date determined by the commissioner, services described in RCW 48.49.020(1) other than air ambulance services are subject to the independent dispute resolution process established in sections 2799A-1 and 2799A-2 of the public health service act (42 U.S.C. Secs. 300gg-111 and 300gg-112) and implementing federal regulations in effect on July 1, 2023, or a later date determined by the commissioner. Until July 1, 2023, or a later date determined by the commissioner, the arbitration process in this section governs the dispute resolution process for those services.

(2) Effective July 1, 2023, or a later date determined by the commissioner, services described in RCW 48.49.020(3) are subject to the independent dispute resolution process established in section 2799A-1 and 2799A-2 of the public health service act (42 U.S.C. Secs. 300gg-111 and 300gg-112) and implementing federal regulations in effect on July 1, 2023, or a later date determined by the commissioner. Until July 1, 2023, or a later date determined by the commissioner or if the federal independent dispute resolution process is not available to the state for resolution of these disputes, the arbitration process in this section governs the dispute resolution process for those services.

(3)

(a) Notwithstanding RCW 48.43.055 and 48.18.200, if good faith negotiation, as described in RCW 48.49.030, does not result in resolution of the dispute, and the carrier or nonparticipating provider, facility, or behavioral health emergency services provider chooses to pursue further action to resolve the dispute, the carrier or nonparticipating provider, facility, or behavioral health emergency services provider shall initiate arbitration to determine a commercially reasonable payment amount. To initiate arbitration, the carrier or nonparticipating provider, facility, or behavioral health emergency services provider must provide written notification to the commissioner and the noninitiating party no later than ten calendar days following completion of the period of good faith negotiation under RCW 48.49.030. The notification to the noninitiating party must state the initiating party's final offer. No later than thirty calendar days following receipt of the notification, the non-initiating party must provide its final offer to the initiating party. The parties may reach an agreement on reimbursement during this time and before the arbitration proceeding.

(b) Notwithstanding (a) of this subsection (3), where a dispute resolution matter initiated under sections 2799A-1 and 2799A-2 of the public health service act (42 U.S.C. Secs. 300gg-111 and 300gg-112) and implementing federal regulations in effect on March 31, 2022, results in a determination by a certified independent dispute resolution entity that such process does not apply to the dispute or to portions thereof, a carrier, provider, facility, or behavioral health emergency services provider may initiate arbitration described in this section for such dispute:
    (i) Without completing good faith negotiation under RCW 48.49.160 if the open negotiation period required under sections 2799A-1 and 2799A-2 of the public health service act (42 U.S.C. Secs. 300gg-111 and 300gg-112) and implementing federal regulations in effect on March 31, 2022, has been completed; and
    (ii) By providing written notification to the commissioner and the noninitiating party no later than 10 calendar days following the date notice is received by the parties from the certified independent dispute resolution entity that the federal independent dispute resolution process is not applicable to the dispute.

(4) Multiple claims may be addressed in a single arbitration proceeding if the claims at issue:
    (a) Involve identical carrier and provider, provider group, facility, or behavioral health emergency services provider parties;
    (b) Involve claims with the same procedural code, or a comparable code under a different procedural code system; and
    (c) Occur within the same 30 business day period.

(5) Within seven calendar days of receipt of notification from the initiating party, the commissioner must provide the parties with a list of approved arbitrators or entities that provide arbitration. The arbitrators on the list must be trained by the American arbitration association or the American health lawyers association and must have experience in matters related to medical or health care services. The parties may agree on an arbitrator from the list provided by the commissioner. If the parties do not agree on an arbitrator, they must notify

the commissioner who must provide them with the names of five arbitrators from the list. Each party may veto two of the five named arbitrators. If one arbitrator remains, that person is the chosen arbitrator. If more than one arbitrator remains, the commissioner must choose the arbitrator from the remaining arbitrators. The parties and the commissioner must complete this selection process within twenty calendar days of receipt of the original list from the commissioner.

(6) Each party must make written submissions to the arbitrator in support of its position no later than thirty calendar days after the final selection of the arbitrator. Each party must include in their written submission the evidence and methodology for asserting that the amount proposed to be paid is or is not commercially reasonable. A party that fails to make timely written submissions under this section without good cause shown shall be considered to be in default and the arbitrator shall require the party in default to pay the final offer amount submitted by the party not in default and may require the party in default to pay expenses incurred to date in the course of arbitration, including the arbitrator's expenses and fees and the reasonable attorneys' fees of the party not in default.

(7) If the parties agree on an out-of-network rate for the services at issue after providing the arbitration initiation notice to the commissioner but before the arbitrator has made their decision, the amount agreed to by the parties for the service will be treated as the out-of-network rate for the service. The initiating party must send a notification to the commissioner and to the arbitrator, as soon as possible, but no later than three business days after the date of the agreement. The notification must include the out-of-network rate for the service and signatures from authorized signatories for both parties.

(8)

(a) No later than thirty calendar days after the receipt of the parties' written submissions, the arbitrator must: Issue a written decision requiring payment of the final offer amount of either the initiating party or the noninitiating party; notify the parties of its decision; and provide the decision and the information described in *RCW 48.49.050 regarding the decision to the commissioner. The arbitrator's decision must include an explanation of the elements of the parties' submissions the arbitrator relied upon to make their decision and why those elements were relevant to their decision.

(b) In reviewing the submissions of the parties and making a decision related to whether payment should be made at the final offer amount of the initiating party or the noninitiating party, the arbitrator must consider the following factors:

(i) The evidence and methodology submitted by the parties to assert that their final offer amount is reasonable; and

(ii) Patient characteristics and the circumstances and complexity of the case, including time and place of service and whether the service was delivered at a level I or level II trauma center or a rural facility, that are not already reflected in the provider's billing code for the service.

(c) The arbitrator may not require extrinsic evidence of authenticity for admitting data from the Washington state all-payer claims database data set developed under RCW 43.371.100 into evidence.

(d) The arbitrator may also consider other information that a party believes is relevant to the factors included in (b) of this subsection or other factors the arbitrator requests and information provided by the parties that is relevant to such request, including the Washington state all-payer claims database data set developed under RCW 43.371.100.

(9) Expenses incurred in the course of arbitration, including the arbitrator's expenses and fees, but not including attorneys' fees, must be divided equally among the parties to the arbitration. The commissioner may establish allowable arbitrator fee ranges or an arbitrator fee schedule by rule. Arbitrator fees must be paid to the arbitrator by a party within 30 calendar days following receipt of the arbitrator's decision by the party. The enrollee is not liable for any of the costs of the arbitration and may not be required to participate in the arbitration proceeding as a witness or otherwise.

(10) Within 10 business days of a party notifying the commissioner and the noninitiating party of intent to initiate arbitration, both parties shall agree to and execute a nondisclosure agreement. The nondisclosure agreement must not preclude the arbitrator from submitting the arbitrator's decision to the commissioner under subsection (6) of this section or impede the commissioner's duty to prepare the annual report under *RCW 48.49.050.

(11) The decision of the arbitrator is final and binding on the parties to the arbitration and is not subject to judicial review.

(12) Chapter 7.04A RCW applies to arbitrations conducted under this section, but in the event of a conflict between this section and chapter 7.04A RCW, this section governs.

(13) For dispute resolution proceedings initiated under RCW 48.49.135(2)(b), the arbitration provisions of this section apply except that:

(a) The issue before the arbitrator will be the commercially reasonable payment for applicable services addressed in the alternate access delivery request rather than the commercially reasonable payment for single or multiple claims under subsection (4) of this section. The arbitrator shall issue a decision related to whether payment for the applicable services should be made at the final offer amount of the carrier or the final offer amount of the provider or facility. The arbitrator's decision is final and binding on the parties for services rendered to enrollees from the effective date of the amended alternate access delivery request approved under RCW 48.49.135(2)(b) to either the expiration date of the amended alternate access delivery request, or at the time that a provider contract and provider compensation agreement are executed between the parties, whichever occurs first;

(b) During the period from the effective date of the amended alternate access delivery request to issuance of the arbitrator's decision, the allowed amount paid to providers or facilities for the applicable services addressed in the amended alternate access delivery request shall be a commercially reasonable amount, based on payments for the same or similar services provided in a similar geographic area; and

(c) The proceedings are subject to the arbitration process described in this section, and not to the independent dispute resolution process established in sections 2799A-1 and 2799A-2 of the public health service act (42 U.S.C. Secs. 300gg-111 and 300gg-112) and implementing federal regulations in effect on March 31, 2022.

(14) Air ambulance services are subject to the independent dispute resolution process established in sections 2799A-1 and 2799A-2 of the public health service act (42 U.S.C. Secs. 300gg-111 and 300gg-112) and implementing federal regulations in effect on March 31, 2022.

(15) This section applies to health care providers, facilities, or behavioral health emergency services providers providing services to members of entities administering a self-funded group health plan and its plan members only if the entity has elected to participate in RCW 48.49.020 and 48.49.030, 48.49.160, and this section as provided in RCW 48.49.130.

(16) An entity administering a self-funded group health plan that has elected to participate in this section pursuant to RCW 48.49.130 shall comply with the provisions of this section. [2022 c 263 § 11; 2019 c 427 § 8.]

*Reviser's note: RCW 48.49.050 expired January 1, 2023.
Effective date—2022 c 263: See note following RCW 43.371.100.

§ 48.49.060 Notice of consumer rights—development of standard template language by commissioner

(1) The commissioner, in consultation with health carriers, health care providers, health care facilities, and consumers, must develop standard template language for a notice of consumer rights notifying consumers of their rights under this chapter, and sections 2799A-1 and 2799A-2 of the public health service act (42 U.S.C. Secs. 300gg-111 and 300gg-112) and implementing federal regulations in effect on March 31, 2022.

(2) The standard template language must include contact information for the office of the insurance commissioner so that consumers may contact the office of the insurance commissioner if they believe they have received a balance bill in violation of this chapter.

(3) The office of the insurance commissioner shall determine by rule when and in what format health carriers, health care providers, and health care facilities must provide consumers with the notice developed under this section. [2022 c 263 § 13; 2019 c 427 § 10.]

Effective date—2022 c 263: See note following RCW 43.371.100.

§ 48.49.070 Requirement to provide certain information on website or upon consumer request—requirement to provide carriers with nonemployed provider lists

(1)

(a) A hospital, ambulatory surgical facility, behavioral health emergency services provider, or ground ambulance services organization must post the following information on its website, if one is available:

(i) The listing of the carrier health plan provider networks with which the hospital, ambulatory surgical facility, behavioral health emergency services provider, or ground ambulance services organization is an in-network provider, based upon the information provided by the carrier pursuant to RCW 48.43.730(7); and

(ii) The notice of consumer rights developed under RCW 48.49.060.

(b) If the hospital, ambulatory surgical facility, behavioral health emergency services provider, or ground ambulance services organization does not maintain a website, this information must be provided to consumers upon an oral or written request.

(2) Posting or otherwise providing the information required in this section does not relieve a hospital, ambulatory surgical facility, behavioral health emergency services provider, or ground ambulance services organization of its obligation to comply with the provisions of this chapter.

(3) Not less than 30 days prior to executing a contract with a carrier, a hospital or ambulatory surgical facility must provide the carrier with a list of the nonemployed providers or provider groups contracted to provide emergency medicine, anesthesiology, pathology, radiology, neonatology, surgery, hospitalist, intensivist, and diagnostic services, including radiology and laboratory services at the hospital or ambulatory surgical facility. The hospital or ambulatory surgical facility must notify the carrier within thirty days of a removal from or addition to the nonemployed provider list. A hospital or ambulatory surgical facility also must provide an updated list of these providers within 14 calendar days of a request for an updated list by a carrier.

§ 48.49.080 Health care provider—requirement to provide certain information on website or upon consumer request—requirement to submit network status information to carriers

(1)
  (a) A health care provider must provide the following information on its website, if one is available:
    (i) The listing of the carrier health plan provider networks with which the provider contracts, based upon the information provided by the carrier pursuant to RCW 48.43.730(7); and
    (ii) The notice of consumer rights developed under RCW 48.49.060.
  (b) If the health care provider does not maintain a website, this information must be provided to consumers upon an oral or written request.

(2) Posting or otherwise providing the information required in this section does not relieve a provider of its obligation to comply with the provisions of this chapter.

(3) An in-network provider must submit accurate information to a carrier regarding the provider's network status in a timely manner, consistent with the terms of the contract between the provider and the carrier. [2019 c 427 § 12.]

§ 48.49.090 Carrier—requirement to update website and provider directory—requirement to provide enrollee with certain information

(1) A carrier must update its website and provider directory no later than thirty days after the addition or termination of a facility or provider.

(2) A carrier must provide an enrollee with:
  (a) A clear description of the health plan's out-of-network health benefits;
  (b) The notice of consumer rights developed under RCW 48.49.060;
  (c) Notification that if the enrollee receives services from an out-of-network provider, facility, or behavioral health emergency services provider, under circumstances other than those described in RCW 48.49.020, the enrollee will have the financial responsibility applicable to services provided outside the health plan's network in excess of applicable cost-sharing amounts and that the enrollee may be responsible for any costs in excess of those allowed by the health plan;
  (d) Information on how to use the carrier's member transparency tools under RCW 48.43.007;
  (e) Upon request, information regarding whether a health care provider is in-network or out-of-network, and whether there are in-network providers available to provide emergency medicine, anesthesiology,

pathology, radiology, neonatology, surgery, hospitalist, intensivist[,] and diagnostic services, including radiology and laboratory services at specified in-network hospitals or ambulatory surgical facilities; and

(f) Upon request, an estimated range of the out-of-pocket costs for an out-of-network benefit. [2022 c 263 § 15; 2019 c 427 § 13.]

Effective date—2022 c 263: See note following RCW 43.371.100.

§ 48.49.110 Rule-making authority

(1) The commissioner may adopt rules to implement and administer this chapter, including rules governing the dispute resolution process established in RCW 48.49.040.

(2) The commissioner may adopt rules to adopt or incorporate by reference without material change federal regulations adopted on or after March 31, 2022, that implement P.L. 116-260 (enacted December 27, 2020). [2022 c 263 § 20; 2019 c 427 § 15.]

Effective date—2022 c 263: See note following RCW 43.371.100.

§ 48.49.120 No application of chapter to health plans under chapter 74.09 RCW

This chapter does not apply to health plans that provide benefits under chapter 74.09 RCW. [2019 c 427 § 22.]

§ 48.49.130 Application of chapter to self-funded group health plans that elect to participate in balance billing protection provisions—annual notice to commissioner

As authorized in 45 C.F.R. Sec. 149.30 as in effect on March 31, 2022, the provisions of this chapter apply to a self-funded group health plan whether governed by or exempt from the provisions of the federal employee retirement income security act of 1974 (29 U.S.C. Sec. 1001 et seq.) only if the self-funded group health plan elects to participate in the provisions of RCW 48.49.020 and 48.49.030, 48.49.160, and 48.49.040. To elect to participate in these provisions, the self-funded group health plan shall provide notice, on an annual basis, to the commissioner in a manner prescribed by the commissioner, attesting to the plan's participation and agreeing to be bound by RCW 48.49.020 and 48.49.030, 48.49.160, and 48.49.040. An entity administering a self-funded health benefits plan that elects to participate under this section, shall comply with the provisions of RCW 48.49.020 and 48.49.030, 48.49.160, and 48.49.040. [2022 c 263 § 17; 2019 c 427 § 23.]

Effective date—2022 c 263: See note following RCW 43.371.100.

§ 48.49.135 Determining the adequacy of provider networks—required considerations

(1) When determining the adequacy of a proposed provider network or the ongoing adequacy of an in-force provider network, the commissioner must review the carrier's proposed provider network or in-force provider network to determine whether the network includes a sufficient number of contracted providers of emergency medicine, anesthesiology, pathology, radiology, neonatology, surgery, hospitalist, intensivist[,] and diagnostic services, including radiology and laboratory services at or for the carrier's contracted in-network hospitals or ambulatory surgical facilities to reasonably ensure enrollees have in-network access to covered benefits delivered at that facility.

(2)

(a) When determining the adequacy of a proposed provider network or the ongoing adequacy of an in-force provider network, the commissioner may allow a carrier to submit an alternate access delivery request. The commissioner shall define the circumstances under which a carrier may submit an alternate access delivery request and the requirements for submission and approval of such a request in rule. To submit an alternate access delivery request, a carrier shall:

(i) Ensure that enrollees will not bear any greater cost of receiving services under the alternate access delivery request than if the provider or facility was contracted with the carrier or make other arrangements acceptable to the commissioner;

(ii) Provide substantial evidence of good faith efforts on its part to contract with providers or facilities. If a carrier is submitting an alternate access delivery request for the same service and geographic area as a previously approved request, the carrier shall provide new or additional evidence of good faith efforts to contract associated with the current request;

(iii) Demonstrate that there is not an available provider or facility with which the carrier can contract to meet the commissioner's provider network standards; and

(iv) For services for which balance billing is prohibited under RCW 48.49.020, notify out-of-network providers or facilities that deliver the services referenced in the alternate access delivery request within five days of submitting the request to the commissioner. Any notification provided under this subsection shall include contact information for carrier staff who can provide detailed information to the affected provider or facility regarding the submitted alternate access delivery request.

(b) For services for which balance billing is prohibited under RCW 48.49.020, a carrier may not treat its payment of nonparticipating providers or facilities under this chapter or P.L. 116-260 (enacted

December 27, 2020) as a means to satisfy network access standards established by the commissioner unless all requirements of this subsection are met.

(i) If a carrier is unable to obtain a contract with a provider or facility delivering services addressed in an alternate access delivery request to meet network access requirements, the carrier may ask the commissioner to amend the alternate access delivery request if the carrier's communication to the commissioner occurs at least three months after the effective date of the alternate access delivery request and demonstrates substantial evidence of good faith efforts on its part to contract for delivery of services during that three-month time period. If the carrier has demonstrated substantial evidence of good faith efforts on its part to contract, the commissioner shall allow a carrier to use the dispute resolution process provided in RCW 48.49.040 to determine the amount that will be paid to providers or facilities for services referenced in the alternate access delivery request. The commissioner may determine by rule the associated processes for use of the dispute resolution process under this subsection.

(ii) Once notification is provided by the carrier to a provider or facility under (a) of this subsection, a carrier is not responsible for reimbursing a provider's or facility's charges in excess of the amount charged by the provider or facility for the same or similar service at the time the notification was provided. The provider or facility shall accept this reimbursement as payment in full.

(3) When determining the adequacy of a carrier's proposed provider network or the ongoing adequacy of an in-force provider network, beginning January 1, 2023, the commissioner shall require that the carrier's proposed provider network or in-force provider network include a sufficient number of contracted behavioral health emergency services providers. [2022 c 263 § 18; 2019 c 427 § 25. Formerly RCW 48.49.150.]

Effective date—2022 c 263: See note following RCW 43.371.100.

§ 48.49.140 Liberal construction of chapter to promote public interest

This chapter must be liberally construed to promote the public interest by ensuring that consumers are not billed out-of-network charges and do not receive additional bills from providers under the circumstances described in RCW 48.49.020. [2019 c 427 § 24.]

§ 48.49.160 Allowed amounts paid to nonparticipating providers

(1)

(a) Until July 1, 2023, or a later date determined by the commissioner under RCW 48.49.040, the allowed amount paid to a nonparticipating provider for health care services described under RCW 48.49.020(1) other than air ambulance services shall be a commercially reasonable amount, based on payments for the same or similar services provided in a similar geographic area. Within 30 calendar days of receipt of a claim from a nonparticipating provider or facility, the carrier shall offer to pay the provider or facility a commercially reasonable amount. If the nonparticipating provider or facility wants to dispute the carrier's payment, the provider or facility must notify the carrier no later than 30 calendar days after receipt of payment or payment notification from the carrier. If the nonparticipating provider or facility disputes the carrier's initial offer, the carrier and provider or facility have 30 calendar days from the initial offer to negotiate in good faith. If the carrier and the nonparticipating provider or facility do not agree to a commercially reasonable payment amount within 30 calendar days, and the carrier or nonparticipating provider or facility chooses to pursue further action to resolve the dispute, the dispute shall be resolved as provided in RCW 48.49.040.

(b) The carrier must make payments for health care services described in RCW 48.49.020(1) provided by nonparticipating providers or facilities directly to the provider or facility, rather than the enrollee.

(2)

(a) The allowed amount paid to a nonparticipating behavioral health emergency services provider for behavioral health emergency services shall be a commercially reasonable amount, based on payments for the same or similar services provided in a similar geographic area. Within 30 calendar days of receipt of a claim from a nonparticipating behavioral health emergency services provider, the carrier shall offer to pay the behavioral health emergency services provider a commercially reasonable amount. If the nonparticipating behavioral health emergency services provider wants to dispute the carrier's payment, the behavioral health emergency services provider must notify the carrier no later than 30 calendar days after receipt of payment or payment notification from the carrier. If the nonparticipating behavioral health emergency services provider disputes the carrier's initial offer, the carrier and behavioral health emergency services provider have 30 calendar days from the initial offer to negotiate in good faith. If the carrier and the nonparticipating behavioral health emergency services provider do not agree to a commercially reasonable payment amount within 30 calendar days, and the carrier or nonparticipating behavioral health emergency services provider chooses to pursue further action to resolve the dispute, the dispute shall be resolved as provided in RCW 48.49.040.

(b) The carrier must make payments for behavioral health emergency services provided by nonparticipating behavioral health emergency services providers directly to the provider, rather than the enrollee.

(3) This section shall only apply to health care providers, facilities, or behavioral health emergency services providers providing services to members of entities administering a self-funded group health plan and its plan members if the entity has elected to participate in RCW 48.49.020, 48.49.030, and 48.49.040, and this section as provided in RCW 48.49.130. [2022 c 263 § 9.]

Effective date—2022 c 263: See note following RCW 43.371.100.

§ 48.49.170 Application of state and federal requirements—applicability information access—waivers prohibited

(1) Carriers must make available through electronic and other methods of communication generally used by a provider or facility to verify enrollee eligibility and benefits information regarding whether an enrollee's health plan is subject to the requirements of this chapter or section 2799A-1 et seq. of the public health service act (42 U.S.C. Sec. 300gg-111 et seq.) and implementing federal regulations in effect on March 31, 2022.

(2) A health care provider, health care facility, behavioral health emergency services provider, or air ambulance service provider may not request or require a patient at any time, for any procedure, service, or supply, to sign or otherwise execute by oral, written, or electronic means, any document that would attempt to avoid, waive, or alter any provision of RCW 48.49.020 and 48.49.030 or sections 2799A-1 et seq. of the public health service act (P.L. 116-260) and implementing federal regulations in effect on March 31, 2022.

(3) This section shall only apply to health care providers, facilities, or behavioral health emergency services providers providing services to members of entities administering a self-funded group health plan and its plan members if the entity has elected to participate in RCW 48.49.020, 48.49.030, 48.49.160, and 48.49.040 as provided in RCW 48.49.130. [2022 c 263 § 10.]

Effective date—2022 c 263: See note following RCW 43.371.100.

§ 48.49.180 Commissioner authority—enforcement—penalties

The commissioner is authorized to enforce provisions of P.L. 116-260 (enacted December 27, 2020, as the consolidated appropriations act of 2021) that are applicable to or regulate the conduct of carriers issuing health plans or grandfathered health plans to residents of Washington state on or after January 1, 2022. In addition to the enforcement actions authorized under RCW 48.02.080, the commissioner may impose a civil monetary penalty in an amount not to exceed $100 for each day for each individual with respect to which a failure to comply with these provisions occurs. [2022 c 263 § 19.]

Effective date—2022 c 263: See note following RCW 43.371.100.

§ 48.49.900 Effective date—2019 c 427

Except for section 26 of this act, this act takes effect January 1, 2020. [2019 c 427 § 31.]

WASHINGTON ADMINISTRATIVE CODE

§ 284-43B-010 Definitions

(1) The definitions in RCW 48.43.005 apply throughout this chapter unless the context clearly requires otherwise, or the term is defined otherwise in subsection (2) of this section.

(2) The following definitions shall apply throughout this chapter:

- (a) "Air ambulance service" has the same meaning as defined in RCW 48.43.005.
- (b) "Allowed amount" means the maximum portion of a billed charge a health carrier will pay, including any applicable enrollee cost-sharing responsibility, for a covered health care service or item rendered by a participating provider or facility or by a nonparticipating provider or facility.
- (c) "Balance bill" means a bill sent to an enrollee by a nonparticipating provider, facility, behavioral health emergency services provider or air ambulance service provider for health care services provided to the enrollee after the provider or facility's billed amount is not fully reimbursed by the carrier, exclusive of cost-sharing allowed under WAC 284-43B-020.
- (d) "Behavioral health emergency services provider" has the same meaning as defined in RCW 48.43.005.
- (e) "De-identified" means, for the purposes of this rule, the removal of all information that can be used to identify the patient from whose medical record the health information was derived.
- (f) "Emergency medical condition" has the same meaning as defined in RCW 48.43.005.
- (g) "Emergency services" has the same meaning as defined in RCW 48.43.005.
- (h) "Facility" or "health care facility" means:

(i) With respect to the provision of emergency services, a hospital or freestanding emergency department licensed under chapter 70.41 RCW (including an "emergency department of a hospital" or "independent freestanding emergency department" described in section 2799A-1(a) of the Public Health Service Act (42 U.S.C. Sec. 300gg-111(a) and 45 C.F.R. Sec. 149.30)) or a behavioral health emergency services provider; and

(ii) With respect to provision of nonemergency services, a hospital licensed under chapter 70.41 RCW, a hospital outpatient department, a critical access hospital or an ambulatory surgical facility licensed under chapter 70.230 RCW (including a "health care facility" described in section 2799A-1(b) of the Public Health Service Act (42 U.S.C. Sec. 300gg-111(b) and 45 C.F.R. Sec. 149.30)).

(i) "Hospital outpatient department" means an entity or site that provides outpatient services and:

(i) Is a provider-based facility under 42 C.F.R. Sec. 413.65;

(ii) Charges a hospital facility fee in billing associated with the receipt of outpatient services from the entity or site; or

(iii) Bills the consumer or their health plan under a hospital's national provider identifier or federal tax identification number.

(j) "In-network" or "participating" means a provider or facility that has contracted with a carrier or a carrier's contractor or subcontractor to provide health care services to enrollees and be reimbursed by the carrier at a contracted rate as payment in full for the health care services, including applicable cost-sharing obligations. A single case reimbursement agreement between a provider or facility and a carrier used for the purpose described in WAC 284-170-200 constitutes a contract exclusively for purposes of this definition under the Balance Billing Protection Act and is limited to the services and parties to the agreement.

(k) "Nonemergency health care services performed by nonparticipating providers at certain participating facilities" has the same meaning as defined in RCW 48.43.005.

(l) "Offer to pay," "carrier payment," or "payment notification" means a claim that has been adjudicated and paid by a carrier to a nonparticipating provider for emergency services or for nonemergency health care services performed by nonparticipating providers at certain participating facilities.

(m) "Out-of-network" or "nonparticipating" has the same meaning as defined in RCW 48.43.005.

(n) "Provider" means a person regulated under Title 18 RCW or chapter 70.127 RCW to practice health or health-related services or otherwise practicing health care services in this state consistent with state law, or an employee or agent of a person acting in the course and scope of his or her employment, that provides emergency services, or nonemergency health care services at certain participating facilities.

§ 284-43B-015 Coverage of emergency services

(1) Coverage of emergency services is governed by RCW 48.43.093. Emergency services, as defined in RCW 48.43.005, include services provided after an enrollee is stabilized and as part of outpatient observation or an inpatient or outpatient stay with respect to the visit during which screening and stabilization services have been furnished. Poststabilization services relate to medical, mental health or substance use disorder treatment necessary in the short term to avoid placing the health of the individual, or with respect to a pregnant person, the health of a person or their unborn child, in serious jeopardy, serious impairment to bodily functions, or serious dysfunction of any bodily organ or part.

(2) A carrier may require notification of stabilization or inpatient admission of an enrollee as provided in RCW 48.43.093. Regardless of such notification, payment and cost-sharing for poststabilization services provided by a nonparticipating facility, provider or behavioral health emergency services provider and dispute resolution related to those services are governed by RCW 48.49.040 and 48.49.160.

§ 284-43B-020 Balance billing prohibition and consumer cost-sharing

(1) If an enrollee receives any emergency services from a nonparticipating facility, provider, or behavioral health emergency services provider, any nonemergency health care services performed by a nonparticipating provider at certain participating facilities, or any air ambulance services from a nonparticipating provider:

(a) The enrollee satisfies their obligation to pay for the health care services if they pay the in-network cost-sharing amount specified in the enrollee's or applicable group's health plan contract. The enrollee's obligation must be calculated as if the total amount charged for the services were equal to:

(i) For emergency services other than services provided by emergency behavioral health services providers, for nonemergency health care services performed by a nonparticipating provider at certain participating facilities, and for air ambulance services, the lesser of the qualifying payment amount, as determined in accordance with 45 C.F.R. Sec. 149.140, or billed charges; and

(ii) For services provided by emergency behavioral health services providers, the qualifying payment amount, as determined in accordance with 45 C.F.R. Sec. 149.140. The carrier must provide an explanation of benefits to the enrollee and the nonparticipating provider, facility, emergency behavioral health services provider or air ambulance provider that reflects the cost-sharing amount determined under this subsection.

(b) The carrier, nonparticipating provider, nonparticipating facility, nonparticipating behavioral health emergency services provider or nonparticipating air ambulance provider and any agent, trustee, or assignee of the carrier, nonparticipating provider, nonparticipating facility, nonparticipating emergency behavioral health services provider or nonparticipating air ambulance provider must ensure that the enrollee incurs no greater cost than the amount determined under (a) of this subsection.

(c)

(i) For emergency services provided to an enrollee, the nonparticipating provider, nonparticipating facility, or nonparticipating emergency behavioral health services provider and any agent, trustee, or assignee of the nonparticipating provider, nonparticipating facility or nonparticipating behavioral health emergency services provider may not balance bill or otherwise attempt to collect from the enrollee any amount greater than the amount determined under (a) of this subsection. This does not impact the provider's, facility's, or behavioral health emergency services provider's ability to collect a past due balance for an applicable in-network cost-sharing amount with interest;

(ii) For nonemergency health care services performed by nonparticipating providers at certain participating facilities, the nonparticipating provider and any agent, trustee, or assignee of the nonparticipating provider may not balance bill or otherwise attempt to collect from the enrollee any amount greater than the amount determined under (a) of this subsection. This does not impact the provider's ability to collect a past due balance for an applicable in-network cost-sharing amount with interest.

(d) For emergency services, nonemergency health care services performed by nonparticipating providers at certain participating facilities and air ambulance services, the carrier must treat any cost-sharing amounts determined under (a) of this subsection paid or incurred by the enrollee for a nonparticipating provider's, facility's, behavioral health emergency services provider's or air ambulance provider's services in the same manner as cost-sharing for health care services provided by a participating provider, facility, behavioral health emergency services provider, or air ambulance services provider and must apply any cost-sharing amounts paid or incurred by the enrollee for such services toward the enrollee's deductible and maximum out-of-pocket payment obligation.

(e) If the enrollee pays a nonparticipating provider, nonparticipating facility, nonparticipating behavioral health emergency services provider or nonparticipating air ambulance services provider an amount that exceeds the in-network cost-sharing amount determined under (a) of this subsection, the nonparticipating provider, nonparticipating facility, nonparticipating behavioral health emergency services provider or nonparticipating air ambulance services provider must refund any amount in excess of the in-network cost-sharing amount to the enrollee within 30 business days of the nonparticipating provider, nonparticipating facility, nonparticipating behavioral health emergency services provider or nonparticipating air ambulance services provider's receipt of the enrollee's payment. Simple interest must be paid to the enrollee for any unrefunded payments at a rate of 12 percent beginning on the first calendar day after the 30 business days.

(2) The carrier must make payments for health care services described in RCW 48.49.020, provided by a nonparticipating provider, nonparticipating facility, nonparticipating behavioral health emergency services provider or nonparticipating air ambulance services provider directly to the provider or facility, rather than the enrollee.

(3) A health care provider, health care facility, behavioral health emergency services provider or air ambulance service provider may not request or require a patient at any time, for any procedure, service, or supply, to sign or otherwise execute by oral, written, or electronic means, any document that would attempt to avoid, waive, or alter any provision of RCW 48.49.020 and 48.49.030 or sections 2799A-1 et seq. of the Public Health Service Act and federal regulations adopted to implement those sections of P.L. 116-260. This prohibition supersedes any provision of sections 2799A-1 et seq. of the Public Health Service Act and federal regulations adopted to implement those sections of P.L. 116-260 that would authorize a provider or facility to ask a patient to consent to waive their balance billing protections.

§ 284-43B-030 Out-of-network claim payment and placing a claim into dispute

For services described in RCW 48.49.020(1) (other than air ambulance services) provided prior to July 1, 2023, or a later date determined by the commissioner, and for services provided by a nonparticipating emergency behavioral health services provider if the federal government does not authorize use of the federal independent dispute resolution system for these disputes, the allowed amount paid to a nonparticipating provider or facility for emergency services and nonemergency health care services performed by nonparticipating providers at certain participating facilities, shall be a commercially reasonable amount, based on payments for the same or similar services provided in the same or a similar geographic area.

(1) Within 30 calendar days of receipt of a claim from a nonparticipating provider or facility, the carrier shall offer to pay the provider or facility a commercially reasonable amount. Payment of an adjudicated claim shall be considered an offer to pay. The amount actually paid to a nonparticipating provider by a carrier may be reduced by the applicable consumer cost-sharing determined under WAC 284-43B-020 (1)(a). The date of receipt by the provider or facility of the carrier's offer to pay is five calendar days after a transmittal of the offer is mailed to the provider or facility, or the date of transmittal of an electronic notice of payment. The claim submitted by the nonparticipating provider or facility to the carrier must include the following information:
   (a) Patient name;
   (b) Patient date of birth;
   (c) Provider name;
   (d) Provider location;
   (e) Place of service, including the name and address of the facility in which, or on whose behalf, the service that is the subject of the claim was provided;
   (f) Provider federal tax identification number;
   (g) Federal Center for Medicare and Medicaid Services individual national provider identifier number, and organizational national provider identifier number, if the provider works for an organization or is in a group practice that has an organization number;
   (h) Date of service;
   (i) Procedure code; and
   (j) Diagnosis code.
(2) If the nonparticipating provider or facility wants to dispute the carrier's offer to pay, the provider or facility must notify the carrier no later than 30 calendar days after receipt of the offer to pay or payment notification from the carrier. A carrier may not require a provider or facility to reject or return payment of the adjudicated claim as a condition of putting the payment into dispute.
(3) If the nonparticipating provider or facility disputes the carrier's offer to pay, the carrier and provider or facility have 30 calendar days after the provider or facility receives the offer to pay to negotiate in good faith.
(4) If the carrier and the nonparticipating provider or facility do not agree to a commercially reasonable payment amount within the 30-calendar day period under subsection (3) of this section, and the carrier, nonparticipating provider or nonparticipating facility chooses to pursue further action to resolve the dispute, the dispute shall be resolved through arbitration, as provided in RCW 48.49.040.

§ 284-43B-032 Applicable dispute resolution system

(1) Effective for services provided on or after July 1, 2023, or a later date determined by the commissioner, services described in RCW 48.49.020(1) other than air ambulance services are subject to the independent dispute resolution process established in sections 2799A-1 and 2799A-2 of the Public Health Service Act (42 U.S.C. Secs. 300gg-111 and 300gg-112) and federal regulations implementing those sections of P.L. 116-260 (enacted December 27, 2020). Until July 1, 2023, or a later date determined by the commissioner, the arbitration process in this chapter governs the dispute resolution process for those services.

(2) Effective for services provided on or after July 1, 2023, or a later date determined by the commissioner, if the federal independent dispute resolution process is available to the state, behavioral emergency services provider services described in RCW 48.49.020(3) are subject to the independent dispute resolution process established in section 2799A-1 and 2799A-2 of the Public Health Service Act (42 U.S.C. Secs. 300gg-111 and 300gg-112) and federal regulations implementing those sections of P.L. 116-260 (enacted December 27, 2020). Until July 1, 2023, or a later date determined by the commissioner, or if the federal independent dispute resolution process is not available to the state for resolution of these disputes, the arbitration process in this chapter governs the dispute resolution process for those services.

(3) The office of the insurance commissioner must provide a minimum of four months advance notice of the date on which the dispute resolution process will transition to the federal independent dispute resolution process. The notice must be posted on the website of the office of the insurance commissioner.

§ 284-43B-035 Arbitration initiation and selection of arbitrator

(1)

(a) To initiate arbitration, the carrier, provider, or facility must provide written notification to the commissioner and the noninitiating party no later than 10 calendar days following completion of the period of good faith negotiation under WAC 284-43B-030(3) using the arbitration initiation request form found in Appendix A of this rule. A request must be submitted electronically through the website of the office of the insurance commissioner. When multiple claims are addressed in a single arbitration proceeding, subsection (3) of this section governs calculation of the 10 calendar days. Each arbitration initiation request must be submitted to the commissioner individually and constitutes a distinct arbitration proceeding unless consolidation of requests is authorized by a court under chapter 7.04A RCW. The commissioner will assign a unique number or designation to each arbitration initiation request. The parties must include that designation in all communication related to that request. Any information submitted to the commissioner with the arbitration initiation request must be included in the notice to the noninitiating party under RCW 48.49.040. A provider or facility initiating arbitration must send the arbitration initiation request form to the email address appearing on the website established by the designated lead organization for administration simplification in Washington state under (c) of this subsection. Any patient information submitted to the commissioner with an arbitration initiation request form must be de-identified to ensure that protected health information is not disclosed.

(b) The written notification to the commissioner must be made electronically and provide dates related to each of the time period limitations described in WAC 284-43B-030 (1) through (3) and subsection (1)(a) of this section. The commissioner's review of the arbitration initiation request form is limited to the information necessary to determine that the request has been timely submitted and is complete. The commissioner's review does not include a review of whether particular claims included in the request are subject to chapter 48.49 RCW or whether claims are appropriately bundled under subsection (3) of this section. A party seeking to challenge whether a claim is subject to chapter 48.49 RCW or whether claims are appropriately bundled may raise those issues during arbitration.

(c) Each carrier must provide the designated lead organization for administrative simplification in Washington state with the email address and telephone number of the carrier's designated contact for receipt of notices to initiate arbitration. The email address and phone number provided must be specific to the carrier staff responsible for receipt of notices or other actions related to arbitration proceedings. The initial submission of information to the designated lead organization must be made on or before November 10, 2020. The carrier must keep its contact information accurate and current by submitting updated contact information to the designated lead organization as directed by that organization.

(2) Within 10 business days of a party notifying the commissioner and the noninitiating party of intent to initiate arbitration, both parties shall agree to and execute a nondisclosure agreement. The nondisclosure agreement must prohibit either party from sharing or making use of any confidential or proprietary information acquired or used for purposes of one arbitration in any subsequent arbitration proceedings. The nondisclosure agreement must not preclude the arbitrator from submitting the arbitrator's decision to the commissioner under RCW 48.49.040 or impede the commissioner's duty to prepare the annual report under RCW 48.49.050.

(3) If a nonparticipating provider or nonparticipating facility chooses to address multiple claims in a single arbitration proceeding as provided in RCW 48.49.040, notification must be provided no later than 10 calendar days following completion of the period of good faith negotiation under WAC 284-43B-030(3) for the most recent claim that is to be addressed through the arbitration. All of the claims at issue must:

(a) Involve identical carrier and provider, provider group or facility parties. Items and services are billed by the same provider, provider group or facility if the items or services are billed with the same national provider identifier or tax identification number;

(b) Involve the same or similar items and services. The services are considered to be the same or similar items or services if each is billed under the same service code, or a comparable code under a different procedural code system, such as current procedural terminology (CPT) codes with modifiers, if applicable, health care common procedure coding system (HCPCS) with modifiers, if applicable, or diagnosis-related group (DRG) codes with modifiers, if applicable; and

(c) Occur within the same 30-business-day period of one another, such that the earliest claim that is the subject of the arbitration occurred no more than 30 business days prior to the latest claim that is the subject of the arbitration. For purposes of this subsection, a provider or facility claim occurs on the date the service is provided to a patient or, in the case of inpatient facility admissions, the date the admission ends.

(4) A notification submitted to the commissioner later than 10 calendar days following completion of the period of good faith negotiation will be considered untimely and will be rejected. Any revision to a previously timely submitted arbitration initiation request form must be submitted to the commissioner within the 10 calendar day period applicable to submission of the original request. A party that has submitted an untimely notice is permanently foreclosed from seeking arbitration related to the claim or claims that were the subject of the untimely notice.

(5) Within seven calendar days of receipt of notification from the initiating party, the commissioner must provide the parties with a list of approved arbitrators or entities that provide arbitration. The commissioner will use the email addresses for the initiating party and the noninitiating party indicated on the arbitration initiation request form for all communication related to the arbitration request. The arbitrator selection process must be completed within 20 calendar days of receipt of the original list of arbitrators from the commissioner, as follows:

(a) If the parties are unable to agree on an arbitrator from the original list sent by the commissioner, they must notify the commissioner within five calendar days of receipt of the original list of arbitrators. The commissioner must send the parties a list of two individual arbitrators and three arbitration entities within five calendar days of receipt of notice from the parties under this subsection. Each party is responsible for reviewing the list of five arbitrators and arbitration entities and notifying the commissioner and the other party within three calendar days of receipt of the list:

(i) Whether they are taking the opportunity to veto up to two of the five arbitrators or arbitration entities on this list, and if so, which arbitrators or arbitration entities have been vetoed; and

(ii) If there is a conflict of interest as described in subsection (6) of this section with any of the arbitrators or arbitration entities on the list, to avoid the commissioner assigning an arbitrator or arbitration entity with a conflict of interest to an arbitration.

(b) If, after the opportunity to veto up to two of the five named arbitrators or arbitration entities on the list of five arbitrators and arbitration entities sent by the commissioner to the parties, more than one arbitrator or arbitration entity remains on the list, the parties must notify the commissioner within five calendar days of receipt of the list of five arbitrators or arbitration entities. The commissioner will choose the arbitrator from among the remaining arbitrators on the list. If a party fails to timely provide the commissioner with notice of their veto, the commissioner will choose the arbitrator from among the remaining arbitrators or arbitration entities on the list.

(6) Before accepting any appointment, an arbitrator shall ensure that there is no conflict of interest that would adversely impact the arbitrator's independence and impartiality in rendering a decision in the arbitration. A conflict of interest includes (a) current or recent ownership or employment of the arbitrator or a close family member by any health carrier; (b) serves as or was employed by a physician, health care provider, or a health care facility; (c) has a material professional, familial, or financial conflict of interest with a party to the arbitration to which the arbitrator is assigned.

(7) For purposes of this subsection, the date of receipt of a list of arbitrators is the date of electronic transmittal of the list to the parties by the commissioner. The date of receipt of notice from the parties to the commissioner is the date of electronic transmittal of the notice to the commissioner by the parties.

(8) If a noninitiating party fails to timely respond without good cause to a notice initiating arbitration, the initiating party will choose the arbitrator.

(9) Where a dispute resolution matter initiated under sections 2799A-1 and 2799A-2 of the Public Health Service Act (42 U.S.C. Secs. 300gg-111 and 300gg-112) and federal regulations implementing those provisions of P.L. 116-260 (enacted December 27, 2020) results in a determination by a certified independent dispute resolution entity that such process does not apply to the dispute or to portions thereof, RCW 48.49.040 (3)(b) governs initiation of arbitration under this chapter.

§ 284-43B-037 Arbitration proceedings

(1) For purposes of calculating the date that written submissions to the arbitrator under RCW 48.49.040 are due, final selection of the arbitrator occurs on the date that the commissioner sends by electronic transmittal the notice of selection to the arbitrator. The parties must be copied on such notice.

(2) Good cause for purposes of delay in written submissions to the arbitrator under RCW 48.49.040 includes a stipulation that the parties intend to complete settlement negotiations prior to making such submissions to the arbitrator.

(3) If the parties agree on an out-of-network rate for the services at issue after submitting an arbitration initiation request but before the arbitrator has made a decision, they must provide notice to the commissioner as provided in RCW 48.49.040(7).

(4) If an initiating party withdraws an arbitration initiation request at any point before the arbitrator has made a decision, the party must submit to the commissioner notice of the date of the withdrawal of the request, as soon as possible, but no later than three business days after the date of the withdrawal.

(5) Any enrollee or patient information submitted to the arbitrator in support of the final offer shall be de-identified to ensure that protected health information is not disclosed.

(6) The decision of the arbitrator is final and binding on the parties and is not subject to judicial review. The arbitrator must submit to the commissioner:

   (a) Their decision, including an explanation of the elements of the parties' submissions the arbitrator relied upon to make their decision and why those elements were relevant to their decision; and

   (b) The information required in RCW 48.49.050 using the form found in Appendix B to this rule, or for arbitration proceedings under RCW 48.49.135, using the form found in Appendix C to this rule.

(7)

   (a) For the calendar year beginning January 1, 2023, arbitrators must charge a fixed fee for single claim proceedings within the range of \$200–\$650. If an arbitrator chooses to charge a different fixed fee for bundled claim proceedings, that fee must be within the range of \$268–\$800. Beginning January 1, 2024, and January 1st of each year thereafter, the arbitrator may adjust the fee range by the annual consumer price index-urban as determined annually by the United States Bureau of Labor Statistics.

   (b) Expenses incurred during arbitration, including the arbitrator's expenses and fees, but not including attorneys' fees, must be divided equally among the parties to the arbitration. Arbitrator fees must be paid to the arbitrator by the parties within 30 calendar days of receipt of the arbitrator's decision by the parties.

(c) If the parties reach an agreement before the arbitrator makes their decision, the arbitrator fees must be paid by the parties within 30 calendar days of the date the settlement is reported to the commissioner as required under RCW 48.49.040.

(8) RCW 48.49.040(13) governs arbitration proceedings initiated under RCW 48.49.135. The determination of the rate to be paid to the out-of-network or nonparticipating provider must be accomplished through a single arbitration proceeding.

§ 284-43B-040 Determining whether an enrollee's health plan is subject to the requirements of the act

(1) To implement RCW 48.49.170, carriers must make information regarding whether an enrollee's health plan is subject to the requirements of chapter 48.49 RCW or section 2799A-1 et seq. of the Public Health Service Act (42 U.S.C. Sec. 300gg-111 et seq.) and federal regulations implementing those provisions of P.L. 116-260 available to providers and facilities by:

(a) Using the most current version of the Health Insurance Portability and Accountability Act (HIPAA) mandated X12 Health Care Eligibility Benefit Response (271) transaction information through use of the most appropriate standard message that is placed in a standard location within the 271 transaction;

(b) Beginning April 1, 2021, and until December 31, 2022, using the most current version of the Health Insurance Portability and Accountability Act (HIPAA) mandated X12 Health Care Claim Payment and Remittance Advice (835) transaction through compliant use of the X12 industry standard Remark Code N830 to indicate that the claim was processed in accordance with this state's balance billing rules;

(c) Beginning January 1, 2023, using the appropriate version of the Health Insurance Portability and Accountability Act (HIPAA) mandated X12 Health Care Claim Payment and Remittance Advice (835) transaction through compliant use of the applicable X12 industry standard Remark Code to indicate whether a claim was processed in accordance with this state's balance billing rules or the federal No Surprises Act.

(2) The designated lead organization for administrative simplification in Washington state:

(a) After consultation with carriers, providers and facilities through a new or an existing workgroup or committee, must post the language of the most appropriate standard message and the location within the 271 transaction in which the message is to be placed on its website on or before November 1, 2022;

(b) Must post on its website on or before December 1, 2020, instructions on compliant use of the X12 industry standard Remark Code N830 in the X12 Health Care Claim Payment and Remittance Advice (835) transaction;

(c) Must post on its website on or before December 1, 2022, instructions on compliant use of the appropriate X12 industry standard Remark code or codes as provided in subsection (1)(c) of this section; and

(d) Must post on its website on or before December 1, 2020, the information reported by carriers under WAC 284-43B-035(1).

(3) A link to the information referenced in subsection (2) of this section also must be posted on the website of the office of the insurance commissioner.

§ 284-43B-050 Notice of consumer rights and transparency

(1) The commissioner shall develop a standard template for a notice of consumer protections from balance billing under the Balance Billing Protection Act and the federal No Surprises Act (P.L. 116-260). The notice may be modified periodically, as determined necessary by the commissioner. The notice template will be posted on the public website of the office of the insurance commissioner.

(2) The standard template for the notice of consumer protections developed under subsection (1) of this section must be provided to consumers enrolled in any health plan issued in Washington state as follows:

(a) Carriers must:

(i) Include the notice in the carrier's communication to an enrollee, in electronic or any other format, that authorizes nonemergency services to be provided at facilities referenced in WAC 284-43B-010 (2)(h)(ii);

(ii) Include the notice in each explanation of benefits sent to an enrollee for items or services with respect to which the requirements of RCW 48.49.020 and WAC 284-43B-020 apply;

(iii) Post the notice on their website in a prominent and relevant location, such as in a location that addresses coverage of emergency services and prior authorization requirements for nonemergency health care services performed by nonparticipating providers at certain participating facilities; and

(iv) Provide the notice to any enrollee upon request.

(b) Health care facilities and providers must:

(i) For any facility or provider that is owned and operated independently from all other businesses and that has more than 50 employees, upon confirming that a patient's health plan is subject to the Balance Billing Protection Act or the federal No Surprises Act (P.L. 116-260):

(A) Include the notice in any communication to a patient, in electronic or any other format related to scheduling of nonemergency health care services performed by nonparticipating providers at certain participating facilities. Text messaging used as a reminder or follow-up after a patient has already received the full text of the notice under this subsection may provide the notice through a link to the provider's webpage that takes the patient directly to the notice. Telephone calls to patients following the patient's receipt of the full text of the notice under this subsection do not need to include the notice; and

(B) For facilities providing emergency services, including behavioral health emergency services providers, provide or mail the notice to a patient within 72 hours following a patient's receipt of emergency services.

(ii) Post the notice on their website, if the provider, behavioral health emergency services provider or facility maintains a website, in a prominent and relevant location near the list of the carrier health plan provider networks with which the provider, behavioral health emergency services provider or facility is an in-network provider;

(iii) If services were provided at a health care facility or in connection with a visit to a health care facility, provide the notice to patients no later than the date and time on which the provider or facility requests payment from the patient, or with respect to a patient from who the provider or facility does not request payment, no later than the date on which the provider or facility submits a claim to the carrier; and

(iv) Provide the notice upon request of a patient.

(3) The notice required in this section may be provided to a patient or an enrollee electronically if it includes the full text of the notice and if the patient or enrollee has affirmatively chosen to receive such communications from the carrier, provider, or facility electronically. Except as authorized in subsection (2)(b)(i)(A) of this section, the notice may not be provided through a hyperlink in an electronic communication.

(4) For claims processed on or after July 1, 2020, when processing a claim that is subject to the balance billing prohibition in RCW 48.49.020, the carrier must indicate on any form used by the carrier to notify enrollees of the amount the carrier has paid on the claim:

(a) Whether the claim is subject to the prohibition in the act; and

(b) The federal Center for Medicare and Medicaid Services individual national provider identifier number, and organizational national provider identifier number, if the provider works for an organization or is in a group practice that has an organization number.

(5) Carriers must ensure that notices provided under this subsection are inclusive for those patients who may have disabilities or limited-English proficiency,

consistent with carriers' obligations under WAC 284-43-5940 through 284-43-5965. To assist in meeting this language access requirement, carriers may use translated versions of the notice of consumer protections from balance billing posted on the website of the office of the insurance commissioner.

(6) A facility, behavioral health emergency services provider or health care provider meets its obligation under RCW 48.49.070 or 48.49.080, to include a listing on its website of the carrier health plan provider networks in which the facility or health care provider participates by posting this information on its website for in-force contracts, and for newly executed contracts within 14 calendar days of receipt of the fully executed contract from a carrier. If the information is posted in advance of the effective date of the contract, the date that network participation will begin must be indicated.

(7) Not less than 30 days prior to executing a contract with a carrier:

(a)

(i) A hospital, freestanding emergency department, behavioral health emergency services provider or ambulatory surgical facility must provide the carrier with a list of the nonemployed providers or provider groups that have privileges to practice at the hospital, freestanding emergency department, behavioral health emergency services provider or ambulatory surgical facility;

(ii) A hospital, hospital outpatient department, critical access hospital or ambulatory surgical center must provide the carrier with a list of the nonemployed providers or provider groups that are contracted to provide nonemergency health care services at the facility.

(b) The list must include the name of the provider or provider group, mailing address, federal tax identification number or numbers and contact information for the staff person responsible for the provider's or provider group's contracting.

(c) Any facility providing carriers information under this subsection must notify the carrier within 30 days of a removal from or addition to the nonemployed provider list. The facility also must provide an updated list of these providers within 14 calendar days of a written request for an updated list by a carrier.

(8) A participating provider must submit accurate information to a carrier regarding the provider's network status in a timely manner, consistent with the terms of the contract between the provider and the carrier.

§ 284-43B-060 Enforcement

(1)

(a) If the commissioner has cause to believe that any health facility, behavioral health emergency services provider or provider has engaged in a pattern of unresolved violations of RCW 48.49.020 or 48.49.030, the commissioner may submit information to the department of health or the appropriate disciplining authority for action.

(b) In determining whether there is cause to believe that a health care provider, behavioral health emergency services provider or facility has engaged in a pattern of unresolved violations, the commissioner shall consider, but is not limited to, consideration of the following:

(i) Whether there is cause to believe that the health care provider, behavioral health emergency services provider or facility has committed two or more violations of RCW 48.49.020 or 48.49.030;

(ii) Whether the health care provider, behavioral health emergency services provider or facility has failed to submit claims to carriers containing all of the elements required in WAC 284-43B-030(1) on multiple occasions, putting a consumer or consumers at risk of being billed for services to which the prohibition in RCW 48.49.020 applies;

(iii) Whether the health care provider, behavioral health emergency services provider or facility has been nonresponsive to questions or requests for information from the commissioner related to one or more complaints alleging a violation of RCW 48.49.020 or 48.49.030; and

(iv) Whether, subsequent to correction of previous violations, additional violations have occurred.

(c) Prior to submitting information to the department of health or the appropriate disciplining authority, the commissioner may provide the health care provider, behavioral health emergency services provider or facility with an opportunity to cure the alleged violations or explain why the actions in question did not violate RCW 48.49.020 or 48.49.030.

(2) In determining whether a carrier has engaged in a pattern of unresolved violations of any provision of this chapter, the commissioner shall consider, but is not limited to, consideration of the following:

(a) Whether a carrier has failed to timely respond to arbitration initiation request notifications from providers or facilities;

(b) Whether a carrier has failed to comply with the requirements of WAC 284-43-035 related to choosing an arbitrator or arbitration entity;

(c) Whether a carrier has met its obligation to maintain current and accurate carrier contact information related to initiation of arbitration proceedings under WAC 284-43-035;

(d) Whether a carrier has complied with the requirements of WAC 284-43-040;

(e) Whether a carrier has complied with the consumer notice requirements under WAC 284-43-050; and

(f) Whether a carrier has committed two or more violations of chapter 48.49 RCW or this chapter.

§ 284-43B-070 Self-funded group health plan opt in

(1) A self-funded group health plan that elects to participate in RCW 48.49.020 through 48.49.040 and 48.49.160, shall provide notice to the commissioner of their election decision on a form prescribed by the commissioner. The completed form must include an attestation that the self-funded group health plan has elected to participate in and be bound by RCW 48.49.020 through 48.49.040, 48.49.160 and rules adopted to implement those sections of law. If the form is completed by the self-funded group health plan, the plan must inform any entity that administers the plan of their election to participate. The form will be posted on the commissioner's public website for use by self-funded group health plans.

(2) A self-funded group health plan election to participate is for a full year. The plan may elect to initiate its participation on January 1st of any year or in any year on the first day of the self-funded group health plan's plan year.

(3) A self-funded group health plan's election occurs on an annual basis. On its election form, the plan must indicate whether it chooses to affirmatively renew its election on an annual basis or whether it should be presumed to have renewed on an annual basis until the commissioner receives advance notice from the plan that it is terminating its election as of either December 31st of a calendar year or the last day of its plan year. Notices under this subsection must be submitted to the commissioner at least 15 days in advance of the effective date of the election to initiate participation and the effective date of the termination of participation.

(4) A self-funded plan operated by an out-of-state employer that has at least one employee who resides in Washington state may elect to participate in balance billing protections as provided in RCW 48.49.130 on behalf of their Washington state resident employees and dependents. If a self-funded group health plan established by Washington state employer has elected to participate in balance billing protections under RCW 48.49.130 and has employees that reside in other states, those employees are protected from balance billing when receiving care from a Washington state provider.

(5) Self-funded group health plan sponsors and their third party administrators may develop their own internal processes related to member notification, member appeals and other functions associated with their fiduciary duty to enrollees under the Employee Retirement Income Security Act of 1974 (ERISA).

§ 284-43B-075 Severability

If any provision of this chapter or its application to any person or circumstance is for any reason held to be invalid by a court, the remainder of this chapter and the application of the provisions to other persons or circumstances shall not be affected.

§ 284-43B-085 Appendix A

The Balance Billing Protection Action Arbitration Initiation Request Form is an online form that can be accessed at: https://www.insurance.wa.gov/balance-billing-protection-act-arbitration-initiation-request-appendix.

§ 284-43B-090 Appendix B

The Arbitrator Decisions Reporting Form is an online form that can be accessed at https://app.leg.wa.gov/wac/default.aspx?cite=284-43B-090.

WEST VIRGINIA CODE

§ 16-29D-2 Definitions

(a) "Coordination of benefits" means a provision establishing an order in which two or more insurance contracts, plans or programs covering the same beneficiary pay their claims, with the effect that there is no duplication of benefits.

(b) The term "health care" or "health care services" means clinically related preventive, diagnostic, treatment, or rehabilitative services whether provided in the home, office, hospital, clinic or any other suitable place either inside or outside the State of West Virginia provided or prescribed by any health care provider or providers. Such services include, among others, medical supplies, appliances, laboratory, preventive, diagnostic, therapeutic and rehabilitative services, hospital care, nursing home and convalescent care, medical physicians, osteopathic physicians, chiropractic physicians, and such other surgical including inpatient oral surgery, nursing, and podiatric services and supplies as may be prescribed by such health care providers but not other dental services.

(c) "Health care provider" means a person, partnership, corporation, facility or institution licensed, certified or authorized by law to provide professional health care services in or outside this State to an individual during this individual's medical care, treatment or confinement. For the sole purpose of this article, pharmacists and pharmacies shall not be considered health care providers.

§ 16-29D-4 Prohibition on balance billing; exceptions

(a) Except in instances involving the delivery of health care services immediately needed to resolve an imminent life-threatening medical or surgical emergency, the agreement by a health care provider to deliver services to a beneficiary of any department or division of the State which participates in a plan or plans developed under section three [§ 16-29D-3] of this article shall be considered to also include an agreement by that health care provider:

(1) To accept the assignment by the beneficiary of any rights the beneficiary may have to bill such division or department for, and to receive payment under such plan or plans on account of, such services; and

(2) To accept as payment in full for the delivery of such services the amount specified in plan or plans or as determined by the plan or plans. In such instances, the health care provider shall bill the division or department, or such other person specified in the plan or plans, directly for the services. The health care provider shall not bill the beneficiary or any other person on behalf of the beneficiary and, except for deductibles or other payments specified in the applicable plan or plans, the beneficiary shall not be personally liable for any of the charges, including any balance claimed by the provider to be owed as being the difference between that provider's charge or charges and the amount payable by the applicable department or divisions. The plan or plans may specify what sums are deductibles, copayments or are otherwise payable by the beneficiary and the sums for which the health care provider may bill the beneficiary: In addition, any health care service which is not subject to payment by the plan or plans shall be the responsibility of the beneficiary and for those health care services which are not covered by the plans, there shall be no prohibition against billing the beneficiary directly.

(b) The prohibitions and limitations stated in subsection (a) of this section do not apply to the delivery of health care services immediately needed to resolve an imminent life-threatening medical or surgical emergency. However, once the patient is stabilized, then the delivery of any further health care services shall be subject to subsection (a) of this section for those latter services only.

(c) The exceptions provided in this section for the delivery of health care services immediately needed to resolve an imminent life-threatening medical or surgical emergency shall not apply to health care providers under contract with a department or division plan or plans.